Love Hina

ALSO AVAILABLE FROM TOKYOPOP®

MANGA

HACK//LEGEND OF THE TWILIGHT
@LARGE (October 2003)
ANGELIC LAYER*
BABY BIRTH*
BATTLE ROYALE*
BRAIN POWERED*
BRIGADOON*
CARDCAPTOR SAKURA
CARDCAPTOR SAKURA: MASTER OF THE CLOW*
CHOBITS*
CHRONICLES OF THE CURSED SWORD
CLAMP SCHOOL DETECTIVES*
CLOVER
CONFIDENTIAL CONFESSIONS*
CORRECTOR YUI
COWBOY BEBOP*
COWBOY BEBOP: SHOOTING STAR*
CYBORG 009*
DEMON DIARY
DIGIMON*
DRAGON HUNTER
DRAGON KNIGHTS*
DUKLYON: CLAMP SCHOOL DEFENDERS*
ERICA SAKURAZAWA*
FAKE*
FLCL*
FORBIDDEN DANCE*
GATE KEEPERS*
G GUNDAM*
GRAVITATION*
GTO*
GUNDAM WING
GUNDAM WING: BATTLEFIELD OF PACIFISTS
GUNDAM WING: ENDLESS WALTZ*
GUNDAM WING: THE LAST OUTPOST*
HAPPY MANIA*
HARLEM BEAT
I.N.V.U.
INITIAL D*
ISLAND
JING: KING OF BANDITS*
JULINE
KARE KANO*
KINDAICHI CASE FILES, THE*
KING OF HELL
KODOCHA: SANA'S STAGE*
LOVE HINA*
LUPIN III*
MAGIC KNIGHT RAYEARTH*

MAGIC KNIGHT RAYEARTH II* (COMING SOON)
MAN OF MANY FACES*
MARMALADE BOY*
MARS*
MIRACLE GIRLS
MIYUKI-CHAN IN WONDERLAND* (October 2003)
MONSTERS, INC.
PARADISE KISS*
PARASYTE
PEACH GIRL
PEACH GIRL: CHANGE OF HEART*
PET SHOP OF HORRORS*
PLANET LADDER*
PLANETES* (October 2003)
PRIEST
RAGNAROK
RAVE MASTER*
REALITY CHECK
REBIRTH
REBOUND*
RISING STARS OF MANGA
SABER MARIONETTE J*
SAILOR MOON
SAINT TAIL
SAMURAI DEEPER KYO*
SAMURAI GIRL: REAL BOUT HIGH SCHOOL*
SCRYED*
SHAOLIN SISTERS*
SHIRAHIME-SYO: SNOW GODDESS TALES* (Dec. 2003)
SHUTTERBOX (November 2003)
SORCERER HUNTERS
THE SKULL MAN*
THE VISION OF ESCAFLOWNE
TOKYO MEW MEW*
UNDER THE GLASS MOON
VAMPIRE GAME*
WILD ACT*
WISH*
WORLD OF HARTZ (COMING SOON)
X-DAY*
ZODIAC P.I. *

For more information visit www.TOKYOPOP.com

*INDICATES 100% AUTHENTIC MANGA (RIGHT-TO-LEFT FORMAT)

CINE-MANGA™

CARDCAPTORS
JACKIE CHAN ADVENTURES (November 2003)
JIMMY NEUTRON
KIM POSSIBLE
LIZZIE MCGUIRE
POWER RANGERS: NINJA STORM
SPONGEBOB SQUAREPANTS
SPY KIDS 2

NOVELS

KARMA CLUB (April 2004)
SAILOR MOON

TOKYOPOP KIDS

STRAY SHEEP

ART BOOKS

CARDCAPTOR SAKURA*
MAGIC KNIGHT RAYEARTH*

ANIME GUIDES

COWBOY BEBOP ANIME GUIDES
GUNDAM TECHNICAL MANUALS
SAILOR MOON SCOUT GUIDES

062703

Love Hina

By
Ken Akamatsu

Vol. 1

TOKYOPOP®

Los Angeles • Tokyo • London

Translator - Anita Sengupta
Copy Editors - Robert Coyner and Paul Morrissey
Associate Editor - Mark Paniccia
Retouch and Lettering - Dolly Chan
Cover Layout - Anna Kernbaum

Editor - Jake Forbes
Managing Editor - Jill Freshney
Production Coordinator - Antonio DePietro
Production Managers - Jennifer Miller & Mario M. Rodriguez
Art Director - Matt Alford
Editorial Director - Jeremy Ross
VP of Production - Ron Klamert
President & C.O.O. - John Parker
Publisher & C.E.O. - Stuart Levy

Email: editor@TOKYOPOP.com
Come visit us online at www.TOKYOPOP.com

A  Manga

TOKYOPOP Inc.
5900 Wilshire Blvd. Suite 2000
Los Angeles, CA 90036

ISBN: 1-931514-94-1

First TOKYOPOP printing: May 2002

10 9 8 7 6

Printed in the USA

CONTENTS

LOVE♡HINA

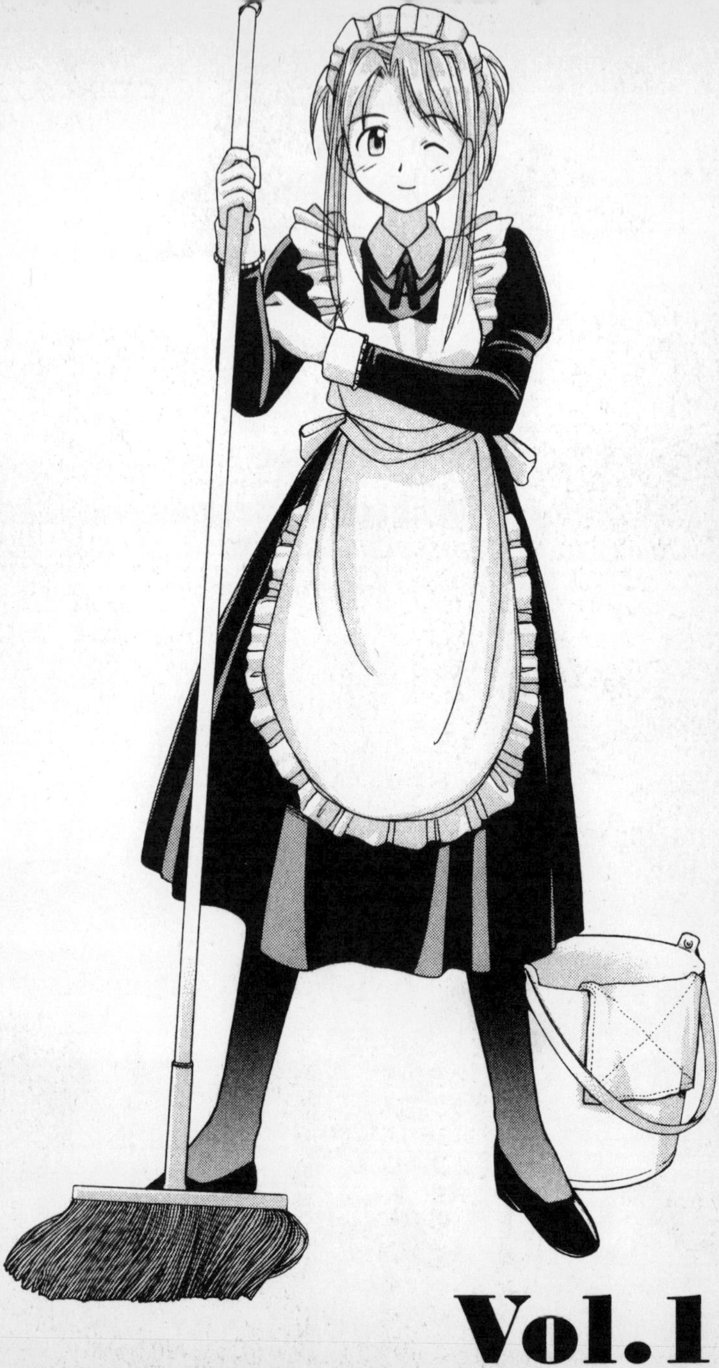

Vol.1

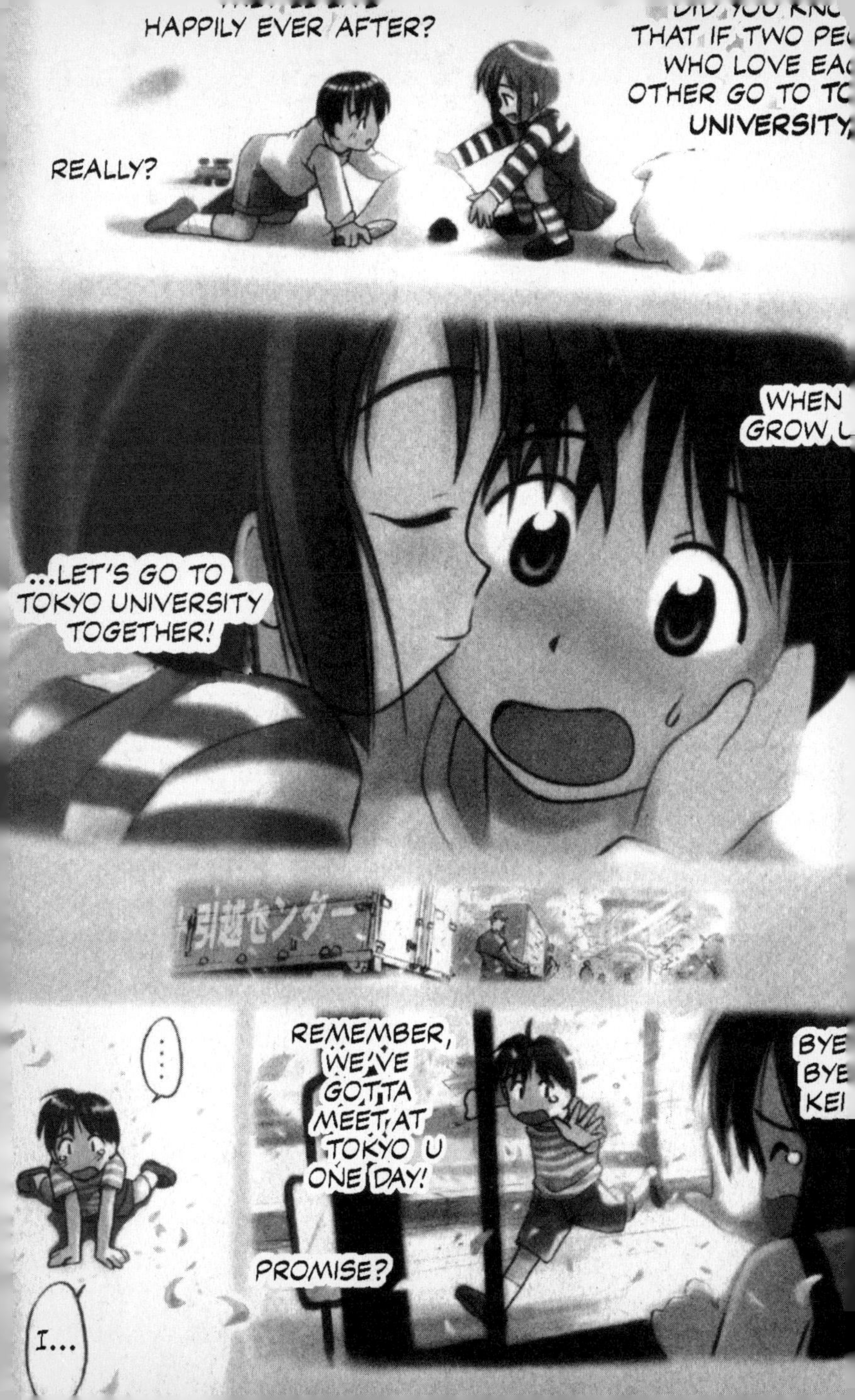

DID YOU KN
THAT IF TWO PE
WHO LOVE EA
OTHER GO TO TO
UNIVERSITY,
HAPPILY EVER AFTER?
REALLY?
WHEN
GROW U
...LET'S GO TO TOKYO UNIVERSITY TOGETHER!
引越センター
BYE BYE KEI
REMEMBER, WE'VE GOTTA MEET AT TOKYO U ONE DAY!
PROMISE?
....
I...

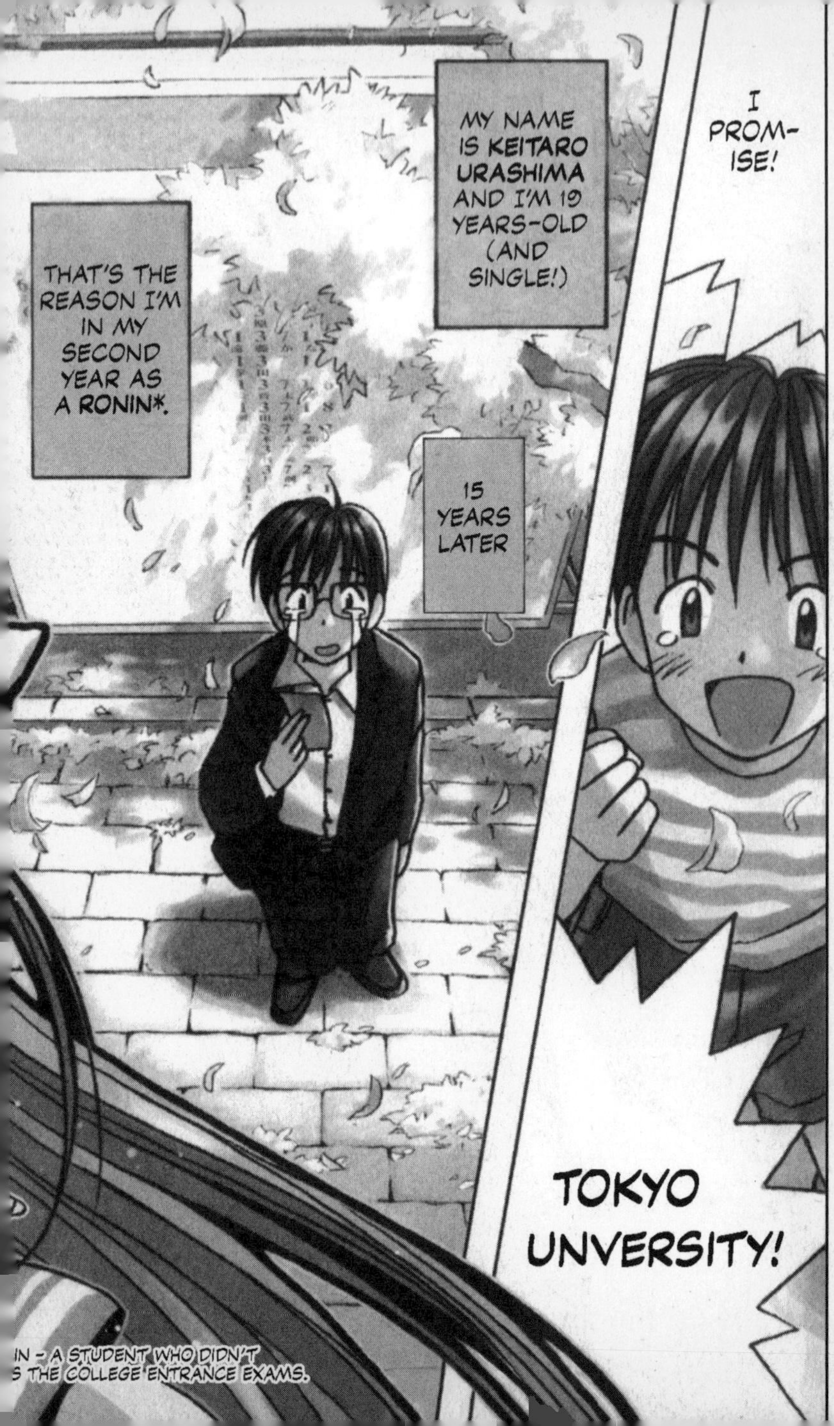
I PROMISE!
TOKYO UNVERSITY!
15 YEARS LATER
MY NAME IS KEITARO URASHIMA AND I'M 19 YEARS-OLD (AND SINGLE!)
THAT'S THE REASON I'M IN MY SECOND YEAR AS A RONIN*.

IN - A STUDENT WHO DIDN'T
S THE COLLEGE ENTRANCE EXAMS.

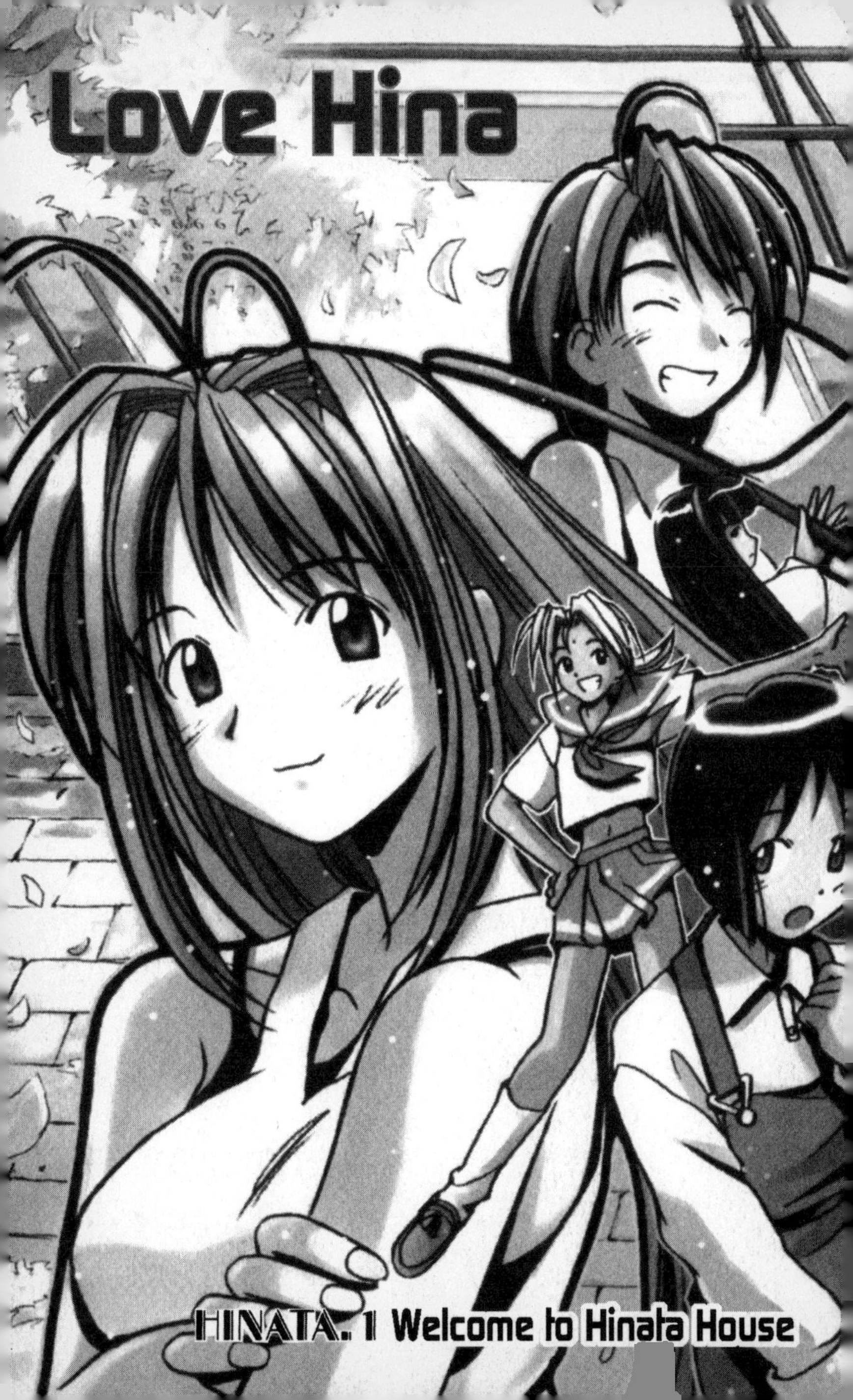
Love Hina
HINATA. 1 Welcome to Hinata House

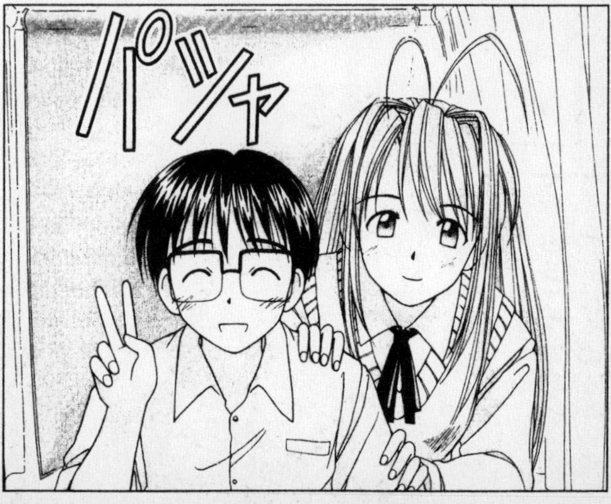
パシャ

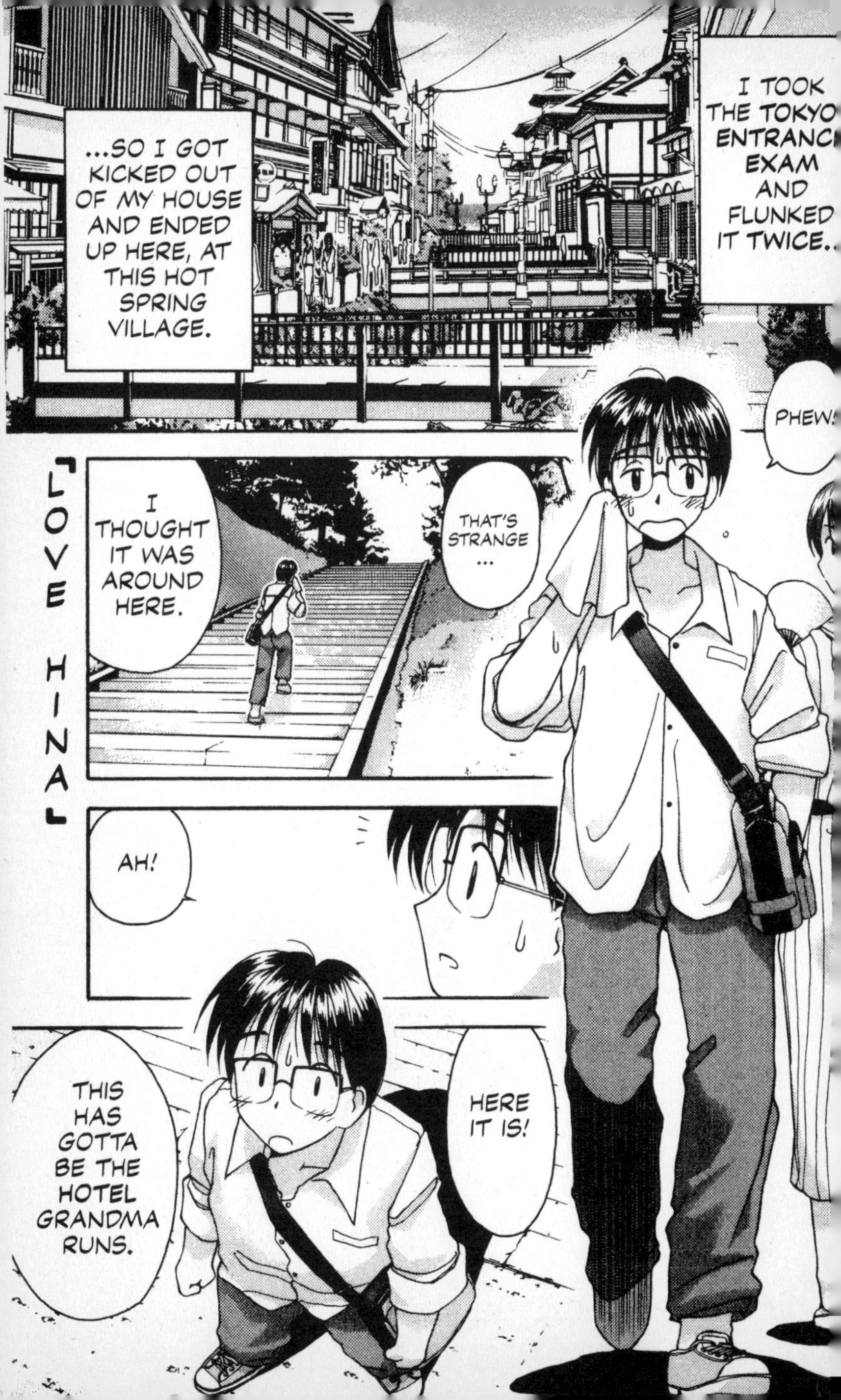
I TOOK THE TOKYO ENTRANC EXAM AND FLUNKED IT TWICE..
...SO I GOT KICKED OUT OF MY HOUSE AND ENDED UP HERE, AT THIS HOT SPRING VILLAGE.
PHEW!
THAT'S STRANGE ...
I THOUGHT IT WAS AROUND HERE.
AH!
HERE IT IS!
THIS HAS GOTTA BE THE HOTEL GRANDMA RUNS.
「LOVE HINA」

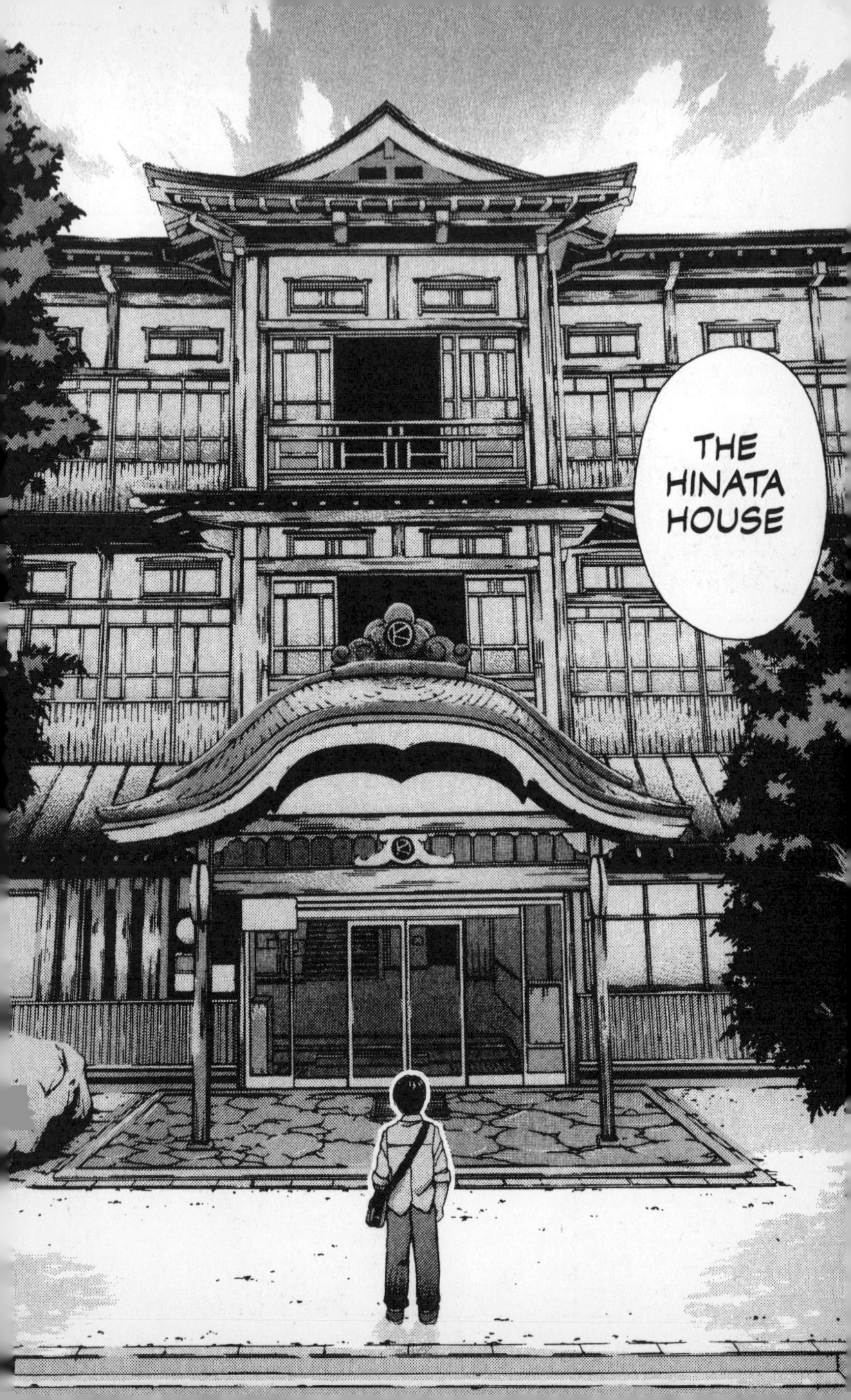
THE HINATA HOUSE

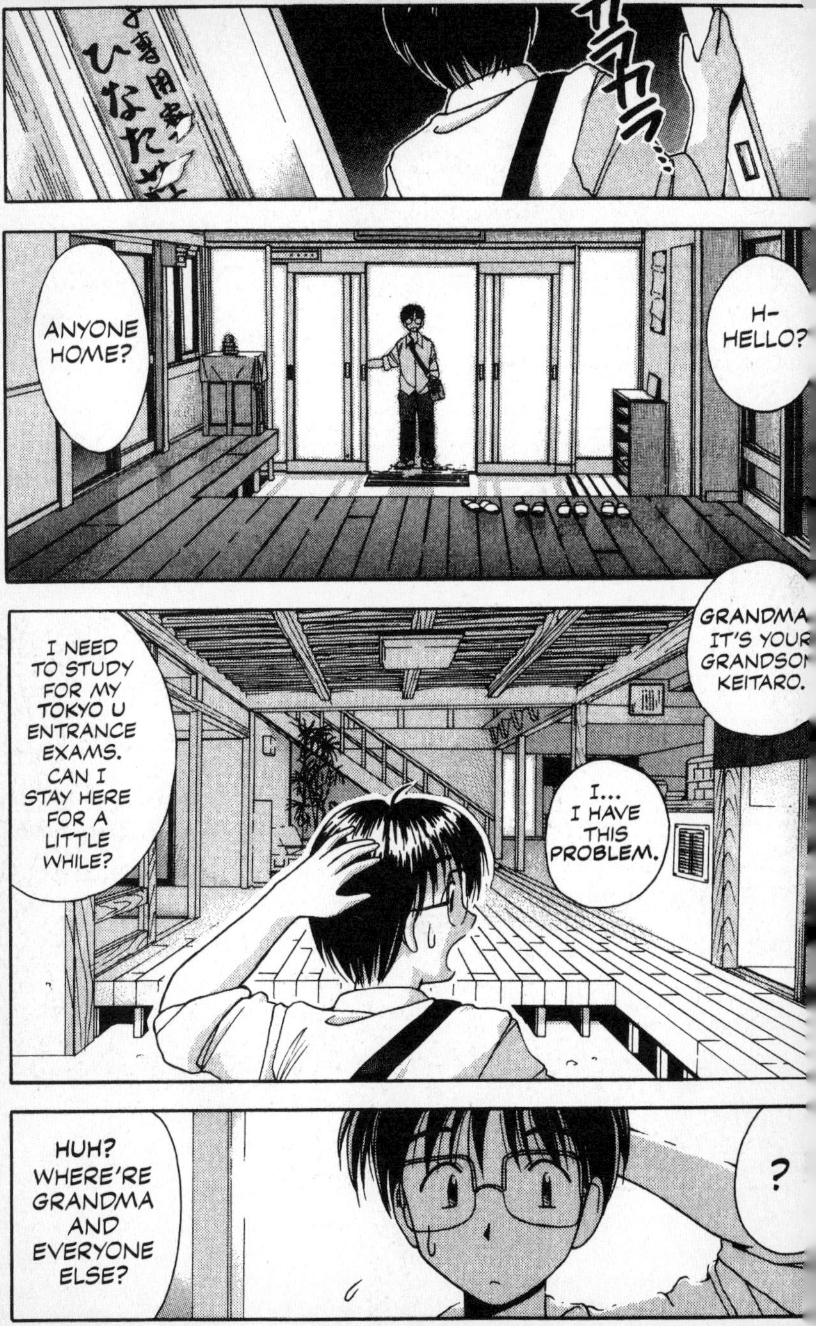
カラカラ…
専用寮
ひなた
H- HELLO?
ANYONE HOME?
GRANDMA IT'S YOUR GRANDSON KEITARO.
I... I HAVE THIS PROBLEM.
I NEED TO STUDY FOR MY TOKYO U ENTRANCE EXAMS. CAN I STAY HERE FOR A LITTLE WHILE?
?
HUH? WHERE'RE GRANDMA AND EVERYONE ELSE?

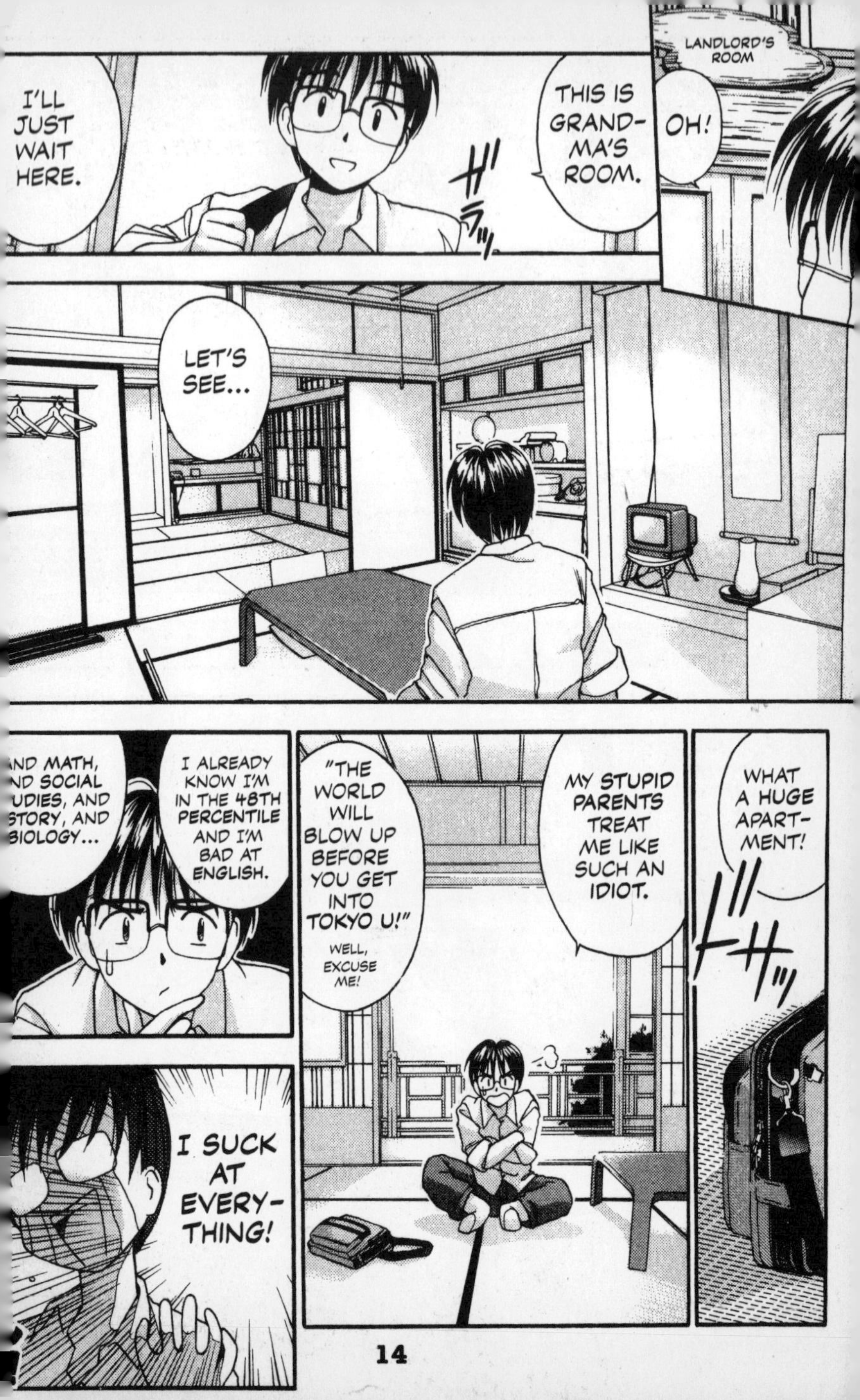
LANDLORD'S ROOM
OH!
THIS IS GRAND-MA'S ROOM.
I'LL JUST WAIT HERE.
LET'S SEE...
WHAT A HUGE APART-MENT!
MY STUPID PARENTS TREAT ME LIKE SUCH AN IDIOT.
"THE WORLD WILL BLOW UP BEFORE YOU GET INTO TOKYO U!"
WELL, EXCUSE ME!
I ALREADY KNOW I'M IN THE 48TH PERCENTILE AND I'M BAD AT ENGLISH.
ND MATH, ND SOCIAL UDIES, AND STORY, AND BIOLOGY...
I SUCK AT EVERY-THING!

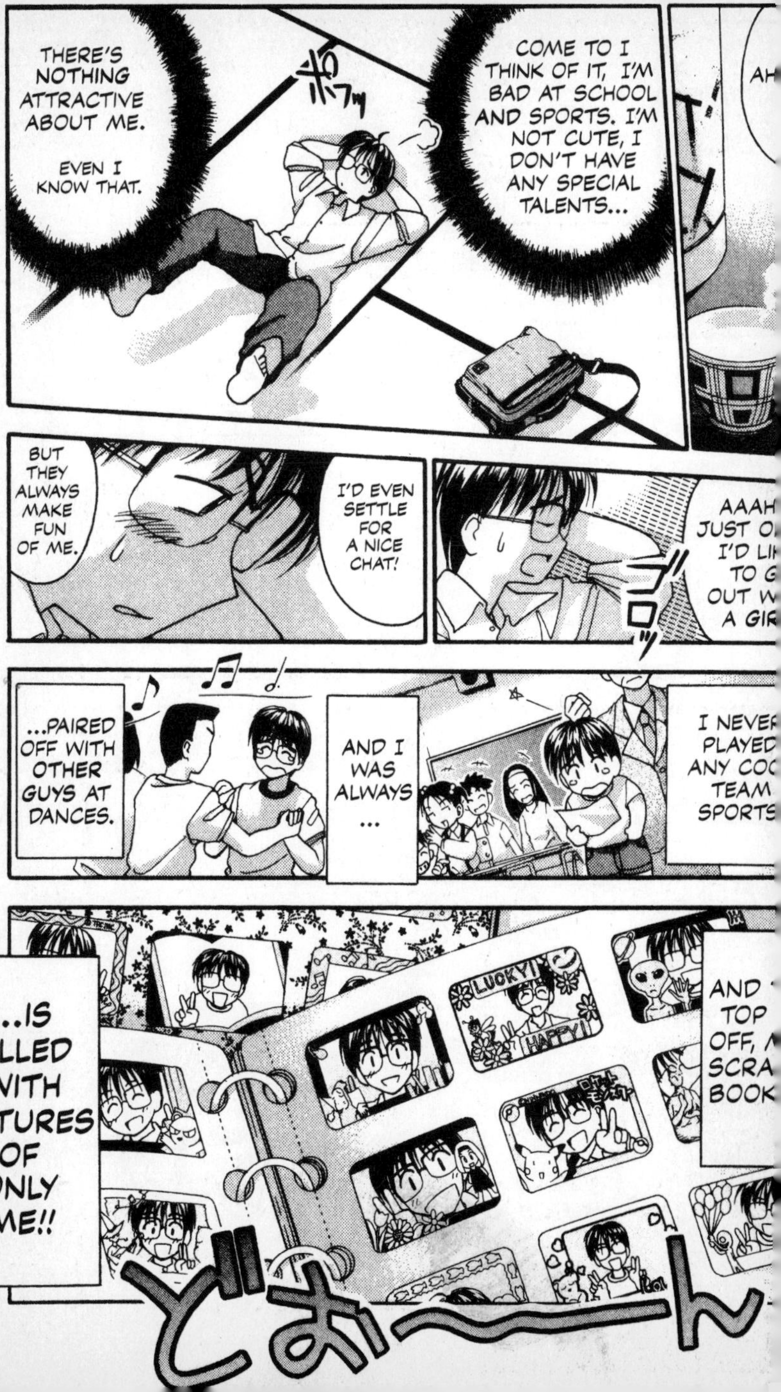
AH
COME TO I THINK OF IT, I'M BAD AT SCHOOL AND SPORTS. I'M NOT CUTE, I DON'T HAVE ANY SPECIAL TALENTS...
ボフッ
THERE'S NOTHING ATTRACTIVE ABOUT ME.
EVEN I KNOW THAT.
AAAH JUST O I'D LI TO G OUT W A GIR
ゴロッ
I'D EVEN SETTLE FOR A NICE CHAT!
BUT THEY ALWAYS MAKE FUN OF ME.
I NEVER PLAYED ANY COO TEAM SPORTS
AND I WAS ALWAYS ...
...PAIRED OFF WITH OTHER GUYS AT DANCES.
AND T TOP OFF, M SCRA BOOK
LUCKY!
HAPPY!
...IS FILLED WITH PICTURES OF ONLY ME!!
どお〜〜ん

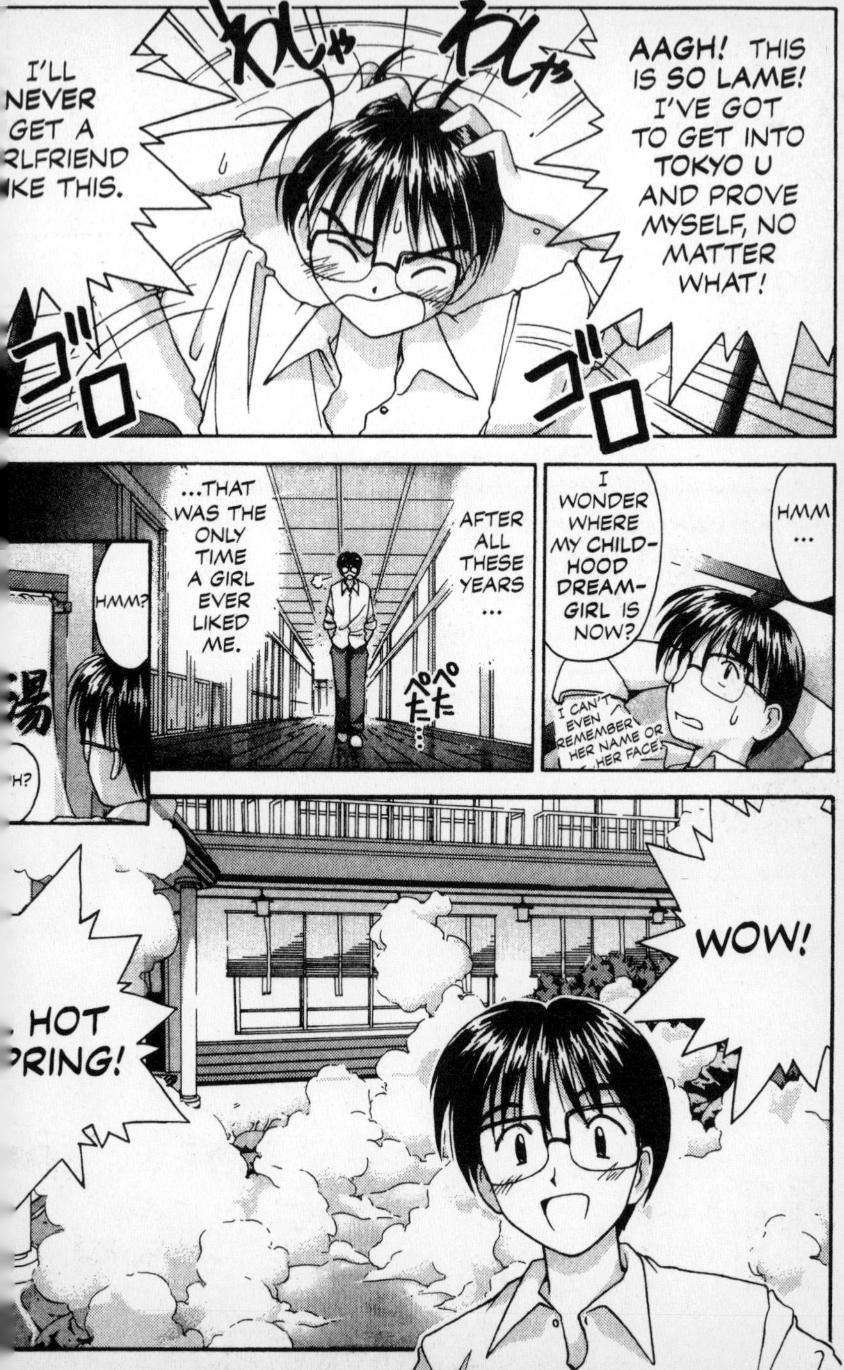
わしゃわしゃ
AAGH! THIS IS SO LAME! I'VE GOT TO GET INTO TOKYO U AND PROVE MYSELF, NO MATTER WHAT!
I'LL NEVER GET A RLFRIEND IKE THIS.
ゴロ
ゴロ
HMM ...
I WONDER WHERE MY CHILD-HOOD DREAM-GIRL IS NOW?
I CAN'T EVEN REMEMBER HER NAME OR HER FACE.
AFTER ALL THESE YEARS ...
...THAT WAS THE ONLY TIME A GIRL EVER LIKED ME.
ぺたぺた...
HMM?
湯
H?
WOW!
HOT PRING!

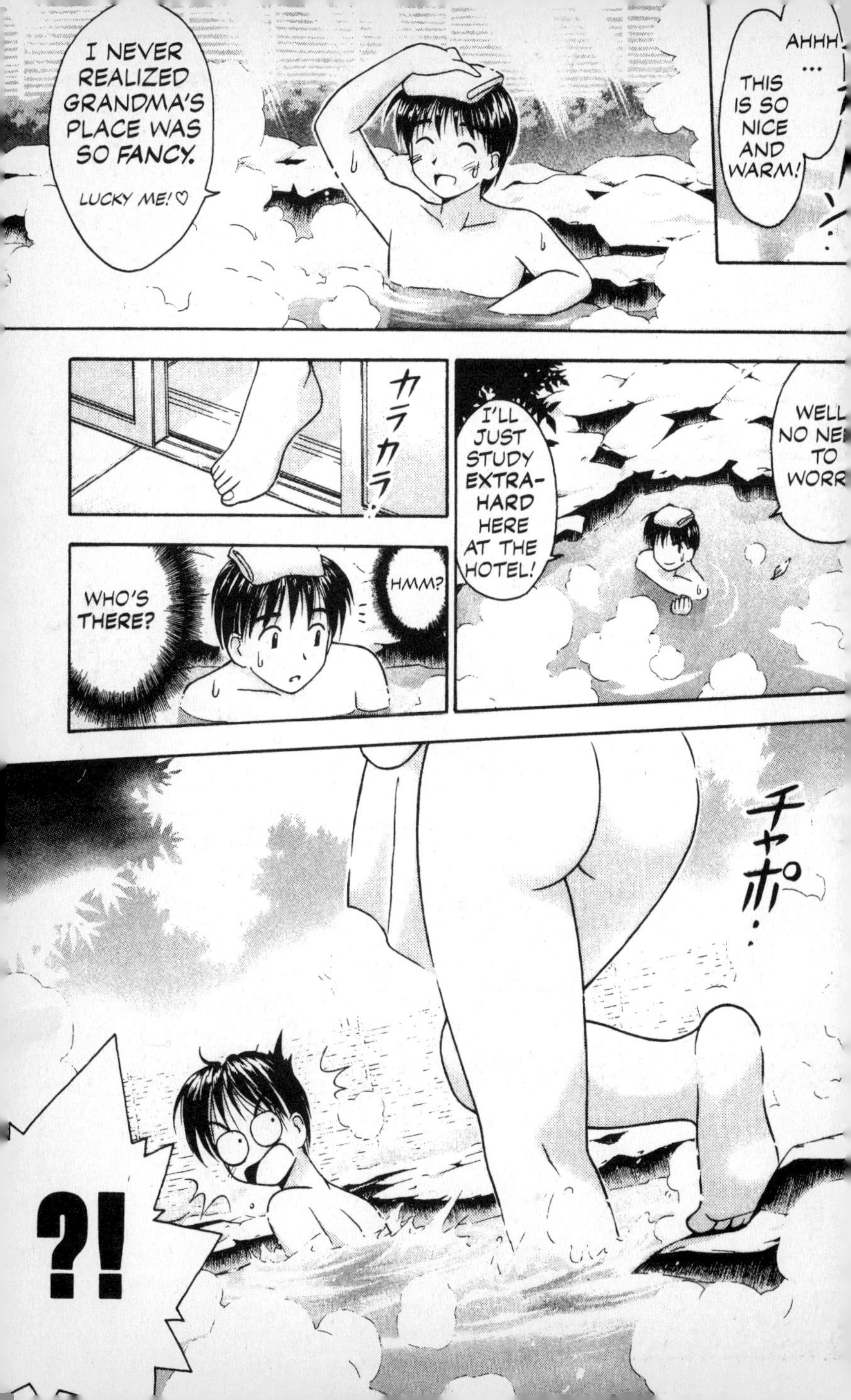
AHHH... THIS IS SO NICE AND WARM!
I NEVER REALIZED GRANDMA'S PLACE WAS SO FANCY.
LUCKY ME! ♡
WELL NO NE TO WORR
I'LL JUST STUDY EXTRA-HARD HERE AT THE HOTEL!
カラカラ
HMM?
WHO'S THERE?
チャポ…
?!

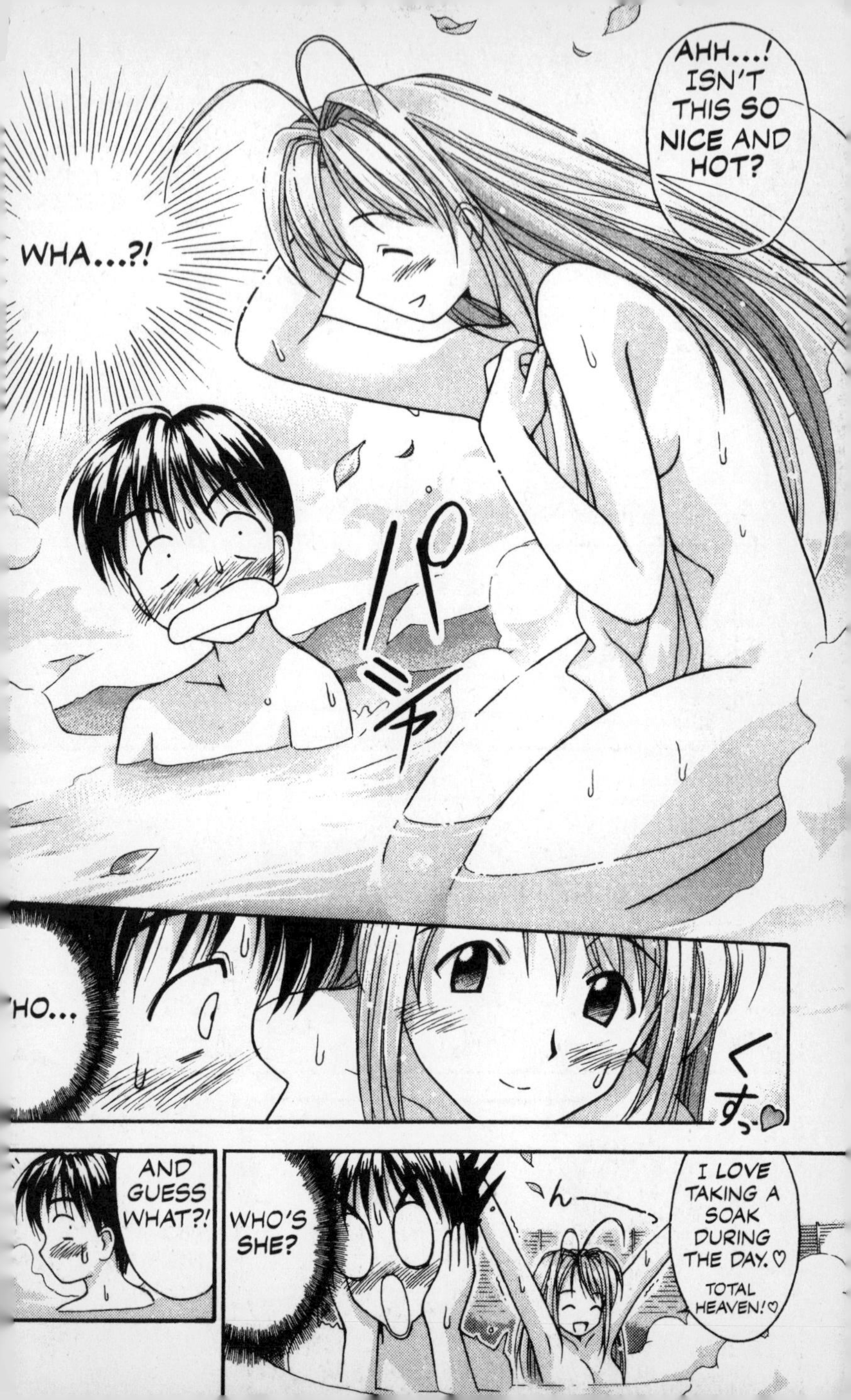
AHH...! ISN'T THIS SO NICE AND HOT?
WHA...?!
くすっ♡
HO...
I LOVE TAKING A SOAK DURING THE DAY. ♡
TOTAL HEAVEN! ♡
ん—
WHO'S SHE?
AND GUESS WHAT?!

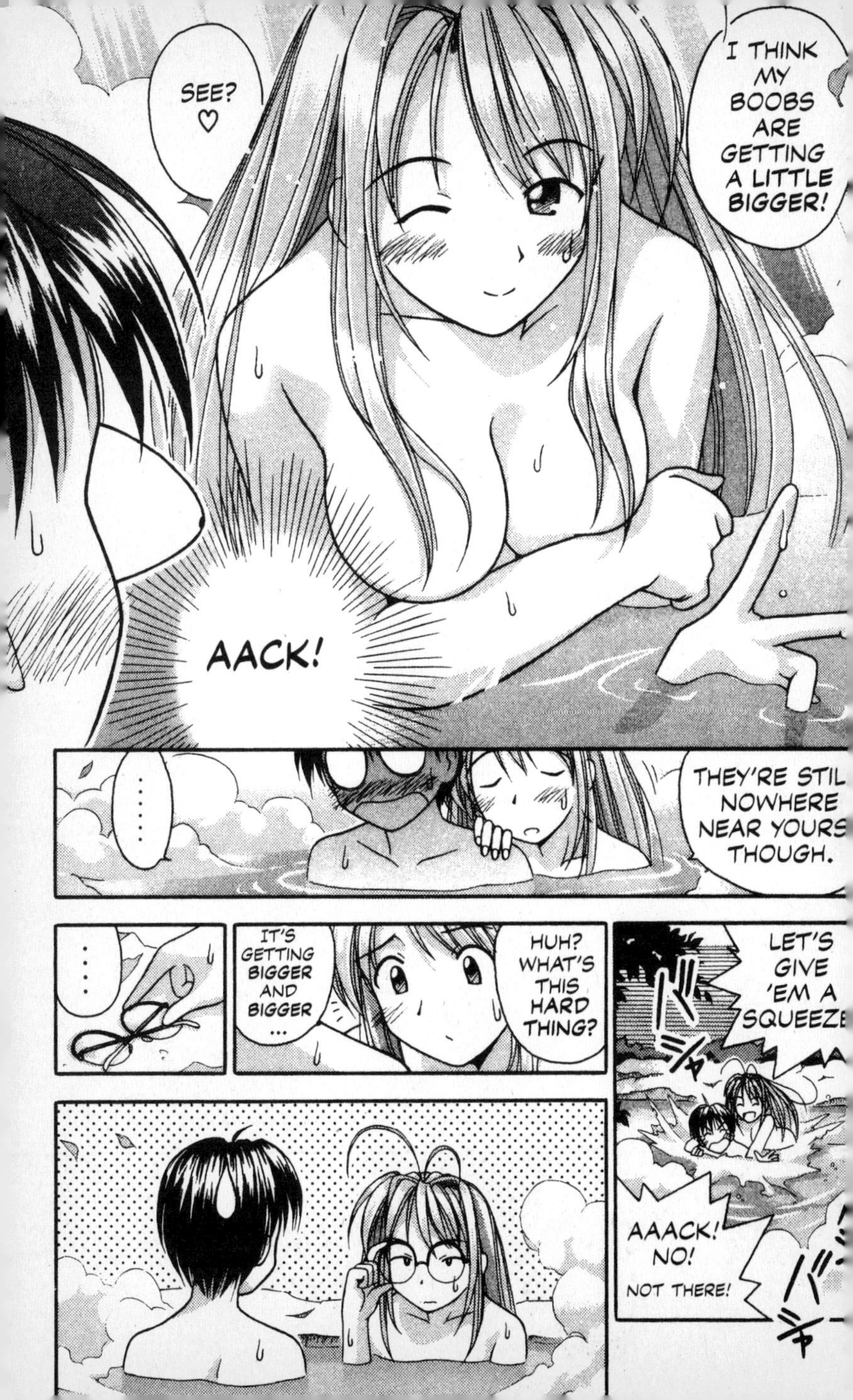
I THINK MY BOOBS ARE GETTING A LITTLE BIGGER!
SEE? ♡
AACK!
THEY'RE STIL NOWHERE NEAR YOURS THOUGH.
......
LET'S GIVE 'EM A SQUEEZE
AAACK! NO! NOT THERE!
HUH? WHAT'S THIS HARD THING?
IT'S GETTING BIGGER AND BIGGER ...
....

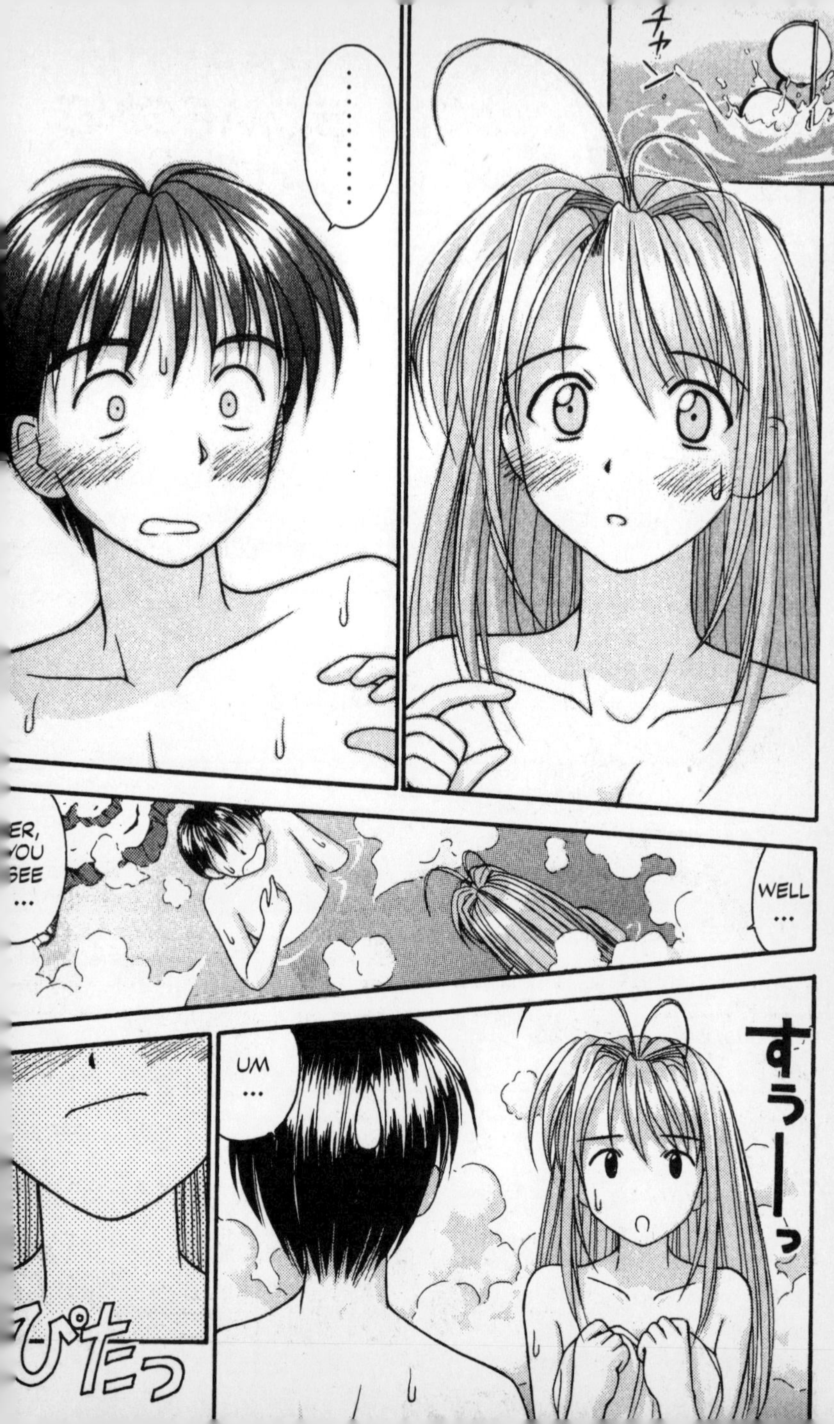

チャン
……
WELL …
ER, YOU SEE …
すうーっ
UM …
ぴたっ

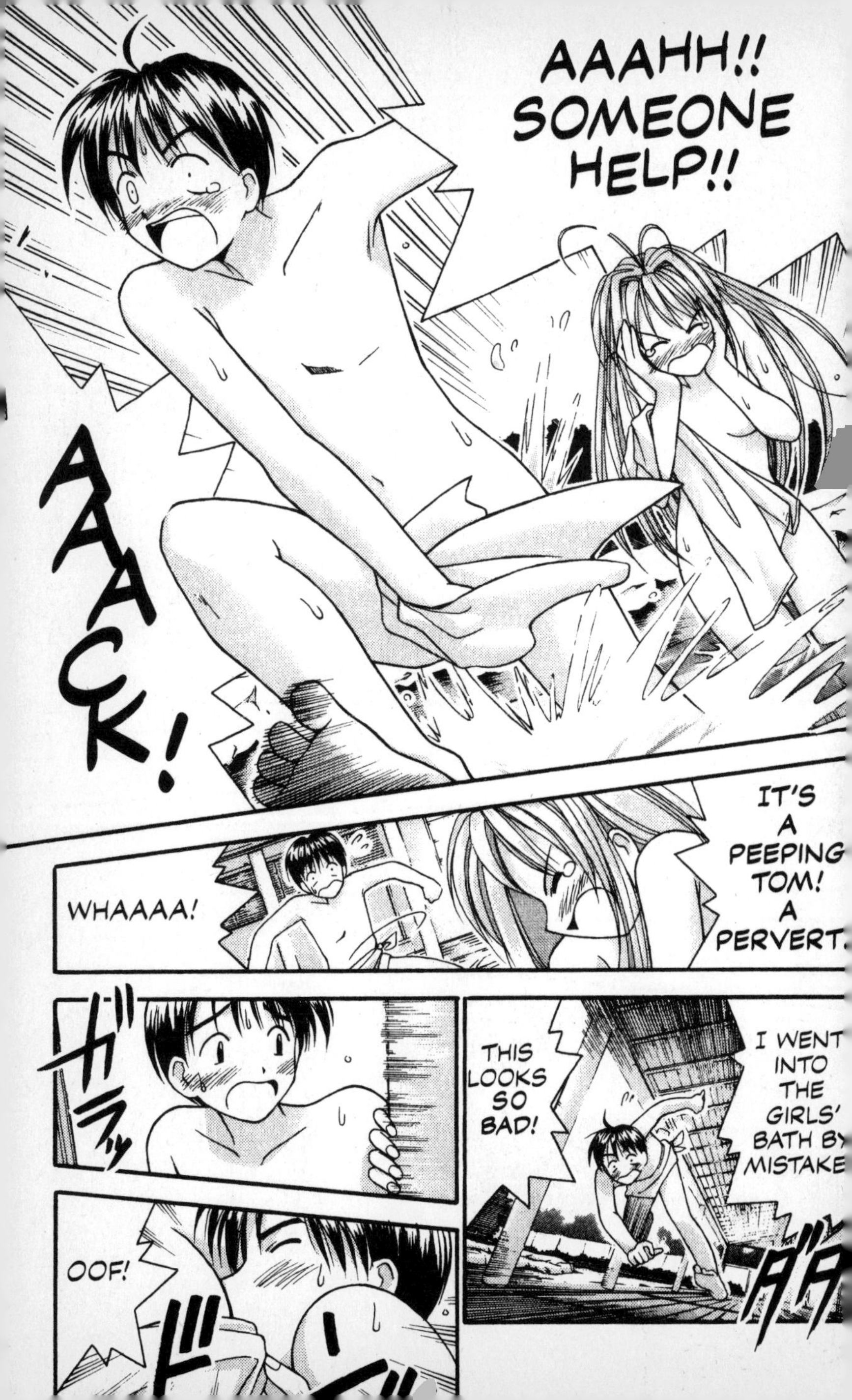
AAAH!! SOMEONE HELP!!
AAACK!
IT'S A PEEPING TOM! A PERVERT.
WHAAAA!
I WENT INTO THE GIRLS' BATH BY MISTAKE
THIS LOOKS SO BAD!
ガラッ
OOF!

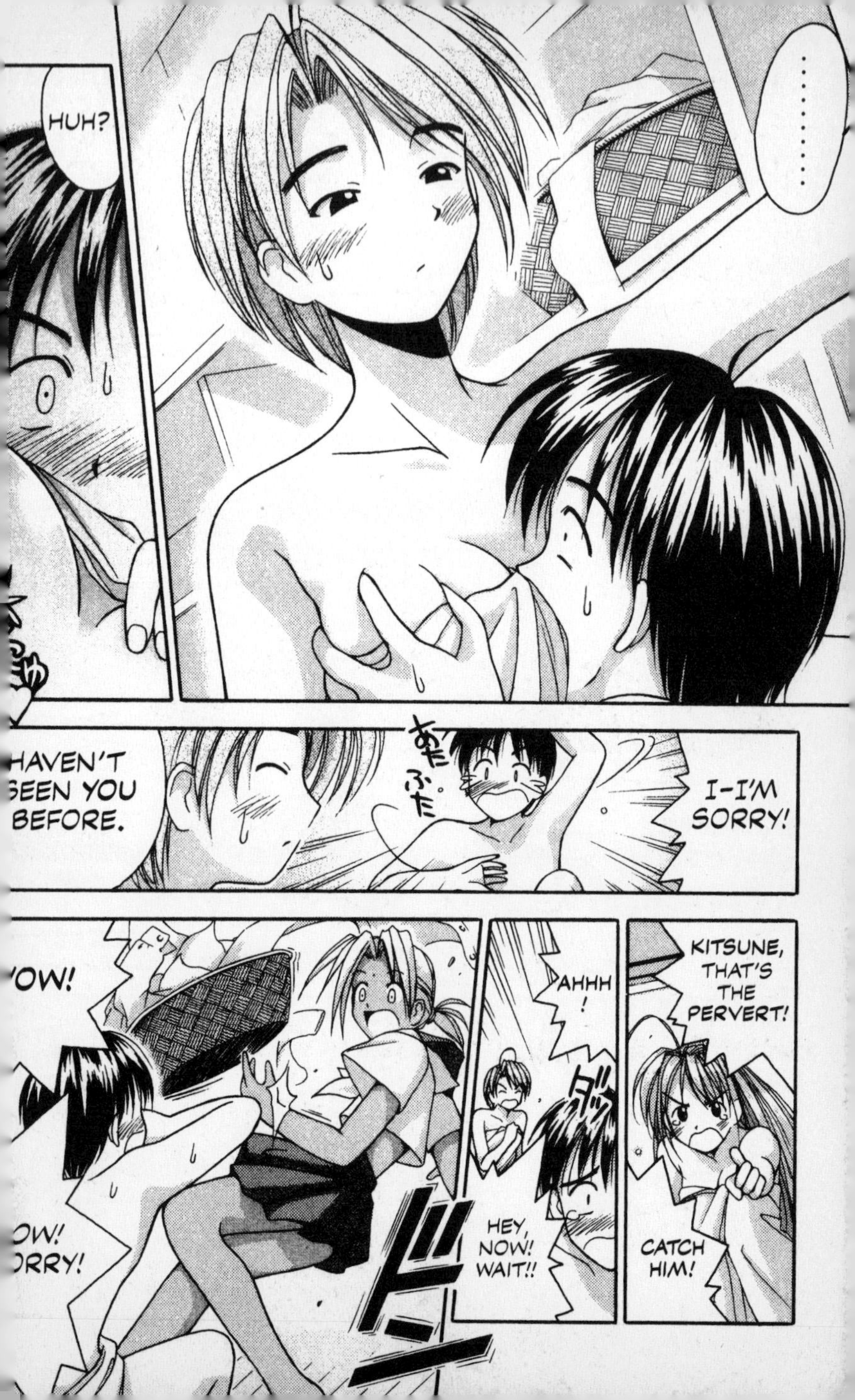
......
HUH?
I-I'M SORRY!
あたふた
HAVEN'T SEEN YOU BEFORE.
KITSUNE, THAT'S THE PERVERT!
CATCH HIM!
AHHH!
ダッ
HEY, NOW! WAIT!!
OW!
ドドー
OW! ORRY!

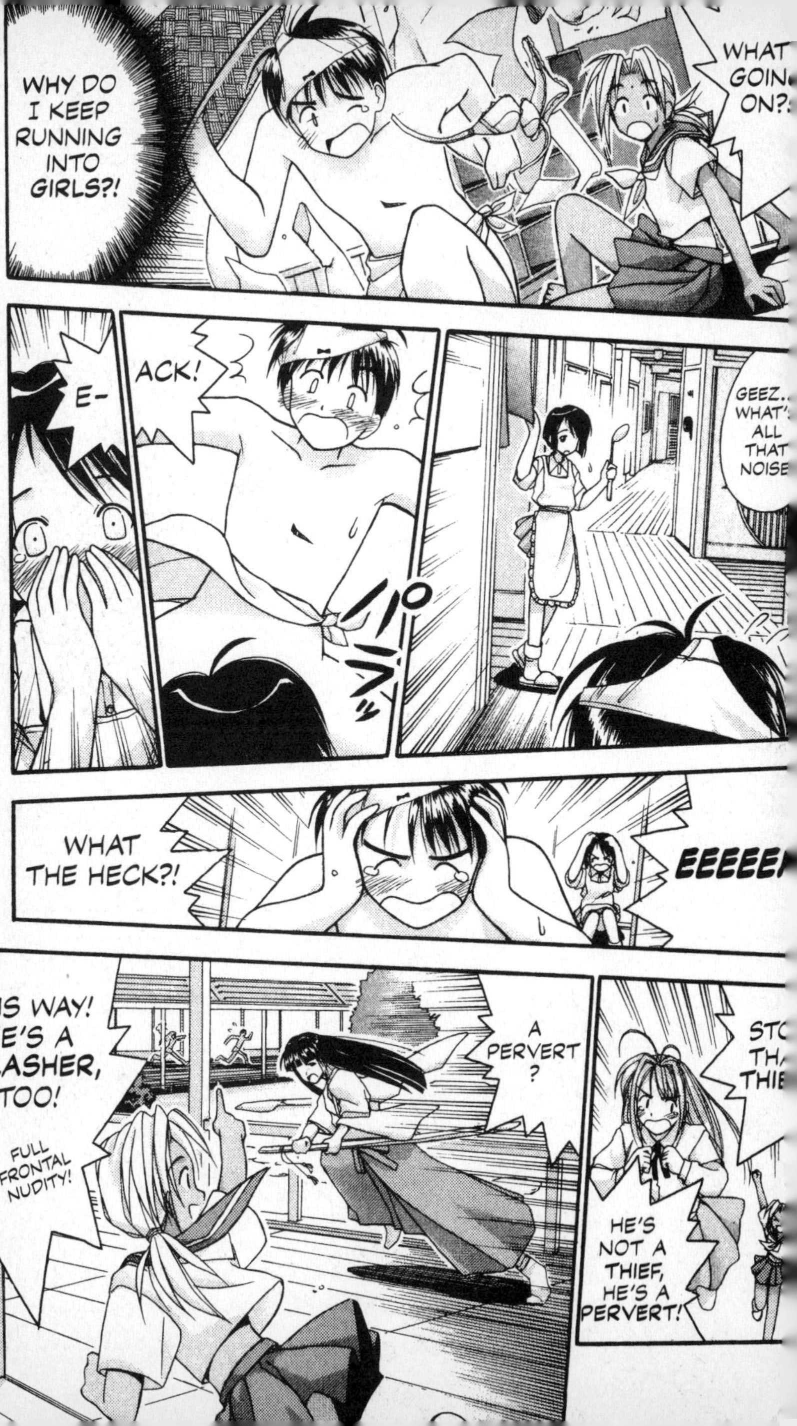

WHAT GOIN ON?!
WHY DO I KEEP RUNNING INTO GIRLS?!
GEEZ... WHAT'S ALL THAT NOISE
ACK!
E-
EEEEE
WHAT THE HECK?!
STO THA THIE
HE'S NOT A THIEF, HE'S A PERVERT!
A PERVERT?
THIS WAY! HE'S A FLASHER, TOO!
FULL FRONTAL NUDITY!

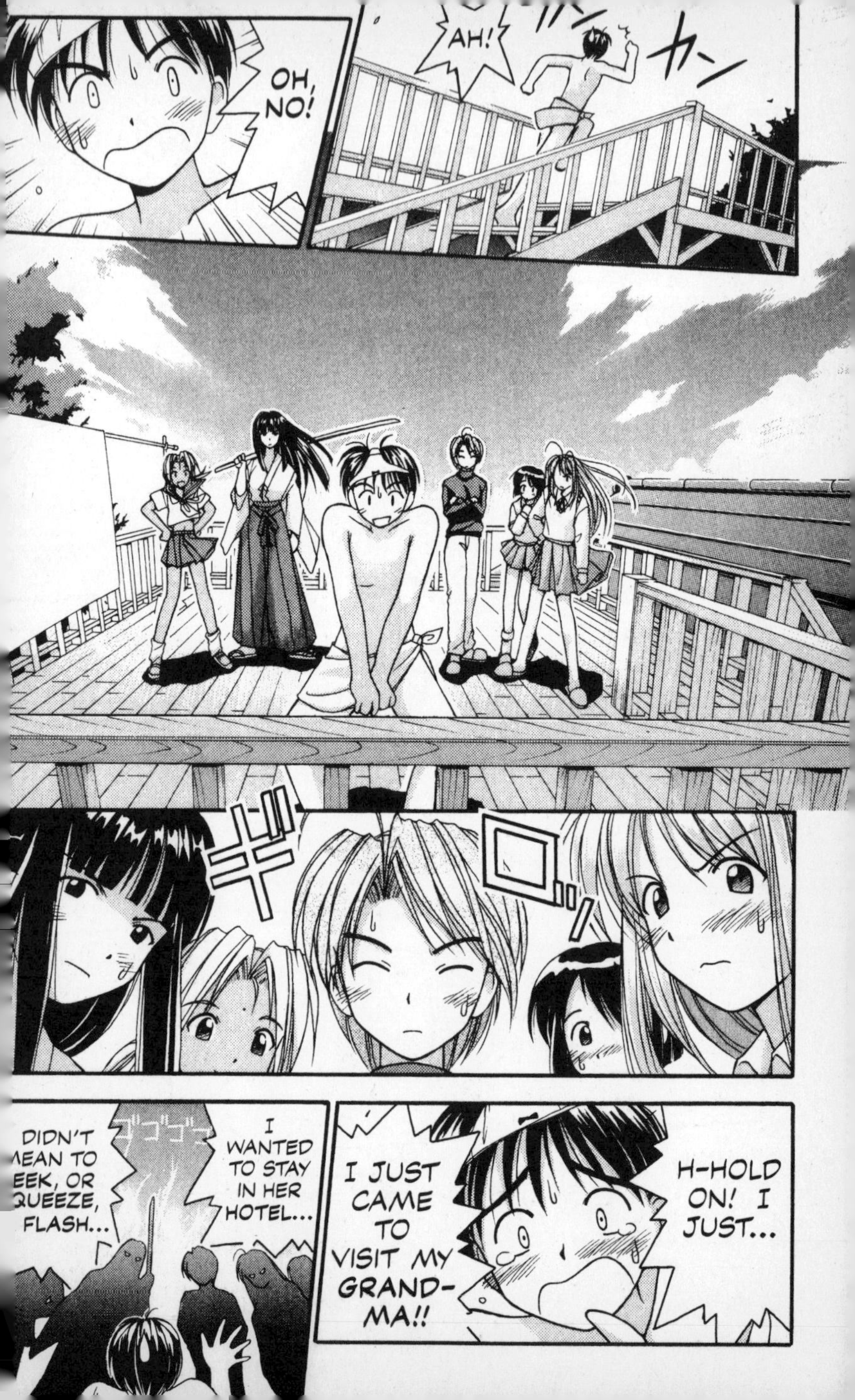
AH!
OH, NO!
H-HOLD ON! I JUST...
I JUST CAME TO VISIT MY GRAND-MA!!
I WANTED TO STAY IN HER HOTEL...
DIDN'T MEAN TO EEK, OR QUEEZE, FLASH...

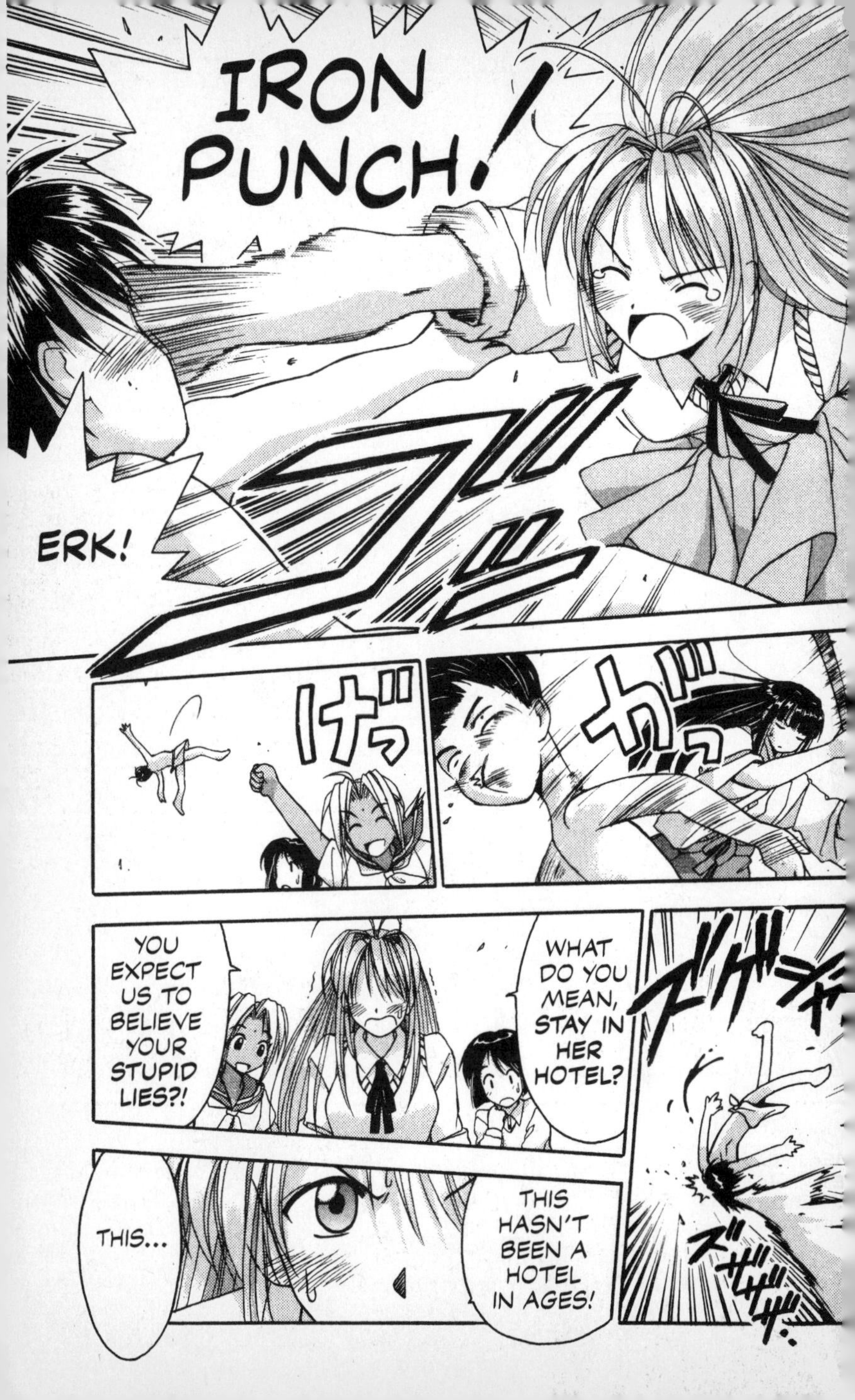
IRON PUNCH!
ERK!
WHAT DO YOU MEAN, STAY IN HER HOTEL?
YOU EXPECT US TO BELIEVE YOUR STUPID LIES?!
THIS HASN'T BEEN A HOTEL IN AGES!
THIS...

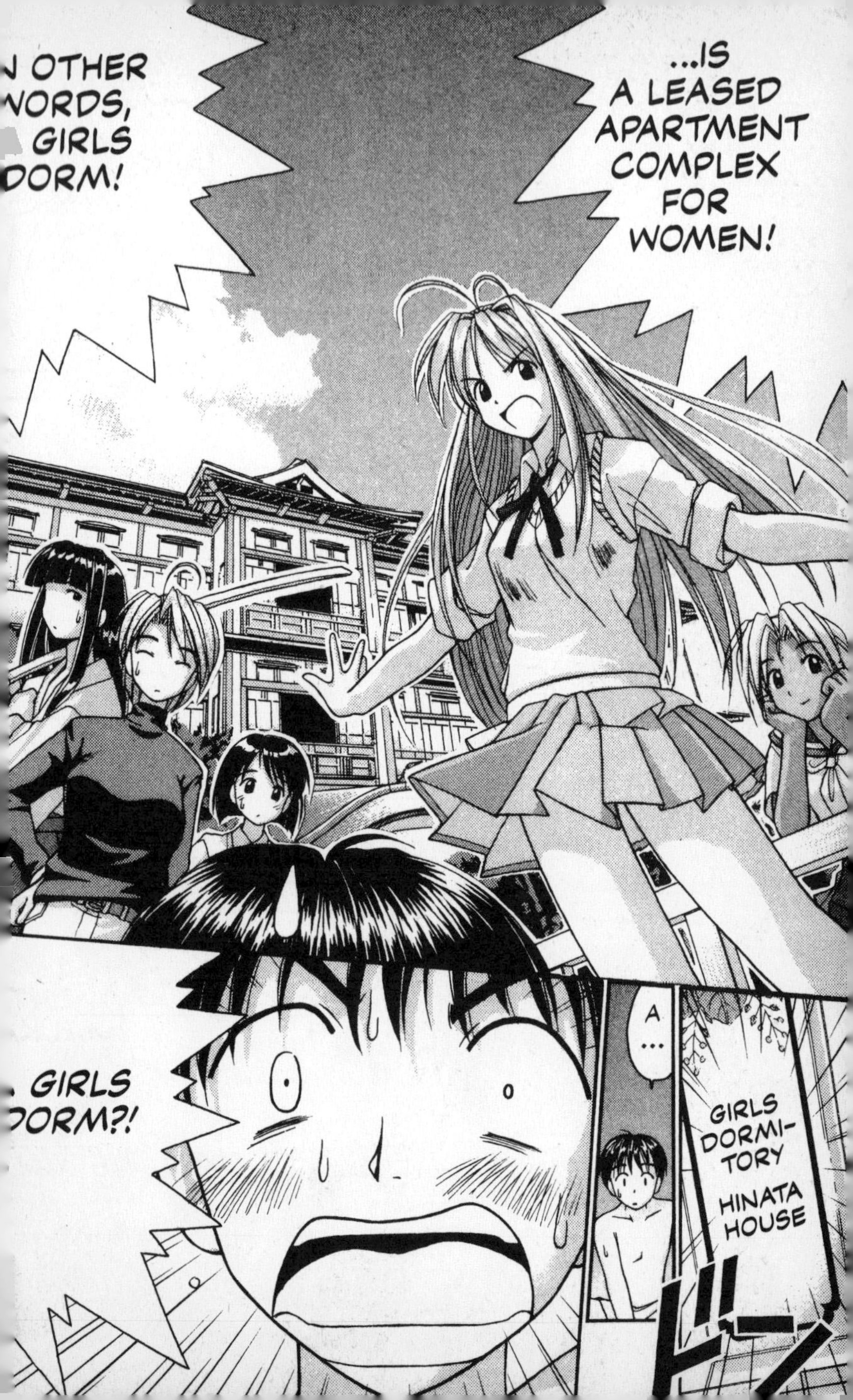
...IS A LEASED APARTMENT COMPLEX FOR WOMEN!
N OTHER WORDS, GIRLS DORM!
GIRLS DORMI-TORY
HINATA HOUSE
A ...
GIRLS DORM?!

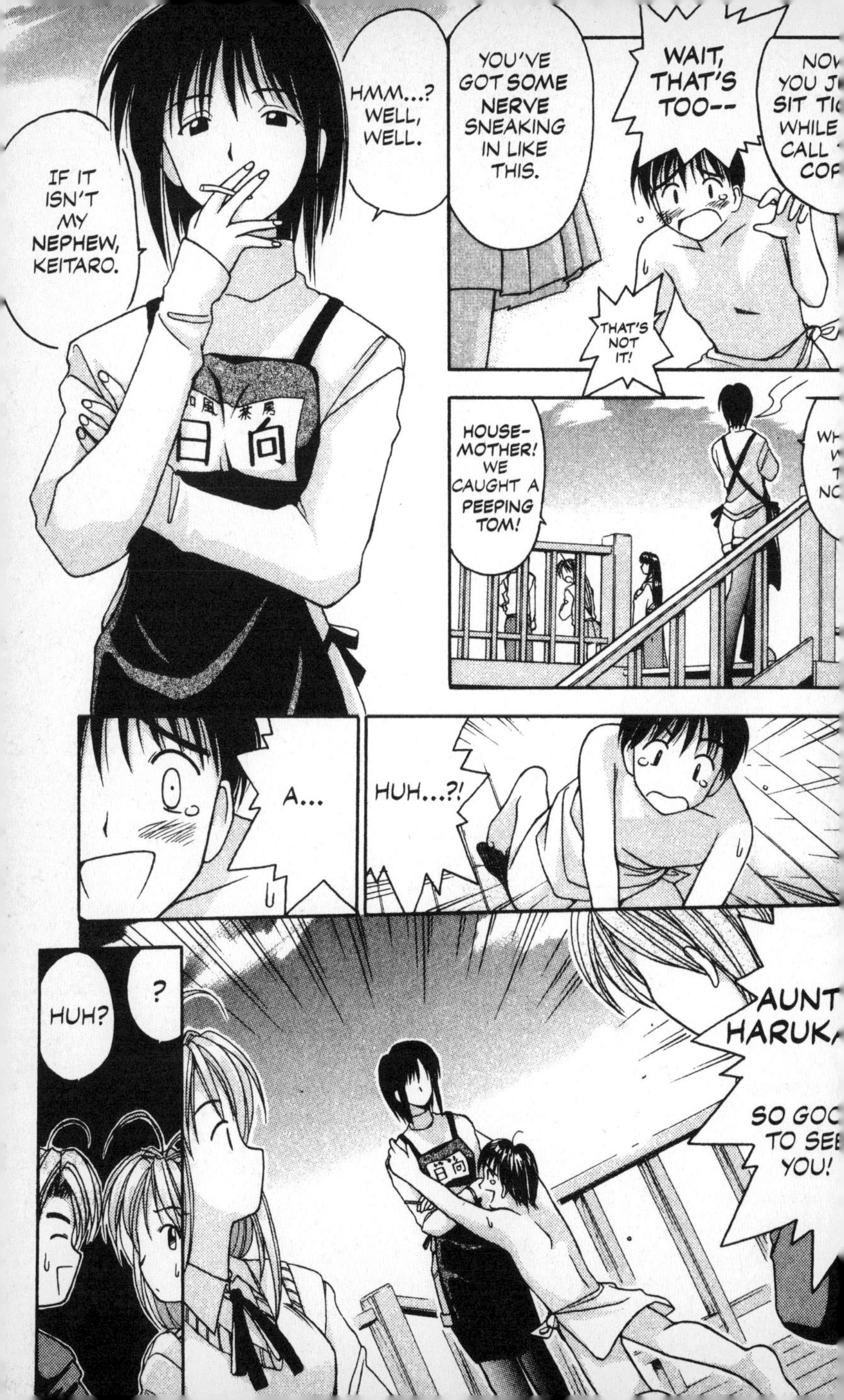
NOW YOU J SIT TI WHILE CALL COP
WAIT, THAT'S TOO--
YOU'VE GOT SOME NERVE SNEAKING IN LIKE THIS.
THAT'S NOT IT!
HOUSE-MOTHER! WE CAUGHT A PEEPING TOM!
HMM...? WELL, WELL.
IF IT ISN'T MY NEPHEW, KEITARO.
日向
HUH...?!
A...
AUNT HARUK
SO GOO TO SEE YOU!
?
HUH?

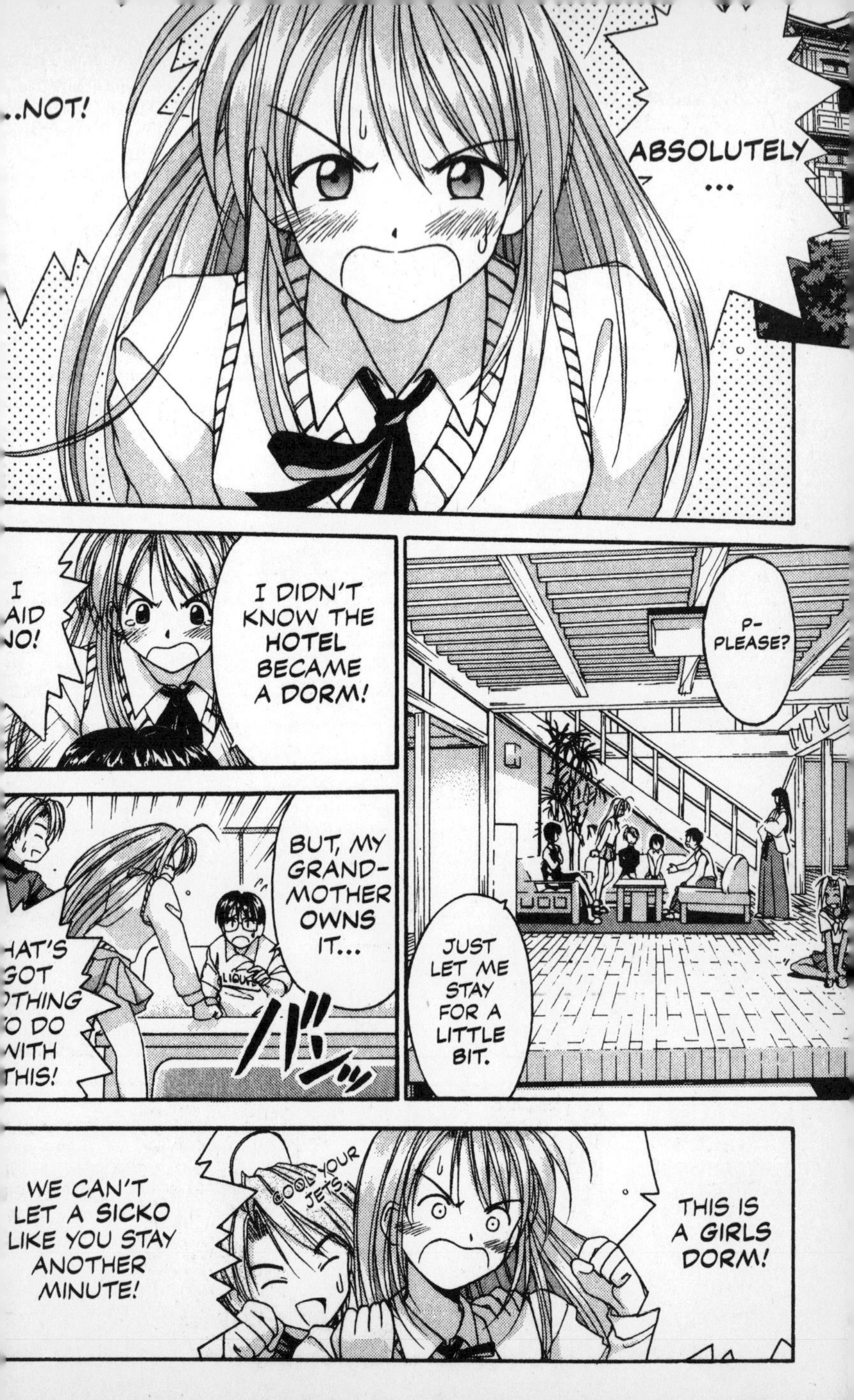
ABSOLUTELY...
..NOT!
P-PLEASE?
JUST LET ME STAY FOR A LITTLE BIT.
I DIDN'T KNOW THE HOTEL BECAME A DORM!
I AID NO!
BUT, MY GRAND-MOTHER OWNS IT...
バンッ
HAT'S GOT THING O DO WITH THIS!
THIS IS A GIRLS DORM!
COOL YOUR JETS!
WE CAN'T LET A SICKO LIKE YOU STAY ANOTHER MINUTE!

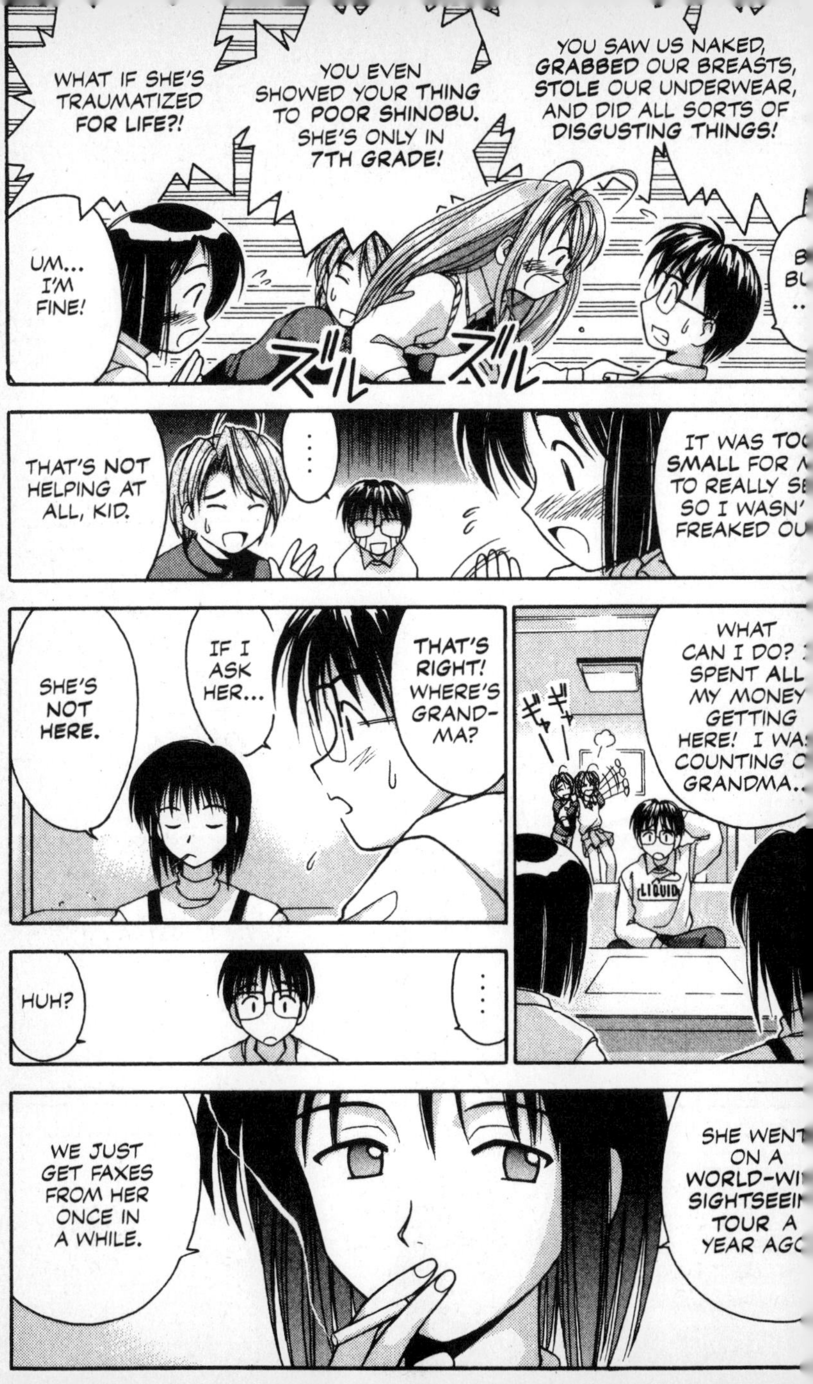
YOU SAW US NAKED, GRABBED OUR BREASTS, STOLE OUR UNDERWEAR, AND DID ALL SORTS OF DISGUSTING THINGS!
YOU EVEN SHOWED YOUR THING TO POOR SHINOBU. SHE'S ONLY IN 7TH GRADE!
WHAT IF SHE'S TRAUMATIZED FOR LIFE?!
UM... I'M FINE!
ズル
ズル
IT WAS TO SMALL FOR M TO REALLY SE SO I WASN' FREAKED OU
....
THAT'S NOT HELPING AT ALL, KID.
WHAT CAN I DO? SPENT ALL MY MONEY GETTING HERE! I WA COUNTING O GRANDMA..
ギャー
ギャー
THAT'S RIGHT! WHERE'S GRAND-MA?
IF I ASK HER...
SHE'S NOT HERE.
....
HUH?
SHE WENT ON A WORLD-WI SIGHTSEEI TOUR A YEAR AG
WE JUST GET FAXES FROM HER ONCE IN A WHILE.

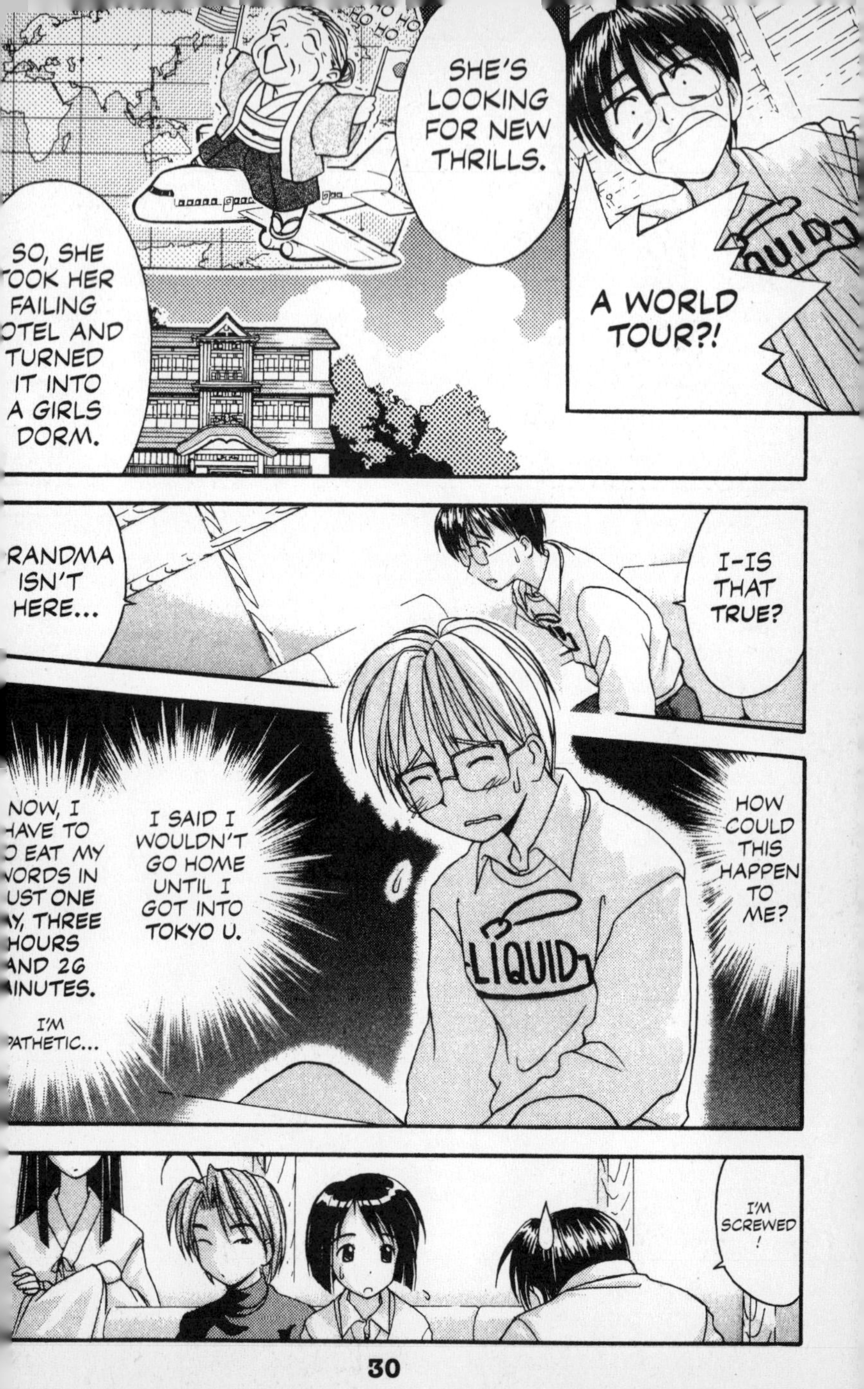
A WORLD TOUR?!
SHE'S LOOKING FOR NEW THRILLS.
SO, SHE OOK HER FAILING OTEL AND TURNED IT INTO A GIRLS DORM.
I-IS THAT TRUE?
RANDMA ISN'T HERE...
HOW COULD THIS HAPPEN TO ME?
I SAID I WOULDN'T GO HOME UNTIL I GOT INTO TOKYO U.
NOW, I HAVE TO EAT MY ORDS IN UST ONE Y, THREE HOURS AND 26 INUTES.
I'M PATHETIC...
I'M SCREWED!

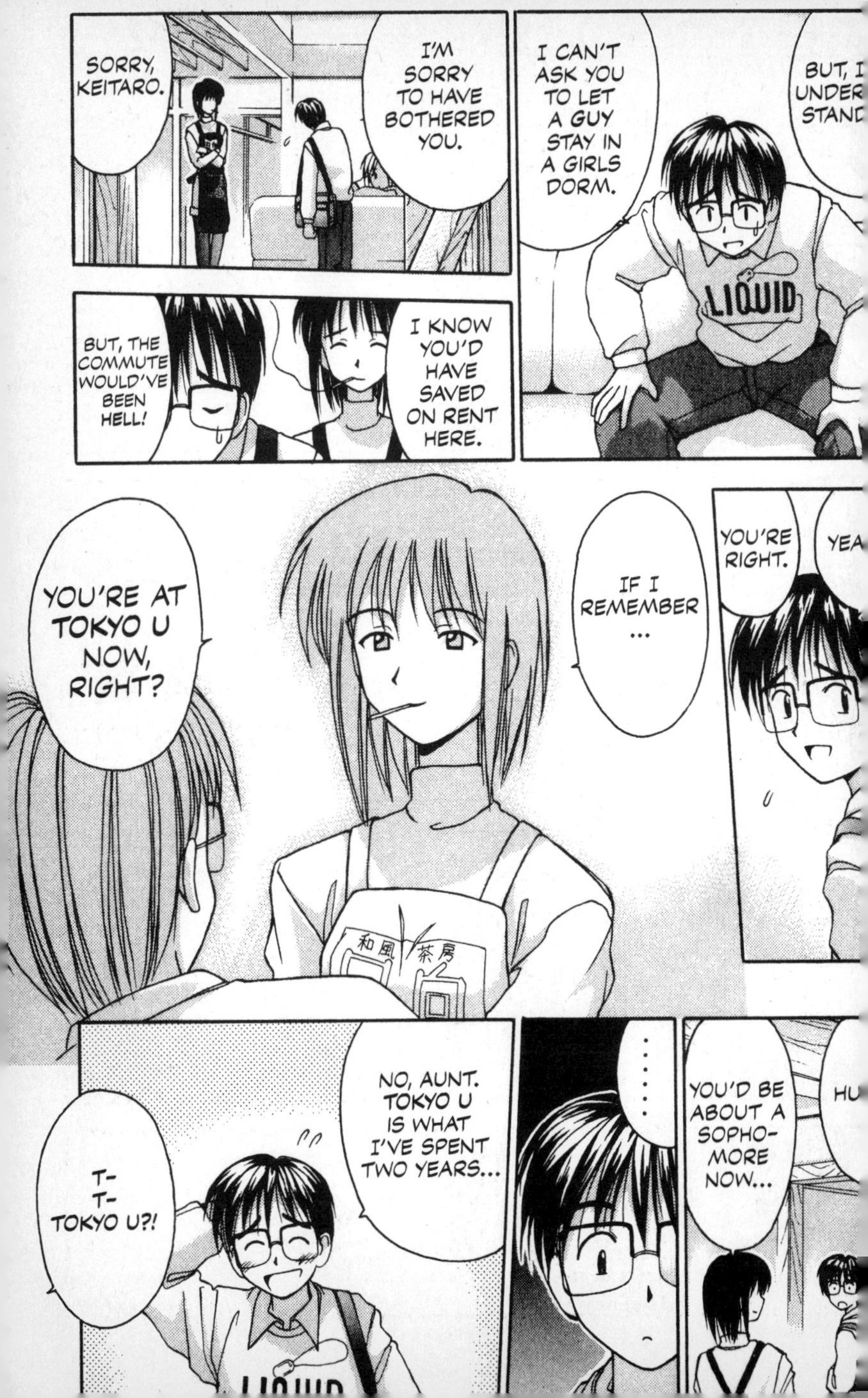
BUT, I UNDER STAND
I CAN'T ASK YOU TO LET A GUY STAY IN A GIRLS DORM.
LIQUID
I'M SORRY TO HAVE BOTHERED YOU.
SORRY, KEITARO.
I KNOW YOU'D HAVE SAVED ON RENT HERE.
BUT, THE COMMUTE WOULD'VE BEEN HELL!
YEA
YOU'RE RIGHT.
IF I REMEMBER ...
YOU'RE AT TOKYO U NOW, RIGHT?
和風 茶房
HU
YOU'D BE ABOUT A SOPHOMORE NOW...
......
NO, AUNT. TOKYO U IS WHAT I'VE SPENT TWO YEARS...
T- T- TOKYO U?!

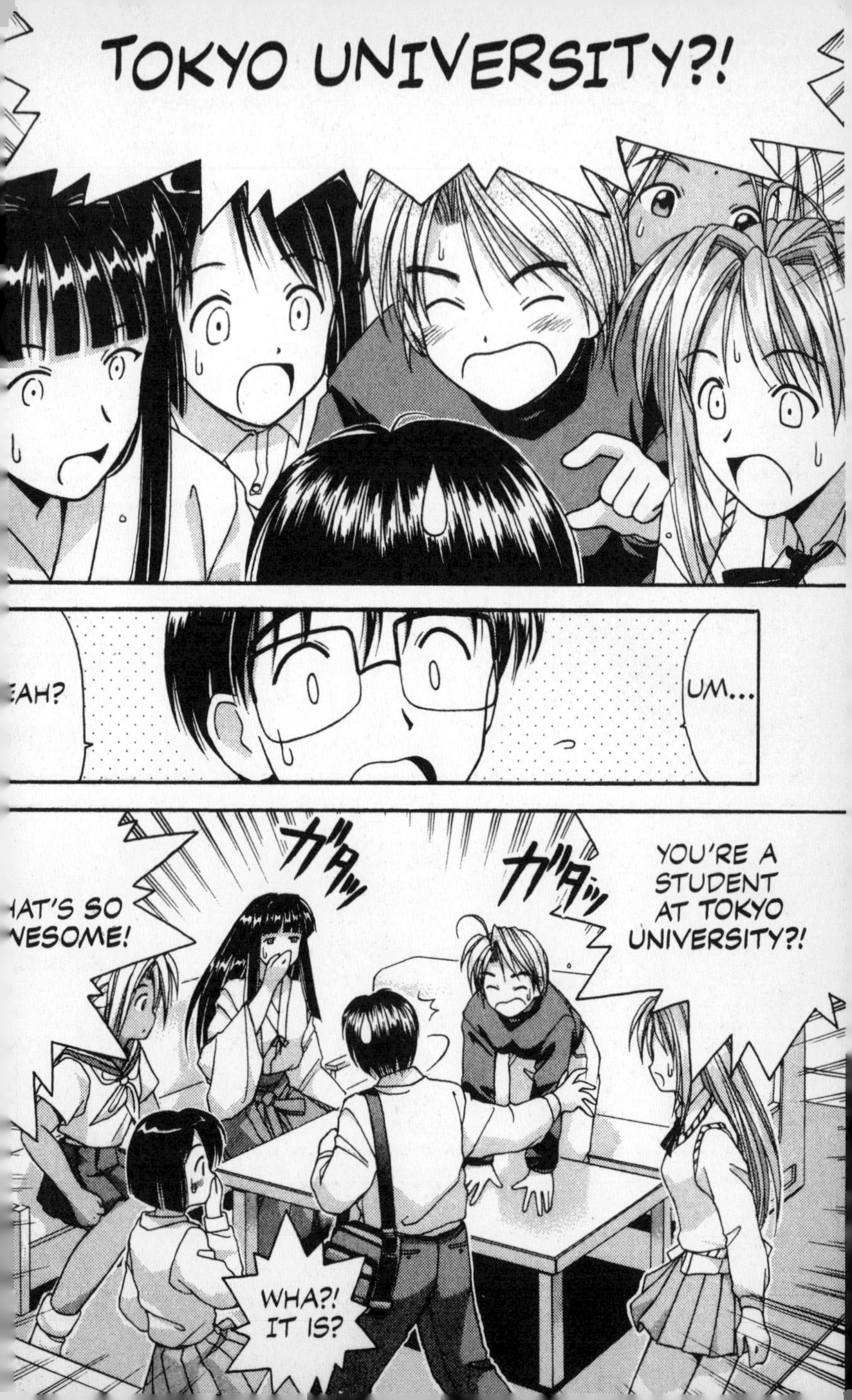
TOKYO UNIVERSITY?!
UM...
EAH?
YOU'RE A STUDENT AT TOKYO UNIVERSITY?!
ガタッ
ガタッ
HAT'S SO WESOME!
WHA?! IT IS?

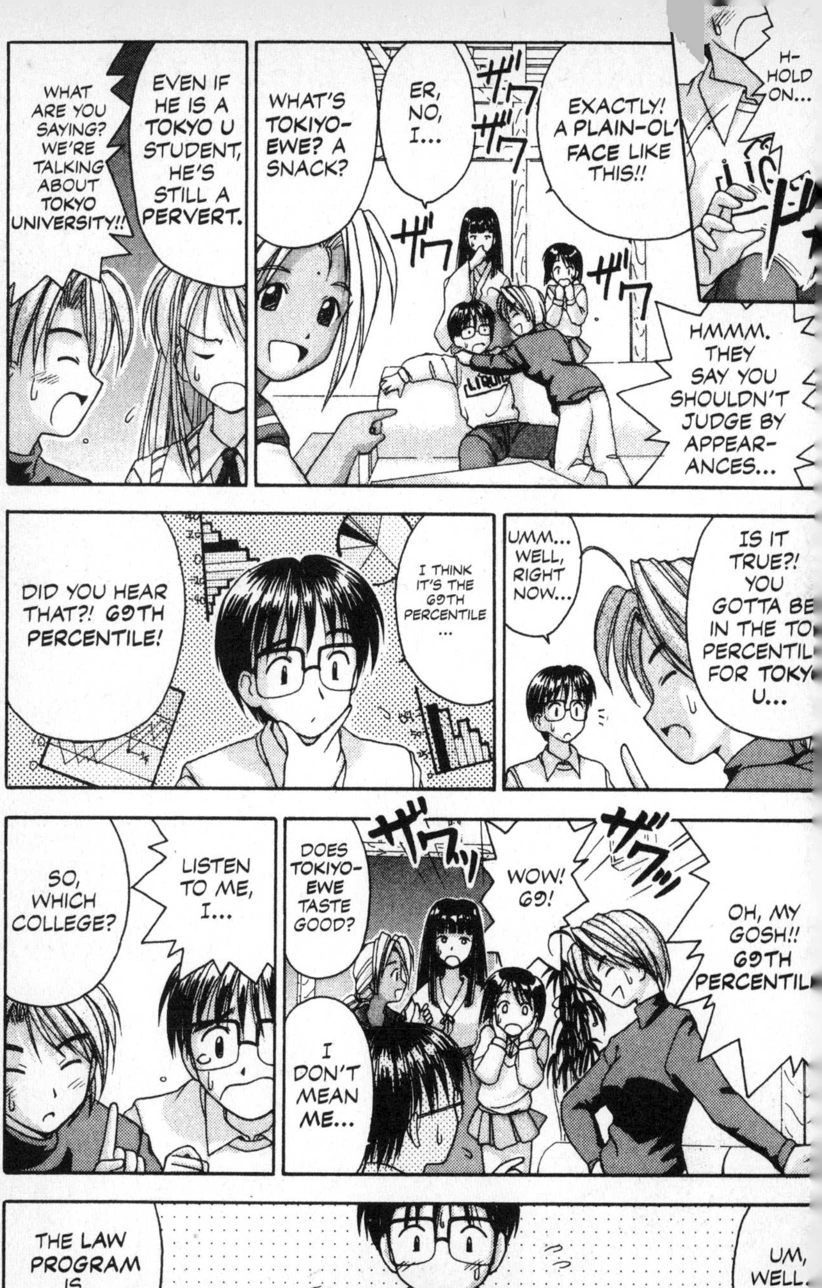
H- HOLD ON...
EXACTLY! A PLAIN-OL' FACE LIKE THIS!!
HMMM. THEY SAY YOU SHOULDN'T JUDGE BY APPEARANCES...
ER, NO, I...
WHAT'S TOKIYO-EWE? A SNACK?
EVEN IF HE IS A TOKYO U STUDENT, HE'S STILL A PERVERT.
WHAT ARE YOU SAYING? WE'RE TALKING ABOUT TOKYO UNIVERSITY!!
IS IT TRUE?! YOU GOTTA BE IN THE TO PERCENTIL FOR TOKY U...
UMM... WELL, RIGHT NOW...
I THINK IT'S THE 69TH PERCENTILE ...
DID YOU HEAR THAT?! 69TH PERCENTILE!
OH, MY GOSH!! 69TH PERCENTIL
WOW! 69!
DOES TOKIYO-EWE TASTE GOOD?
I DON'T MEAN ME...
LISTEN TO ME, I...
SO, WHICH COLLEGE?
UM, WELL.
THE LAW PROGRAM IS...

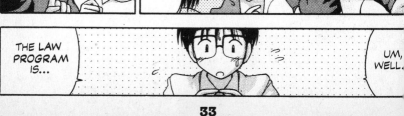

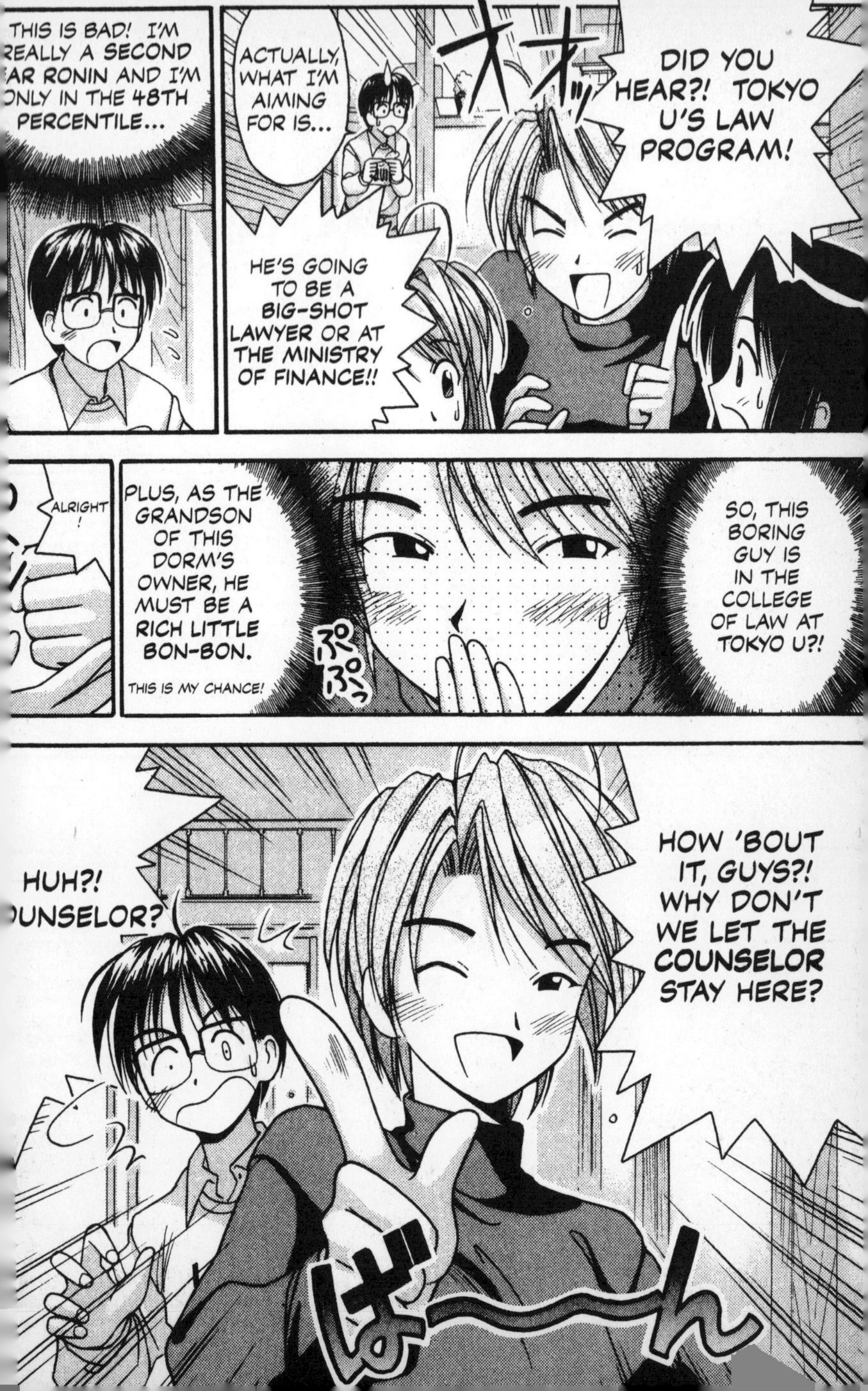
DID YOU HEAR?! TOKYO U'S LAW PROGRAM!
オオッ
HE'S GOING TO BE A BIG-SHOT LAWYER OR AT THE MINISTRY OF FINANCE!!
ACTUALLY, WHAT I'M AIMING FOR IS...
THIS IS BAD! I'M REALLY A SECOND EAR RONIN AND I'M ONLY IN THE 48TH PERCENTILE...
SO, THIS BORING GUY IS IN THE COLLEGE OF LAW AT TOKYO U?!
ぷぷっ
PLUS, AS THE GRANDSON OF THIS DORM'S OWNER, HE MUST BE A RICH LITTLE BON-BON.
THIS IS MY CHANCE!
ALRIGHT!
HOW 'BOUT IT, GUYS?! WHY DON'T WE LET THE COUNSELOR STAY HERE?
HUH?! OUNSELOR?

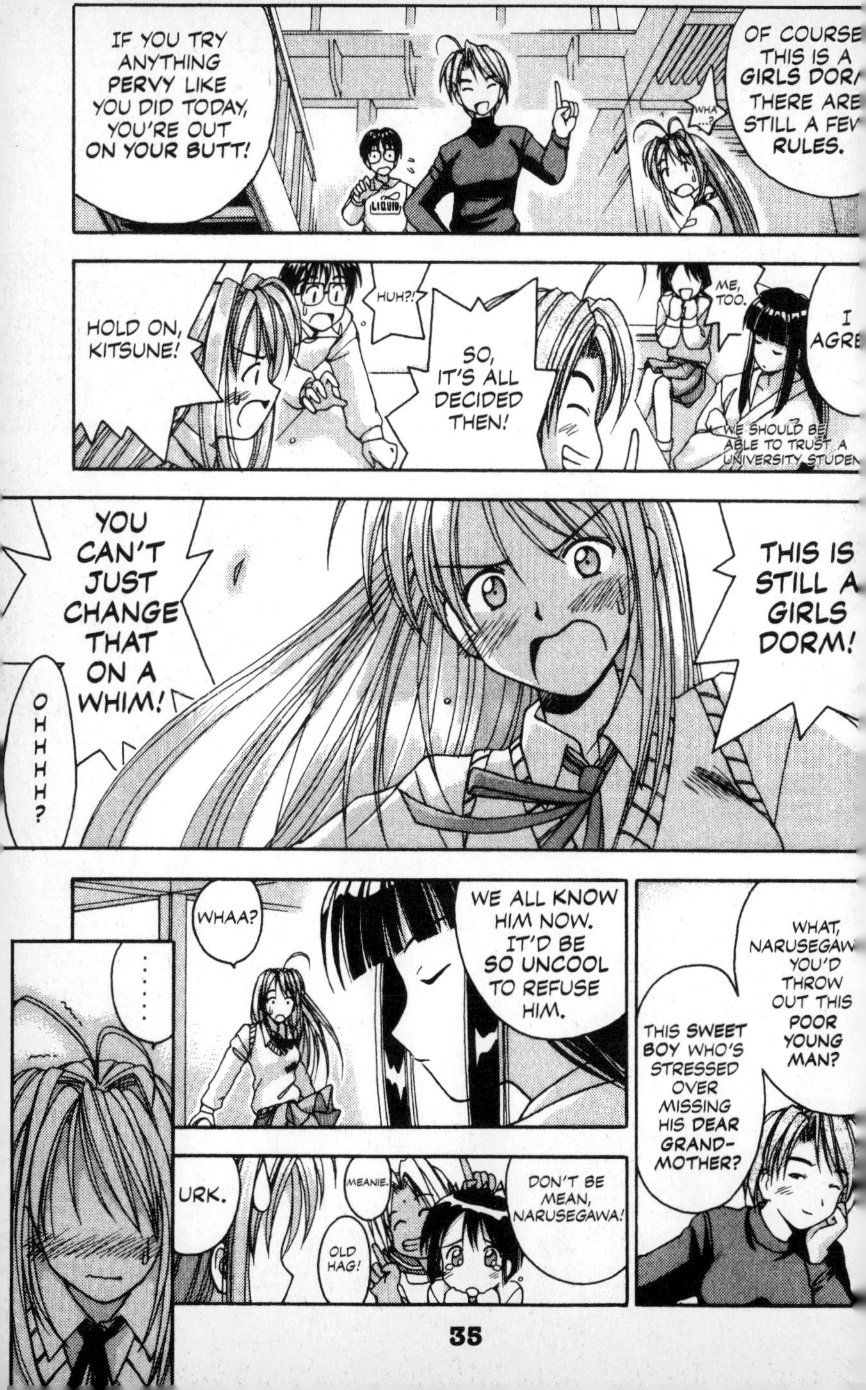
OF COURSE THIS IS A GIRLS DOR/ THERE ARE STILL A FEV RULES.
WHA...?
IF YOU TRY ANYTHING PERVY LIKE YOU DID TODAY, YOU'RE OUT ON YOUR BUTT!
I AGRE
WE SHOULD BE ABLE TO TRUST A UNIVERSITY STUDEN
ME, TOO.
SO, IT'S ALL DECIDED THEN!
HUH?!
HOLD ON, KITSUNE!
THIS IS STILL A GIRLS DORM!
YOU CAN'T JUST CHANGE THAT ON A WHIM!
OHHHH?
WHAT, NARUSEGAW YOU'D THROW OUT THIS POOR YOUNG MAN?
THIS SWEET BOY WHO'S STRESSED OVER MISSING HIS DEAR GRAND-MOTHER?
WE ALL KNOW HIM NOW. IT'D BE SO UNCOOL TO REFUSE HIM.
WHAA?
DON'T BE MEAN, NARUSEGAWA!
MEANIE.
OLD HAG!
URK.
......

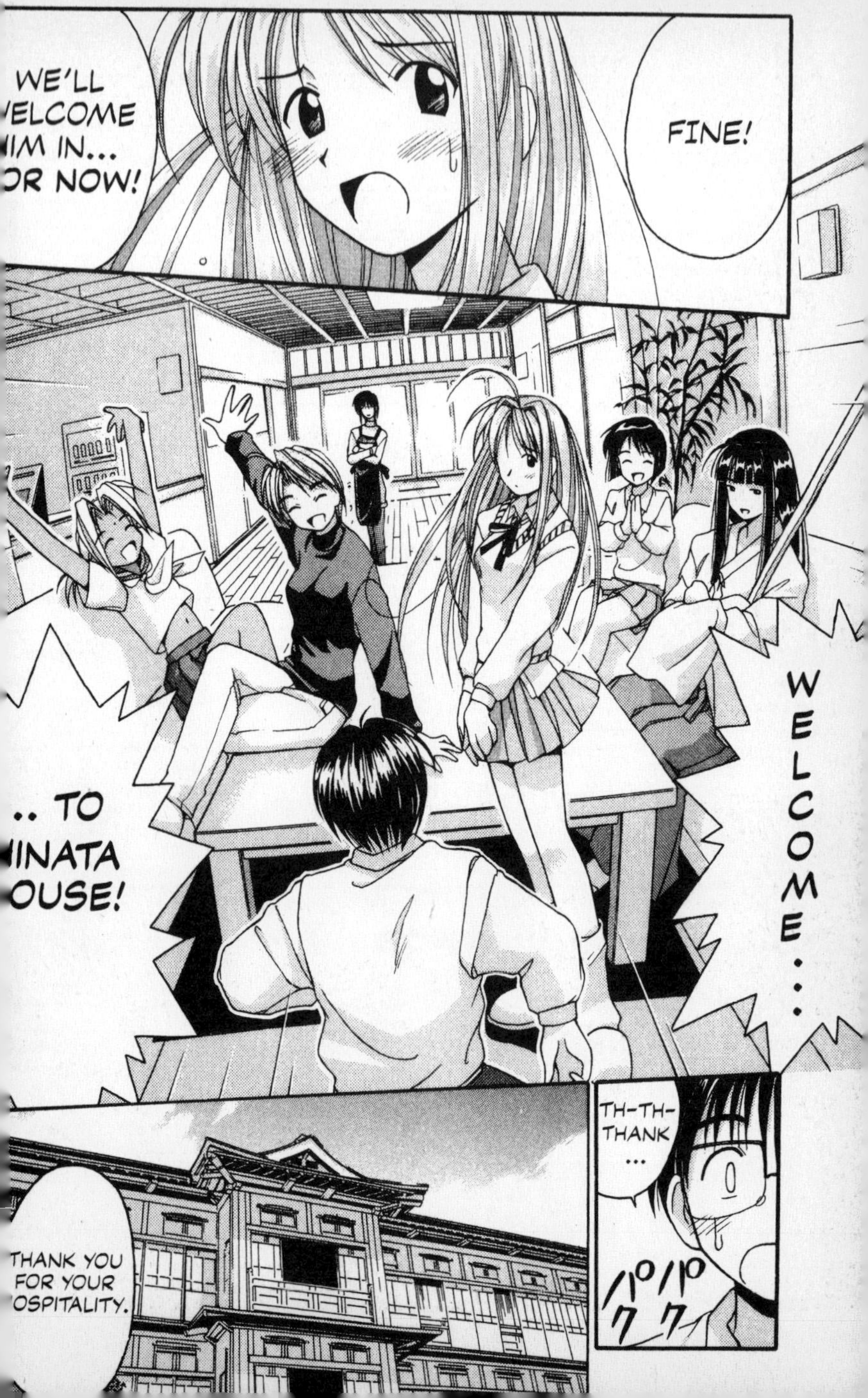
FINE!
WE'LL ELCOME IM IN... R NOW!
WELCOME...
.. TO INATA OUSE!
TH-TH-THANK ...
パクパク
THANK YOU FOR YOUR OSPITALITY.

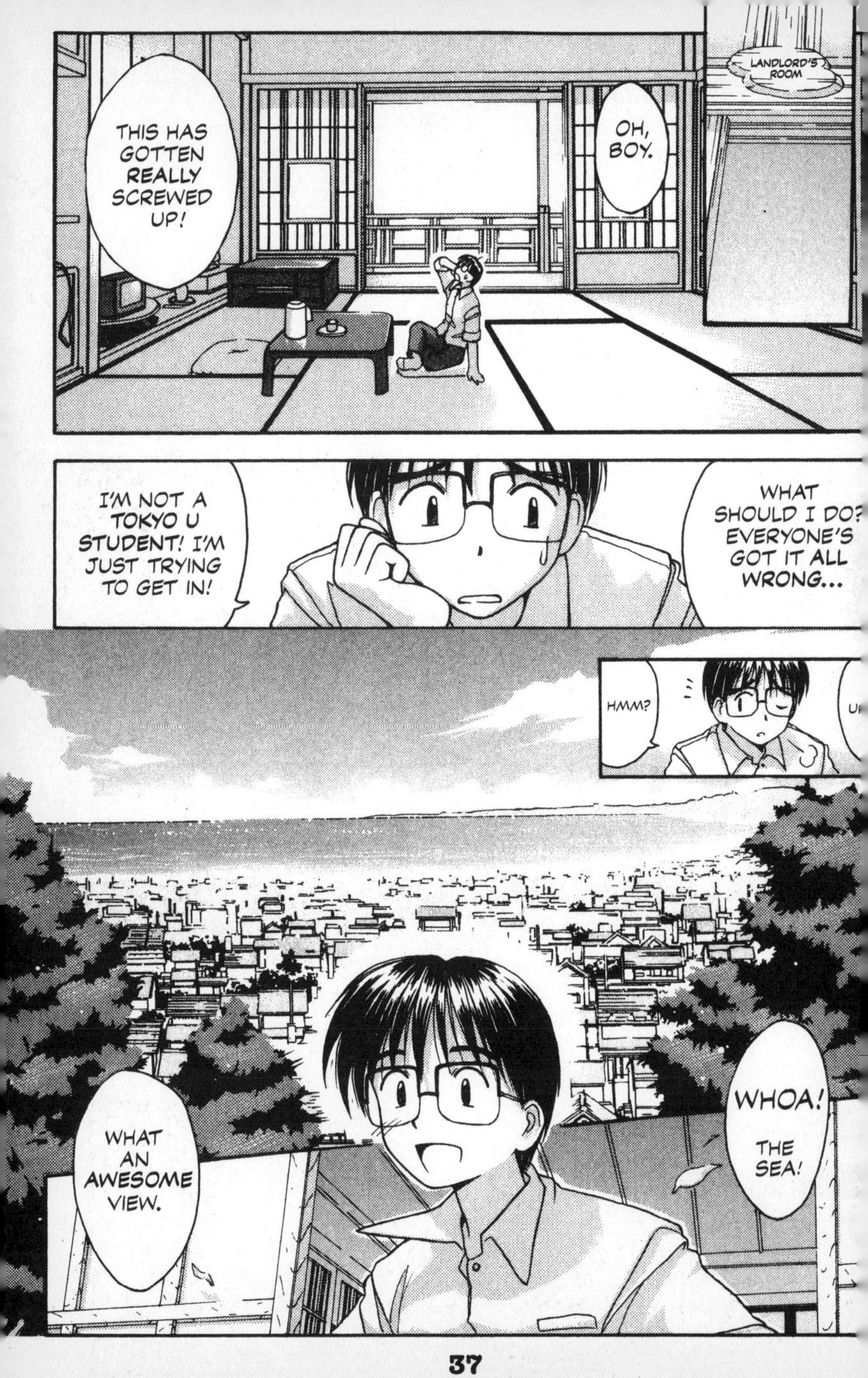
LANDLORD'S ROOM
OH, BOY.
THIS HAS GOTTEN REALLY SCREWED UP!
WHAT SHOULD I DO? EVERYONE'S GOT IT ALL WRONG...
I'M NOT A TOKYO U STUDENT! I'M JUST TRYING TO GET IN!
HMM?
WHOA! THE SEA!
WHAT AN AWESOME VIEW.

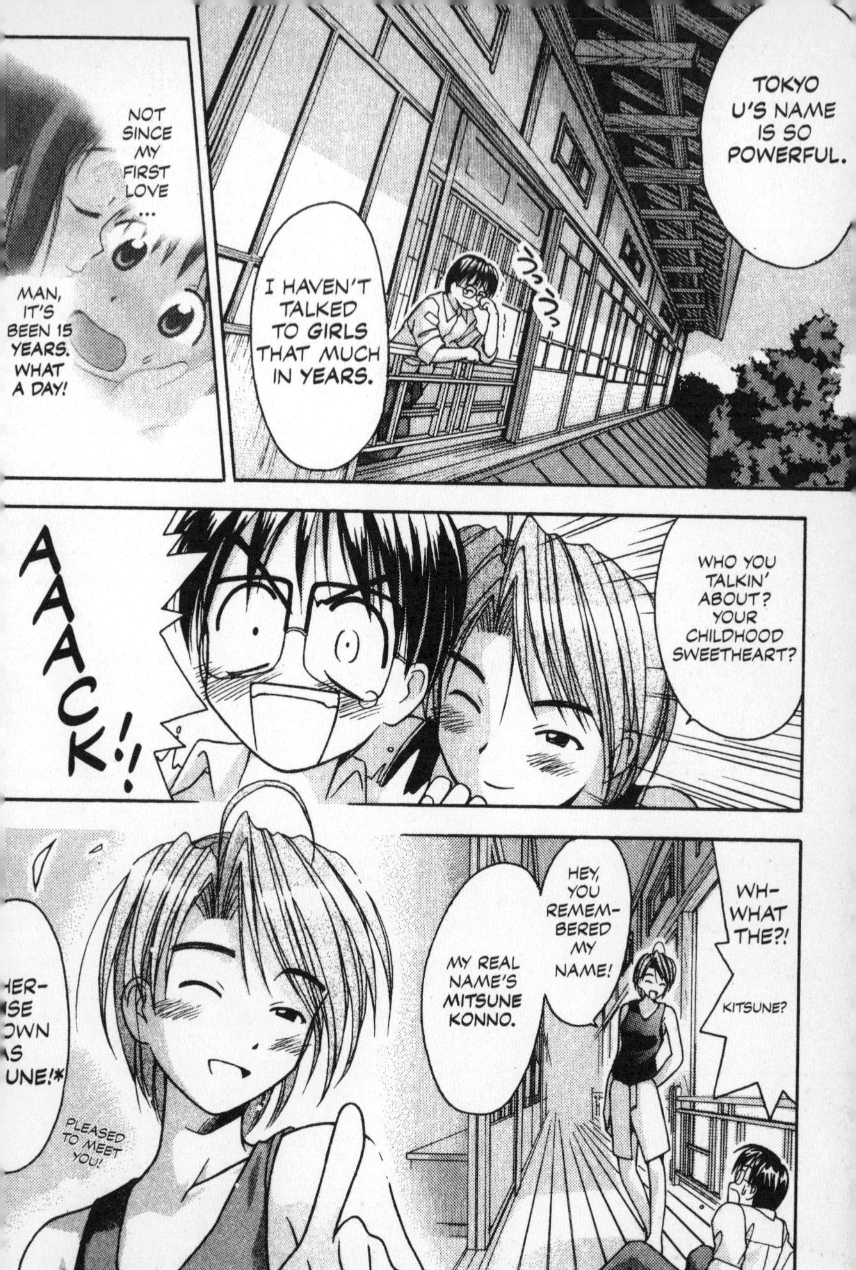
TOKYO U'S NAME IS SO POWERFUL.
I HAVEN'T TALKED TO GIRLS THAT MUCH IN YEARS.
NOT SINCE MY FIRST LOVE ...
MAN, IT'S BEEN 15 YEARS. WHAT A DAY!
WHO YOU TALKIN' ABOUT? YOUR CHILDHOOD SWEETHEART?
AAACK!!
WH-WHAT THE?!
KITSUNE?
HEY, YOU REMEMBERED MY NAME!
MY REAL NAME'S MITSUNE KONNO.
PLEASED TO MEET YOU!

* KITSUNE - JAPANESE FOR "FOX"

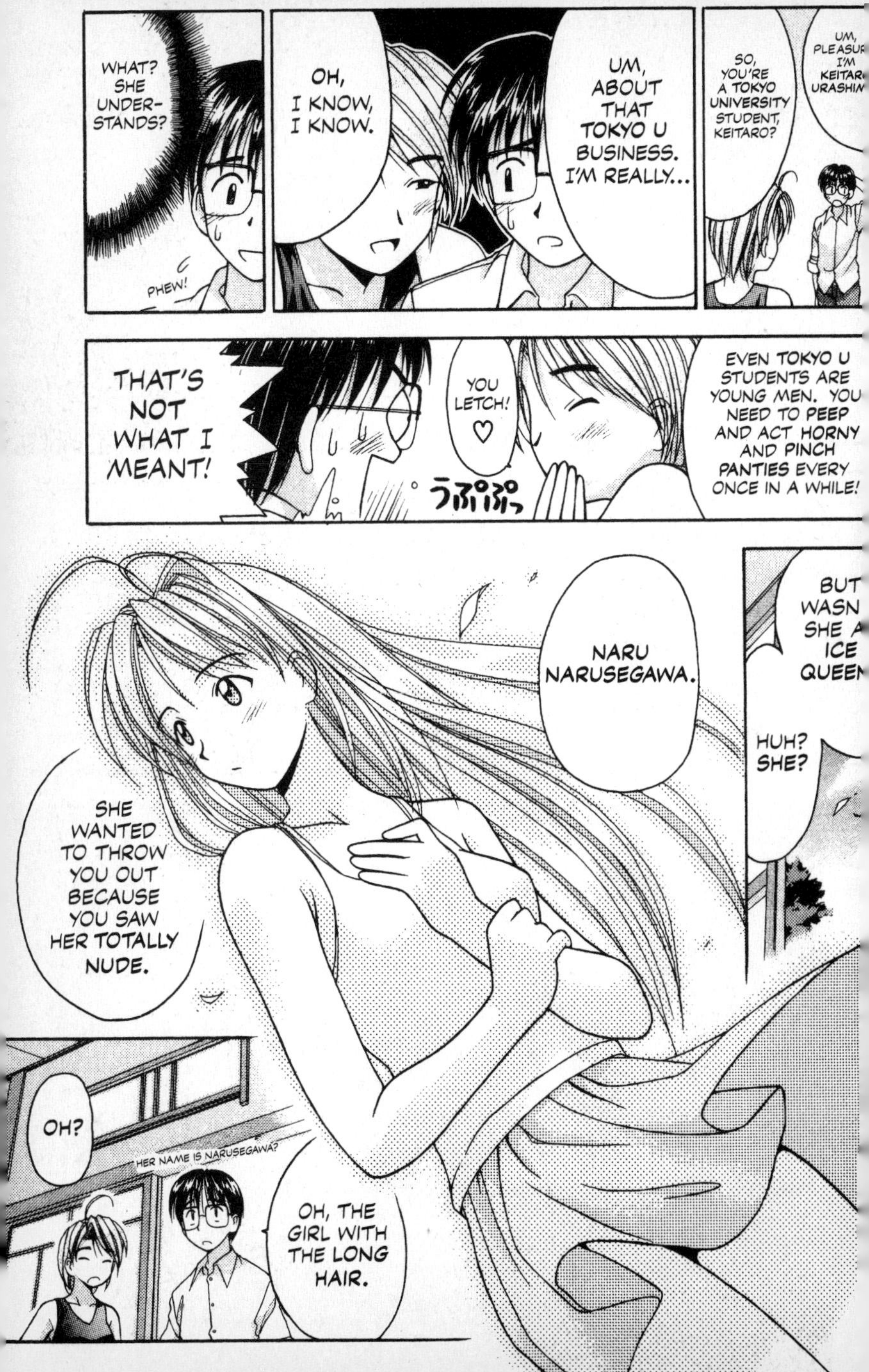
UM, PLEASUR I'M KEITAR URASHIM
SO, YOU'RE A TOKYO UNIVERSITY STUDENT, KEITARO?
UM, ABOUT THAT TOKYO U BUSINESS. I'M REALLY...
OH, I KNOW, I KNOW.
WHAT? SHE UNDER-STANDS?
PHEW!
EVEN TOKYO U STUDENTS ARE YOUNG MEN. YOU NEED TO PEEP AND ACT HORNY AND PINCH PANTIES EVERY ONCE IN A WHILE!
YOU LETCH! ♡
うぷぷっ
THAT'S NOT WHAT I MEANT!
BUT WASN SHE A ICE QUEEN
HUH? SHE?
NARU NARUSEGAWA.
SHE WANTED TO THROW YOU OUT BECAUSE YOU SAW HER TOTALLY NUDE.
OH?
HER NAME IS NARUSEGAWA?
OH, THE GIRL WITH THE LONG HAIR.

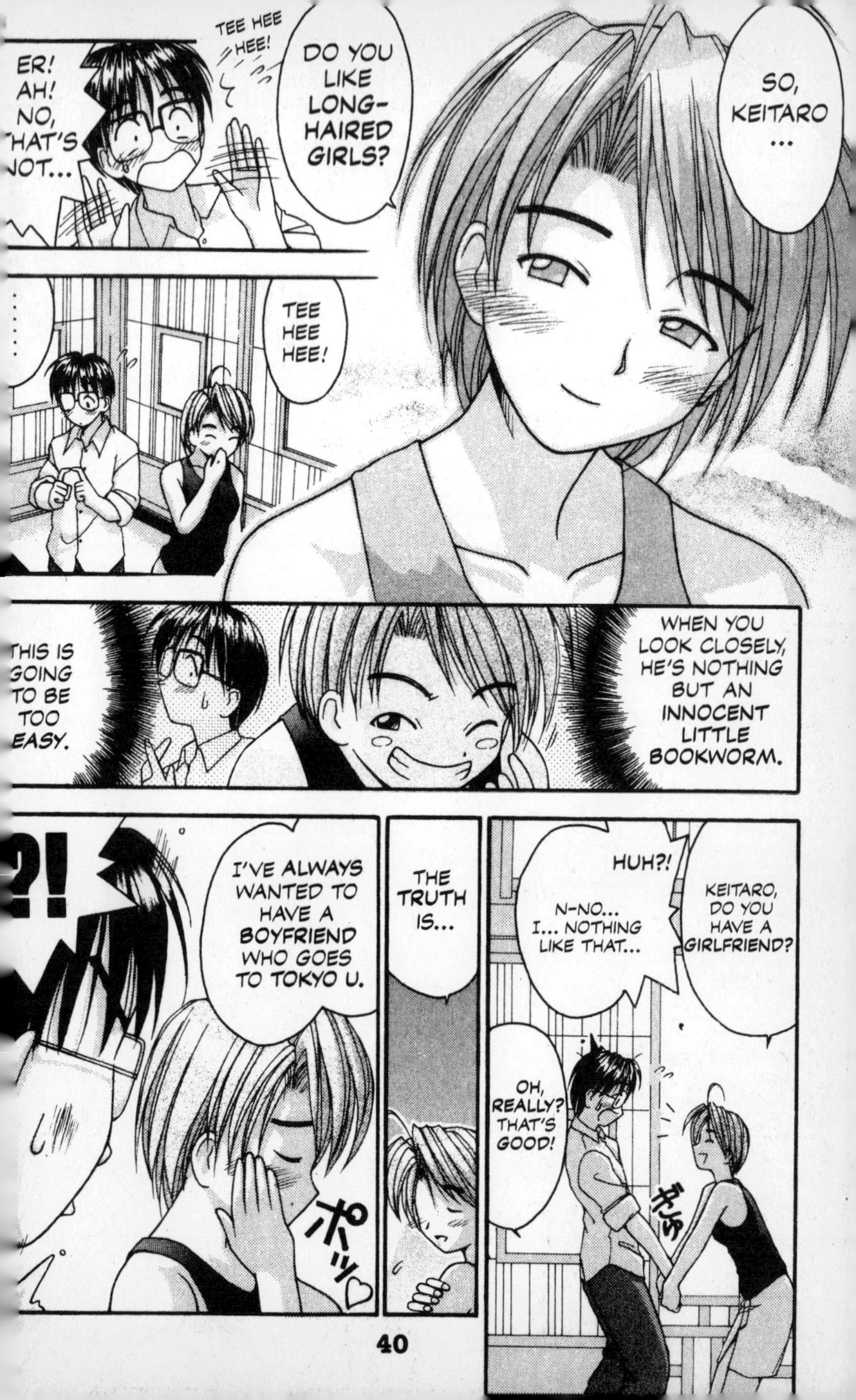
SO, KEITARO ...
DO YOU LIKE LONG-HAIRED GIRLS?
TEE HEE HEE!
ER! AH! NO, THAT'S NOT...
TEE HEE HEE!
......
WHEN YOU LOOK CLOSELY, HE'S NOTHING BUT AN INNOCENT LITTLE BOOKWORM.
THIS IS GOING TO BE TOO EASY.
KEITARO, DO YOU HAVE A GIRLFRIEND?
HUH?!
N-NO... I... NOTHING LIKE THAT...
OH, REALLY? THAT'S GOOD!
THE TRUTH IS...
I'VE ALWAYS WANTED TO HAVE A BOYFRIEND WHO GOES TO TOKYO U.
?!
ポッ♡

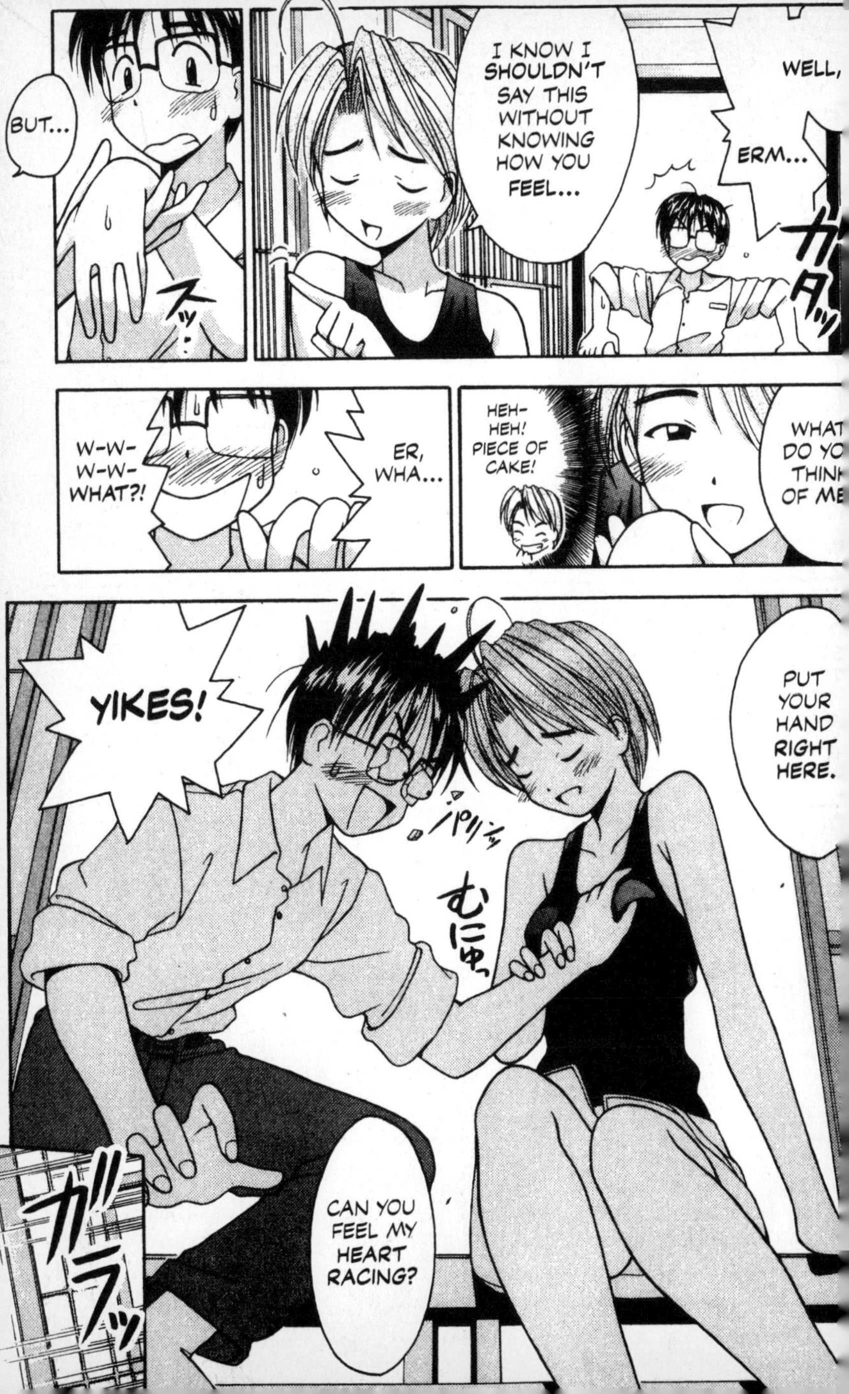
WELL,
ERM...
カタッ
I KNOW I SHOULDN'T SAY THIS WITHOUT KNOWING HOW YOU FEEL...
BUT...
スッ・・・
WHAT DO YO THINK OF ME
HEH-HEH! PIECE OF CAKE!
ER, WHA...
W-W-W-W-WHAT?!
PUT YOUR HAND RIGHT HERE.
YIKES!
パリッ
むにゅっ
CAN YOU FEEL MY HEART RACING?
ガラッ

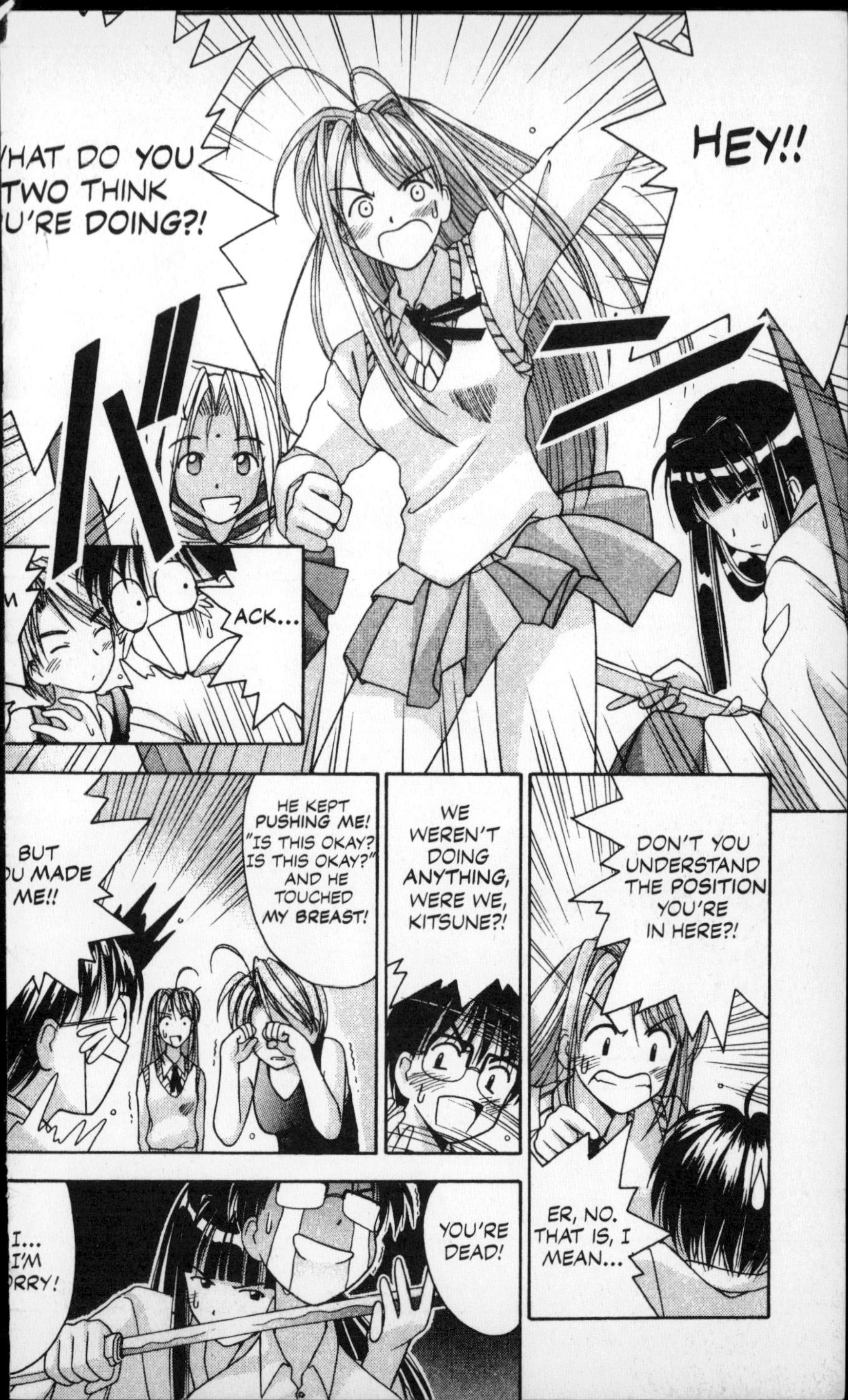
HEY!!
HAT DO YOU TWO THINK U'RE DOING?!
ACK...
DON'T YOU UNDERSTAND THE POSITION YOU'RE IN HERE?!
WE WEREN'T DOING ANYTHING, WERE WE, KITSUNE?!
HE KEPT PUSHING ME! "IS THIS OKAY? IS THIS OKAY?" AND HE TOUCHED MY BREAST!
BUT U MADE ME!!
ER, NO. THAT IS, I MEAN...
YOU'RE DEAD!
I... I'M RRY!

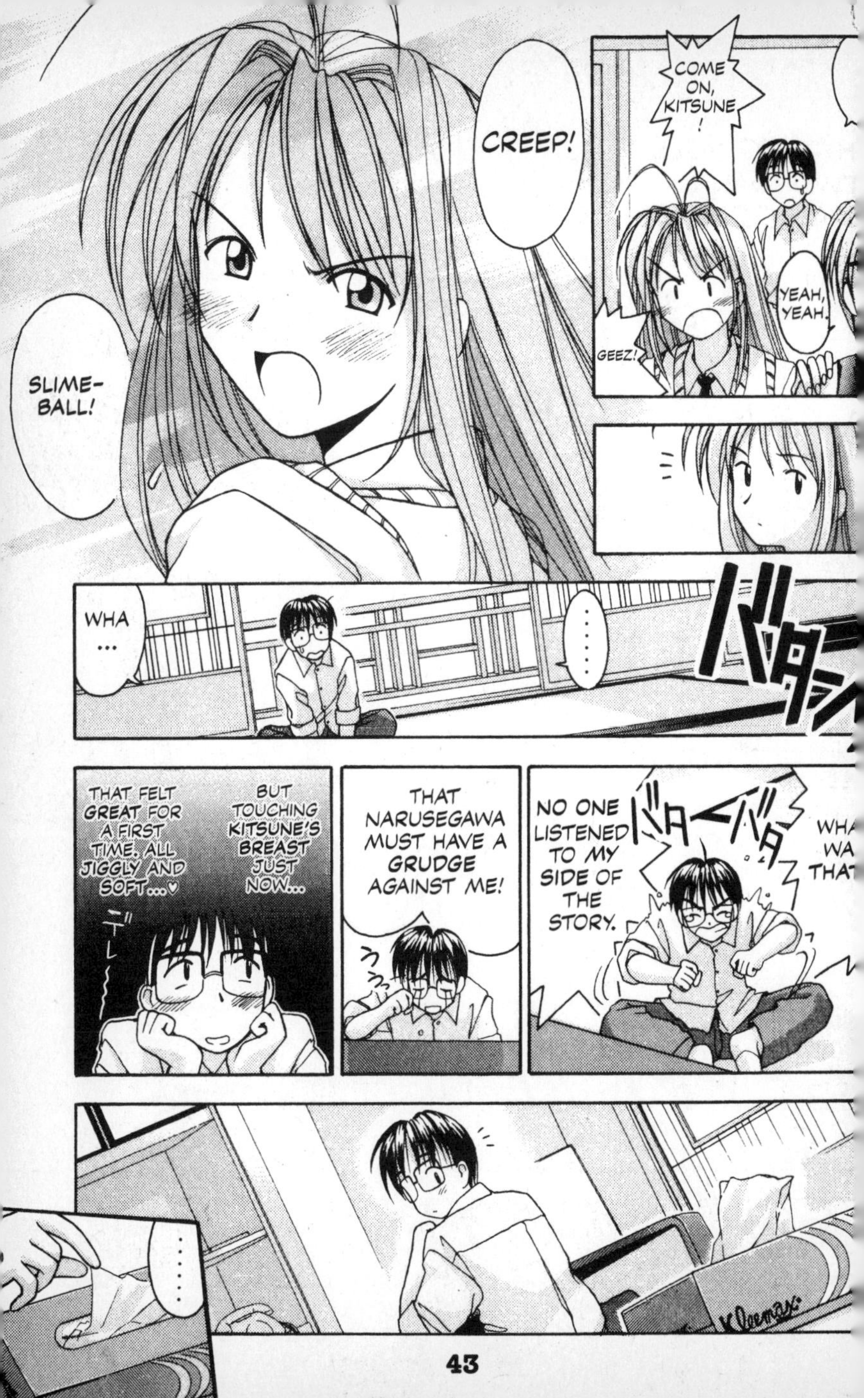
COME ON, KITSUNE!
YEAH, YEAH.
GEEZ!
CREEP!
SLIME-BALL!
.....
WHA ...
WHA WA THA
NO ONE LISTENED TO MY SIDE OF THE STORY.
THAT NARUSEGAWA MUST HAVE A GRUDGE AGAINST ME!
BUT TOUCHING KITSUNE'S BREAST JUST NOW...
THAT FELT GREAT FOR A FIRST TIME. ALL JIGGLY AND SOFT...♥
.....

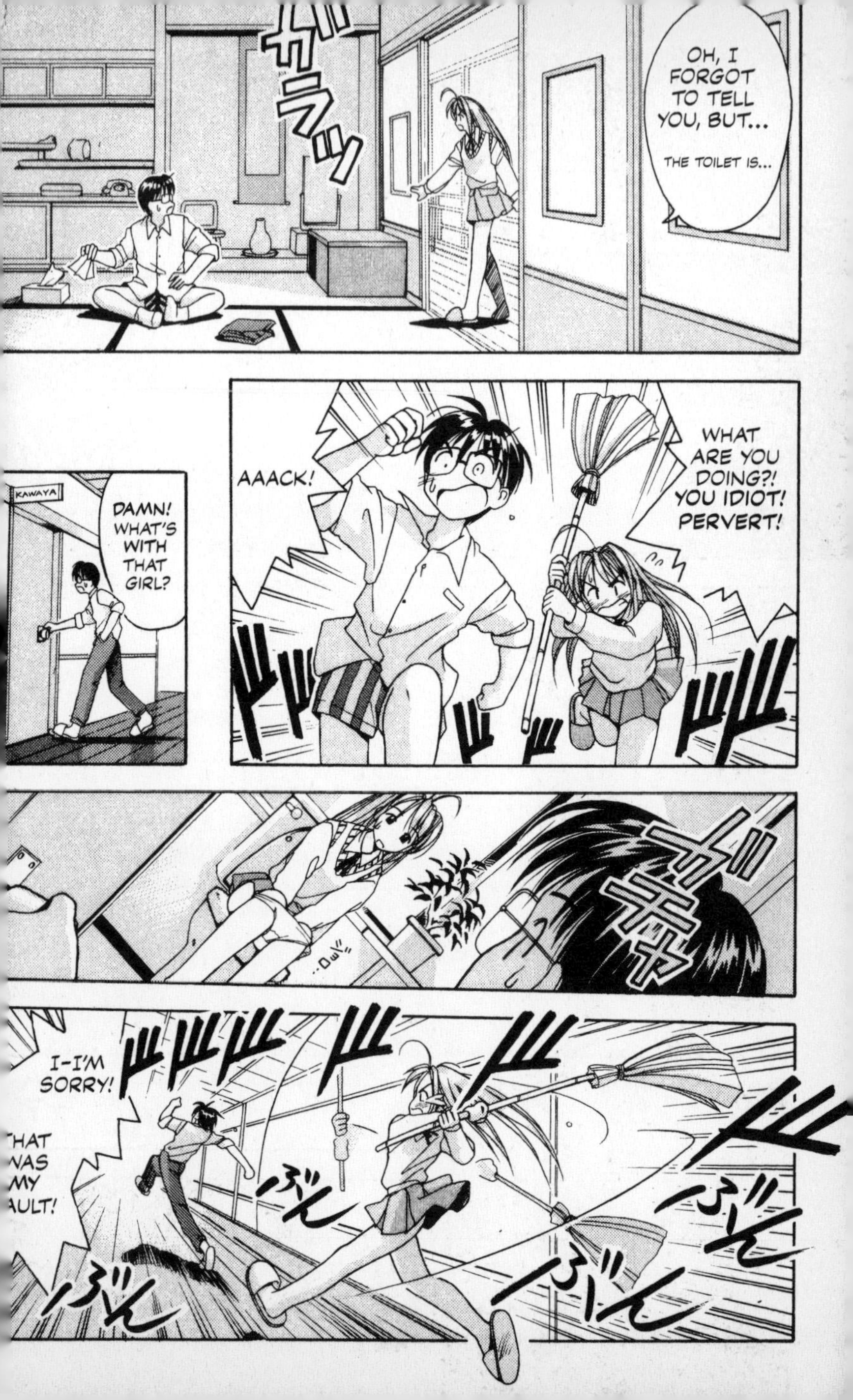
ガラッ
OH, I FORGOT TO TELL YOU, BUT... THE TOILET IS...
WHAT ARE YOU DOING?! YOU IDIOT! PERVERT!
AAACK!
KAWAYA
DAMN! WHAT'S WITH THAT GIRL?
I-I'M SORRY!
THAT WAS MY AULT!
ぶん
ぶん
ぶん
ぶん

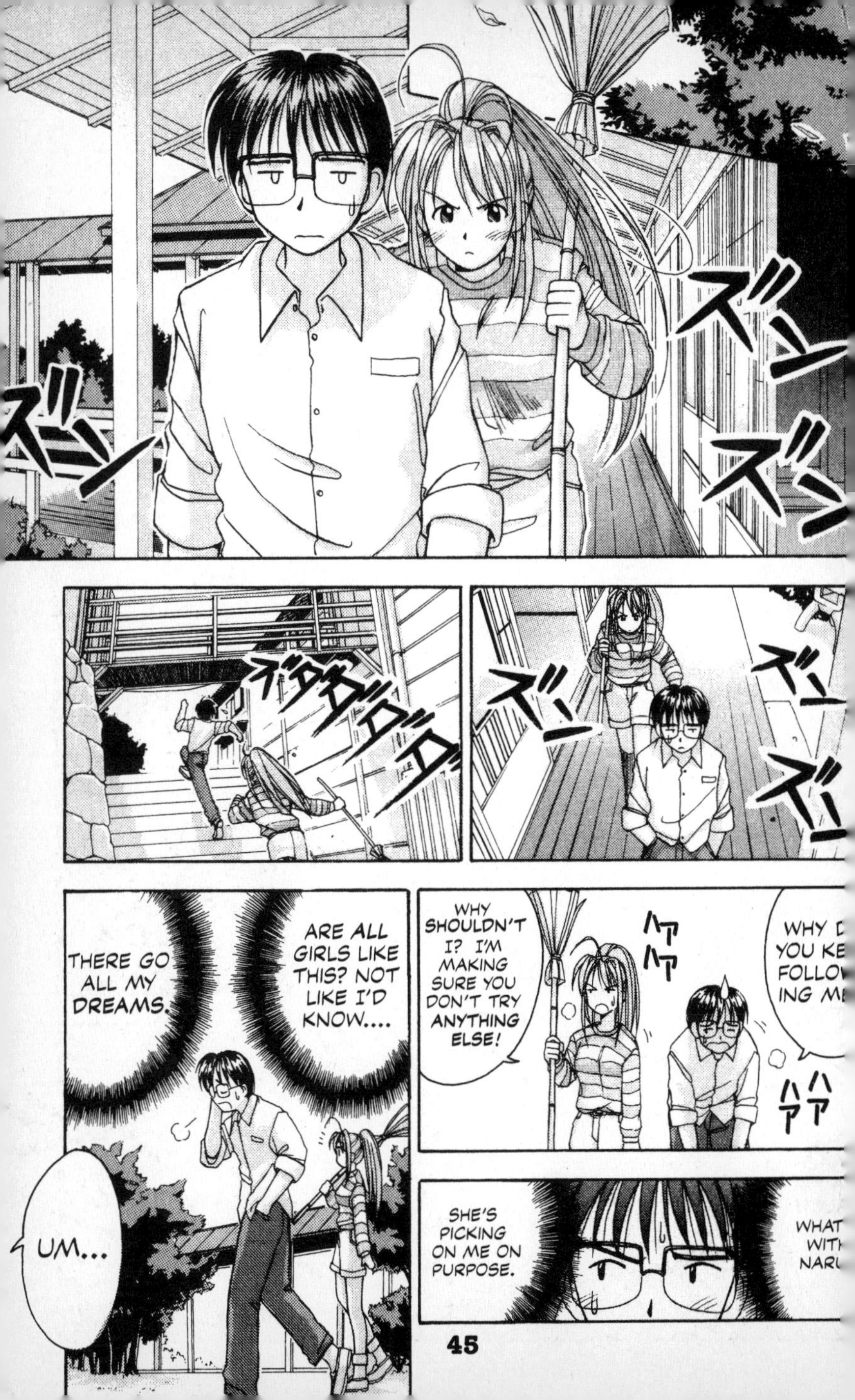
ズーン
ズーン
ズーン
ズーン
ズーン
ズーン
ドタタタ
WHY D YOU KE FOLLOW ING ME
ハァハァ
ハァハァ
WHY SHOULDN'T I? I'M MAKING SURE YOU DON'T TRY ANYTHING ELSE!
WHAT WITH NARU
SHE'S PICKING ON ME ON PURPOSE.
ARE ALL GIRLS LIKE THIS? NOT LIKE I'D KNOW....
THERE GO ALL MY DREAMS.
UM...

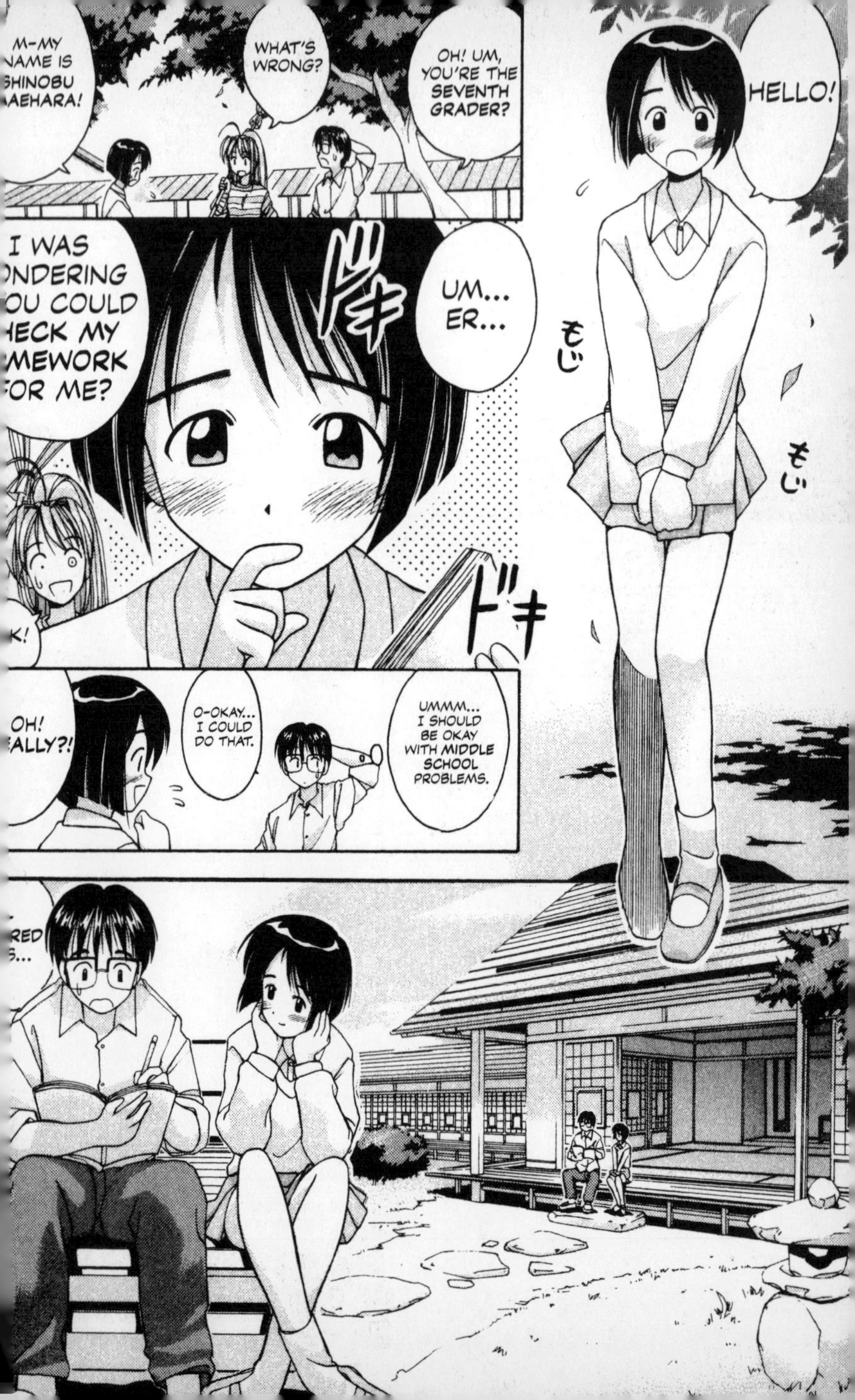
HELLO!
もじ
もじ
OH! UM, YOU'RE THE SEVENTH GRADER?
WHAT'S WRONG?
M-MY NAME IS SHINOBU AEHARA!
ドキ
UM... ER...
ドキ
I WAS ONDERING OU COULD HECK MY MEWORK FOR ME?
K!
UMMM... I SHOULD BE OKAY WITH MIDDLE SCHOOL PROBLEMS.
O-OKAY... I COULD DO THAT.
OH! EALLY?!
RED S...

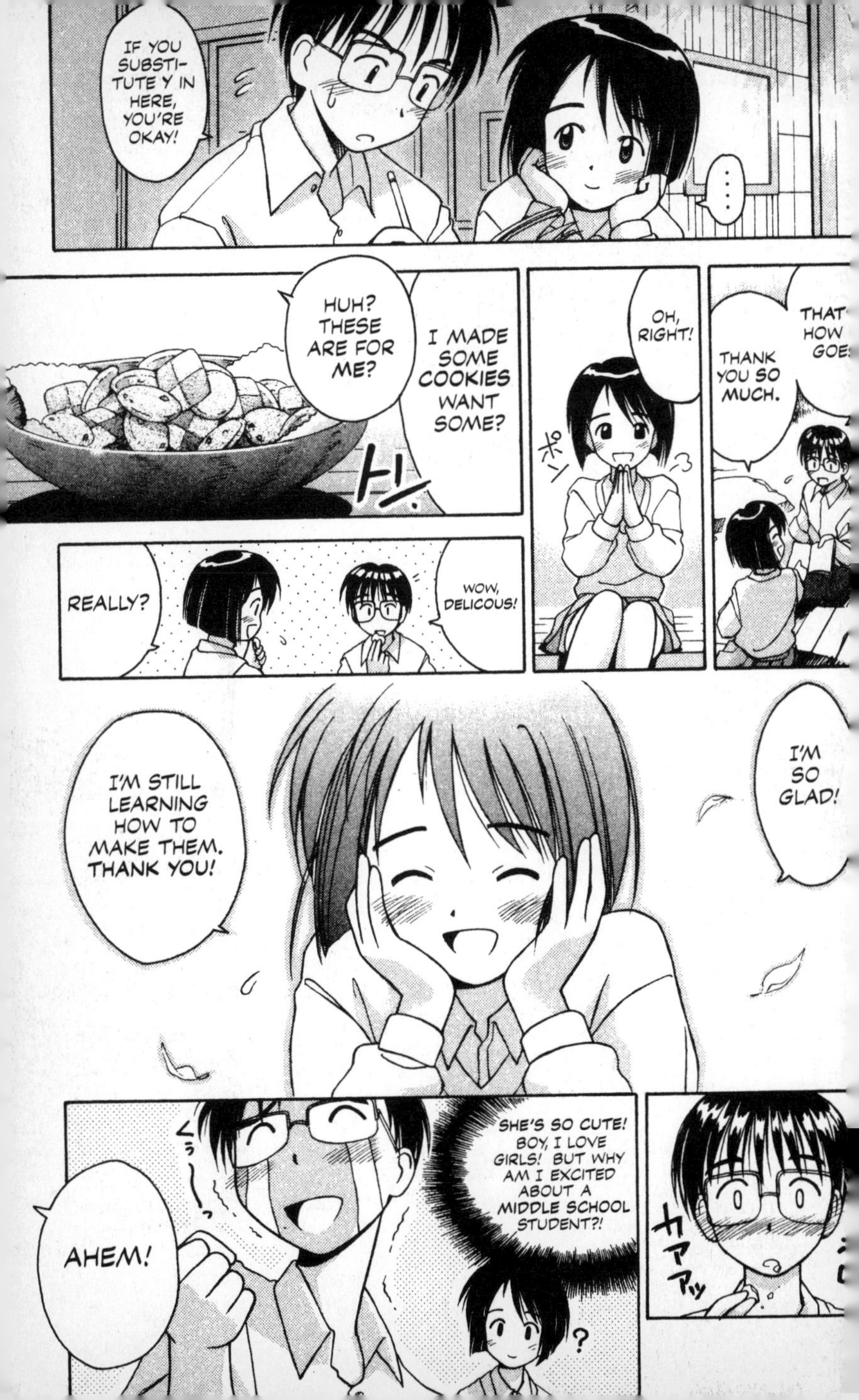
IF YOU SUBSTI-TUTE Y IN HERE, YOU'RE OKAY!
....
THAT' HOW GOE
THANK YOU SO MUCH.
OH, RIGHT!
ポン
I MADE SOME COOKIES WANT SOME?
HUH? THESE ARE FOR ME?
ト!
WOW, DELICOUS!
REALLY?
I'M SO GLAD!
I'M STILL LEARNING HOW TO MAKE THEM. THANK YOU!
カァアッ
SHE'S SO CUTE! BOY, I LOVE GIRLS! BUT WHY AM I EXCITED ABOUT A MIDDLE SCHOOL STUDENT?!
くぅ～っ
AHEM!
?

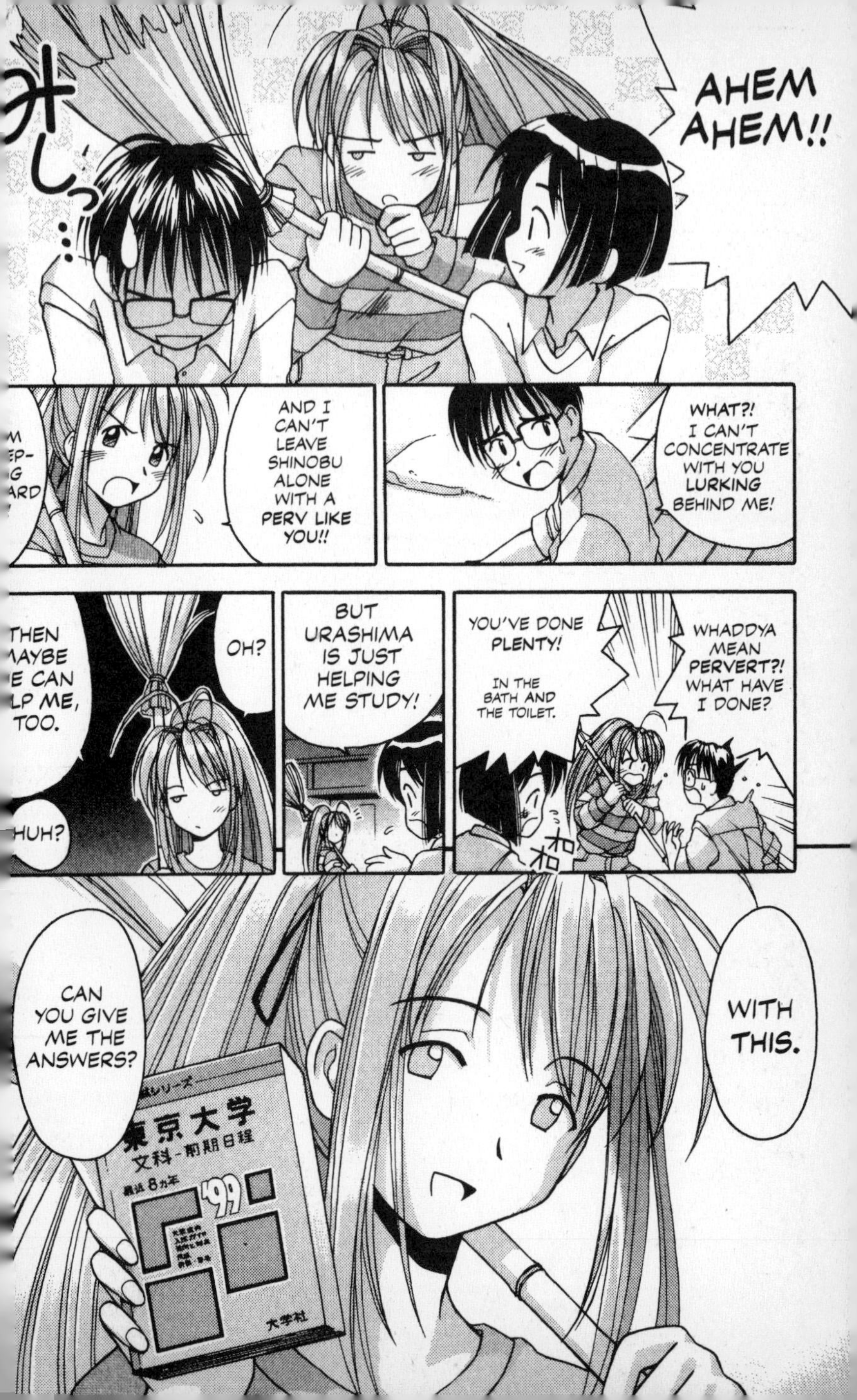
AHEM AHEM!!
WHAT?! I CAN'T CONCENTRATE WITH YOU LURKING BEHIND ME!
AND I CAN'T LEAVE SHINOBU ALONE WITH A PERV LIKE YOU!!
WHADDYA MEAN PERVERT?! WHAT HAVE I DONE?
YOU'VE DONE PLENTY!
IN THE BATH AND THE TOILET.
BUT URASHIMA IS JUST HELPING ME STUDY!
OH?
THEN MAYBE E CAN LP ME, TOO.
HUH?
WITH THIS.
CAN YOU GIVE ME THE ANSWERS?
東京大学
文科-前期日程
'99
大学社

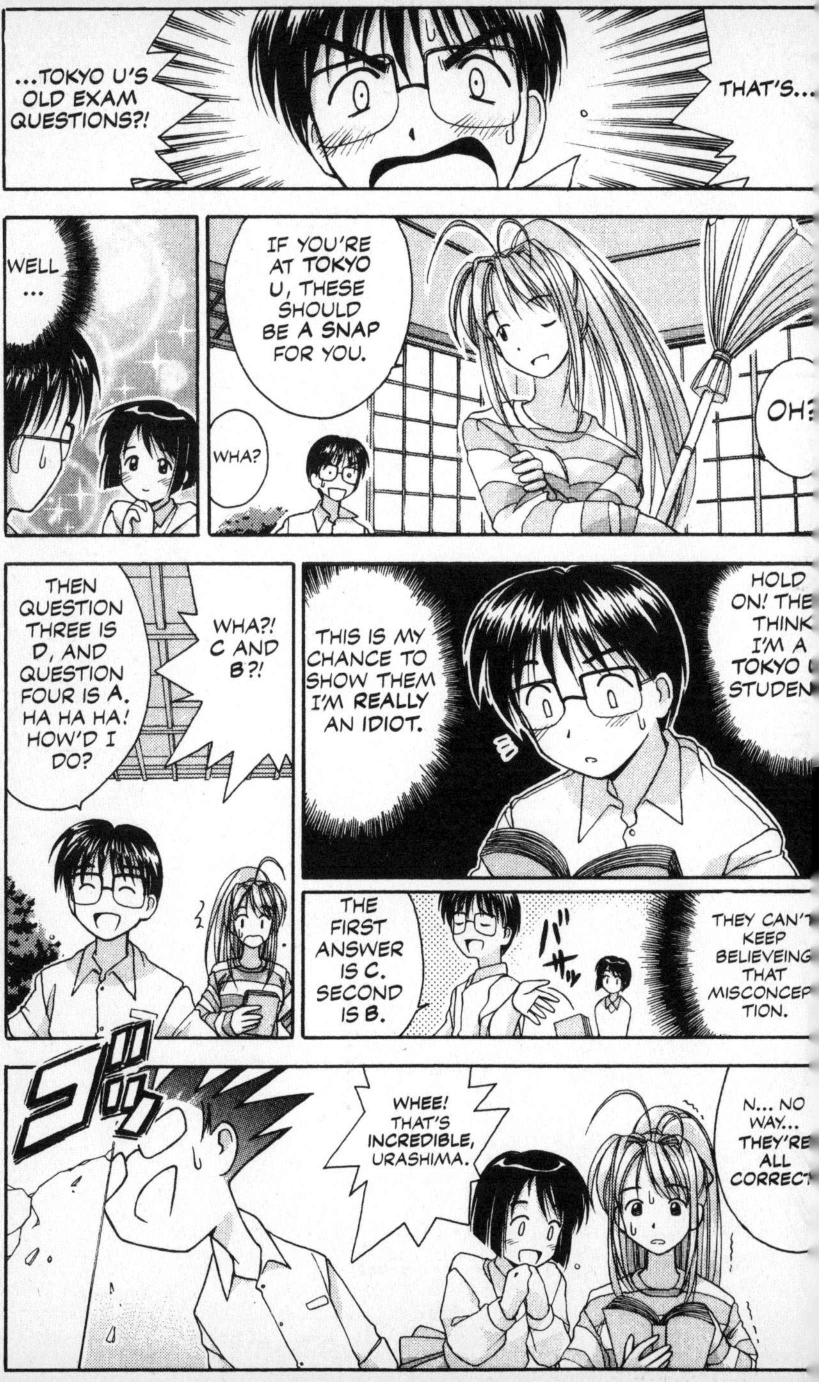
THAT'S...
...TOKYO U'S OLD EXAM QUESTIONS?!
OH?
IF YOU'RE AT TOKYO U, THESE SHOULD BE A SNAP FOR YOU.
WHA?
WELL ...
HOLD ON! THE THINK I'M A TOKYO STUDEN
THIS IS MY CHANCE TO SHOW THEM I'M REALLY AN IDIOT.
THEY CAN'T KEEP BELIEVEING THAT MISCONCEP TION.
THE FIRST ANSWER IS C. SECOND IS B.
バサッ
WHA?! C AND B?!
THEN QUESTION THREE IS D, AND QUESTION FOUR IS A. HA HA HA! HOW'D I DO?
N... NO WAY... THEY'RE ALL CORREC
WHEE! THAT'S INCREDIBLE, URASHIMA.

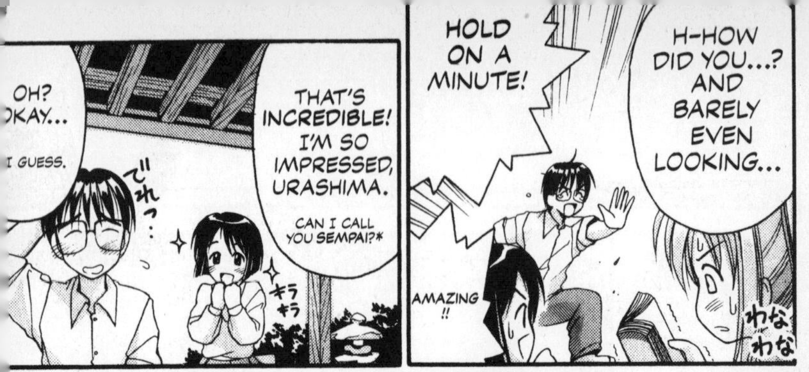
H-HOW DID YOU...? AND BARELY EVEN LOOKING...
HOLD ON A MINUTE!
AMAZING !!
わなわな
THAT'S INCREDIBLE! I'M SO IMPRESSED, URASHIMA.
CAN I CALL YOU SEMPAI?*
でれっ…
キラキラ
OH? OKAY...
I GUESS.

MPAI – A TRADITIONAL JAPANESE EXPRESSION OF RESPECT FOR AN ELDER.

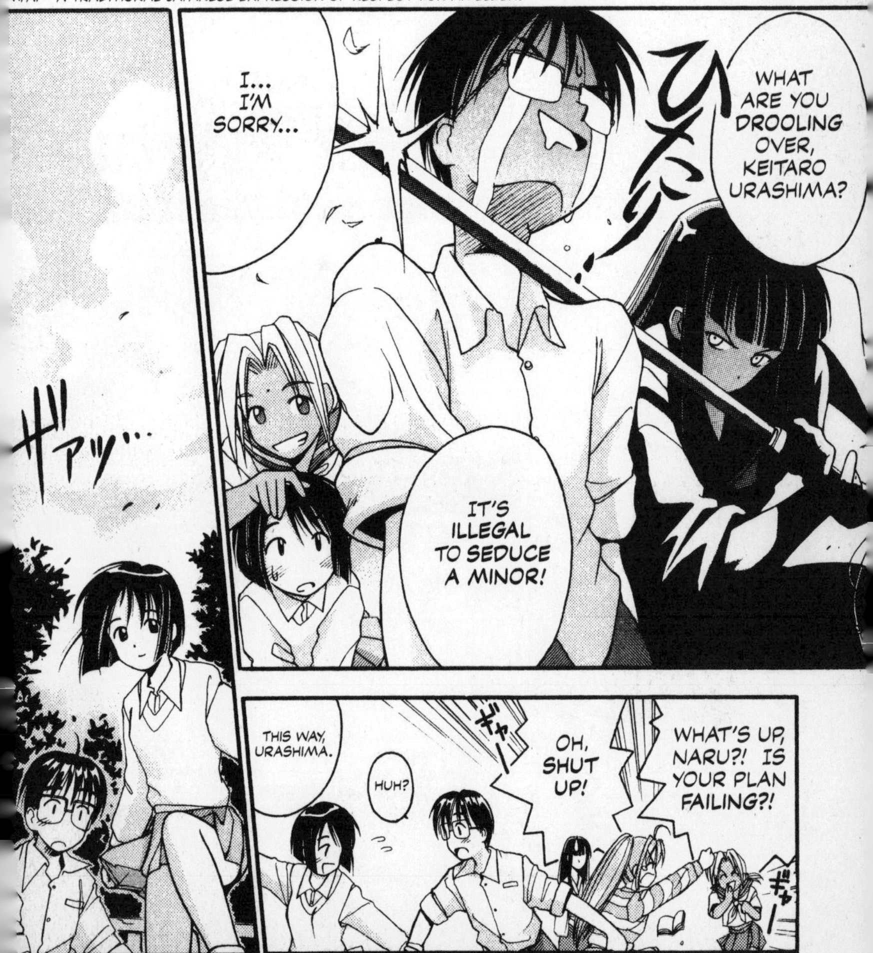
WHAT ARE YOU DROOLING OVER, KEITARO URASHIMA?
I... I'M SORRY...
IT'S ILLEGAL TO SEDUCE A MINOR!
ザアッ…
WHAT'S UP, NARU?! IS YOUR PLAN FAILING?!
ギャー
OH, SHUT UP!
ギャー
HUH?
THIS WAY, URASHIMA.

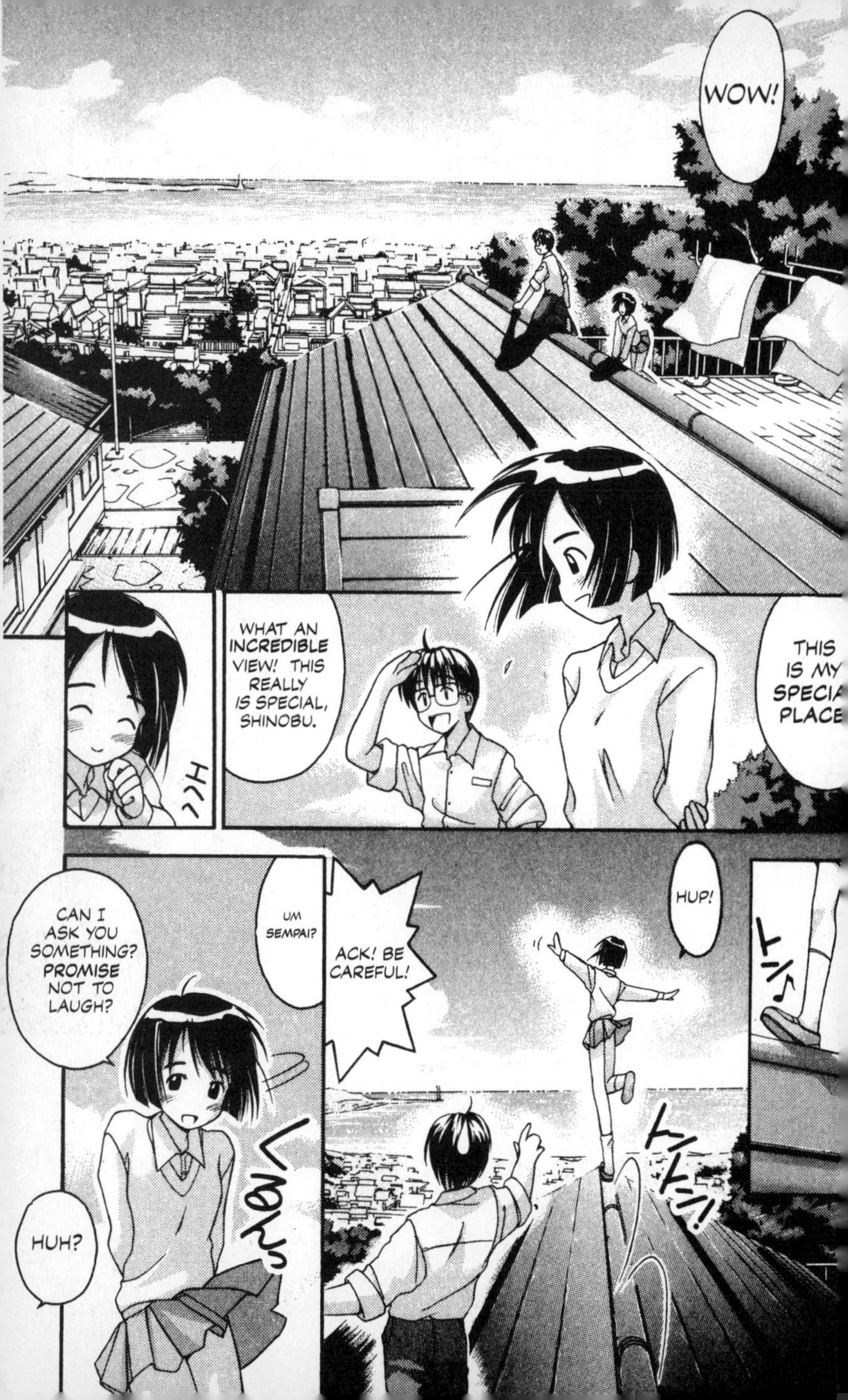
WOW!
THIS IS MY SPECIA PLACE
WHAT AN INCREDIBLE VIEW! THIS REALLY IS SPECIAL, SHINOBU.
HUP!
ACK! BE CAREFUL!
UM SEMPAI?
CAN I ASK YOU SOMETHING? PROMISE NOT TO LAUGH?
HUH?

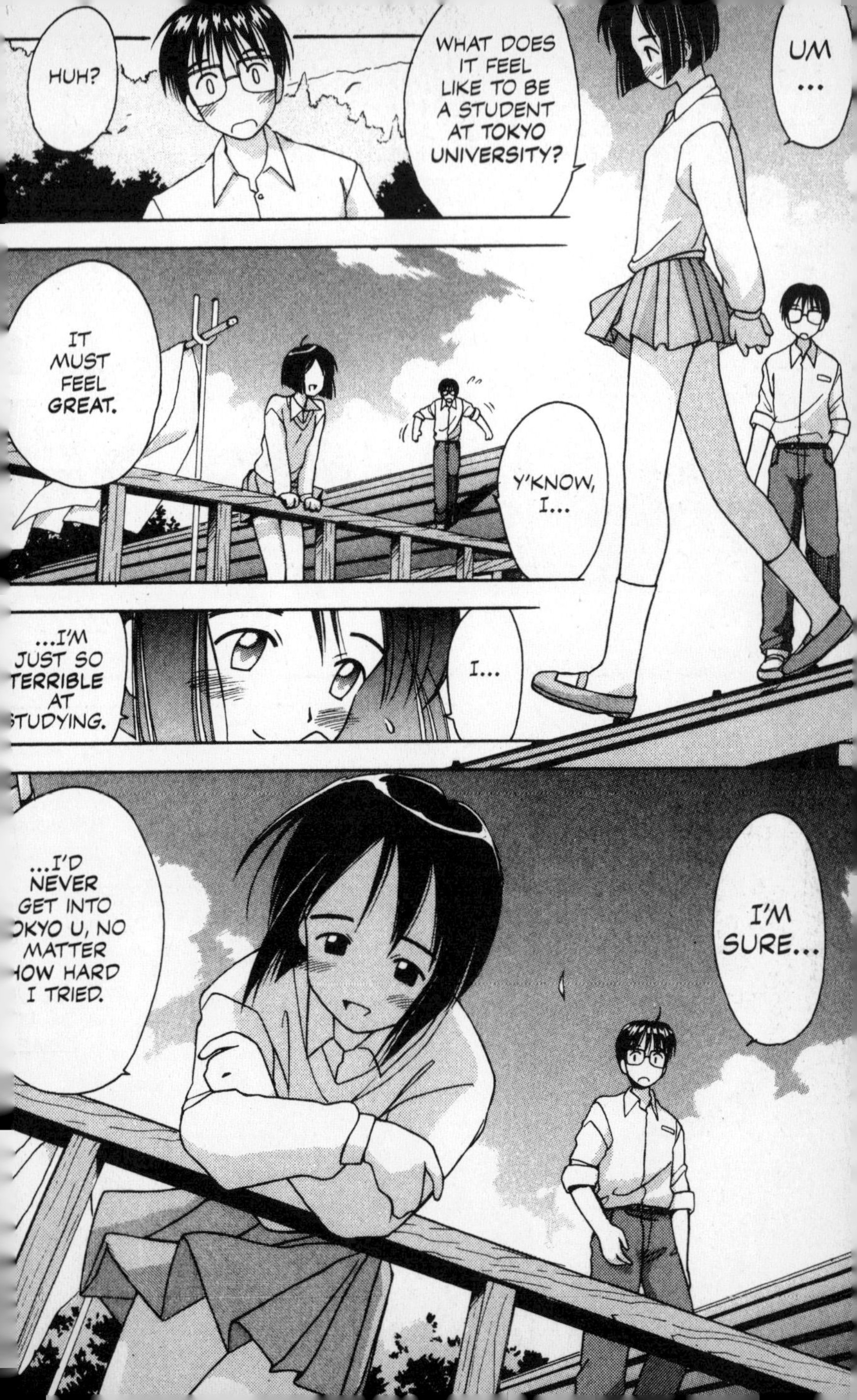
UM...
Y'KNOW, I...
WHAT DOES IT FEEL LIKE TO BE A STUDENT AT TOKYO UNIVERSITY?
HUH?
IT MUST FEEL GREAT.
I...
...I'M JUST SO TERRIBLE AT STUDYING.
I'M SURE...
...I'D NEVER GET INTO TOKYO U, NO MATTER HOW HARD I TRIED.

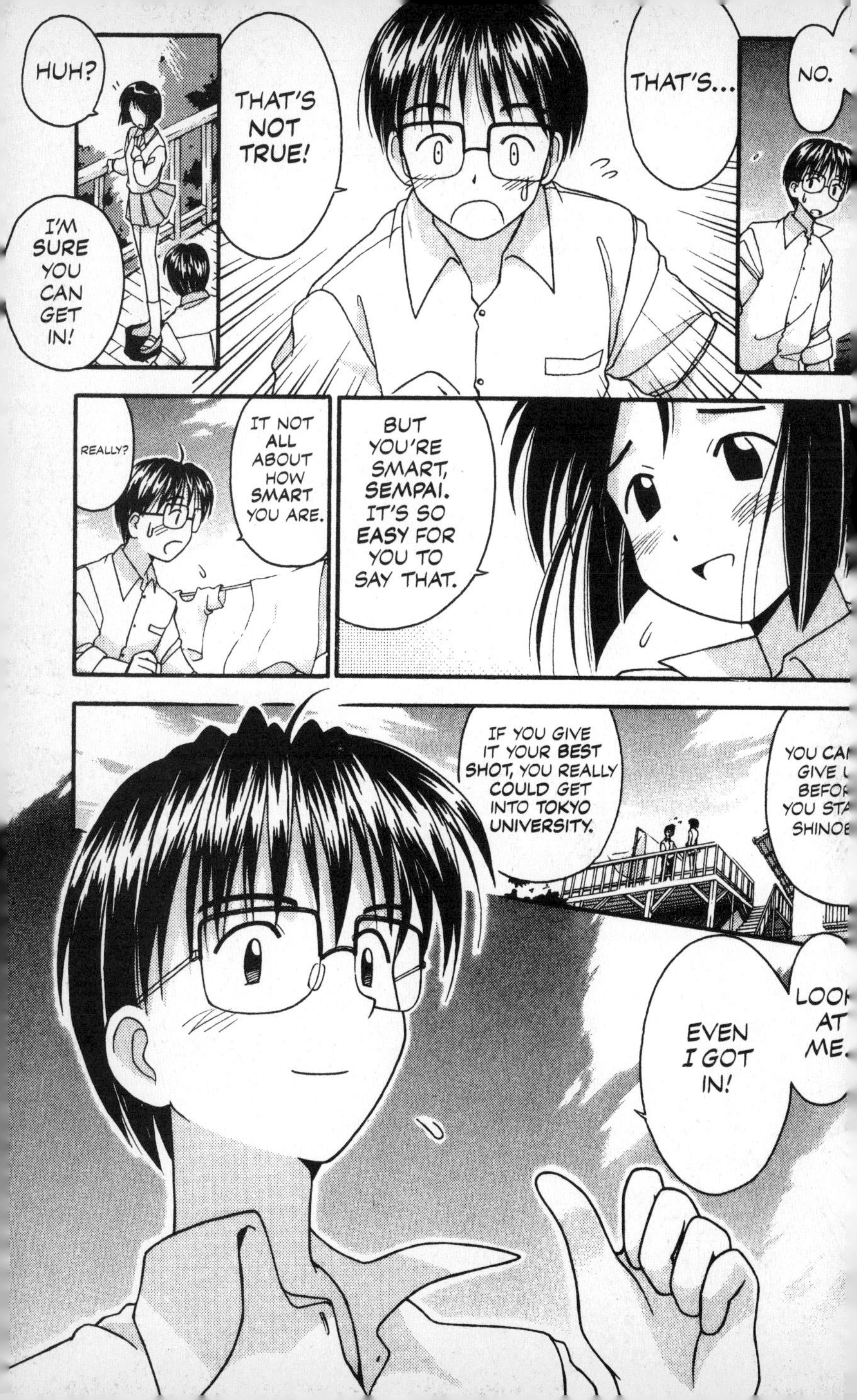
NO.
THAT'S...
THAT'S NOT TRUE!
HUH?
I'M SURE YOU CAN GET IN!
BUT YOU'RE SMART, SEMPAI. IT'S SO EASY FOR YOU TO SAY THAT.
IT NOT ALL ABOUT HOW SMART YOU ARE.
REALLY?
YOU CA GIVE U BEFOR YOU STA SHINOB
IF YOU GIVE IT YOUR BEST SHOT, YOU REALLY COULD GET INTO TOKYO UNIVERSITY.
LOO AT ME.
EVEN I GOT IN!

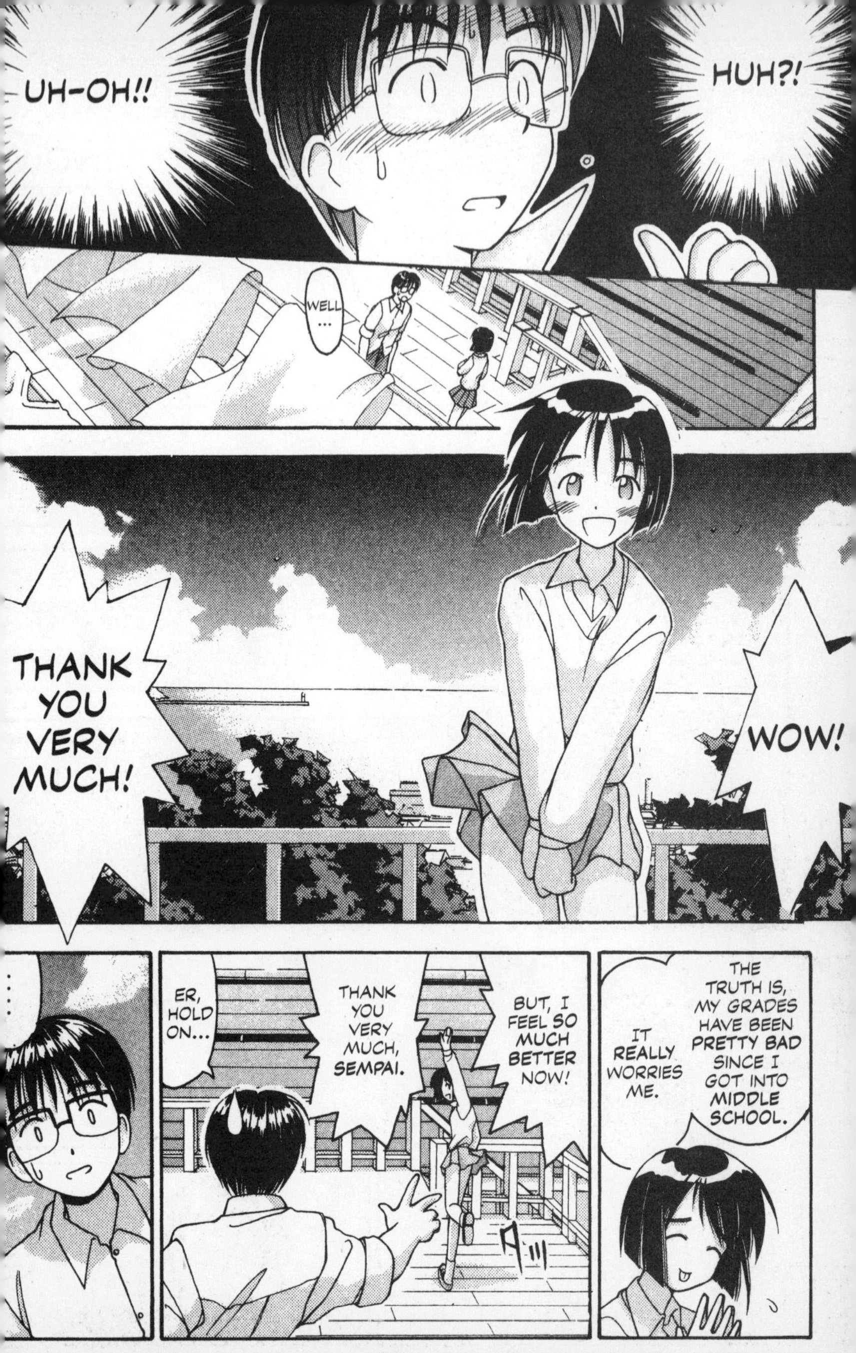
HUH?!
UH-OH!!
WELL ...
WOW!
THANK YOU VERY MUCH!
THE TRUTH IS, MY GRADES HAVE BEEN PRETTY BAD SINCE I GOT INTO MIDDLE SCHOOL.
IT REALLY WORRIES ME.
BUT, I FEEL SO MUCH BETTER NOW!
THANK YOU VERY MUCH, SEMPAI.
ER, HOLD ON...
....

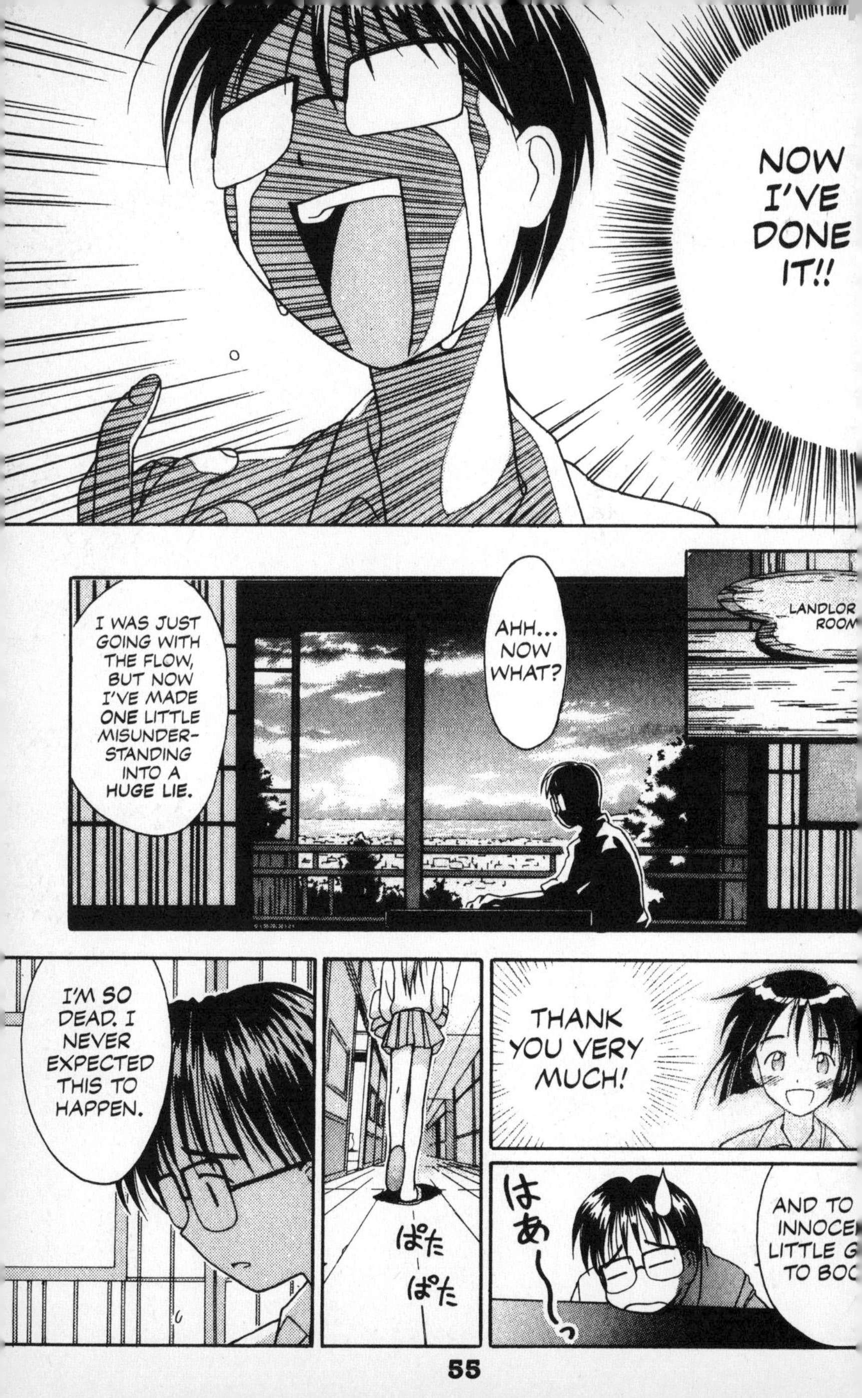
NOW I'VE DONE IT!!
LANDLOR ROOM
AHH... NOW WHAT?
I WAS JUST GOING WITH THE FLOW, BUT NOW I'VE MADE ONE LITTLE MISUNDER-STANDING INTO A HUGE LIE.
THANK YOU VERY MUCH!
AND TO
INNOCE
LITTLE G
TO BOO
はあ～っ
ぱた ぱた
I'M SO DEAD. I NEVER EXPECTED THIS TO HAPPEN.

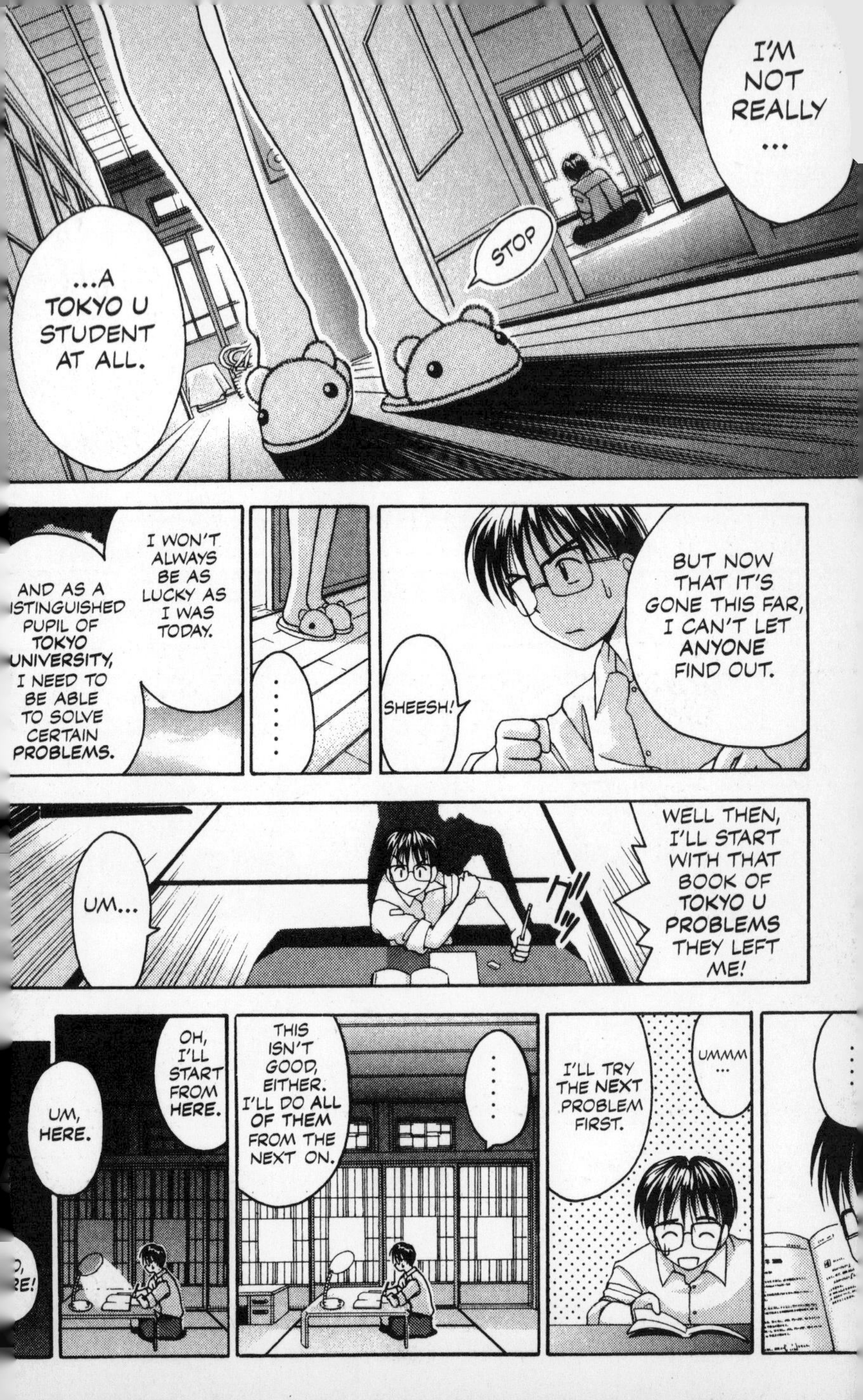
I'M NOT REALLY ...
STOP
...A TOKYO U STUDENT AT ALL.
BUT NOW THAT IT'S GONE THIS FAR, I CAN'T LET ANYONE FIND OUT.
SHEESH!
......
I WON'T ALWAYS BE AS LUCKY AS I WAS TODAY.
AND AS A ISTINGUISHED PUPIL OF TOKYO UNIVERSITY, I NEED TO BE ABLE TO SOLVE CERTAIN PROBLEMS.
WELL THEN, I'LL START WITH THAT BOOK OF TOKYO U PROBLEMS THEY LEFT ME!
UM...
UMMM ...
I'LL TRY THE NEXT PROBLEM FIRST.
......
THIS ISN'T GOOD, EITHER. I'LL DO ALL OF THEM FROM THE NEXT ON.
OH, I'LL START FROM HERE.
UM, HERE.

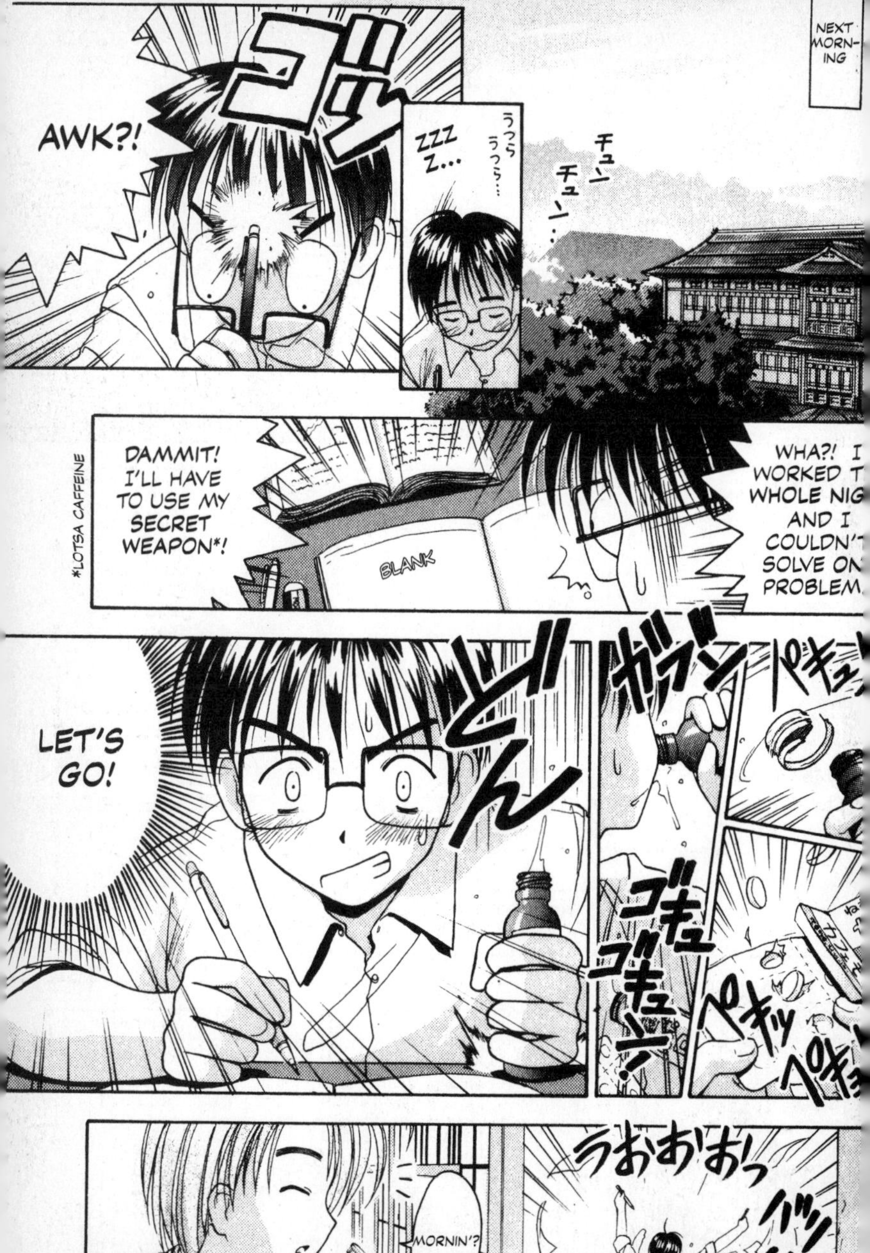
NEXT MORN-ING
チュン チュン…
うつら うつら…
ZZZ Z…
AWK?!
WHA?! I WORKED T WHOLE NIG AND I COULDN'T SOLVE ON PROBLEM.
BLANK
DAMMIT! I'LL HAVE TO USE MY SECRET WEAPON*!
*LOTSA CAFFEINE
ゴキュ ゴキュ〜ッ!
パキッ
どん
LET'S GO!
うおおおっ
MORNIN'?

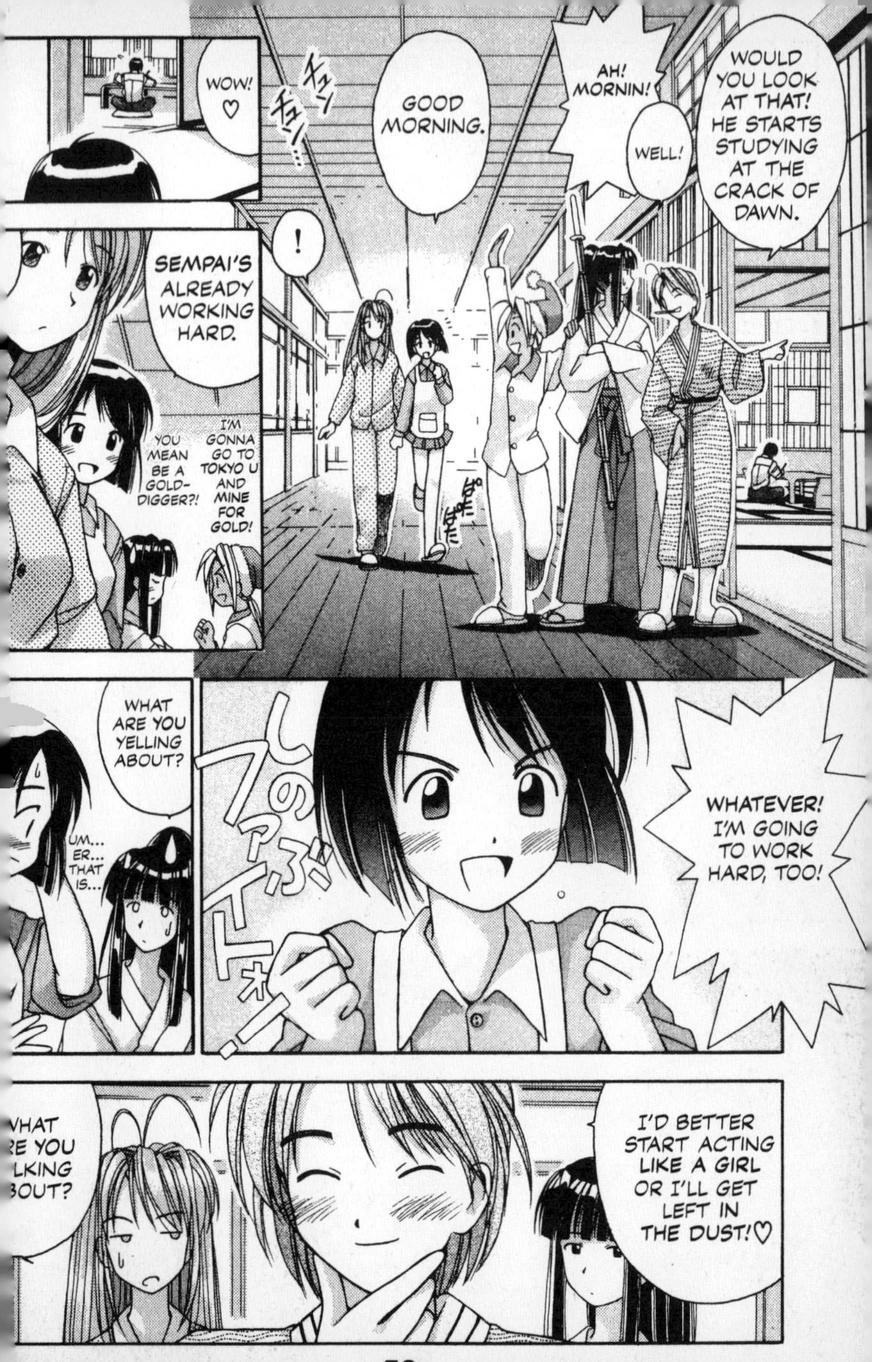
WOULD YOU LOOK AT THAT! HE STARTS STUDYING AT THE CRACK OF DAWN.
WELL!
AH! MORNIN'!
GOOD MORNING.
チュン チュン…
!
WOW! ♡
SEMPAI'S ALREADY WORKING HARD.
I'M GONNA GO TO TOKYO U AND MINE FOR GOLD!
YOU MEAN BE A GOLD-DIGGER?!
WHATEVER! I'M GOING TO WORK HARD, TOO!
しのぶファイトォ
WHAT ARE YOU YELLING ABOUT?
UM... ER... THAT IS...
I'D BETTER START ACTING LIKE A GIRL OR I'LL GET LEFT IN THE DUST! ♡
WHAT RE YOU LKING BOUT?

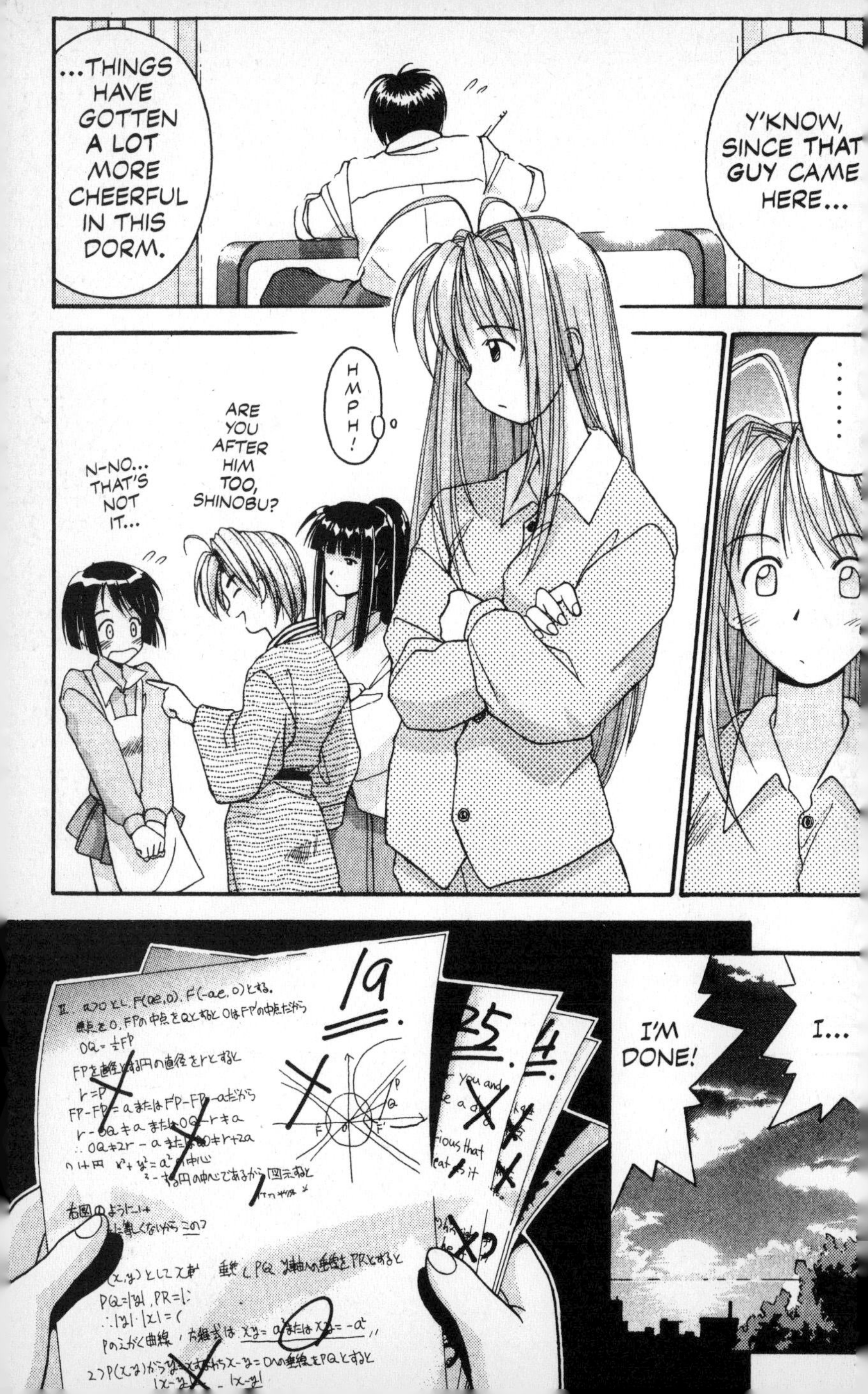
Y'KNOW, SINCE THAT GUY CAME HERE...
...THINGS HAVE GOTTEN A LOT MORE CHEERFUL IN THIS DORM.
......
HMPH!
ARE YOU AFTER HIM TOO, SHINOBU?
N-NO... THAT'S NOT IT...
I...
I'M DONE!
19
25

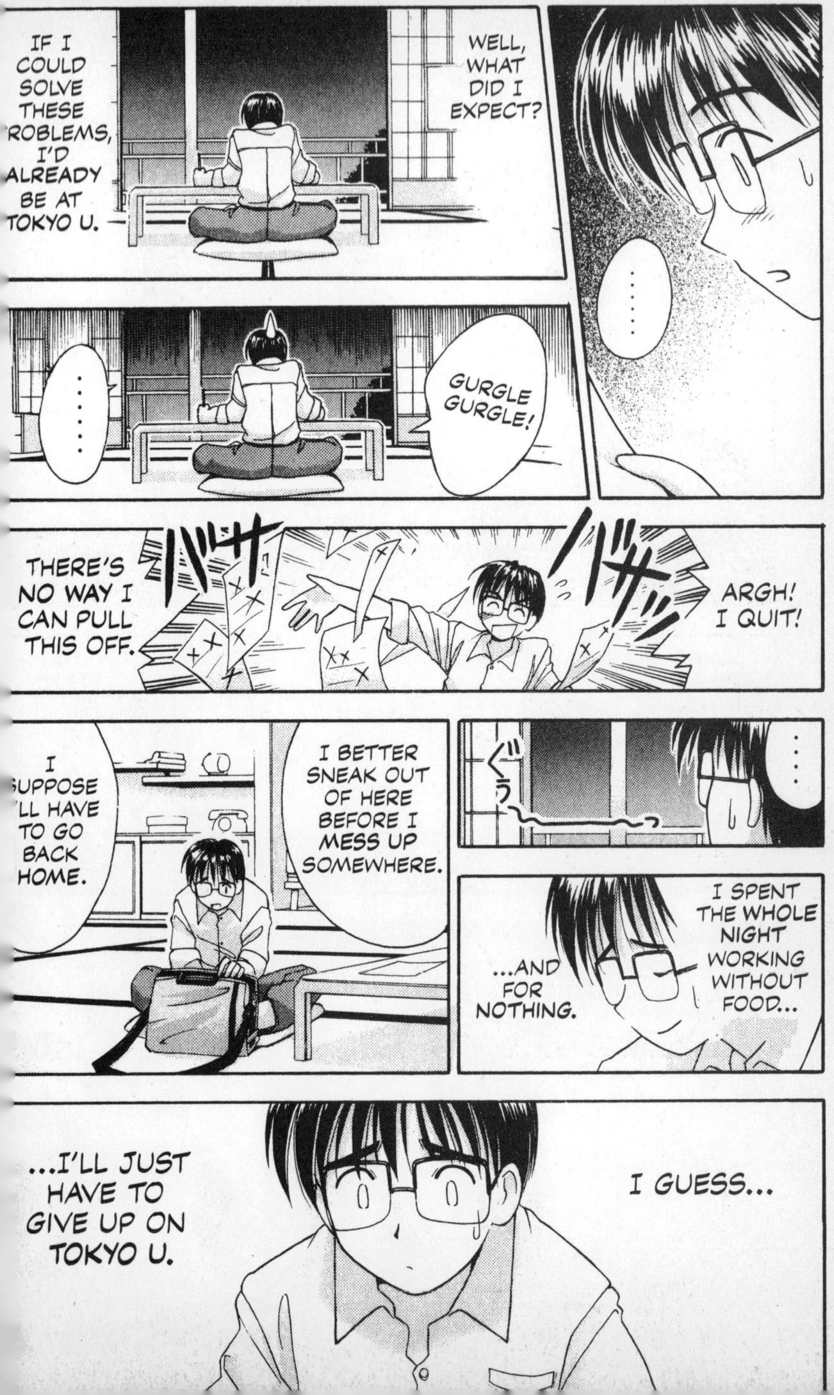
......
WELL, WHAT DID I EXPECT?
IF I COULD SOLVE THESE ROBLEMS, I'D ALREADY BE AT TOKYO U.
GURGLE GURGLE!
......
ARGH! I QUIT!
バサッ
バサ
THERE'S NO WAY I CAN PULL THIS OFF.
....
ぐぅ〜〜っ
I SPENT THE WHOLE NIGHT WORKING WITHOUT FOOD...
...AND FOR NOTHING.
I BETTER SNEAK OUT OF HERE BEFORE I MESS UP SOMEWHERE.
I UPPOSE 'LL HAVE TO GO BACK HOME.
I GUESS...
...I'LL JUST HAVE TO GIVE UP ON TOKYO U.

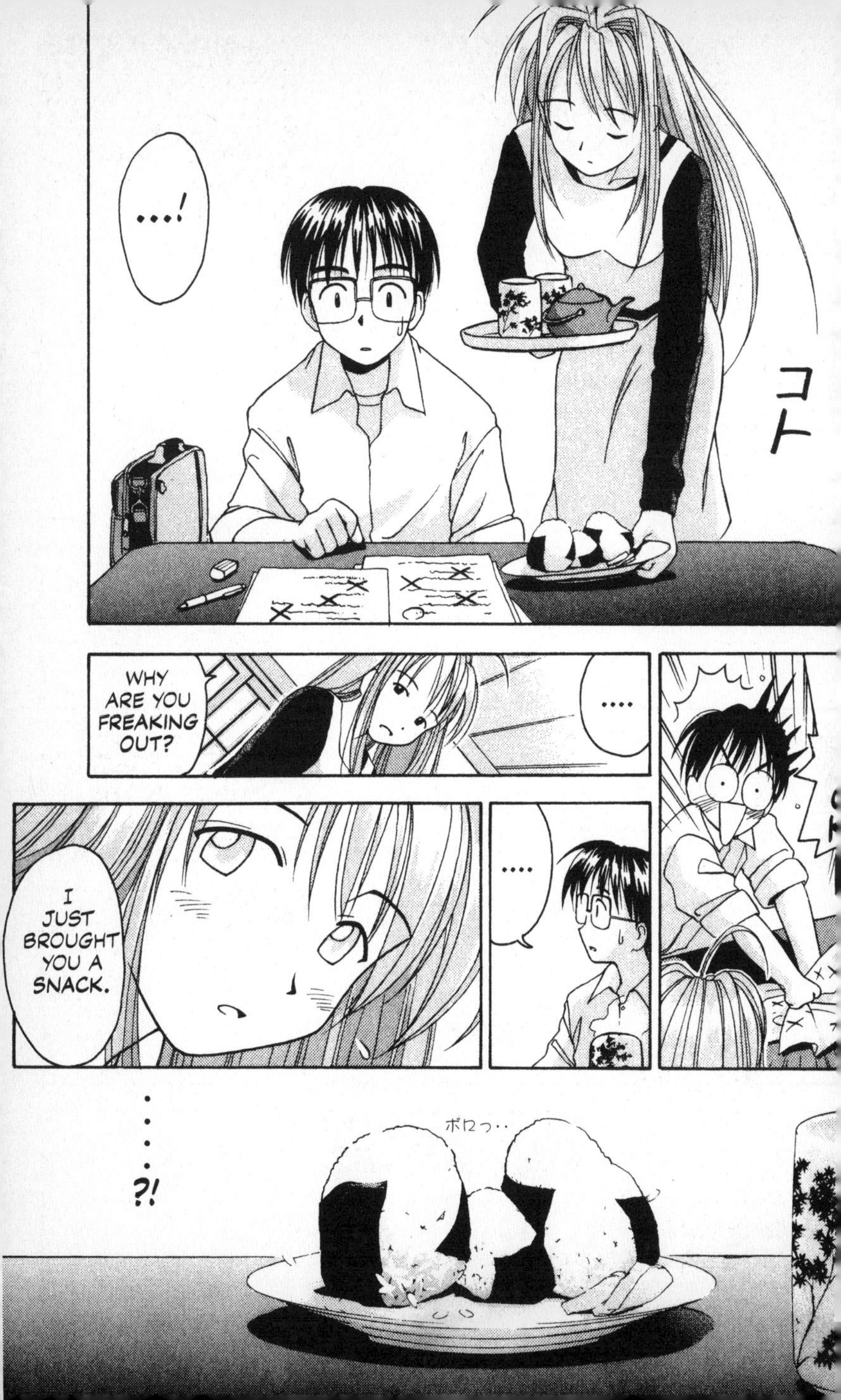
...!
コト
....
WHY ARE YOU FREAKING OUT?
....
I JUST BROUGHT YOU A SNACK.
ボロっ‥
....?!

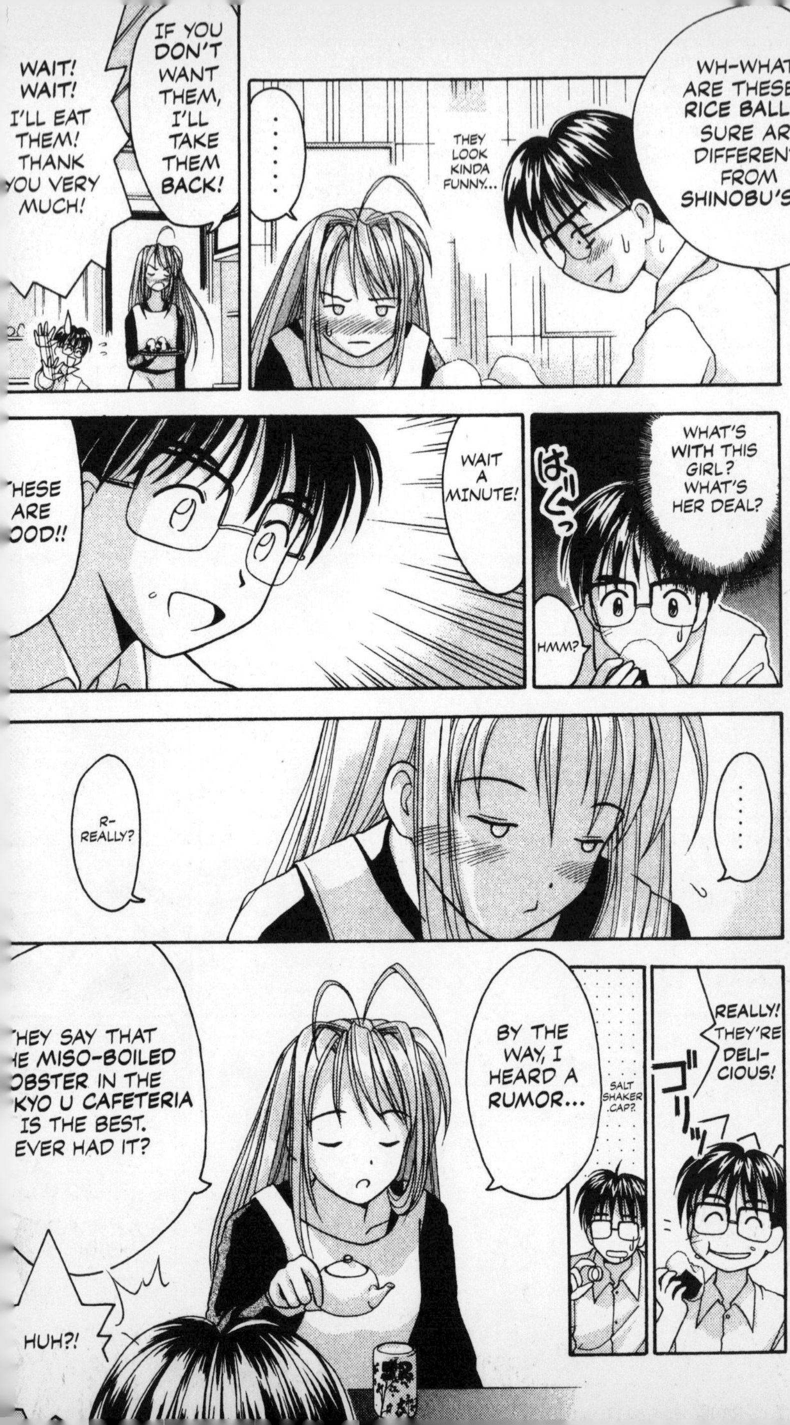

WH-WHAT ARE THESE?! RICE BALLS SURE ARE DIFFERENT FROM SHINOBU'S...
THEY LOOK KINDA FUNNY...
......
IF YOU DON'T WANT THEM, I'LL TAKE THEM BACK!
WAIT! WAIT! I'LL EAT THEM! THANK YOU VERY MUCH!
WHAT'S WITH THIS GIRL? WHAT'S HER DEAL?
はぐっ
HMM?
WAIT A MINUTE!
HESE ARE OOD!!
......
R-REALLY?
REALLY! THEY'RE DELI-CIOUS!
ゴリッ
SALT SHAKER CAP?
BY THE WAY, I HEARD A RUMOR...
HEY SAY THAT E MISO-BOILED OBSTER IN THE KYO U CAFETERIA IS THE BEST. EVER HAD IT?
HUH?!

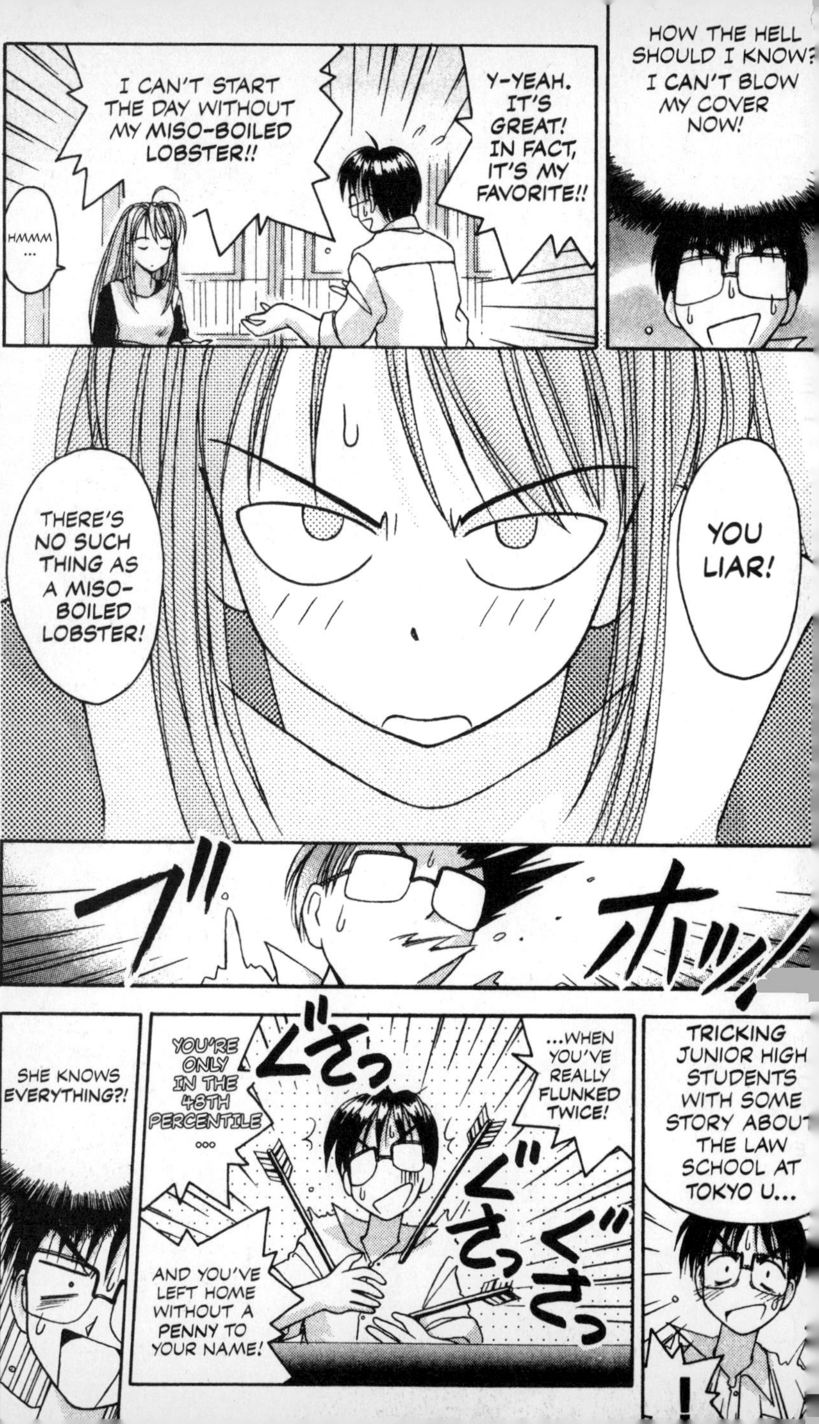
HOW THE HELL SHOULD I KNOW? I CAN'T BLOW MY COVER NOW!
Y-YEAH. IT'S GREAT! IN FACT, IT'S MY FAVORITE!!
I CAN'T START THE DAY WITHOUT MY MISO-BOILED LOBSTER!!
HMMM ...
YOU LIAR!
THERE'S NO SUCH THING AS A MISO-BOILED LOBSTER!
ブホッ!
TRICKING JUNIOR HIGH STUDENTS WITH SOME STORY ABOUT THE LAW SCHOOL AT TOKYO U...
!
...WHEN YOU'VE REALLY FLUNKED TWICE!
ぐさっ
YOU'RE ONLY IN THE 48TH PERCENTILE ...
ぐさっ
ぐさっ
ぐさっ
AND YOU'VE LEFT HOME WITHOUT A PENNY TO YOUR NAME!
SHE KNOWS EVERYTHING?!

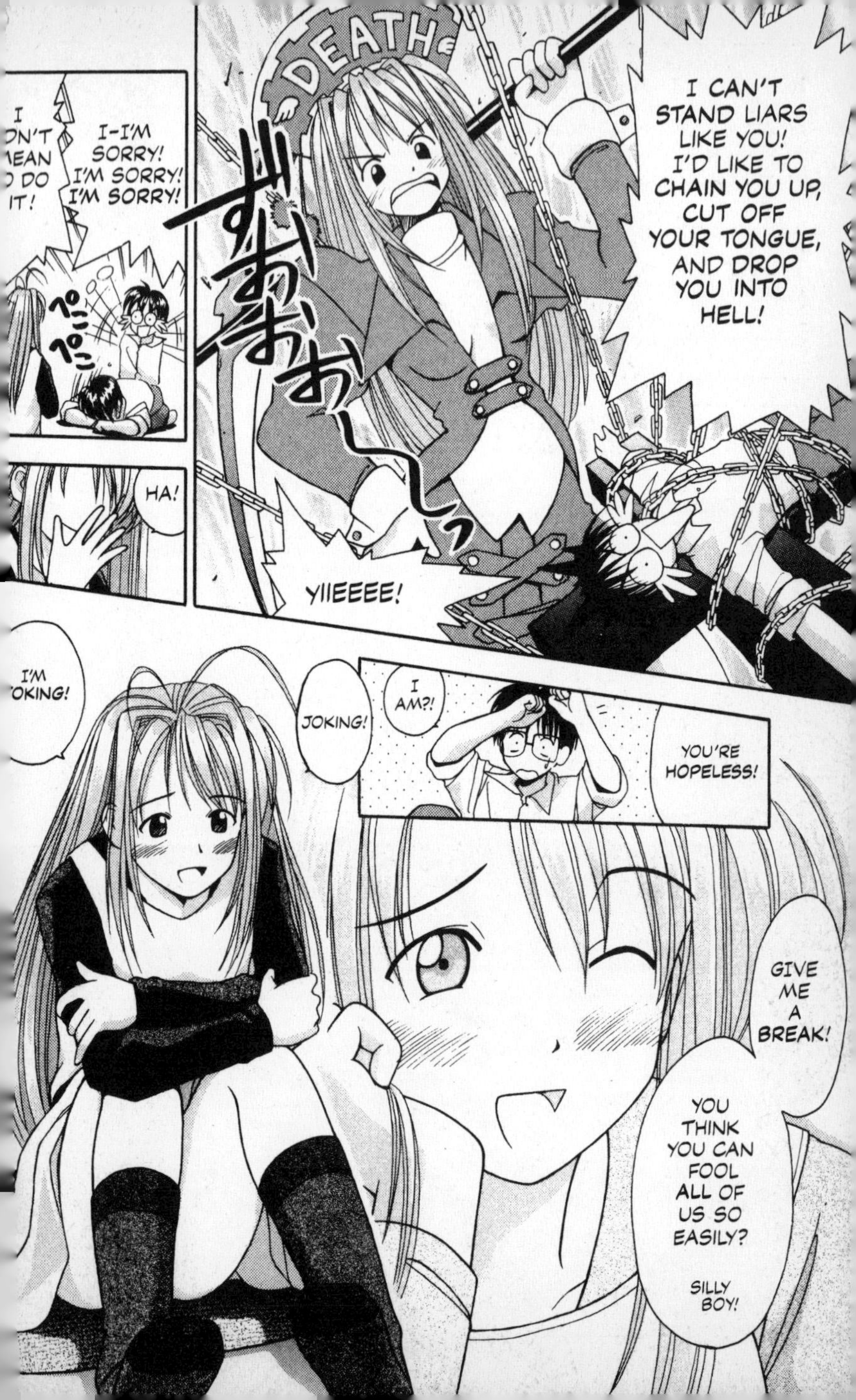
DEATH
I CAN'T STAND LIARS LIKE YOU! I'D LIKE TO CHAIN YOU UP, CUT OFF YOUR TONGUE, AND DROP YOU INTO HELL!
ずあああ〜っ
YIIEEEE!
I-I'M SORRY! I'M SORRY! I'M SORRY!
I ON'T EAN O DO IT!
ぺこぺこ
HA!
GIVE ME A BREAK!
YOU THINK YOU CAN FOOL ALL OF US SO EASILY?
SILLY BOY!
YOU'RE HOPELESS!
I AM?!
JOKING!
I'M OKING!

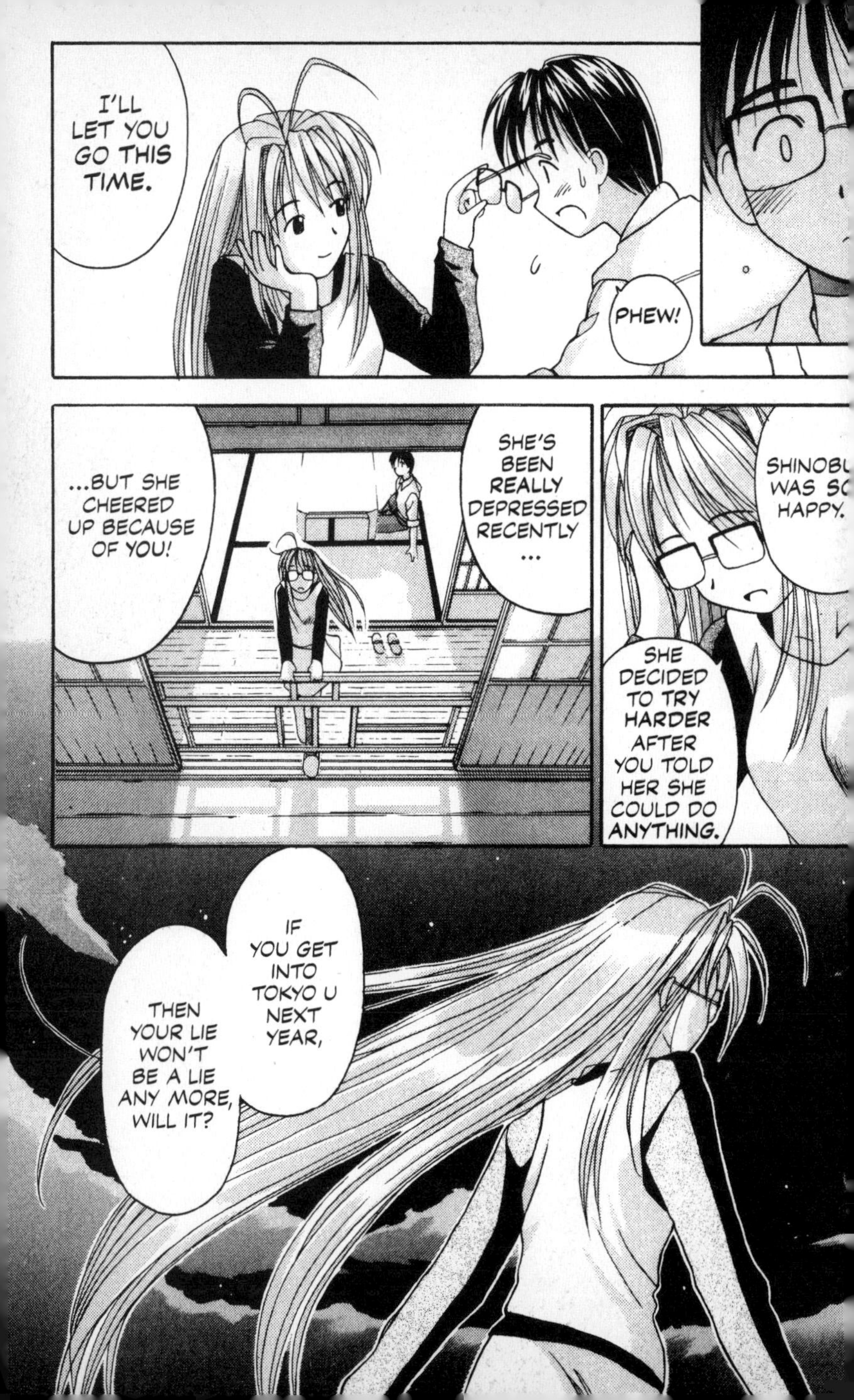
I'LL LET YOU GO THIS TIME.
PHEW!
SHINOBU WAS SO HAPPY.
SHE DECIDED TO TRY HARDER AFTER YOU TOLD HER SHE COULD DO ANYTHING.
SHE'S BEEN REALLY DEPRESSED RECENTLY ...
...BUT SHE CHEERED UP BECAUSE OF YOU!
IF YOU GET INTO TOKYO U NEXT YEAR,
THEN YOUR LIE WON'T BE A LIE ANY MORE, WILL IT?

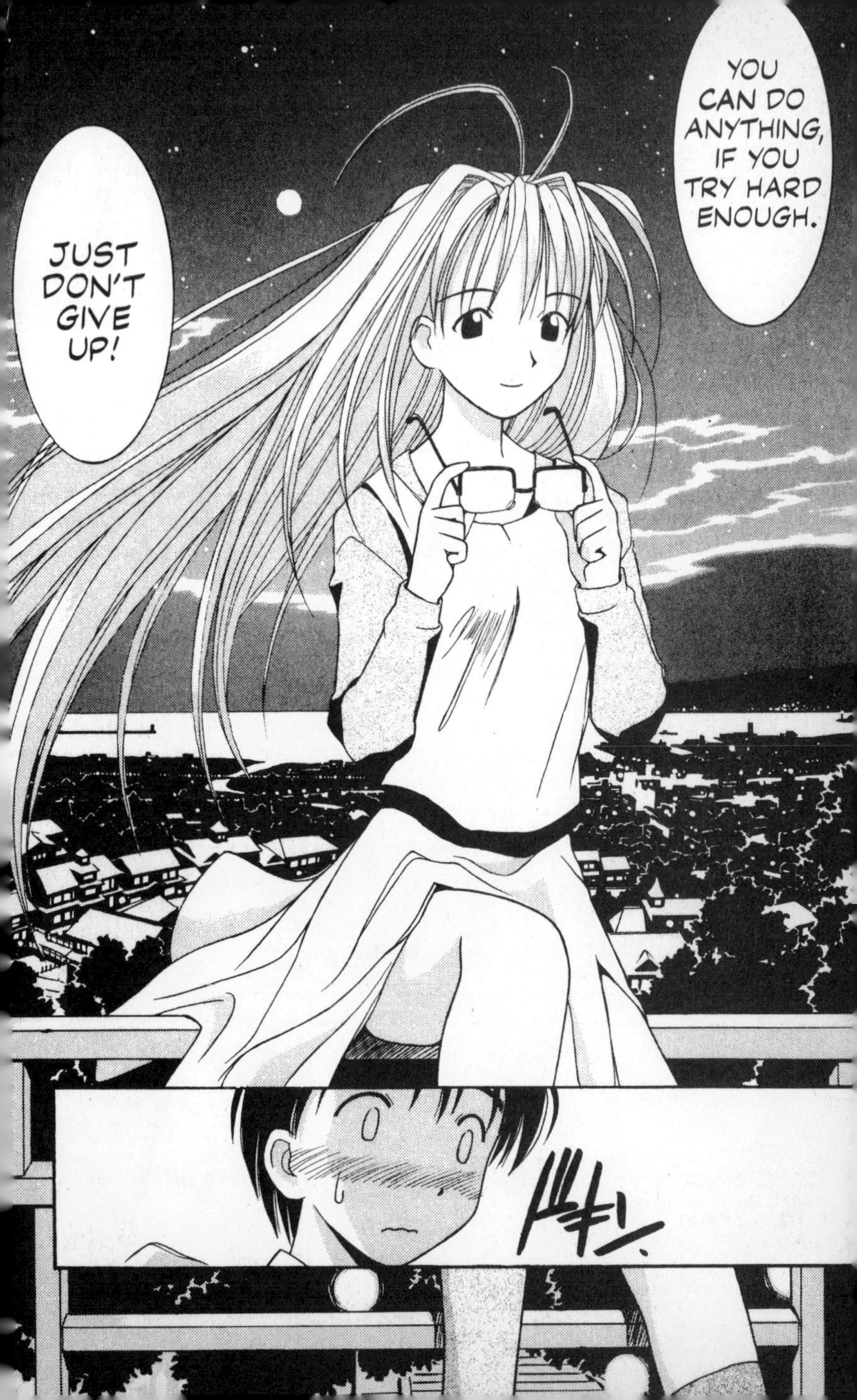
YOU CAN DO ANYTHING, IF YOU TRY HARD ENOUGH.
JUST DON'T GIVE UP!

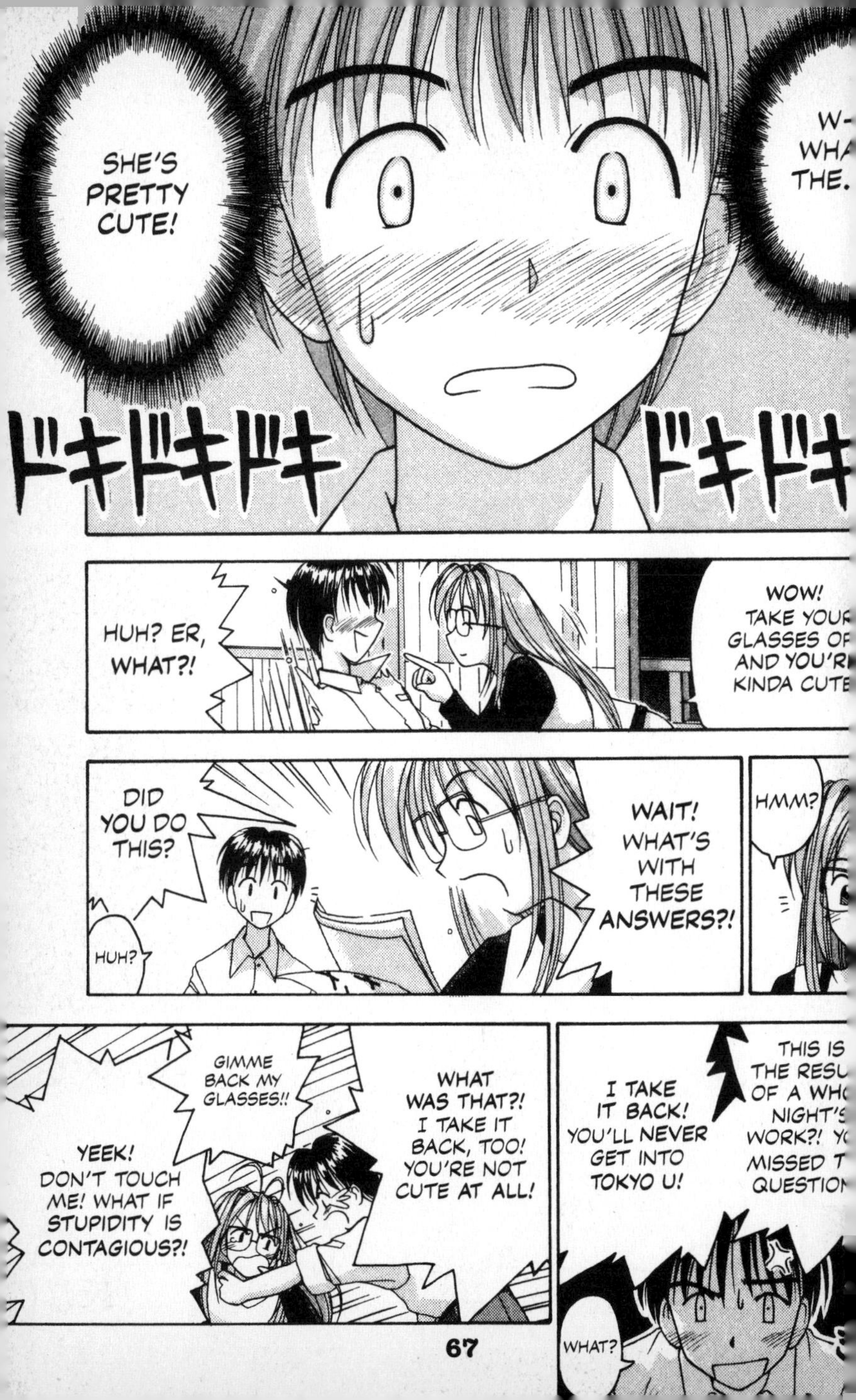

W- WHA THE.
SHE'S PRETTY CUTE!
ドキドキドキ
ドキドキ
WOW! TAKE YOUR GLASSES OF AND YOU'R KINDA CUTE
HUH? ER, WHAT?!
HMM?
WAIT! WHAT'S WITH THESE ANSWERS?!
DID YOU DO THIS?
HUH?
THIS IS THE RESU OF A WHO NIGHT'S WORK?! YO MISSED T QUESTION
I TAKE IT BACK! YOU'LL NEVER GET INTO TOKYO U!
WHAT?
WHAT WAS THAT?! I TAKE IT BACK, TOO! YOU'RE NOT CUTE AT ALL!
GIMME BACK MY GLASSES!!
YEEK! DON'T TOUCH ME! WHAT IF STUPIDITY IS CONTAGIOUS?!

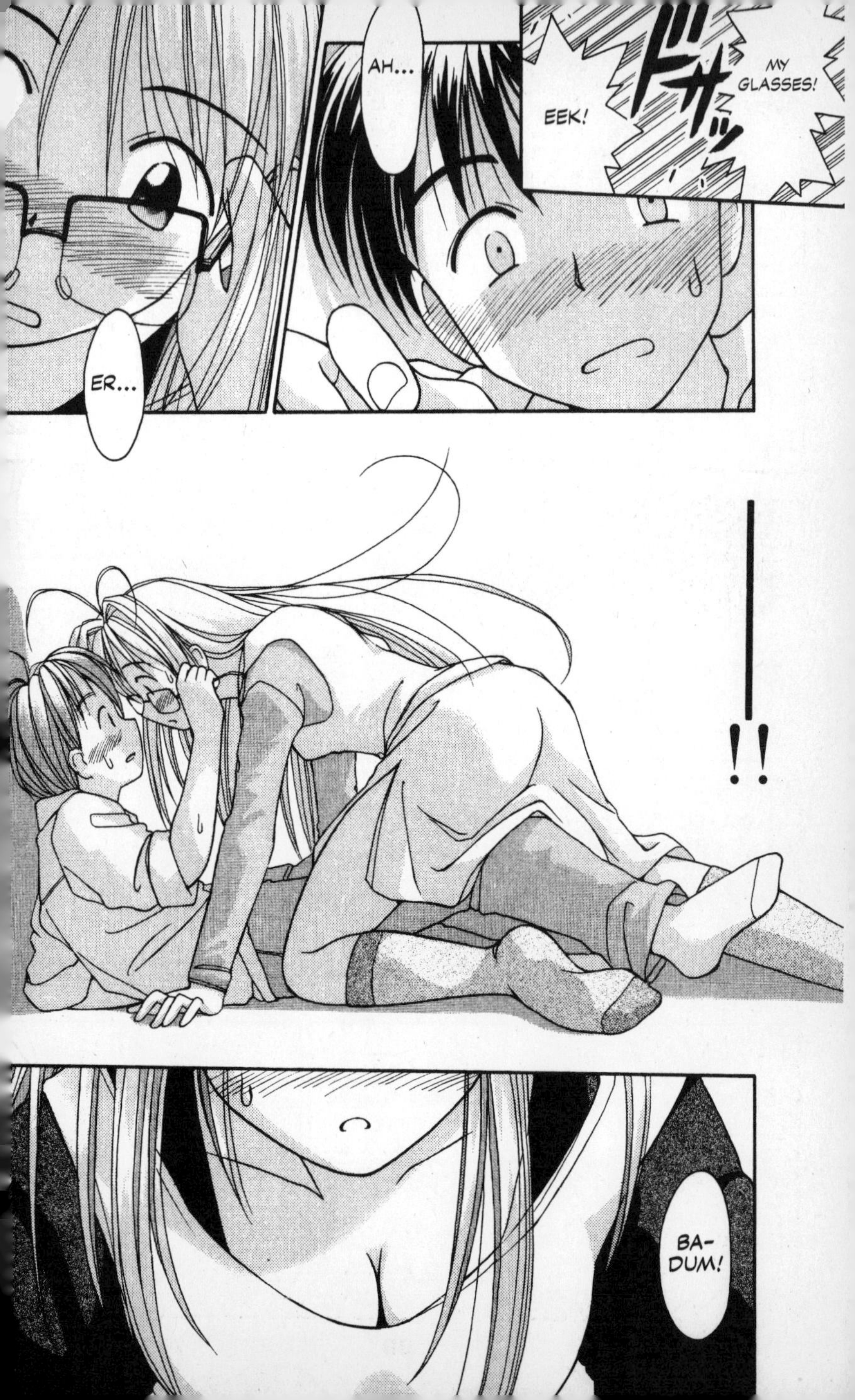

MY GLASSES!
ドサッ
EEK!
AH...
ER...
—!!
BA-DUM!

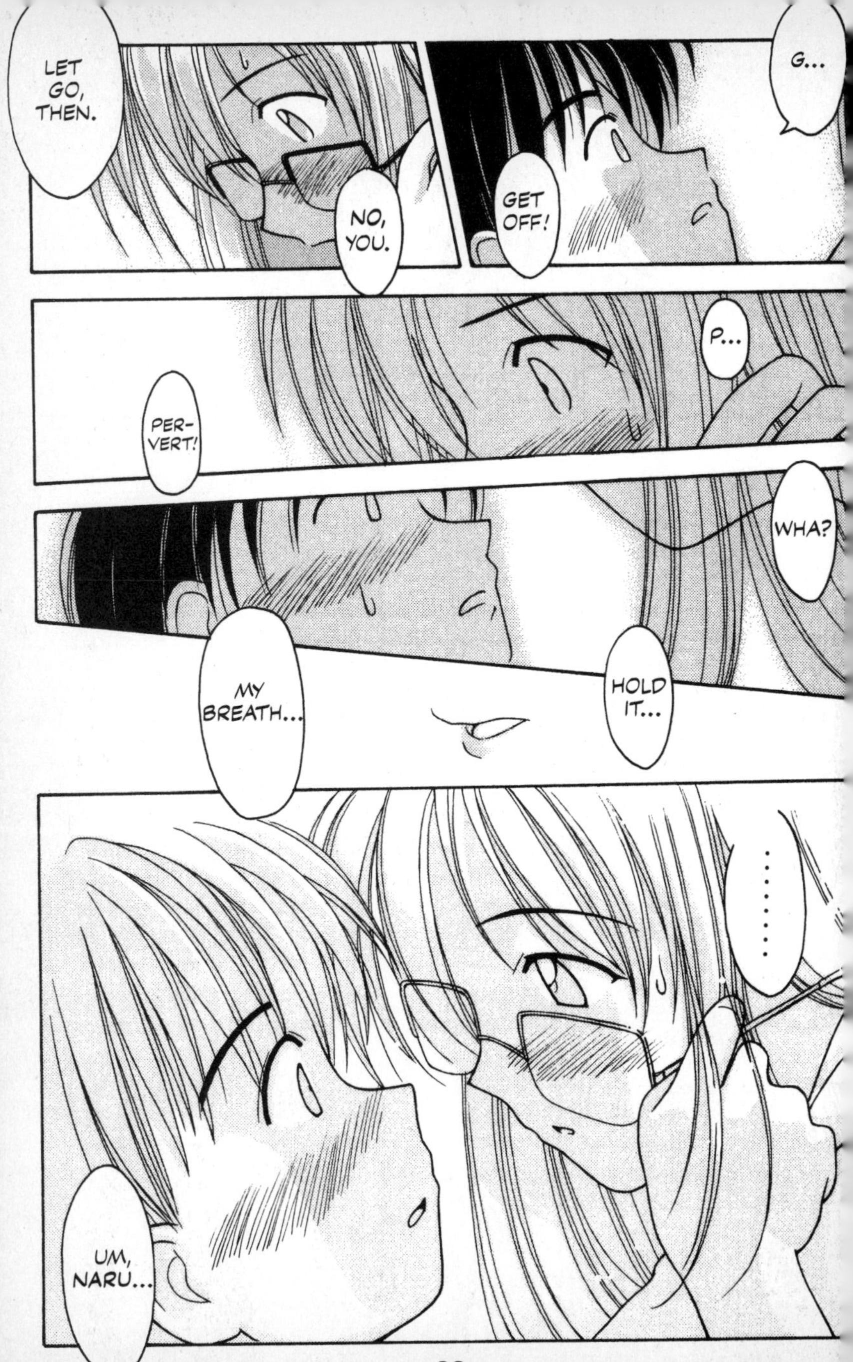
G...
GET OFF!
NO, YOU.
LET GO, THEN.
P...
PER-VERT!
WHA?
HOLD IT...
MY BREATH...
....
UM, NARU...

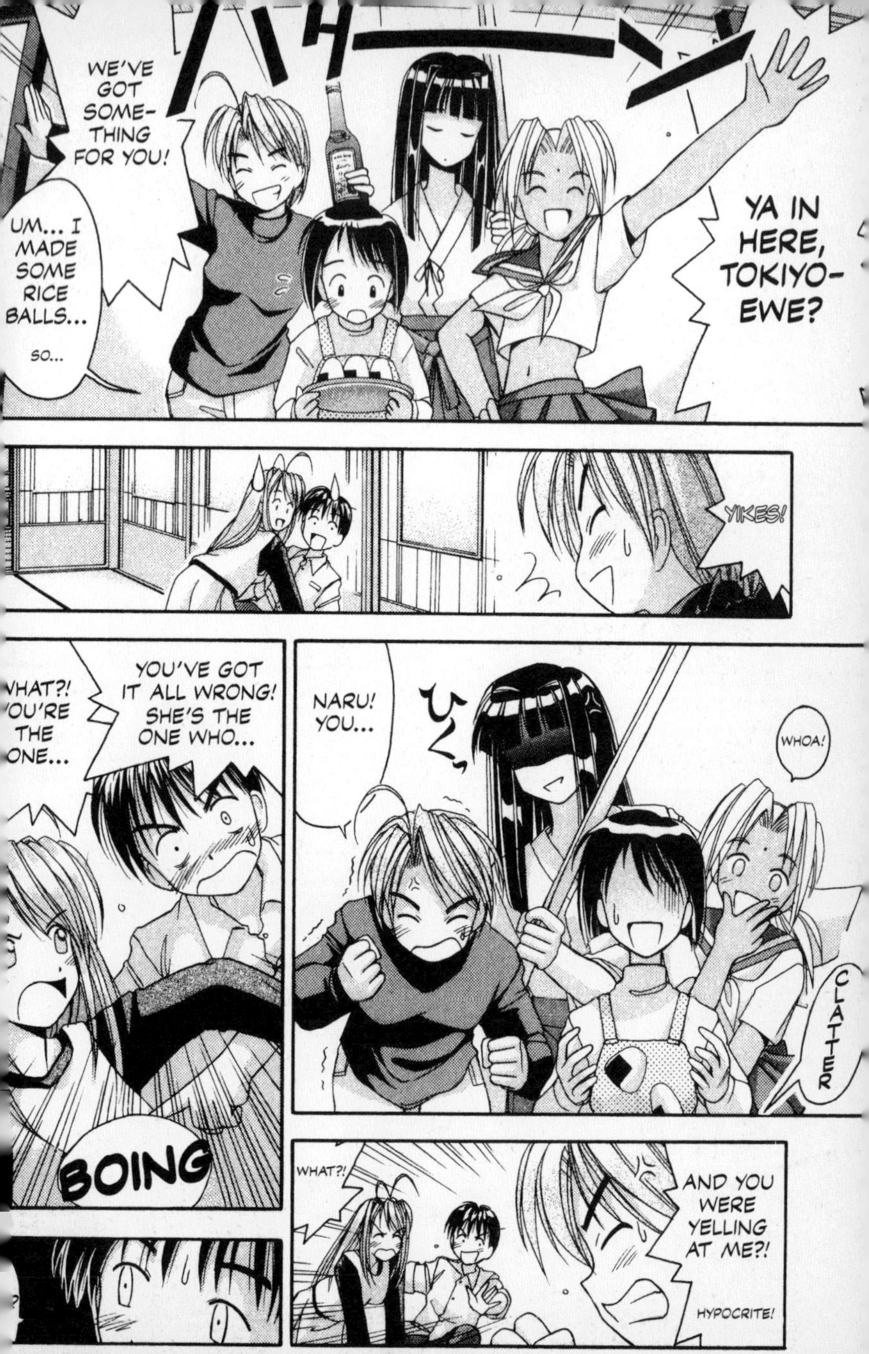
YA IN HERE, TOKIYO-EWE?
WE'VE GOT SOME-THING FOR YOU!
UM... I MADE SOME RICE BALLS...
SO...
YIKES!
NARU! YOU...
WHOA!
CLATTER
WHAT?!
AND YOU WERE YELLING AT ME?!
HYPOCRITE!
YOU'VE GOT IT ALL WRONG! SHE'S THE ONE WHO...
WHAT?! YOU'RE THE ONE...
BOING

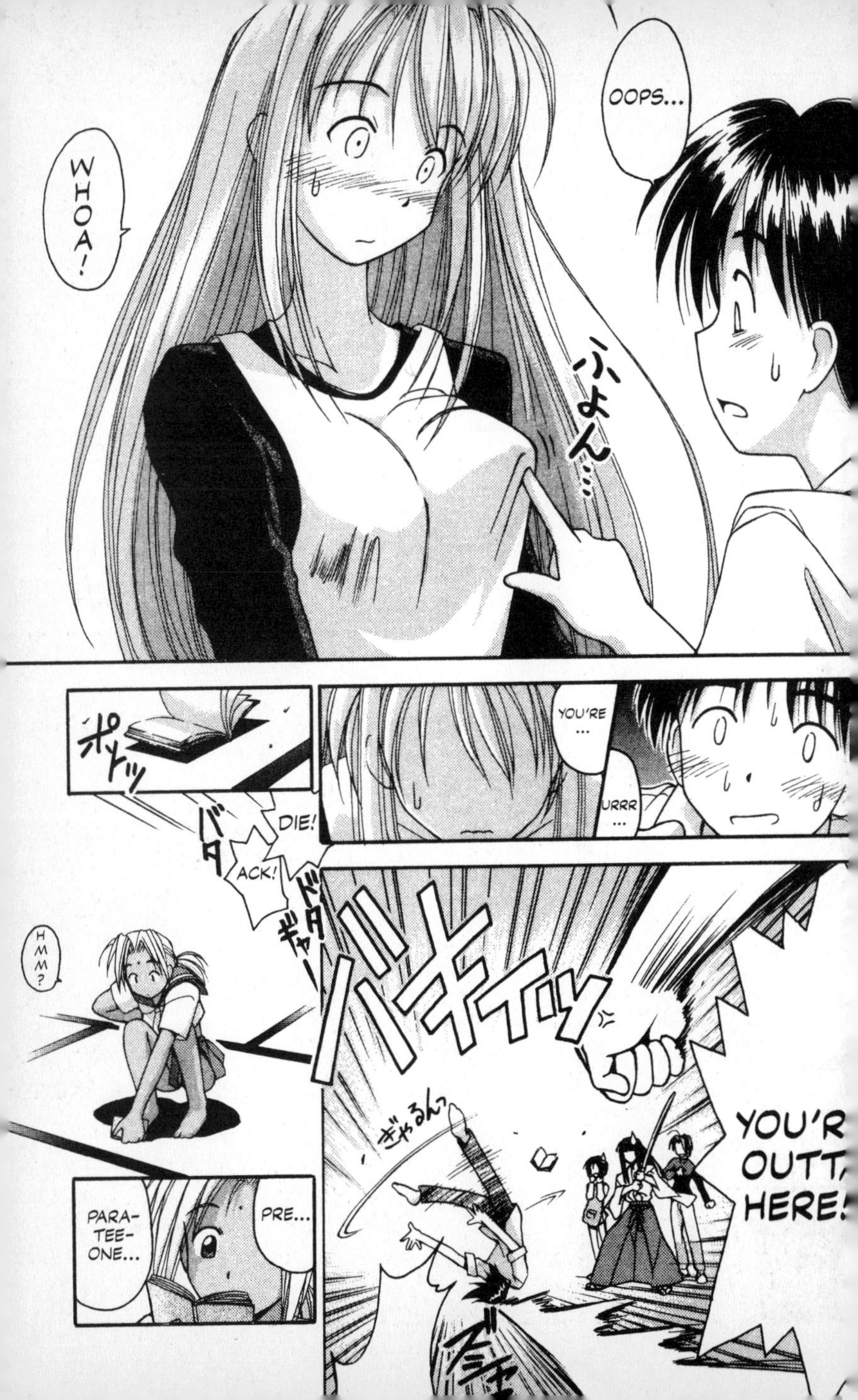
OOPS...
WHOA!
ふよん…
YOU'RE ...
URRR ...
ポトッ
バキィッ
YOU'R OUTTA HERE!
ぎゃるんっ
DIE!
ACK!
バタ
ドタギャー
HMM?
PRE...
PARA-TEE-ONE...

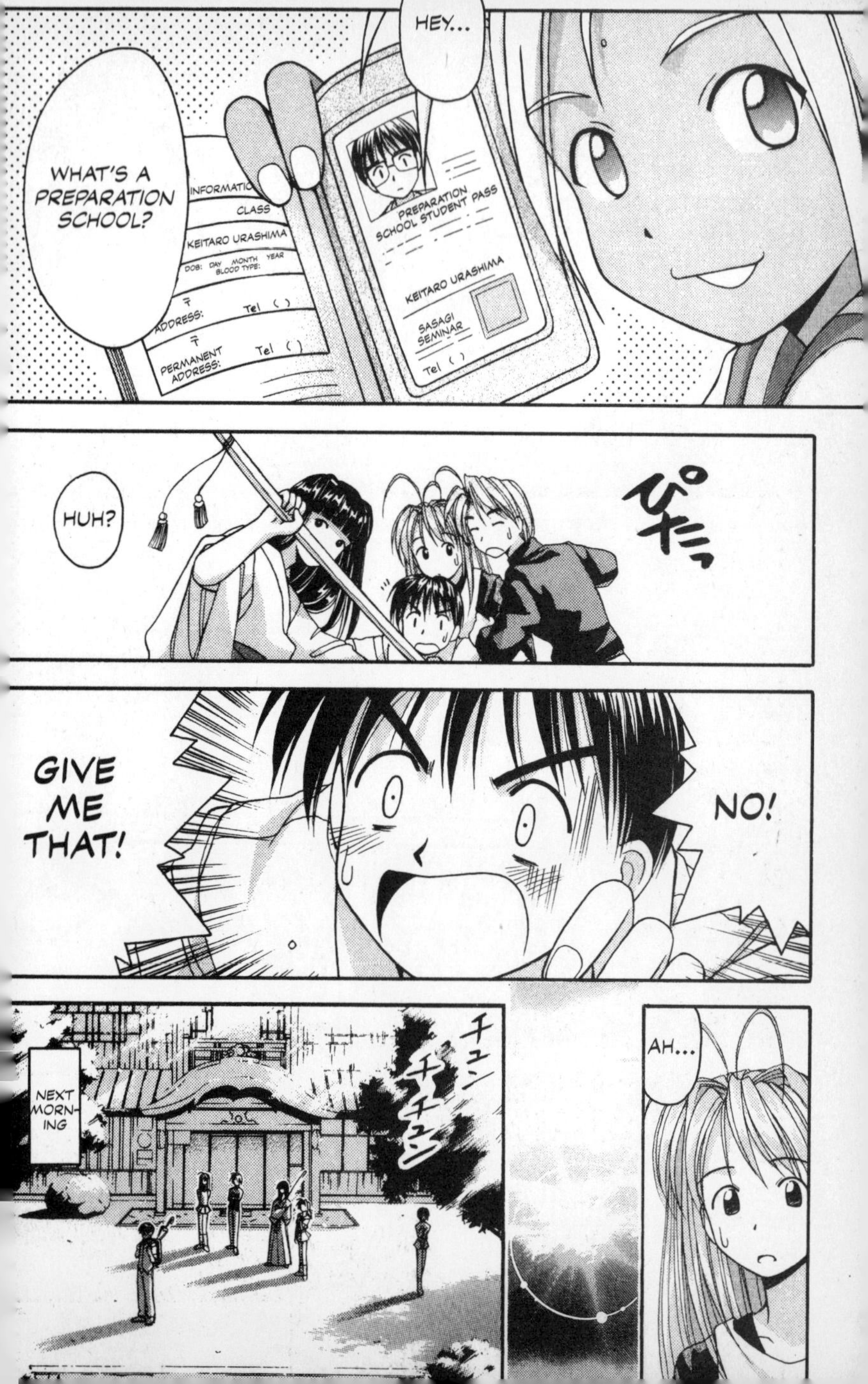
HEY...
WHAT'S A PREPARATION SCHOOL?
PREPARATION SCHOOL STUDENT PASS
KEITARO URASHIMA
SASAGI SEMINAR
Tel ( )
INFORMATIO
CLASS
KEITARO URASHIMA
DOB: DAY MONTH YEAR BLOOD TYPE:
〒
ADDRESS: Tel ( )
〒
PERMANENT ADDRESS: Tel ( )
ぴたっ
HUH?
NO!
GIVE ME THAT!
AH...
チュン
チチュン
NEXT MORNING

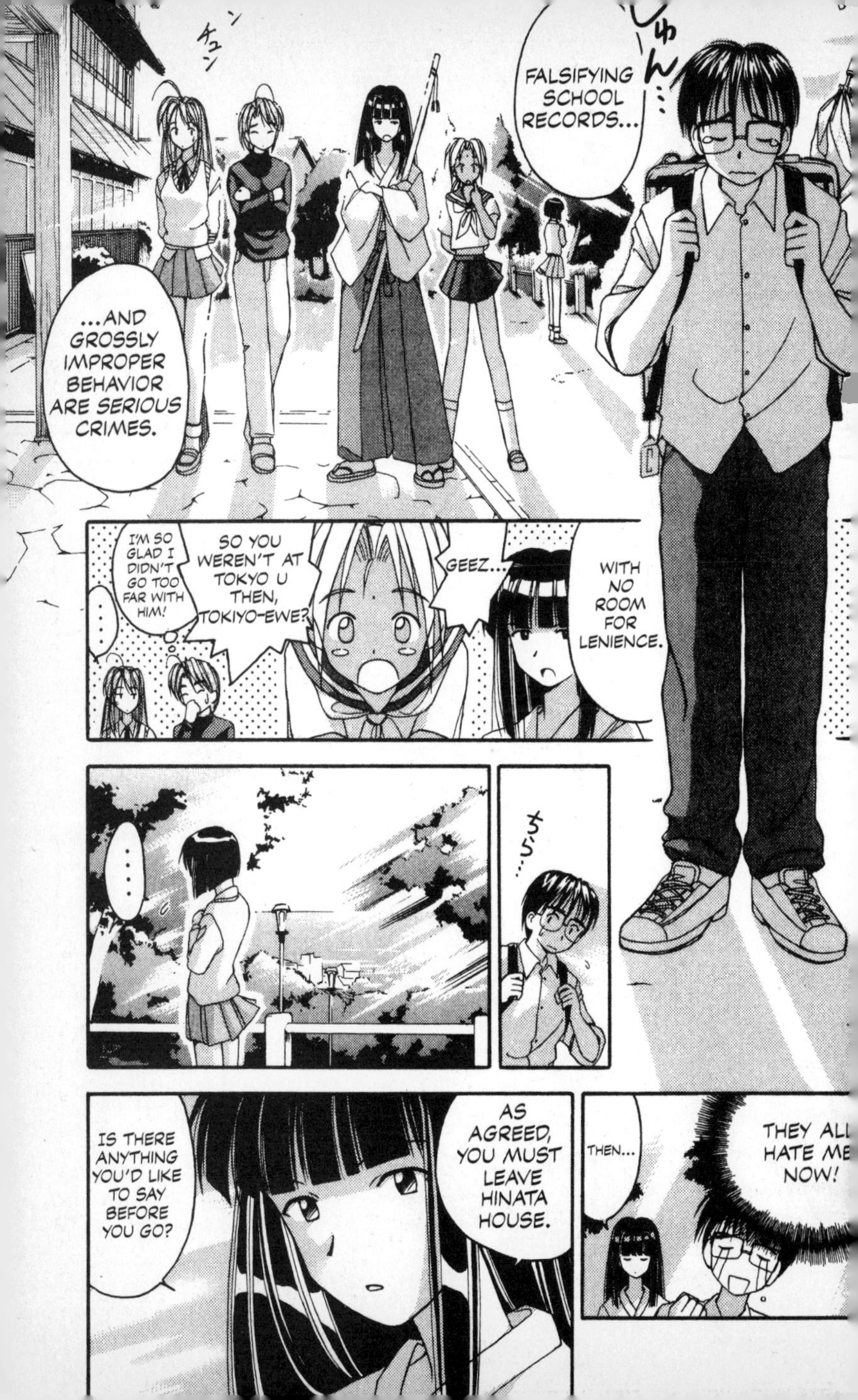

じゅん…
FALSIFYING SCHOOL RECORDS...
チュン
...AND GROSSLY IMPROPER BEHAVIOR ARE SERIOUS CRIMES.
WITH NO ROOM FOR LENIENCE.
GEEZ...
SO YOU WEREN'T AT TOKYO U THEN, TOKIYO-EWE?
I'M SO GLAD I DIDN'T GO TOO FAR WITH HIM!
...
ちら...
...
THEY ALL HATE ME NOW!
THEN...
AS AGREED, YOU MUST LEAVE HINATA HOUSE.
IS THERE ANYTHING YOU'D LIKE TO SAY BEFORE YOU GO?

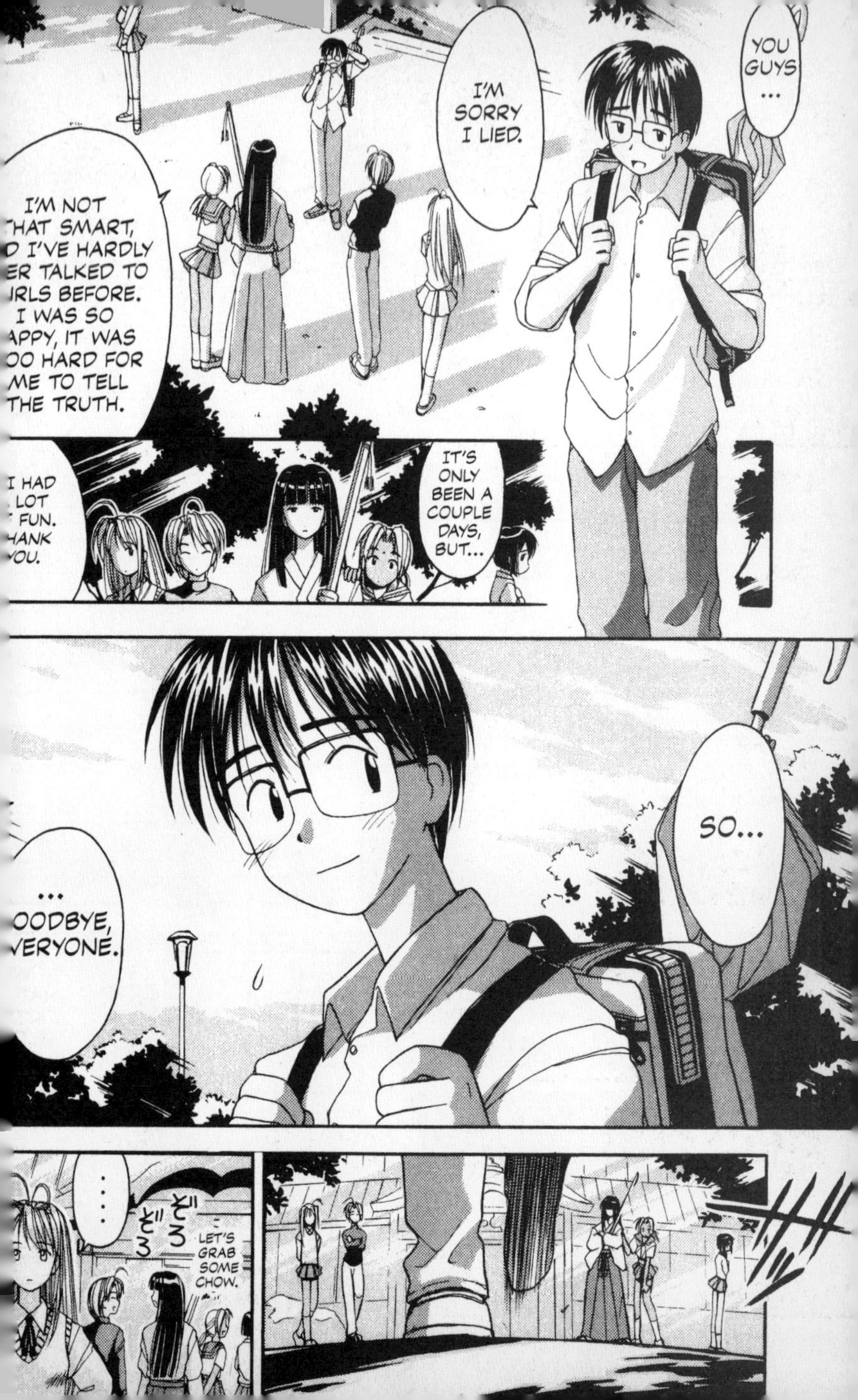

YOU GUYS ...
I'M SORRY I LIED.
I'M NOT HAT SMART, D I'VE HARDLY ER TALKED TO IRLS BEFORE. I WAS SO APPY, IT WAS OO HARD FOR ME TO TELL THE TRUTH.
IT'S ONLY BEEN A COUPLE DAYS, BUT...
I HAD LOT FUN. HANK YOU.
SO...
... OODBYE, VERYONE.
....
ぞろぞろ
LET'S GRAB SOME CHOW.

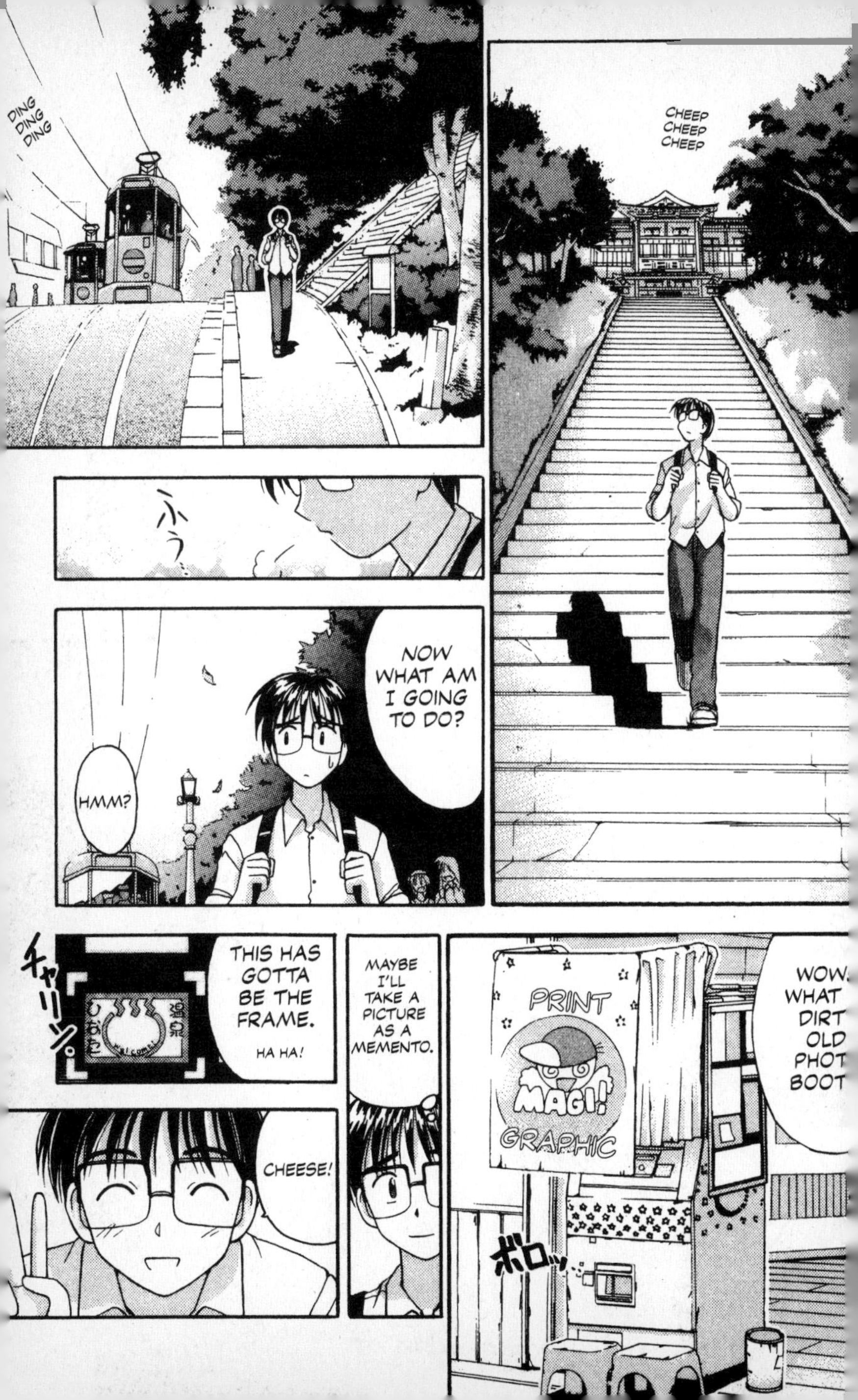
CHEEP CHEEP CHEEP
DING DING DING
ふう…
NOW WHAT AM I GOING TO DO?
HMM?
WOW. WHAT DIRT OLD PHOT BOOT
PRINT MAGI! GRAPHIC
ボロッ
MAYBE I'LL TAKE A PICTURE AS A MEMENTO.
チャリーン。
THIS HAS GOTTA BE THE FRAME.
HA HA!
CHEESE!

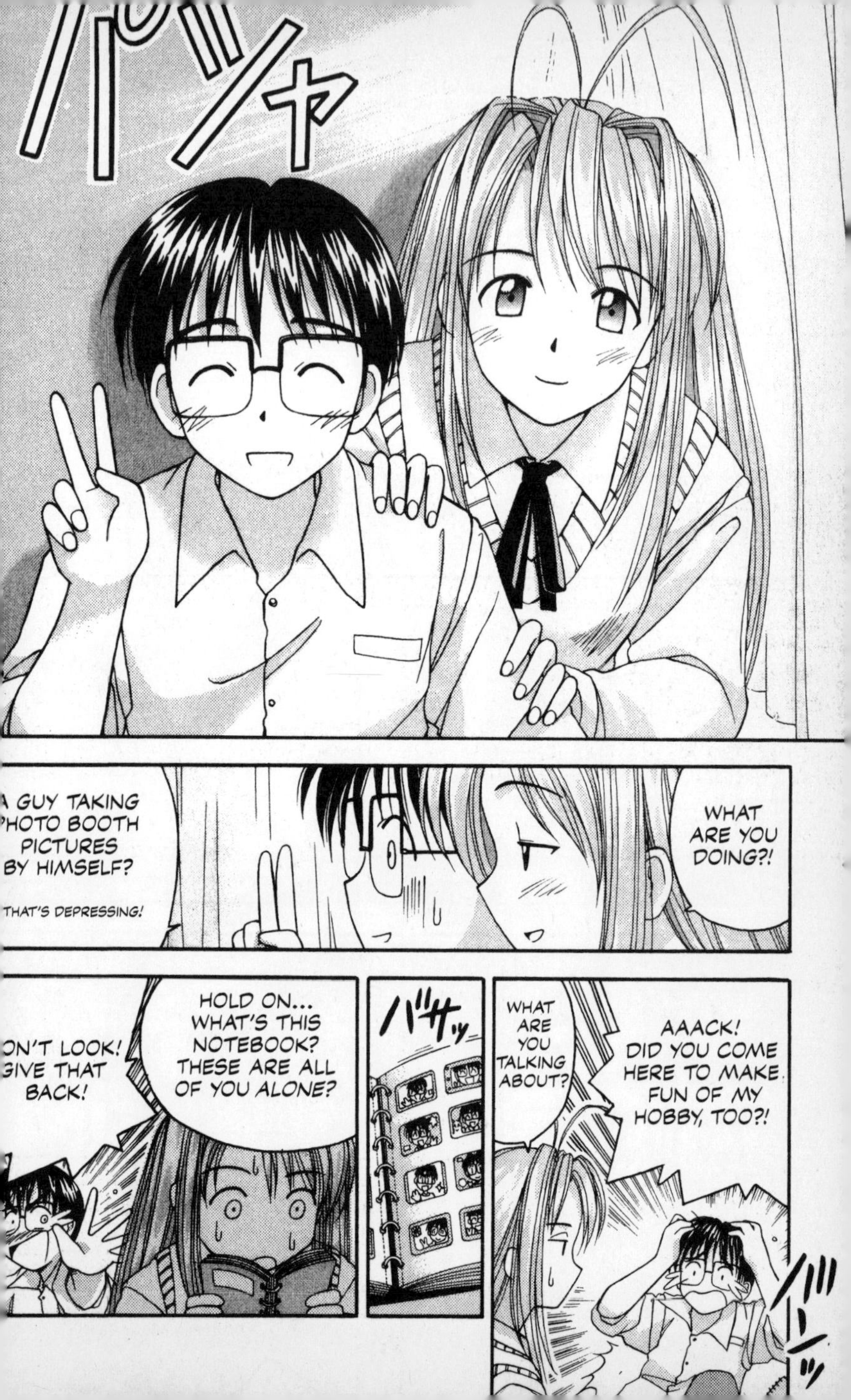
パシャ
WHAT ARE YOU DOING?!
A GUY TAKING PHOTO BOOTH PICTURES BY HIMSELF?
THAT'S DEPRESSING!
AAACK! DID YOU COME HERE TO MAKE FUN OF MY HOBBY, TOO?!
WHAT ARE YOU TALKING ABOUT?
バーッ
バサッ
HOLD ON... WHAT'S THIS NOTEBOOK? THESE ARE ALL OF YOU ALONE?
ON'T LOOK! GIVE THAT BACK!

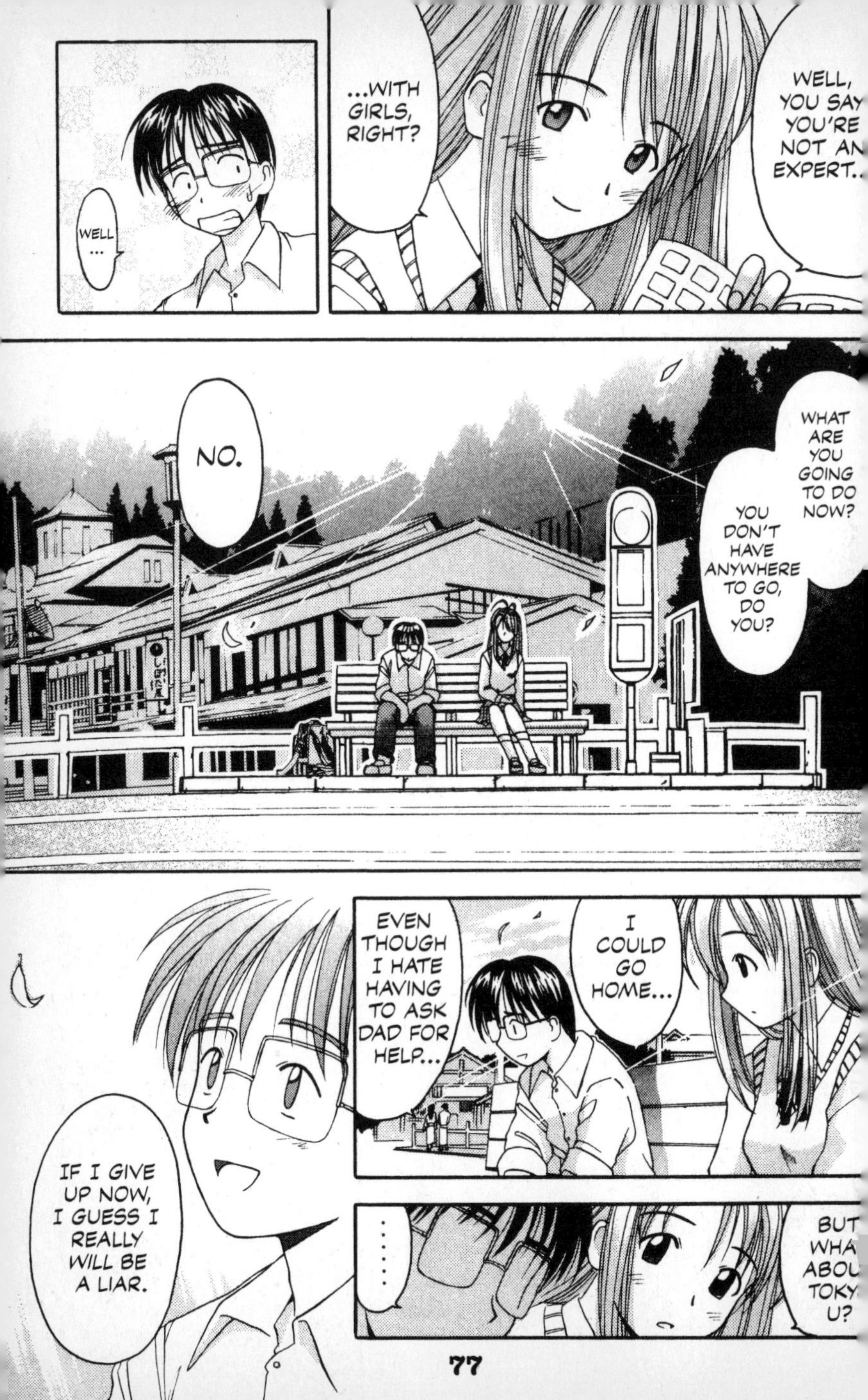
WELL, YOU SAY YOU'RE NOT AN EXPERT..
...WITH GIRLS, RIGHT?
WELL ...
WHAT ARE YOU GOING TO DO NOW?
YOU DON'T HAVE ANYWHERE TO GO, DO YOU?
NO.
I COULD GO HOME...
EVEN THOUGH I HATE HAVING TO ASK DAD FOR HELP...
BUT WHA ABOU TOKY U?
......
IF I GIVE UP NOW, I GUESS I REALLY WILL BE A LIAR.

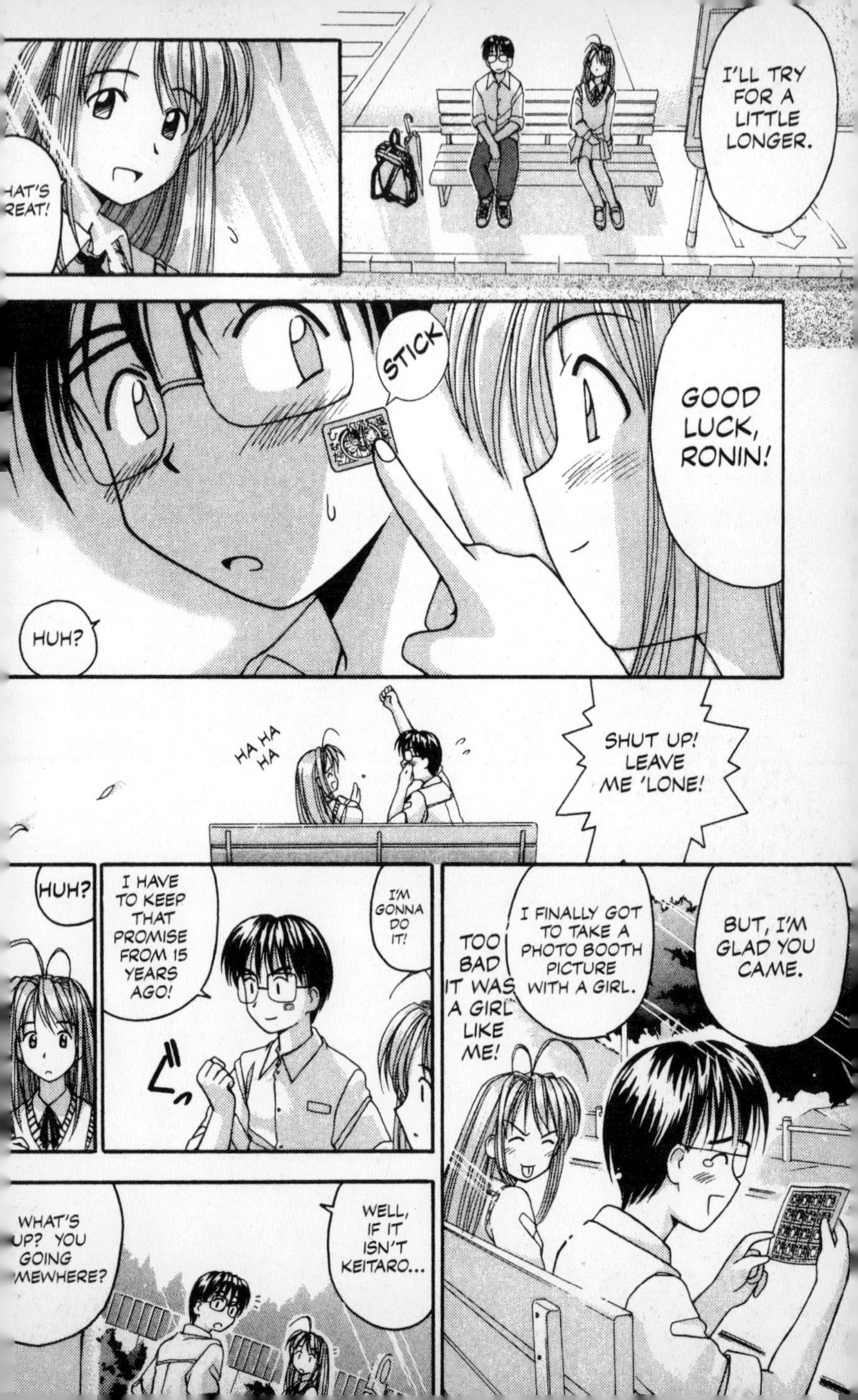

I'LL TRY FOR A LITTLE LONGER.
HAT'S REAT!
GOOD LUCK, RONIN!
STICK
HUH?
SHUT UP! LEAVE ME 'LONE!
HA HA HA
BUT, I'M GLAD YOU CAME.
I FINALLY GOT TO TAKE A PHOTO BOOTH PICTURE WITH A GIRL.
TOO BAD IT WAS A GIRL LIKE ME!
I'M GONNA DO IT!
I HAVE TO KEEP THAT PROMISE FROM 15 YEARS AGO!
HUH?
WELL, IF IT ISN'T KEITARO...
WHAT'S UP? YOU GOING MEWHERE?

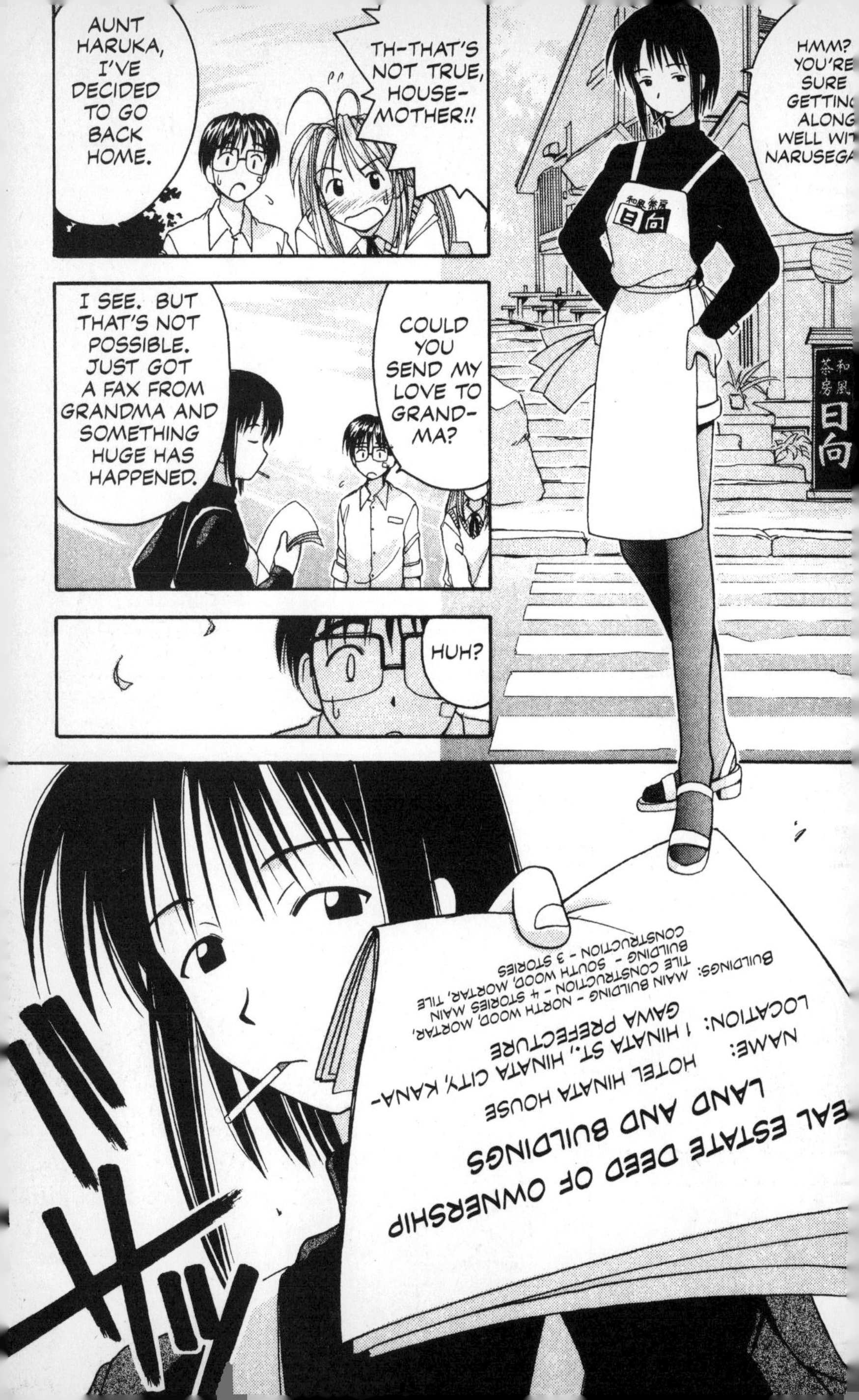
HMM? YOU'RE SURE GETTING ALONG WELL WIT NARUSEGA
TH-THAT'S NOT TRUE, HOUSE-MOTHER!!
AUNT HARUKA, I'VE DECIDED TO GO BACK HOME.
COULD YOU SEND MY LOVE TO GRAND-MA?
I SEE. BUT THAT'S NOT POSSIBLE. JUST GOT A FAX FROM GRANDMA AND SOMETHING HUGE HAS HAPPENED.
HUH?
EAL ESTATE DEED OF OWNERSHIP
LAND AND BUILDINGS
NAME: HOTEL HINATA HOUSE
LOCATION: 1 HINATA ST., HINATA CITY, KANA-GAWA PREFECTURE
BUILDINGS: MAIN BUILDING - NORTH WOOD, MORTAR, TILE CONSTRUCTION - 4 STORIES MAIN BUILDING - SOUTH WOOD, MORTAR, TILE CONSTRUCTION - 3 STORIES

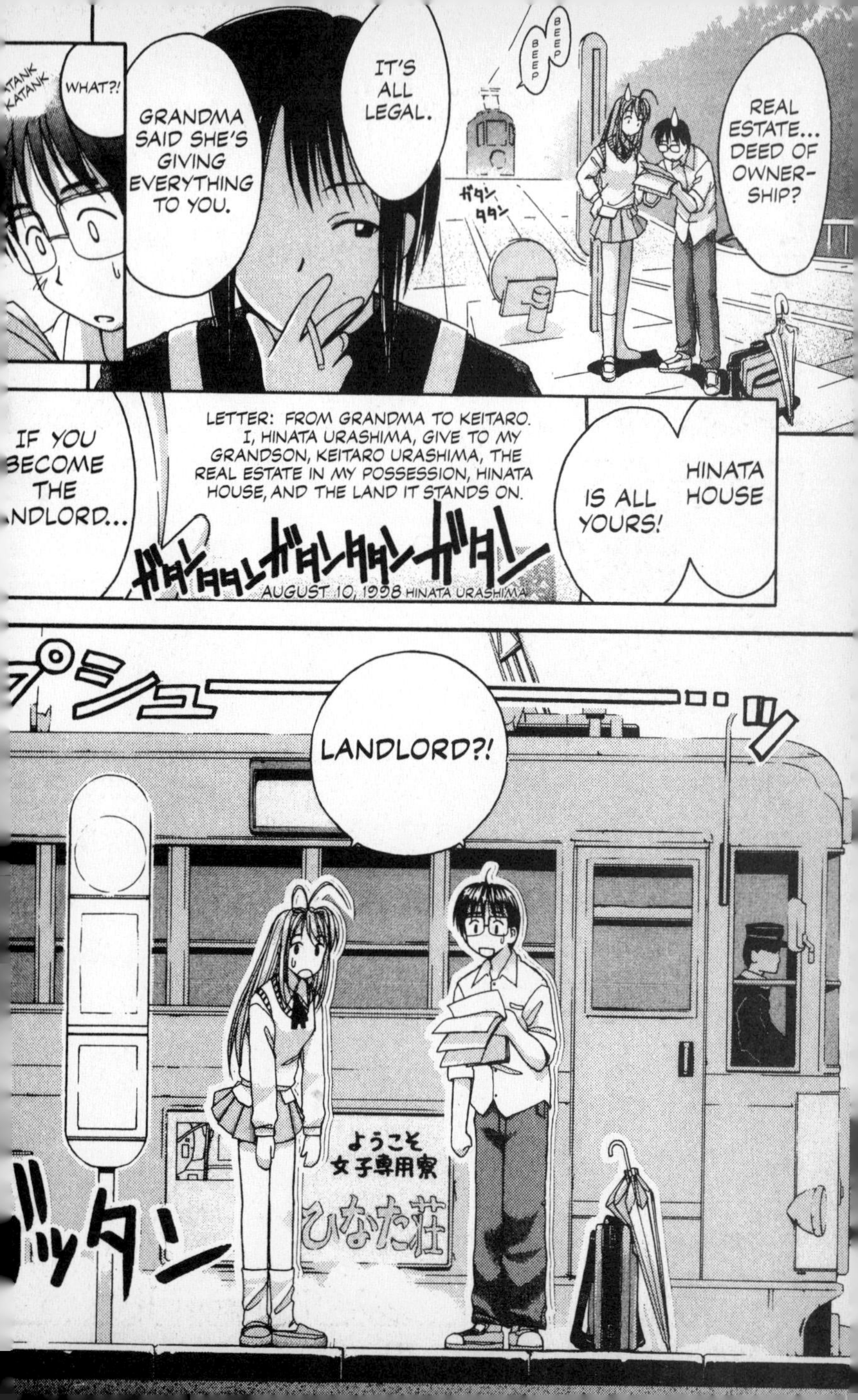
BEEP BEEP
REAL ESTATE... DEED OF OWNERSHIP?
ガタン タタン
IT'S ALL LEGAL.
GRANDMA SAID SHE'S GIVING EVERYTHING TO YOU.
WHAT?!
KATANK KATANK
HINATA HOUSE IS ALL YOURS!
LETTER: FROM GRANDMA TO KEITARO.
I, HINATA URASHIMA, GIVE TO MY GRANDSON, KEITARO URASHIMA, THE REAL ESTATE IN MY POSSESSION, HINATA HOUSE, AND THE LAND IT STANDS ON.
ガタンタタンガタンタタンガタン
AUGUST 10, 1998 HINATA URASHIMA
IF YOU BECOME THE NDLORD...
プシューーーーロロッ
LANDLORD?!
ようこそ 女子専用寮
ひなた荘
ガッタン

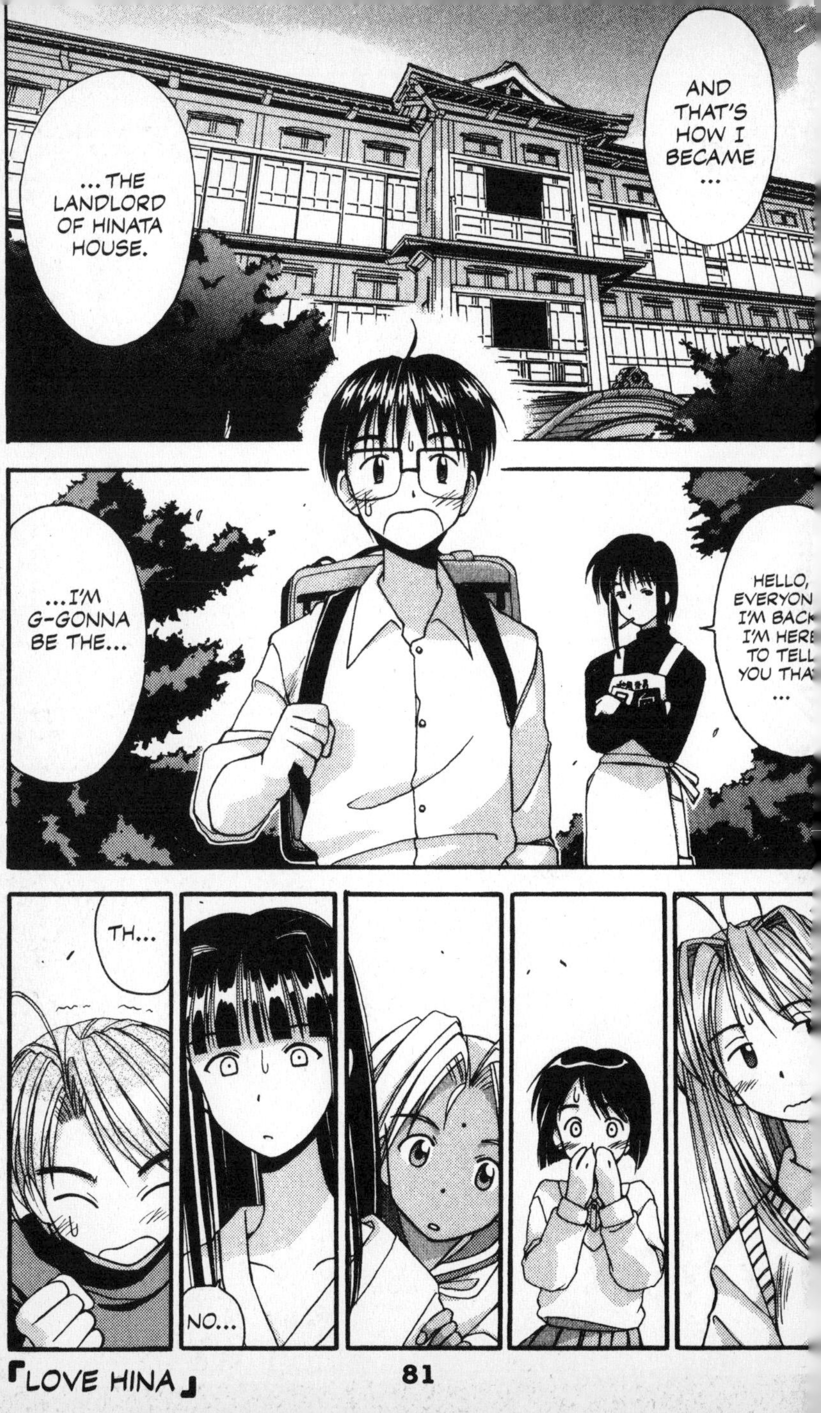
AND THAT'S HOW I BECAME ...
... THE LANDLORD OF HINATA HOUSE.
HELLO, EVERYON I'M BACK I'M HERE TO TELL YOU THA ...
...I'M G-GONNA BE THE...
NO...
TH...

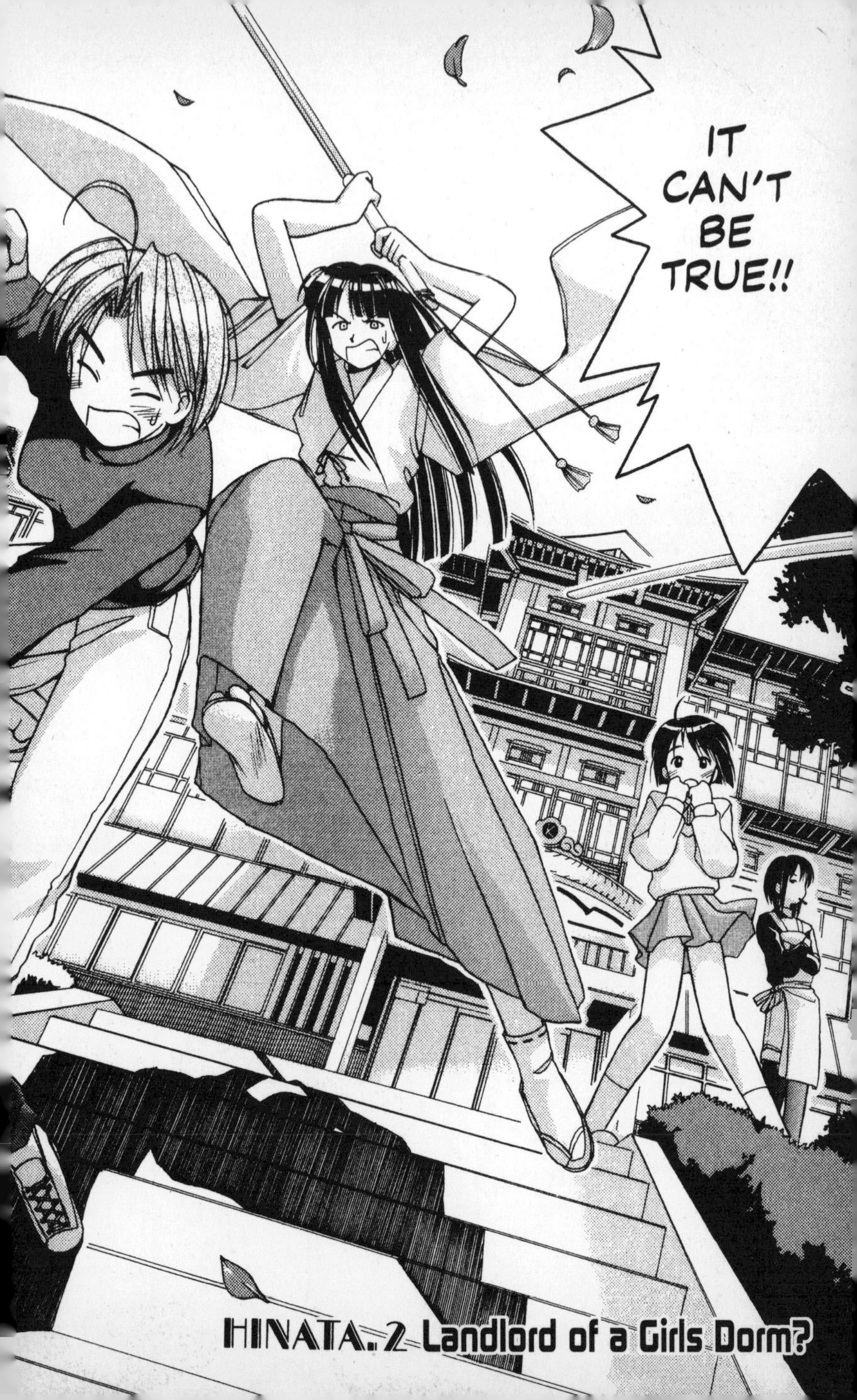
IT CAN'T BE TRUE!!
HINATA. 2 Landlord of a Girls Dorm?

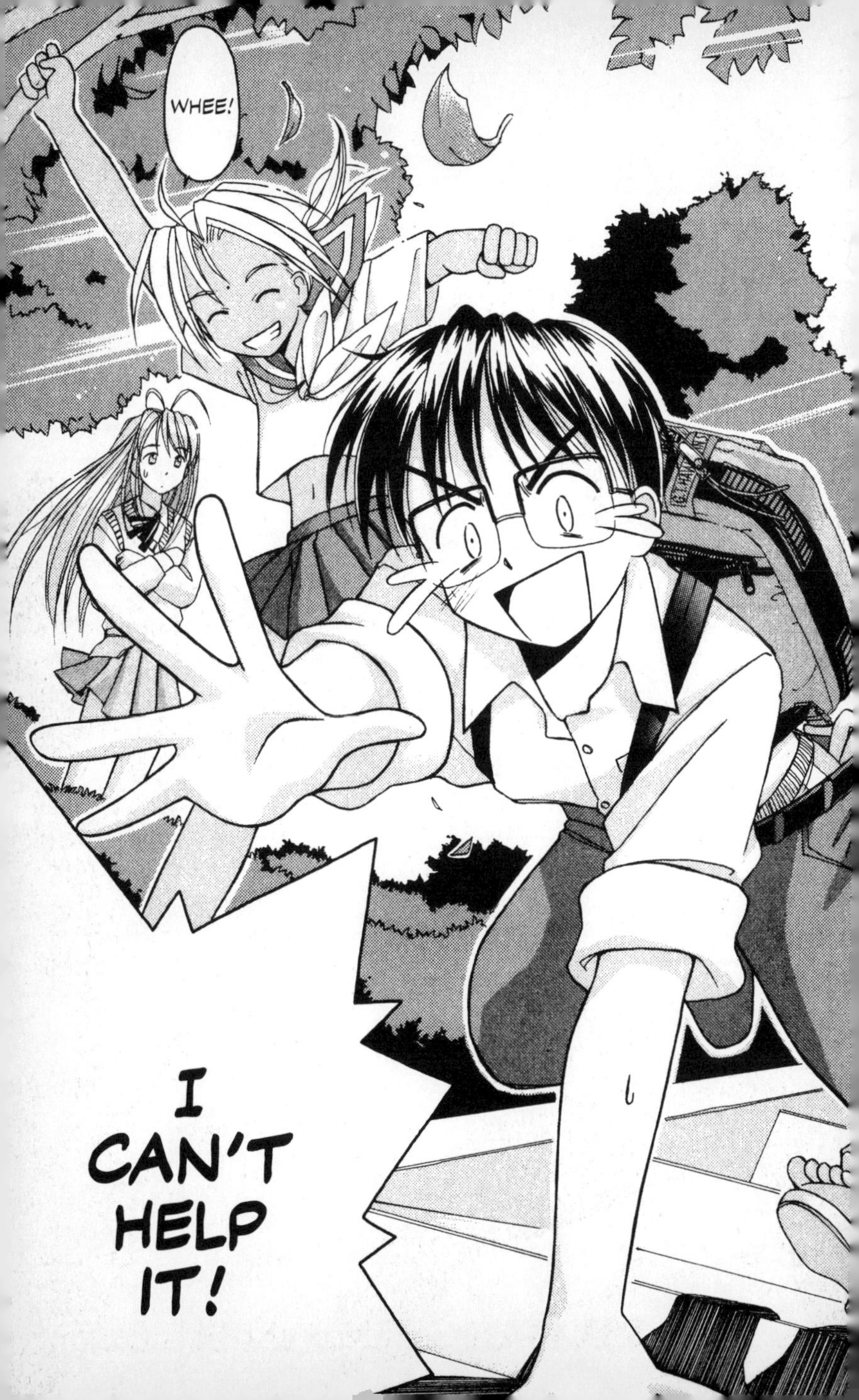
WHEE!
I CAN'T HELP IT!

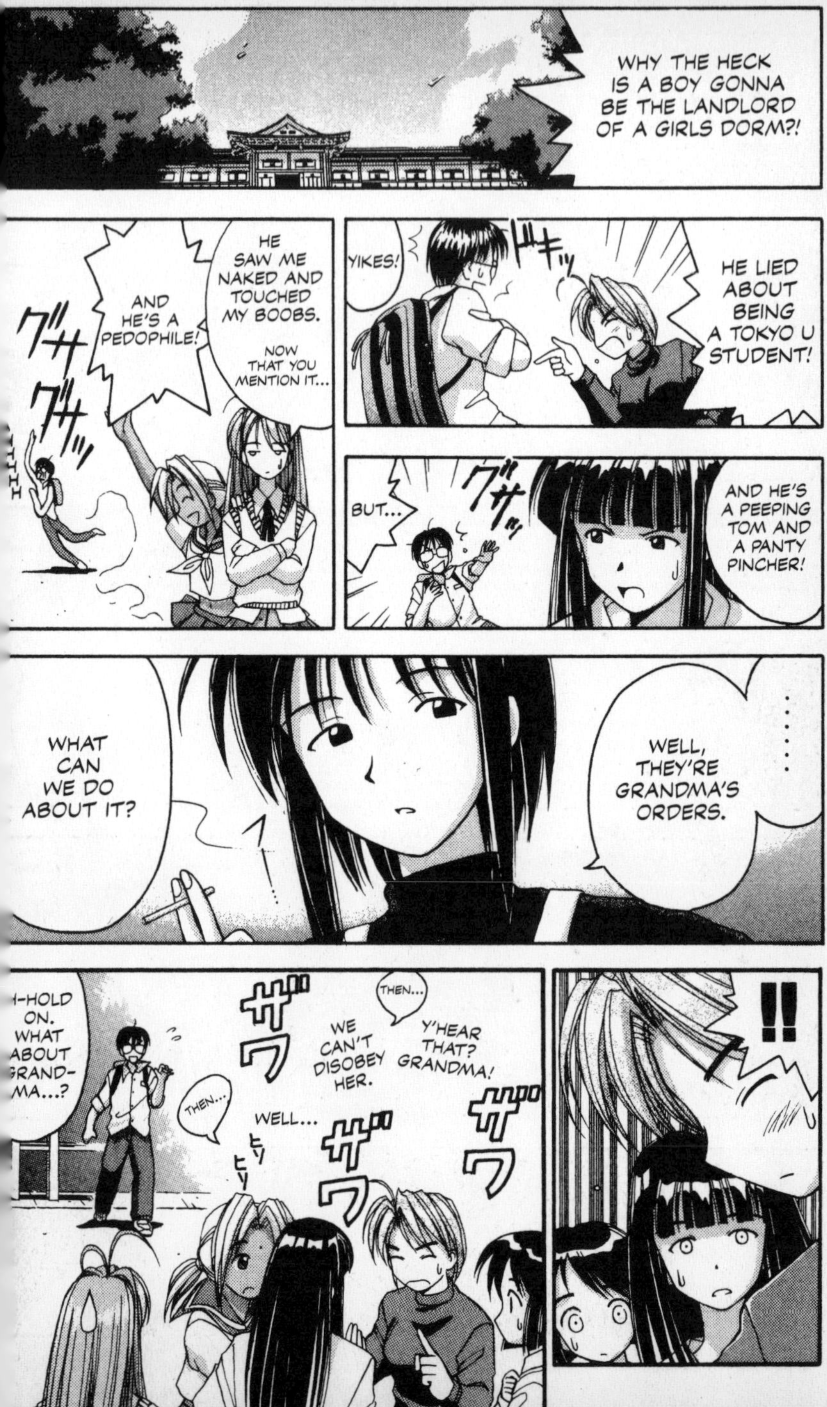
WHY THE HECK IS A BOY GONNA BE THE LANDLORD OF A GIRLS DORM?!
HE LIED ABOUT BEING A TOKYO U STUDENT!
ドキッ
YIKES!
AND HE'S A PEEPING TOM AND A PANTY PINCHER!
グサッ
BUT...
HE SAW ME NAKED AND TOUCHED MY BOOBS.
AND HE'S A PEDOPHILE!
NOW THAT YOU MENTION IT...
グサ
グサッ
WELL, THEY'RE GRANDMA'S ORDERS.
......
WHAT CAN WE DO ABOUT IT?
!!
ザワ
Y'HEAR THAT? GRANDMA!
THEN...
WE CAN'T DISOBEY HER.
ザワ
WELL...
ヒソヒソ
THEN...
ザワ
-HOLD ON. WHAT ABOUT GRAND- MA...?

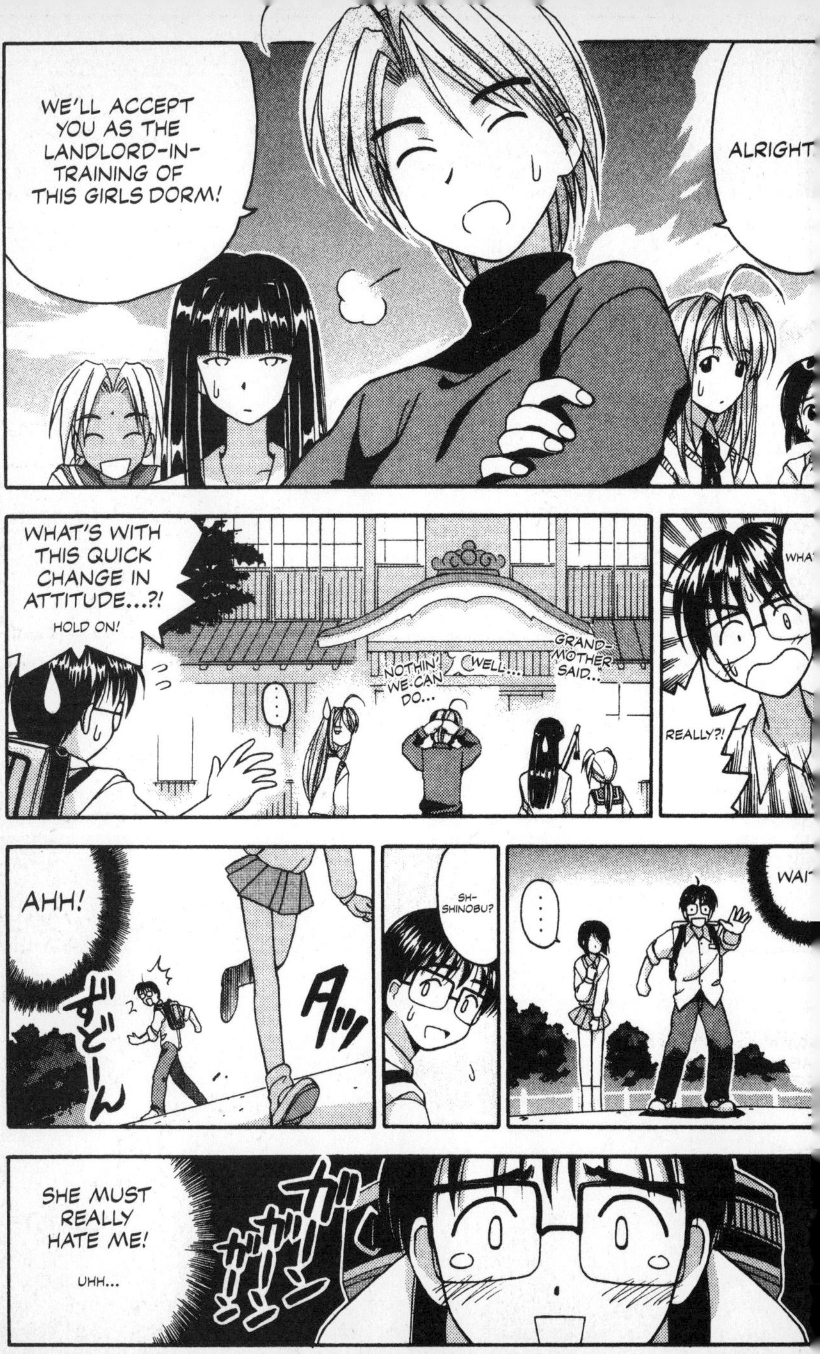
ALRIGHT
WE'LL ACCEPT YOU AS THE LANDLORD-IN-TRAINING OF THIS GIRLS DORM!
REALLY?!
GRAND-MOTHER SAID...
WELL...
NOTHIN' WE CAN DO...
...
WHAT'S WITH THIS QUICK CHANGE IN ATTITUDE...?!
HOLD ON!
...
SH-SHINOBU?
AHH!
ずどーん
SHE MUST REALLY HATE ME!
UHH...

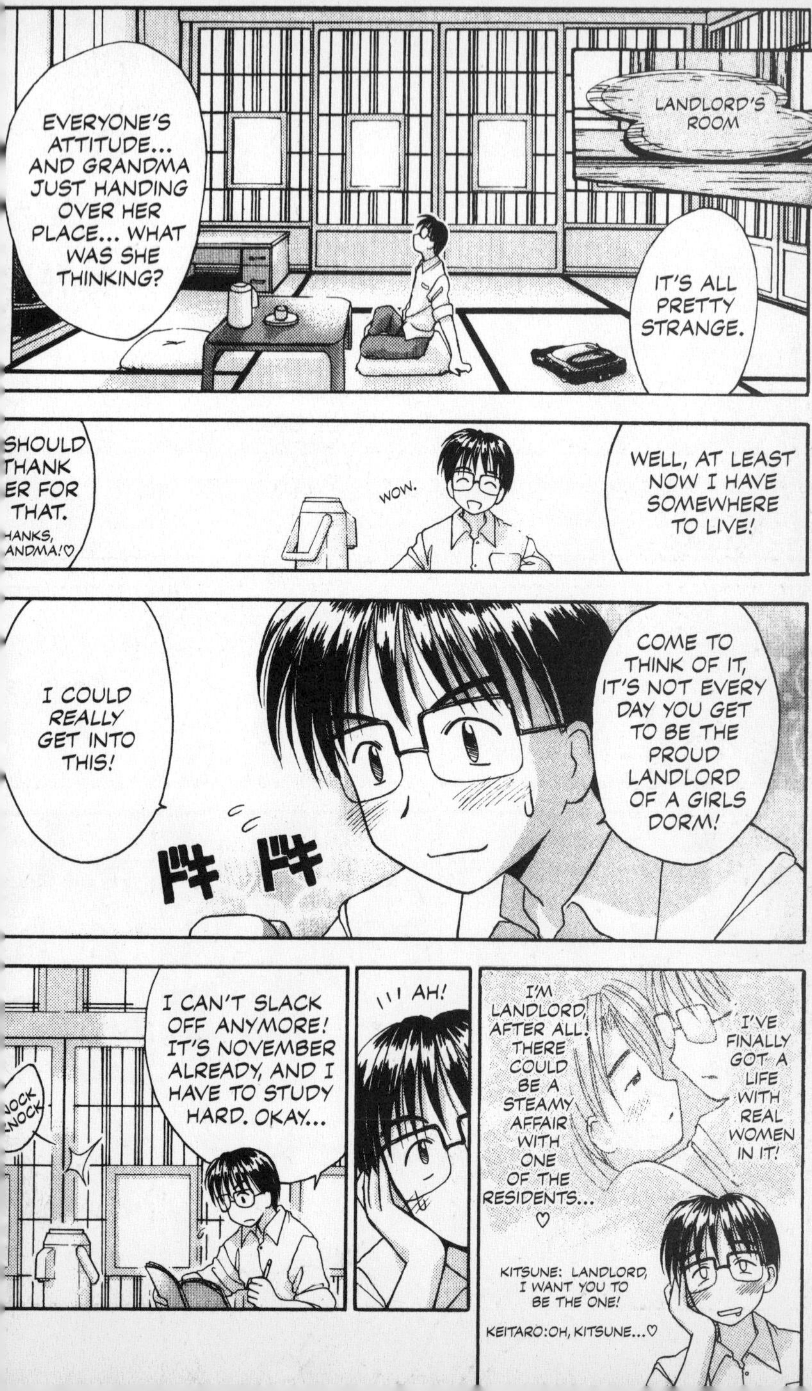
LANDLORD'S ROOM
IT'S ALL PRETTY STRANGE.
EVERYONE'S ATTITUDE... AND GRANDMA JUST HANDING OVER HER PLACE... WHAT WAS SHE THINKING?
WELL, AT LEAST NOW I HAVE SOMEWHERE TO LIVE!
WOW.
SHOULD THANK ER FOR THAT.
HANKS, ANDMA!♡
COME TO THINK OF IT, IT'S NOT EVERY DAY YOU GET TO BE THE PROUD LANDLORD OF A GIRLS DORM!
ドキ ドキ
I COULD REALLY GET INTO THIS!
I'M LANDLORD, AFTER ALL. THERE COULD BE A STEAMY AFFAIR WITH ONE OF THE RESIDENTS... ♡
I'VE FINALLY GOT A LIFE WITH REAL WOMEN IN IT!
KITSUNE: LANDLORD, I WANT YOU TO BE THE ONE!
KEITARO: OH, KITSUNE...♡
AH!
I CAN'T SLACK OFF ANYMORE! IT'S NOVEMBER ALREADY, AND I HAVE TO STUDY HARD. OKAY...
NOCK NOCK

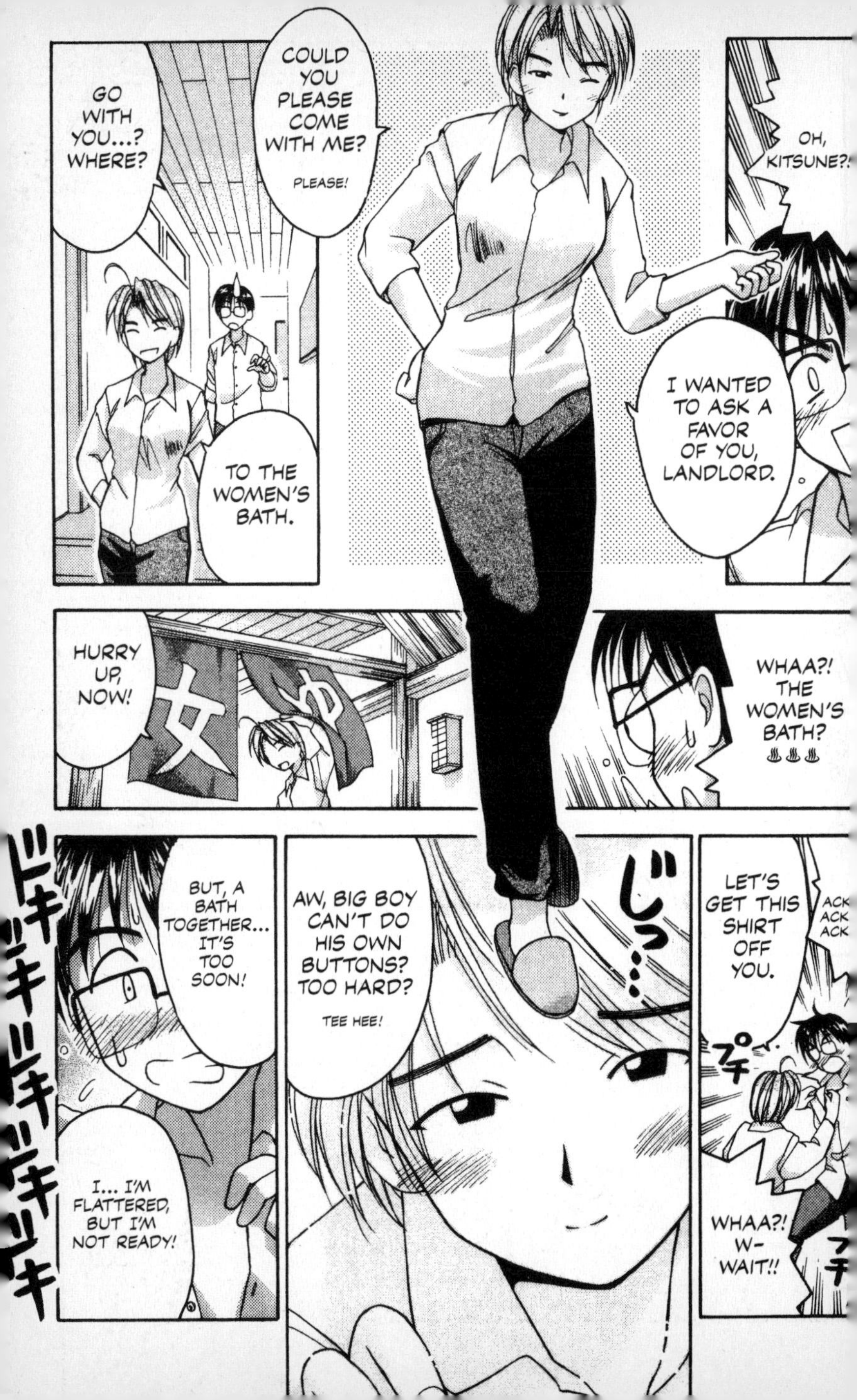
OH, KITSUNE?!
I WANTED TO ASK A FAVOR OF YOU, LANDLORD.
COULD YOU PLEASE COME WITH ME?
PLEASE!
GO WITH YOU...? WHERE?
TO THE WOMEN'S BATH.
WHAA?! THE WOMEN'S BATH? ♨♨♨
HURRY UP, NOW!
女
ゆ
LET'S GET THIS SHIRT OFF YOU.
ACK ACK ACK
プチ
WHAA?! W-WAIT!!
プチ
じっ…
AW, BIG BOY CAN'T DO HIS OWN BUTTONS? TOO HARD?
TEE HEE!
BUT, A BATH TOGETHER... IT'S TOO SOON!
I... I'M FLATTERED, BUT I'M NOT READY!

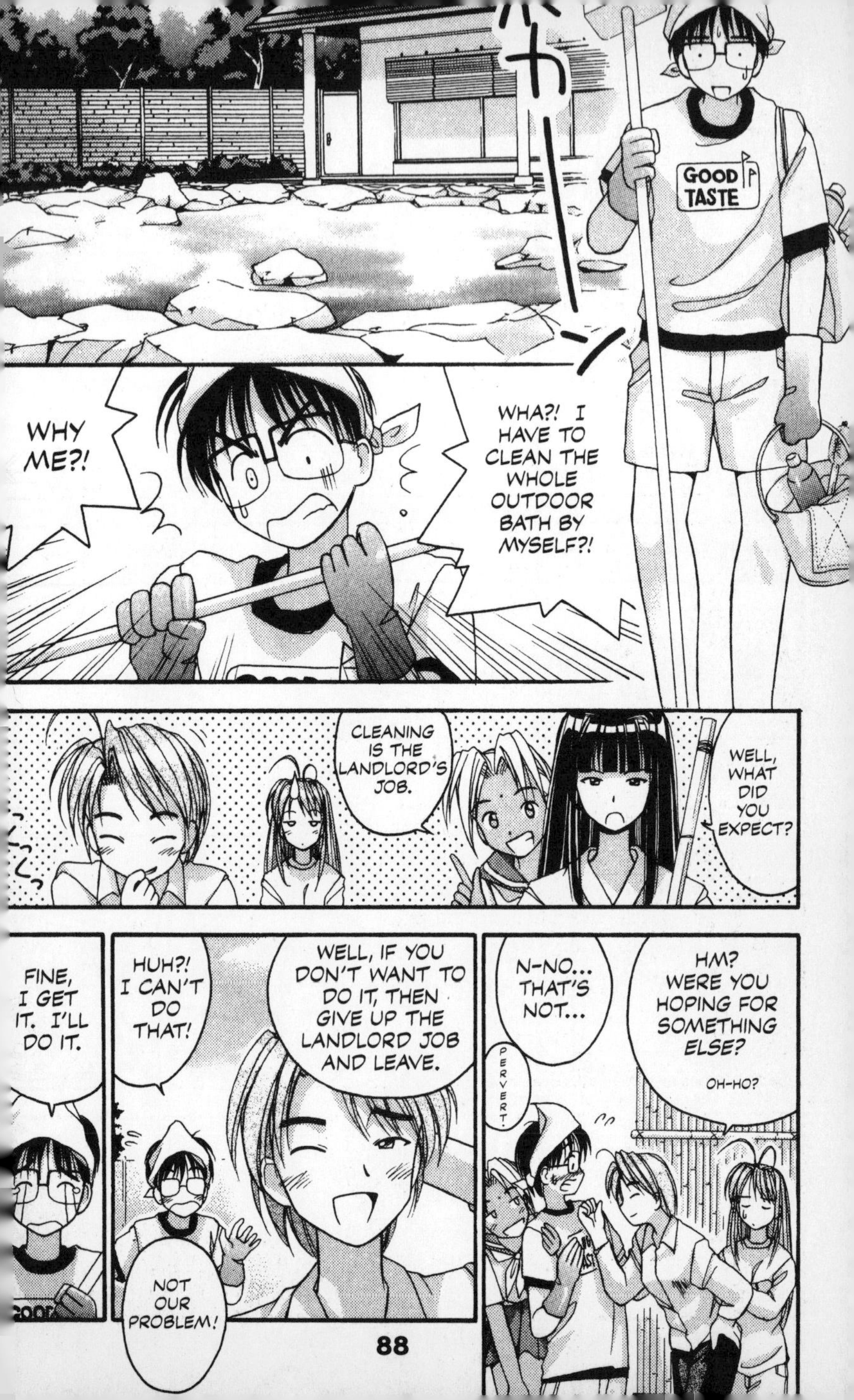
GOOD TASTE
WHA?! I HAVE TO CLEAN THE WHOLE OUTDOOR BATH BY MYSELF?!
WHY ME?!
WELL, WHAT DID YOU EXPECT?
CLEANING IS THE LANDLORD'S JOB.
HM? WERE YOU HOPING FOR SOMETHING ELSE?
OH-HO?
N-NO... THAT'S NOT...
PERVERT.
WELL, IF YOU DON'T WANT TO DO IT, THEN GIVE UP THE LANDLORD JOB AND LEAVE.
HUH?! I CAN'T DO THAT!
NOT OUR PROBLEM!
FINE, I GET IT. I'LL DO IT.

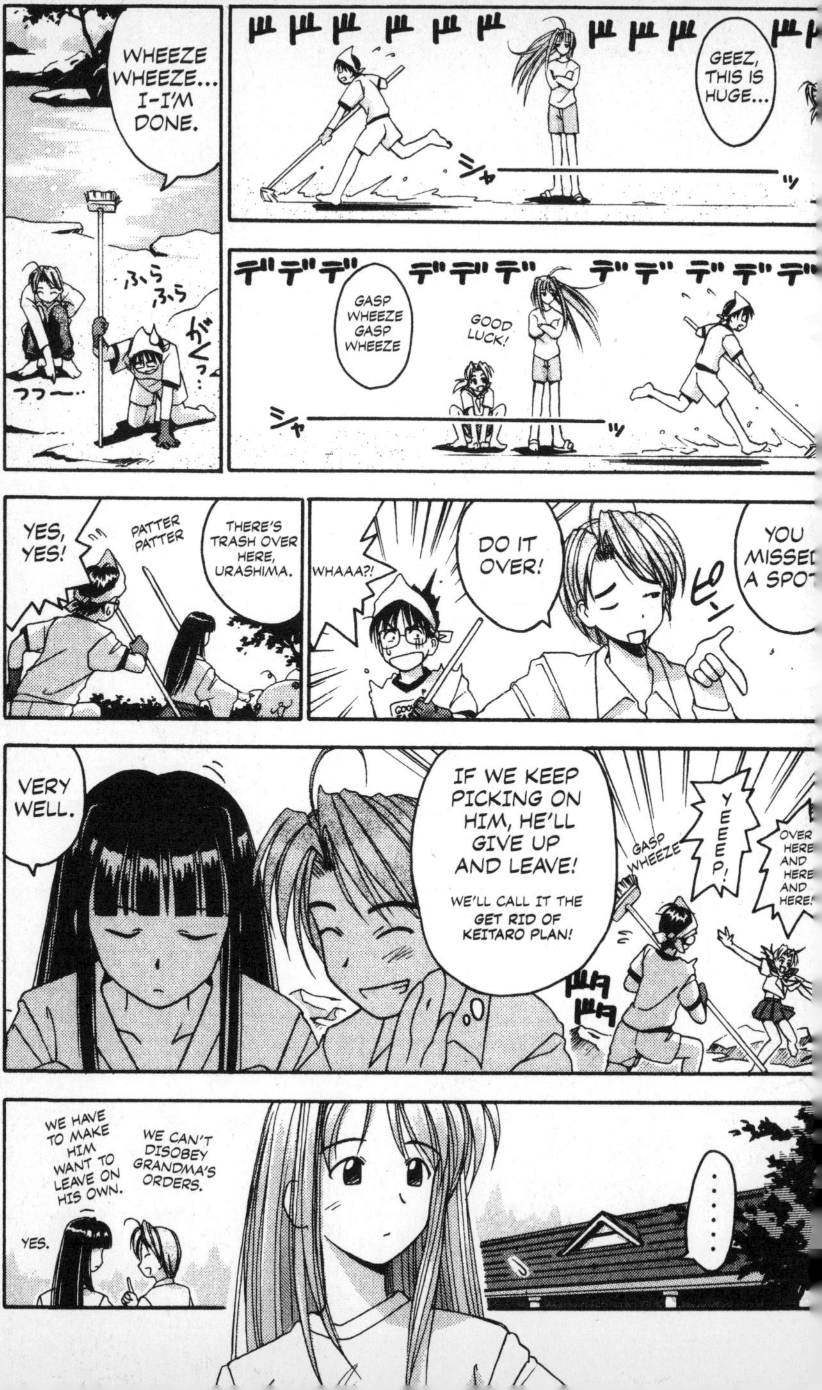
GEEZ, THIS IS HUGE...
シャーーッ
GASP WHEEZE GASP WHEEZE
GOOD LUCK!
シャーーッ
WHEEZE WHEEZE... I-I'M DONE.
ふら ふら
がくっ…
つつー…
YOU MISSED A SPOT
ピーン
DO IT OVER!
WHAAA?!
THERE'S TRASH OVER HERE, URASHIMA.
PATTER PATTER
YES, YES!
OVER HERE AND HERE AND HERE!
YEEEP!
GASP WHEEZE
IF WE KEEP PICKING ON HIM, HE'LL GIVE UP AND LEAVE!
WE'LL CALL IT THE GET RID OF KEITARO PLAN!
VERY WELL.
......
WE CAN'T DISOBEY GRANDMA'S ORDERS.
WE HAVE TO MAKE HIM WANT TO LEAVE ON HIS OWN.
YES.

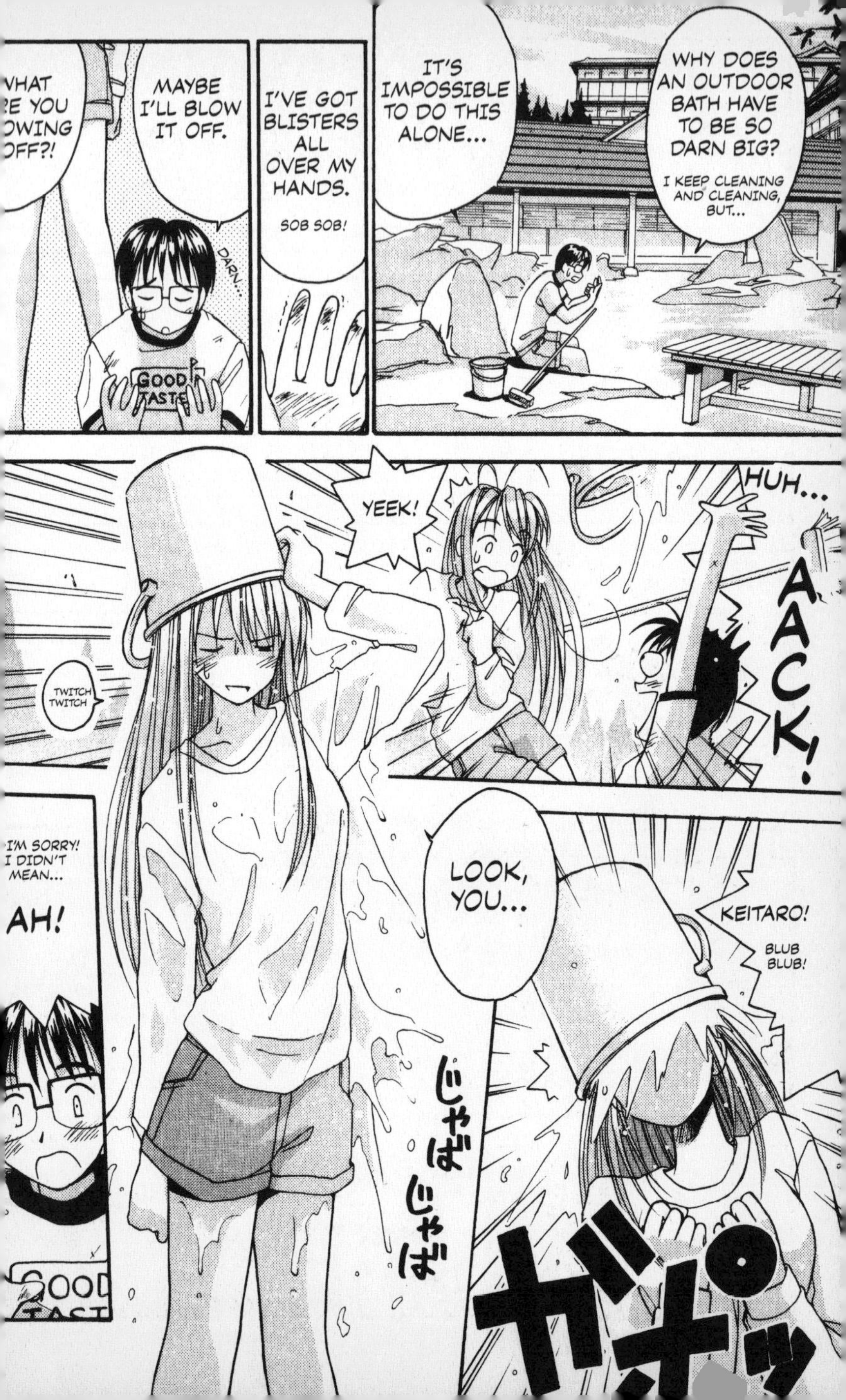
WHY DOES AN OUTDOOR BATH HAVE TO BE SO DARN BIG?
I KEEP CLEANING AND CLEANING, BUT...
IT'S IMPOSSIBLE TO DO THIS ALONE...
I'VE GOT BLISTERS ALL OVER MY HANDS.
SOB SOB!
MAYBE I'LL BLOW IT OFF.
DARN...
GOOD TASTE
VHAT RE YOU OWING OFF?!
HUH...
AACK!
YEEK!
TWITCH TWITCH
KEITARO!
BLUB BLUB!
LOOK, YOU...
じゃばじゃば
ガポッ
I'M SORRY! I DIDN'T MEAN...
AH!

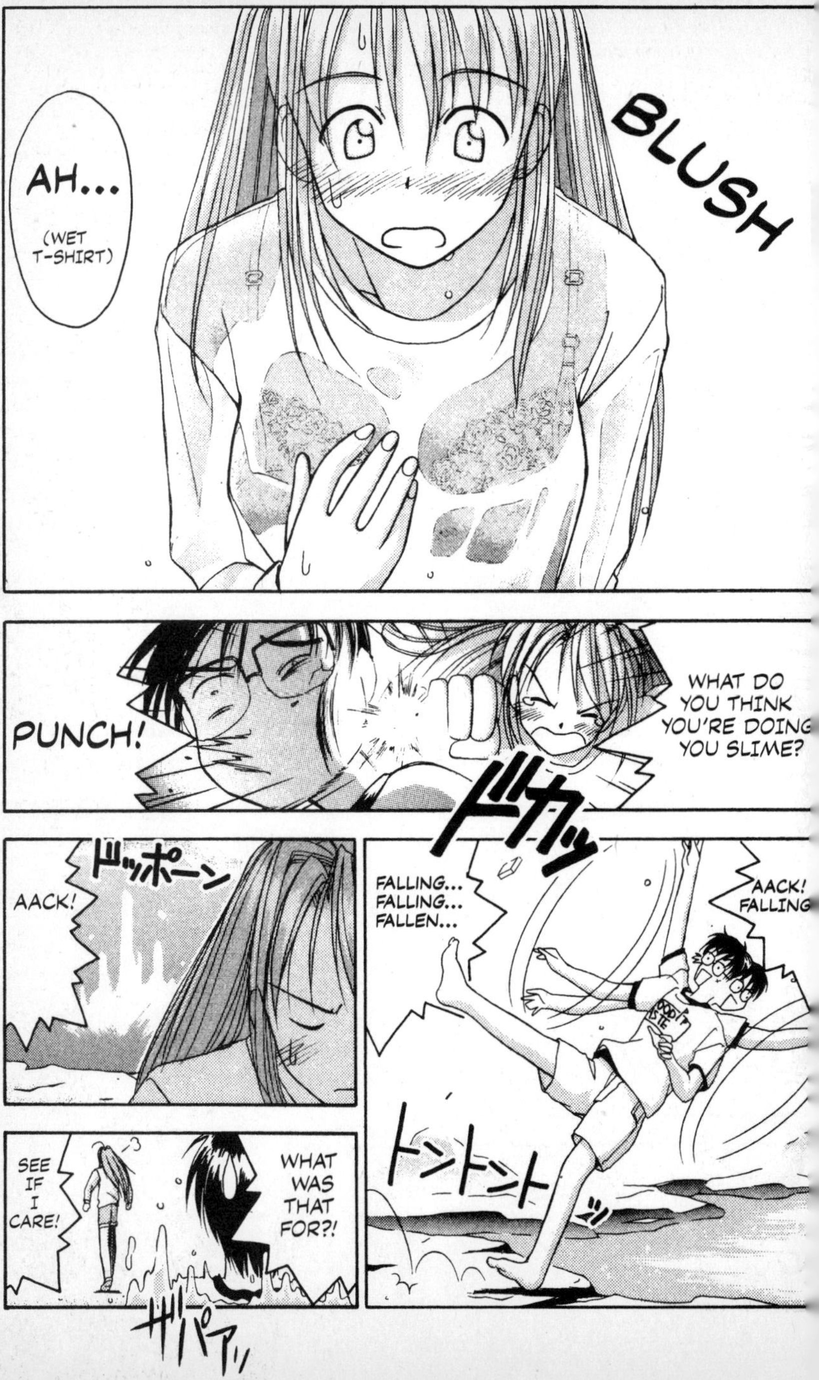
BLUSH
AH...
(WET T-SHIRT)
WHAT DO YOU THINK YOU'RE DOING YOU SLIME?
PUNCH!
ドカッ
AACK! FALLING
FALLING... FALLING... FALLEN...
トントントッ
ドッポーン
AACK!
WHAT WAS THAT FOR?!
SEE IF I CARE!
ザパァッ

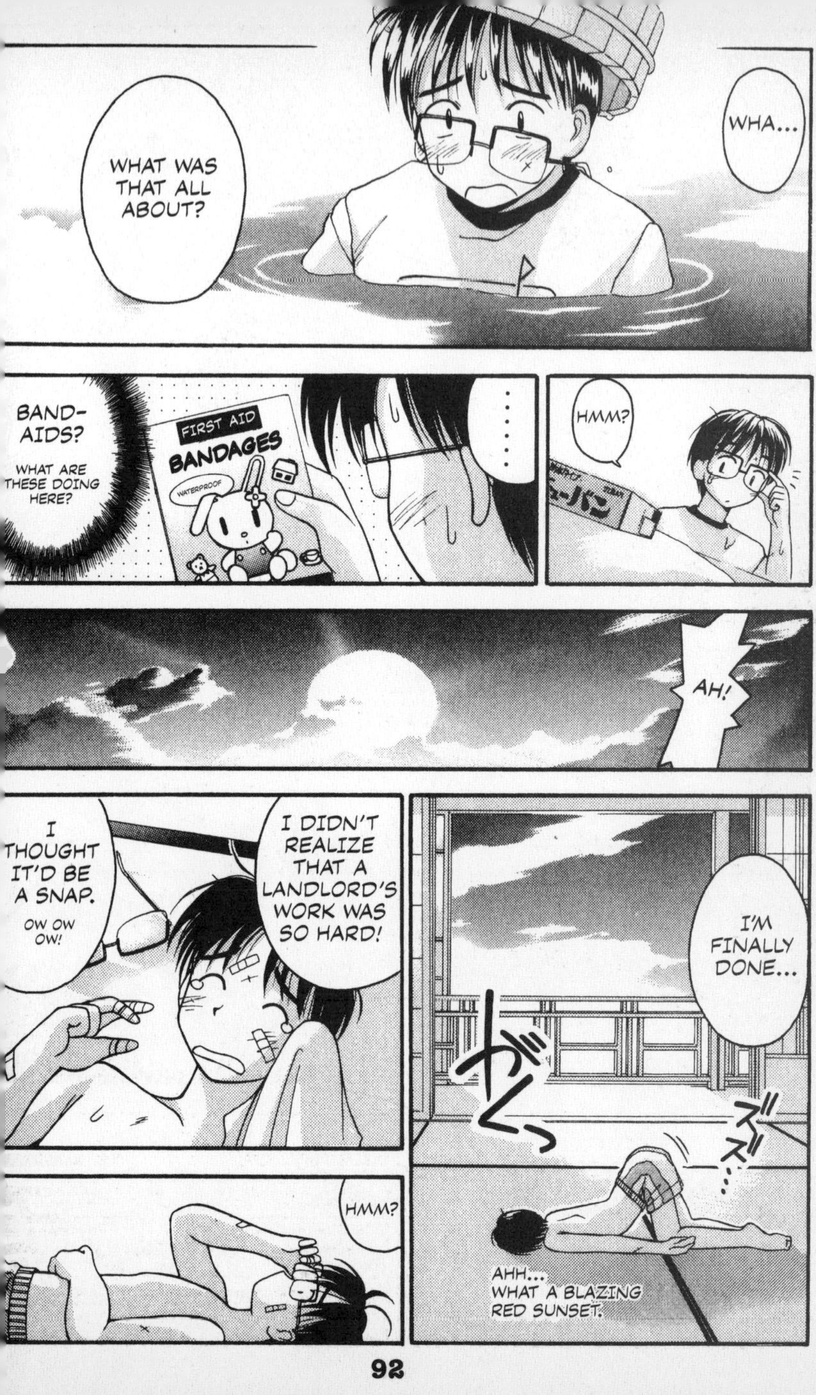
WHA...
WHAT WAS THAT ALL ABOUT?
HMM?
......
FIRST AID
BANDAGES
WATERPROOF
BAND-AIDS?
WHAT ARE THESE DOING HERE?
AH!
I'M FINALLY DONE...
がくっ
ズズ...
AHH... WHAT A BLAZING RED SUNSET.
I DIDN'T REALIZE THAT A LANDLORD'S WORK WAS SO HARD!
I THOUGHT IT'D BE A SNAP.
OW OW OW!
HMM?

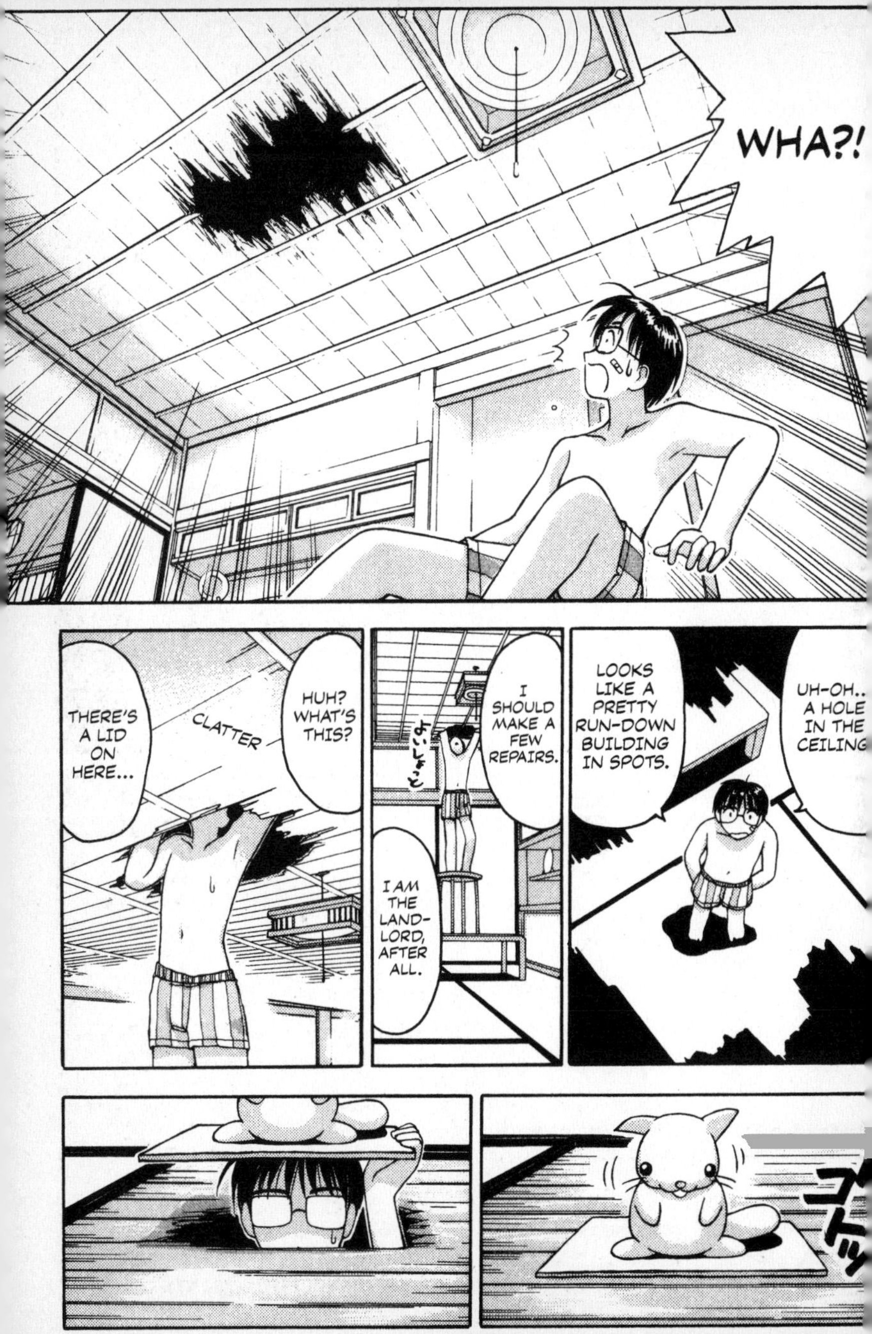
WHA?!
UH-OH.. A HOLE IN THE CEILING
LOOKS LIKE A PRETTY RUN-DOWN BUILDING IN SPOTS.
I SHOULD MAKE A FEW REPAIRS.
よいしょっと
I AM THE LANDLORD, AFTER ALL.
HUH? WHAT'S THIS?
CLATTER
THERE'S A LID ON HERE...
ゴトッ

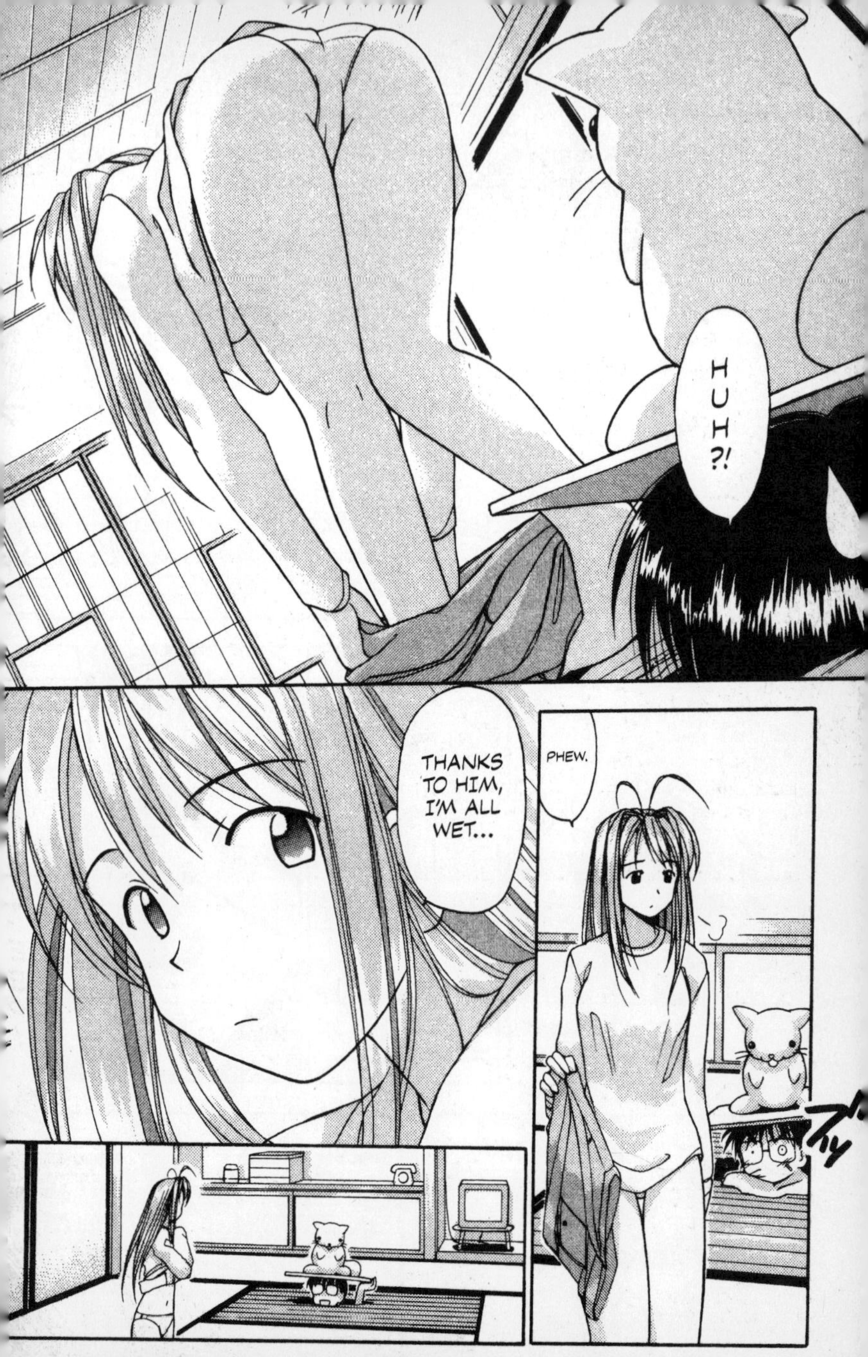
HUH?!
PHEW.
THANKS TO HIM, I'M ALL WET...

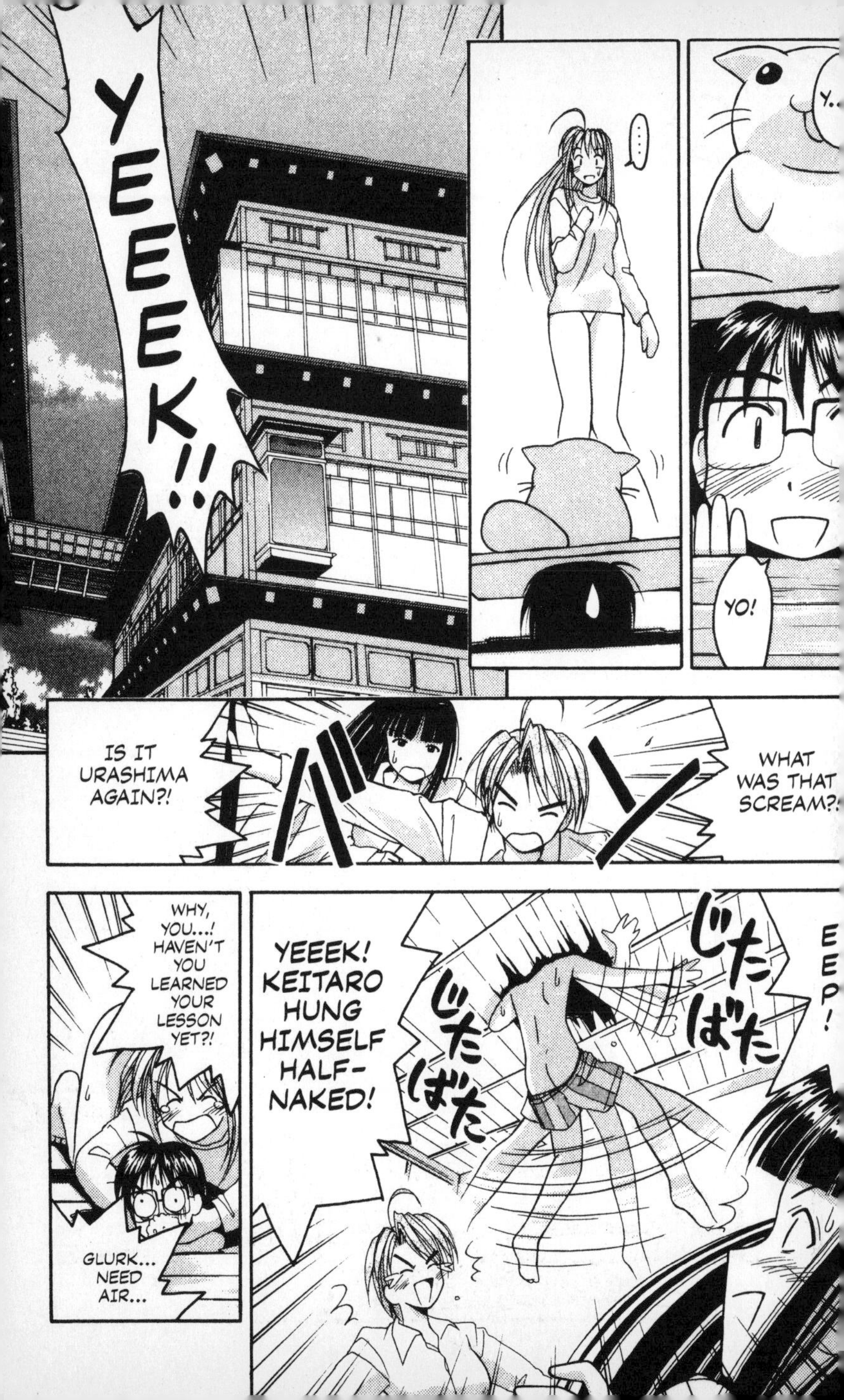

Y...
YO!
...!
YEEEK!!
WHAT WAS THAT SCREAM?!
IS IT URASHIMA AGAIN?!
EEP!
じたばた
じたばた
YEEEK! KEITARO HUNG HIMSELF HALF-NAKED!
WHY, YOU...! HAVEN'T YOU LEARNED YOUR LESSON YET?!
GLURK... NEED AIR...

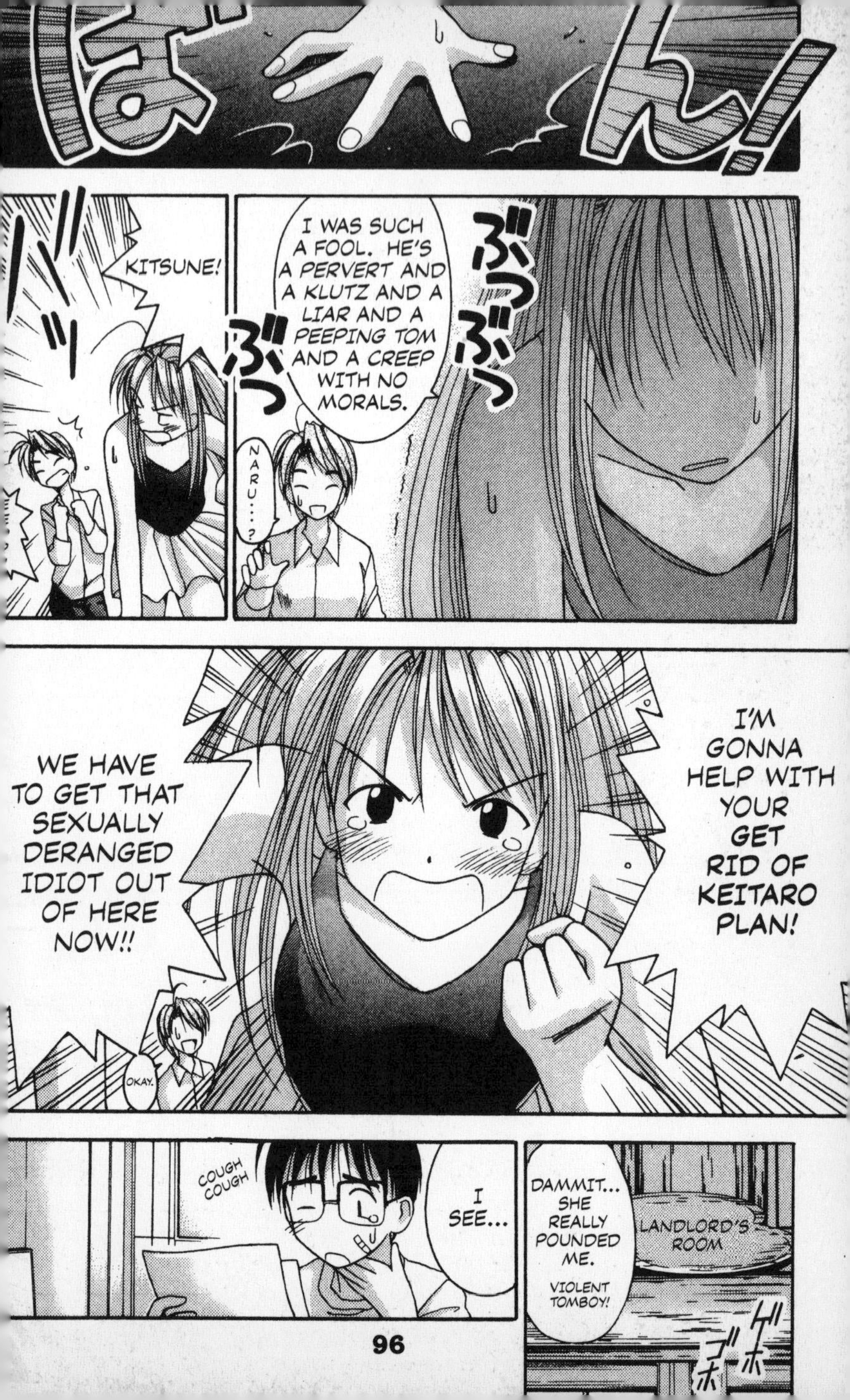
ばん!
I WAS SUCH A FOOL. HE'S A PERVERT AND A KLUTZ AND A LIAR AND A PEEPING TOM AND A CREEP WITH NO MORALS.
ぶつぶつ
ぶつ
NARU...?
KITSUNE!
I'M GONNA HELP WITH YOUR GET RID OF KEITARO PLAN!
WE HAVE TO GET THAT SEXUALLY DERANGED IDIOT OUT OF HERE NOW!!
OKAY.
LANDLORD'S ROOM
DAMMIT... SHE REALLY POUNDED ME.
VIOLENT TOMBOY!
ゲホ
ゴホ
I SEE...
COUGH COUGH

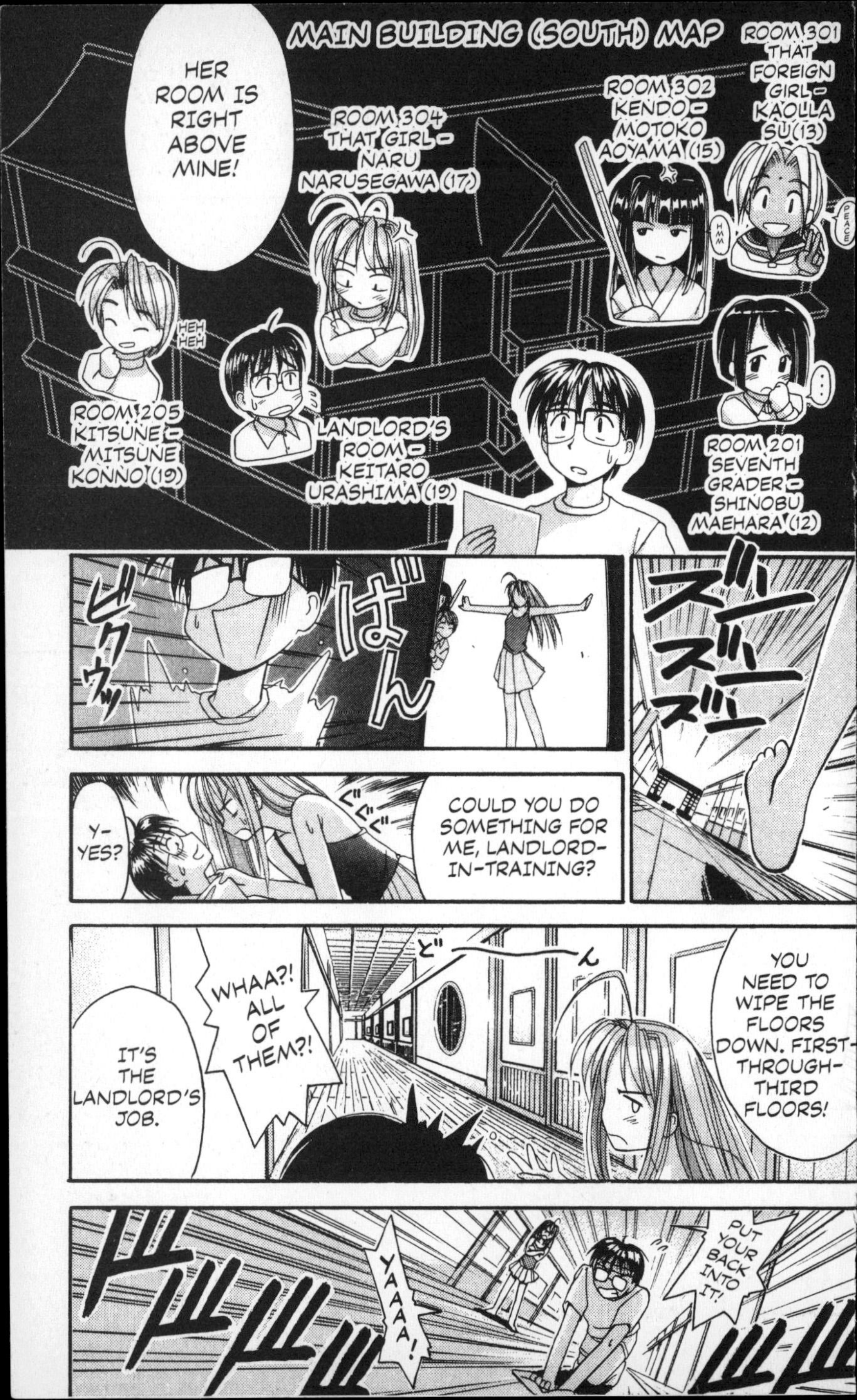
MAIN BUILDING (SOUTH) MAP
ROOM 301 THAT FOREIGN GIRL — KAOLLA SU (13)
PEACE
ROOM 302 KENDO — MOTOKO AOYAMA (15)
HMM
ROOM 304 THAT GIRL — NARU NARUSEGAWA (17)
HER ROOM IS RIGHT ABOVE MINE!
ROOM 201 SEVENTH GRADER — SHINOBU MAEHARA (12)
...
LANDLORD'S ROOM — KEITARO URASHIMA (19)
HEH HEH
ROOM 205 KITSUNE — MITSUNE KONNO (19)
ばん
ビクゥッ
ぐぐぐ
COULD YOU DO SOMETHING FOR ME, LANDLORD-IN-TRAINING?
Y-YES?
YOU NEED TO WIPE THE FLOORS DOWN. FIRST-THROUGH-THIRD FLOORS!
ど———ん
WHAA?! ALL OF THEM?!
IT'S THE LANDLORD'S JOB.
PUT YOUR BACK INTO IT!
YAAAA!

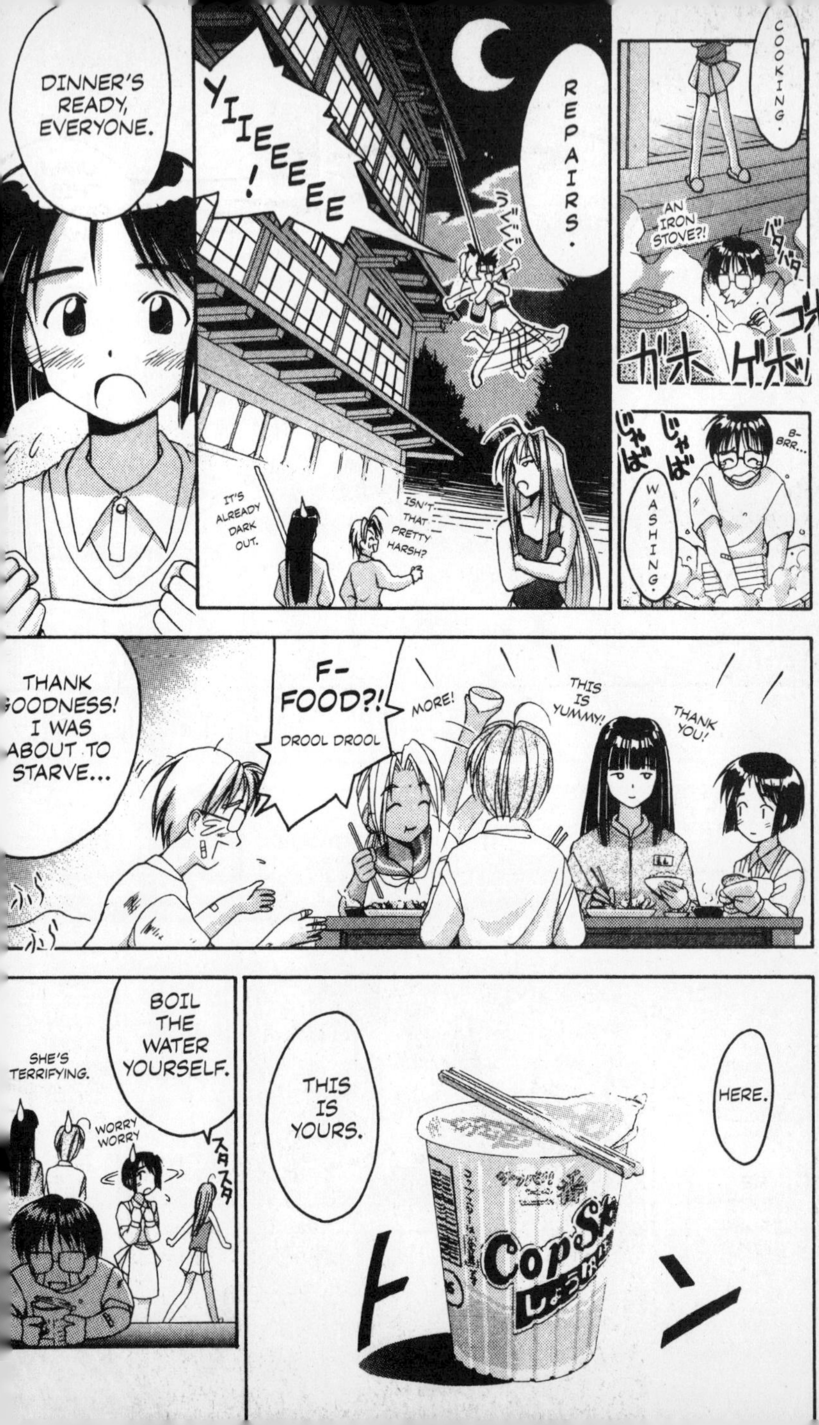
COOKING.
AN IRON STOVE?!
バタバタ
ゴホッ
ガホ
ゲホッ
WASHING.
じゃぶ
じゃぶ
B-BRR...
REPAIRS.
YIIEEEEEE!
ISN'T THAT PRETTY HARSH?
IT'S ALREADY DARK OUT.
DINNER'S READY, EVERYONE.
THANK YOU!
THIS IS YUMMY!
MORE!
F-FOOD?!
DROOL DROOL
THANK GOODNESS! I WAS ABOUT TO STARVE...
HERE.
THIS IS YOURS.
BOIL THE WATER YOURSELF.
スタスタ
SHE'S TERRIFYING.
WORRY WORRY

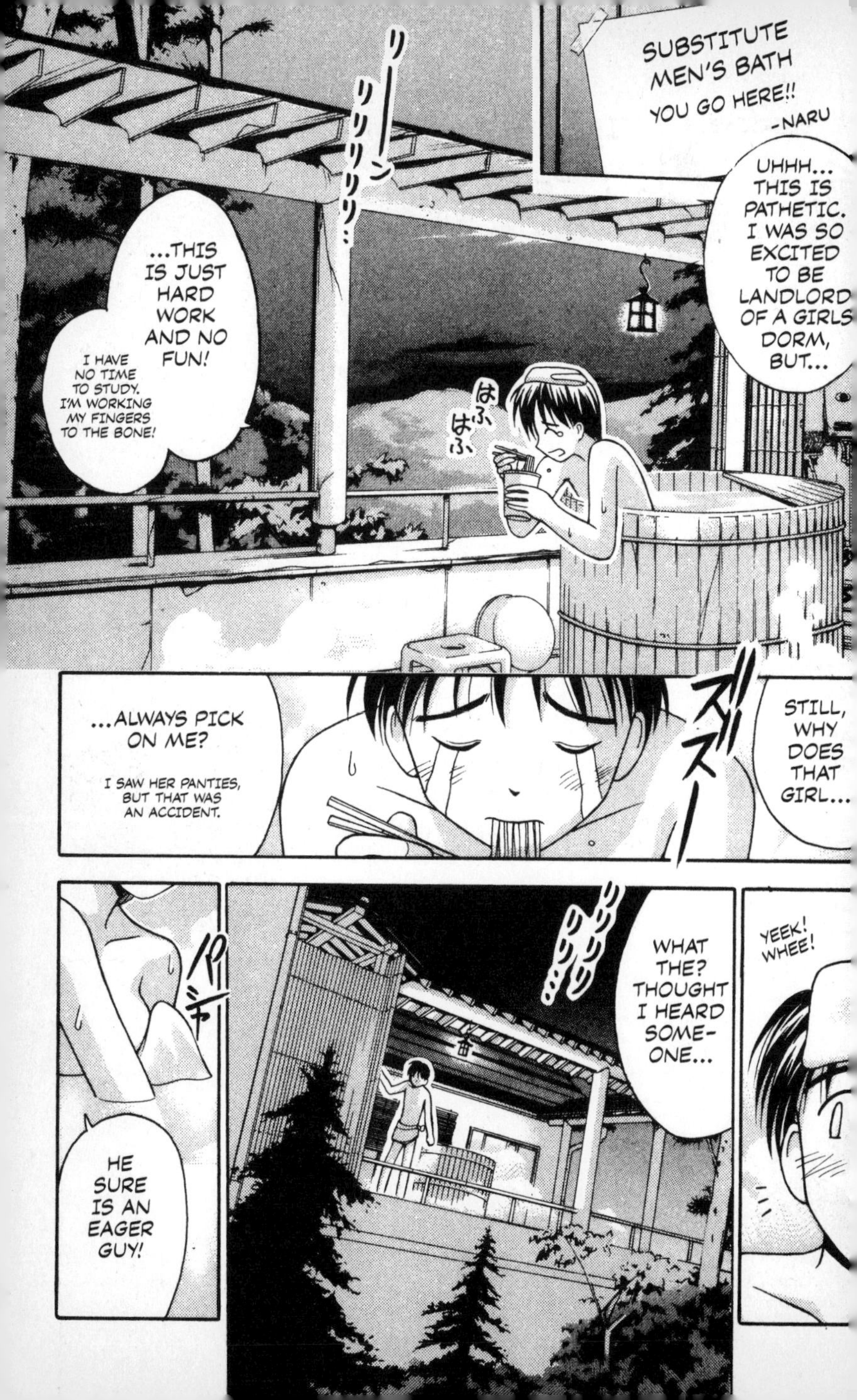
SUBSTITUTE MEN'S BATH
YOU GO HERE!!
-NARU
UHHH... THIS IS PATHETIC. I WAS SO EXCITED TO BE LANDLORD OF A GIRLS DORM, BUT...
リーンリリリリリ…
...THIS IS JUST HARD WORK AND NO FUN!
I HAVE NO TIME TO STUDY. I'M WORKING MY FINGERS TO THE BONE!
はふはふ
ズズズー
STILL, WHY DOES THAT GIRL...
...ALWAYS PICK ON ME?
I SAW HER PANTIES, BUT THAT WAS AN ACCIDENT.
YEEK! WHEE!
WHAT THE? THOUGHT I HEARD SOME-ONE...
パシャ
HE SURE IS AN EAGER GUY!

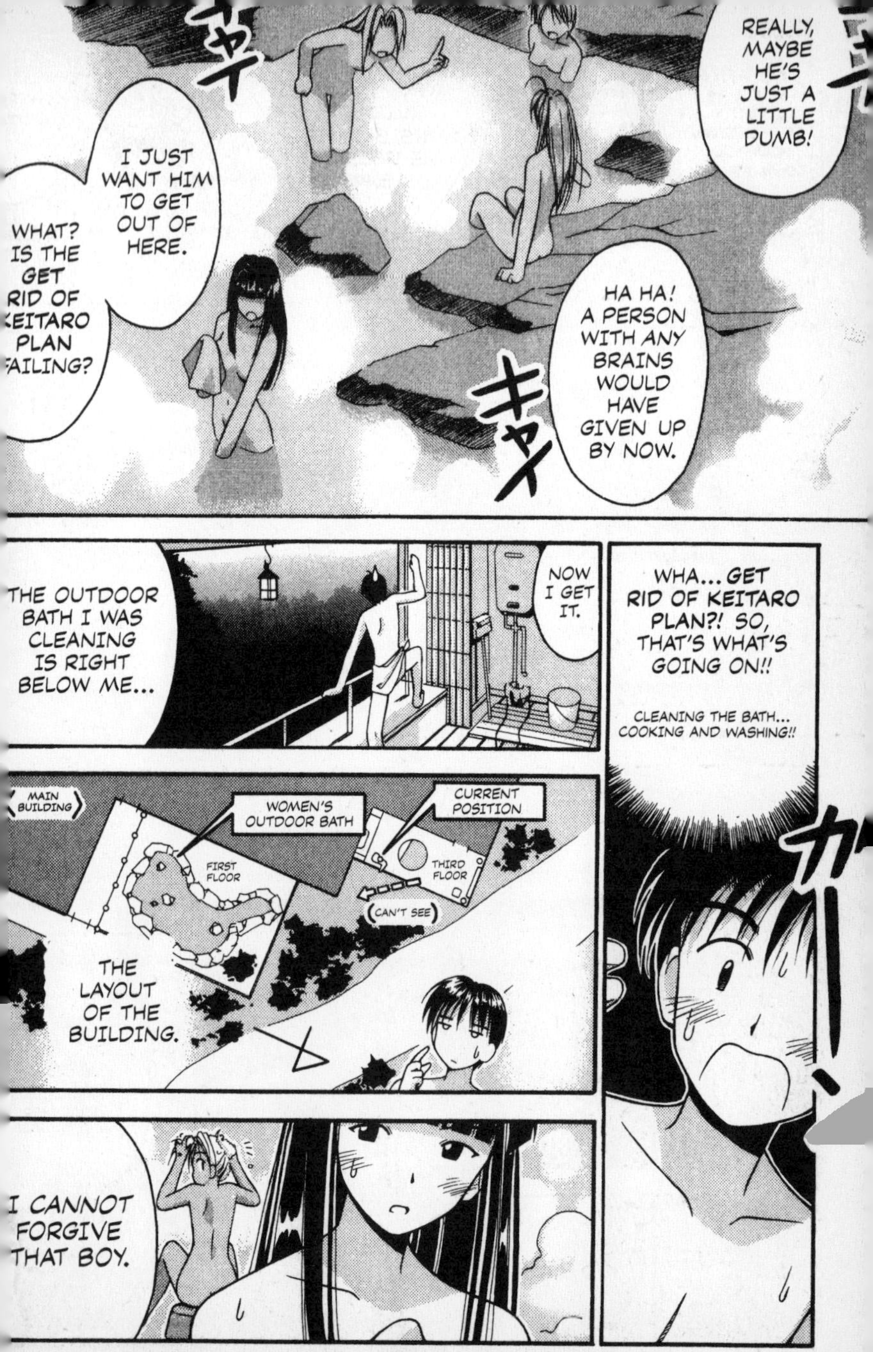
REALLY, MAYBE HE'S JUST A LITTLE DUMB!
HA HA! A PERSON WITH ANY BRAINS WOULD HAVE GIVEN UP BY NOW.
キャイ
I JUST WANT HIM TO GET OUT OF HERE.
キャイ
WHAT? IS THE GET RID OF KEITARO PLAN FAILING?
WHA... GET RID OF KEITARO PLAN?! SO, THAT'S WHAT'S GOING ON!!
CLEANING THE BATH... COOKING AND WASHING!!
カーッ
NOW I GET IT.
THE OUTDOOR BATH I WAS CLEANING IS RIGHT BELOW ME...
CURRENT POSITION
WOMEN'S OUTDOOR BATH
MAIN BUILDING
THIRD FLOOR
FIRST FLOOR
CAN'T SEE
THE LAYOUT OF THE BUILDING.
I CANNOT FORGIVE THAT BOY.

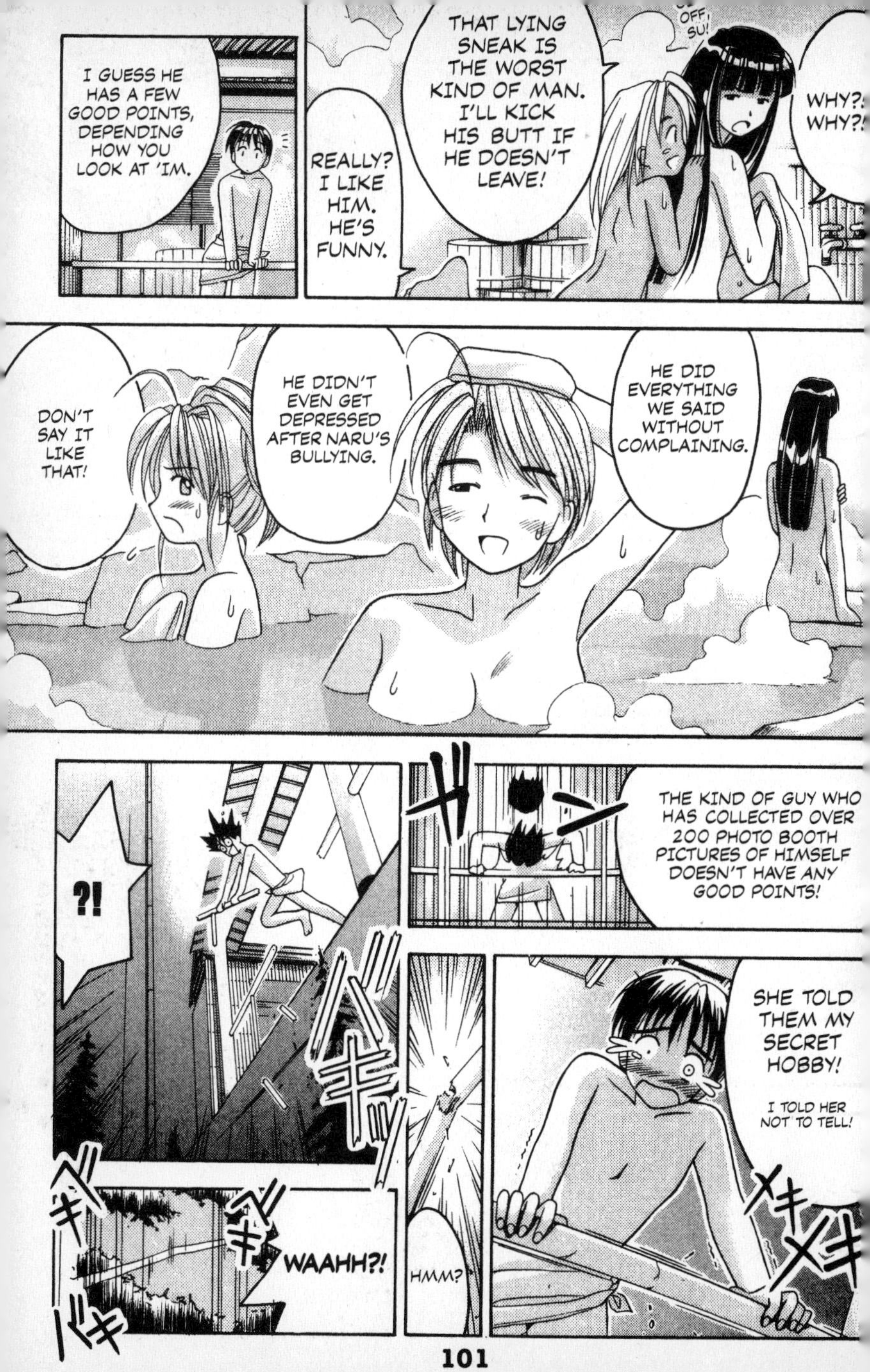

OFF, SU!
WHY?! WHY?!
THAT LYING SNEAK IS THE WORST KIND OF MAN. I'LL KICK HIS BUTT IF HE DOESN'T LEAVE!
REALLY? I LIKE HIM. HE'S FUNNY.
I GUESS HE HAS A FEW GOOD POINTS, DEPENDING HOW YOU LOOK AT 'IM.
HE DID EVERYTHING WE SAID WITHOUT COMPLAINING.
HE DIDN'T EVEN GET DEPRESSED AFTER NARU'S BULLYING.
DON'T SAY IT LIKE THAT!
THE KIND OF GUY WHO HAS COLLECTED OVER 200 PHOTO BOOTH PICTURES OF HIMSELF DOESN'T HAVE ANY GOOD POINTS!
SHE TOLD THEM MY SECRET HOBBY!
I TOLD HER NOT TO TELL!
HMM?
?!
WAAHH?!

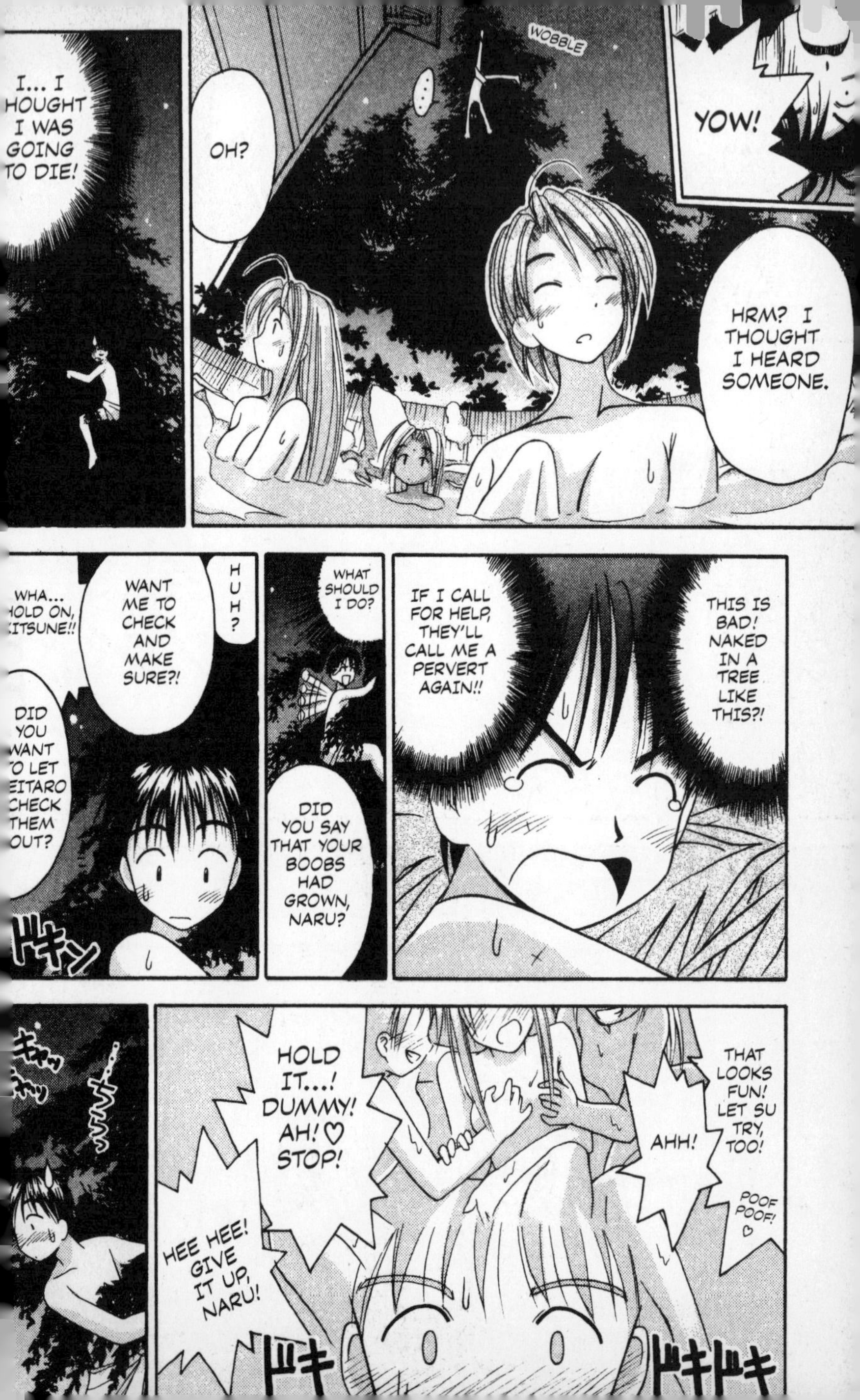
YOW!
HRM? I THOUGHT I HEARD SOMEONE.
WOBBLE
...
OH?
I... I HOUGHT I WAS GOING TO DIE!
THIS IS BAD! NAKED IN A TREE LIKE THIS?!
IF I CALL FOR HELP, THEY'LL CALL ME A PERVERT AGAIN!!
WHAT SHOULD I DO?
DID YOU SAY THAT YOUR BOOBS HAD GROWN, NARU?
HUH?
WANT ME TO CHECK AND MAKE SURE?!
WHA... HOLD ON, ITSUNE!!
DID YOU WANT TO LET EITARO CHECK THEM OUT?
ドキン
THAT LOOKS FUN! LET SU TRY, TOO!
POOF POOF! ♡
AHH!
HOLD IT...! DUMMY! AH! ♡ STOP!
HEE HEE! GIVE IT UP, NARU!
ドキドキ
ドキ
キャッキャッ

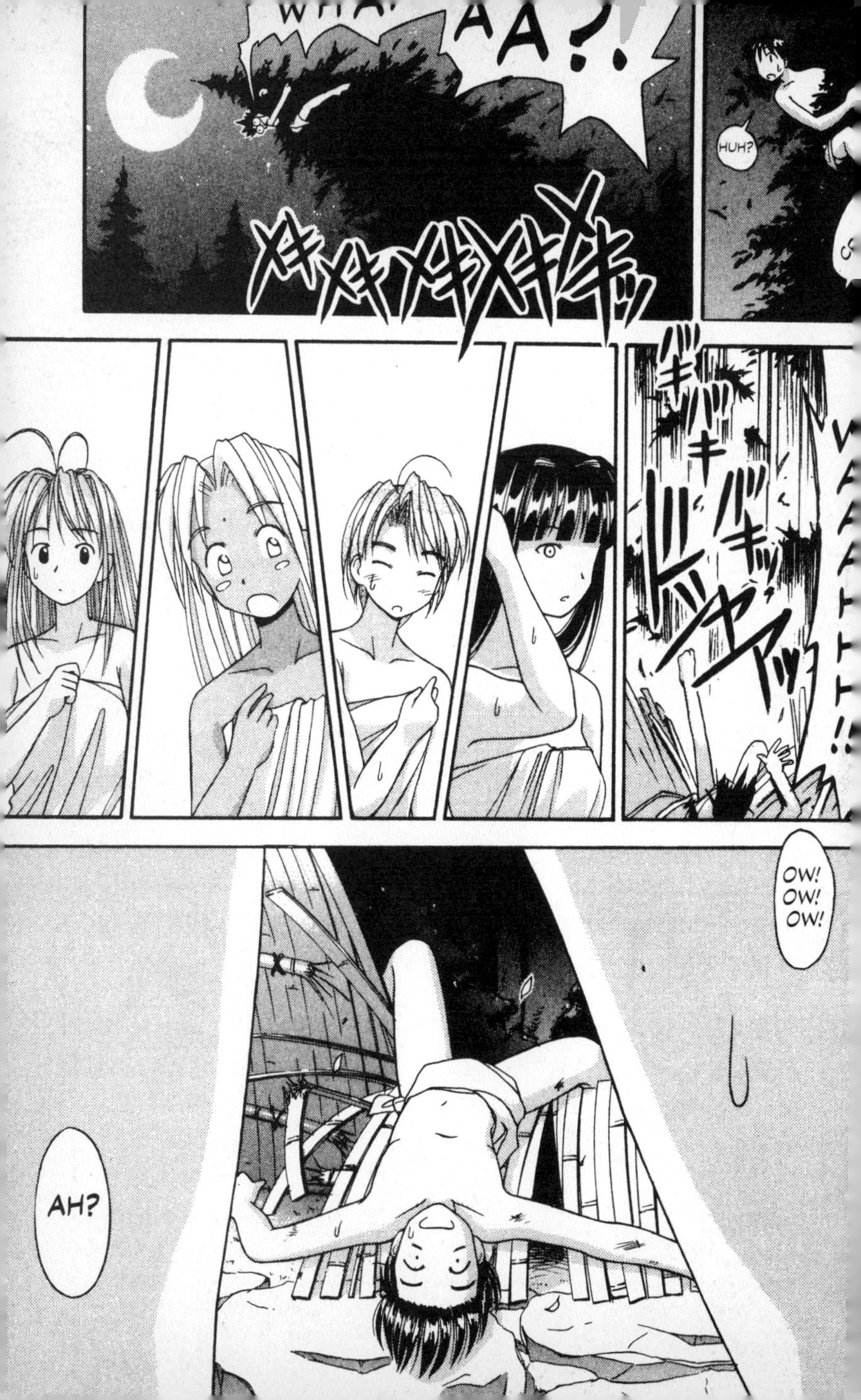

HUH?
AA?!
メキメキメキメキメキッ
バキバキバキッ
ドシャアッ
!!
OW! OW! OW!
AH?

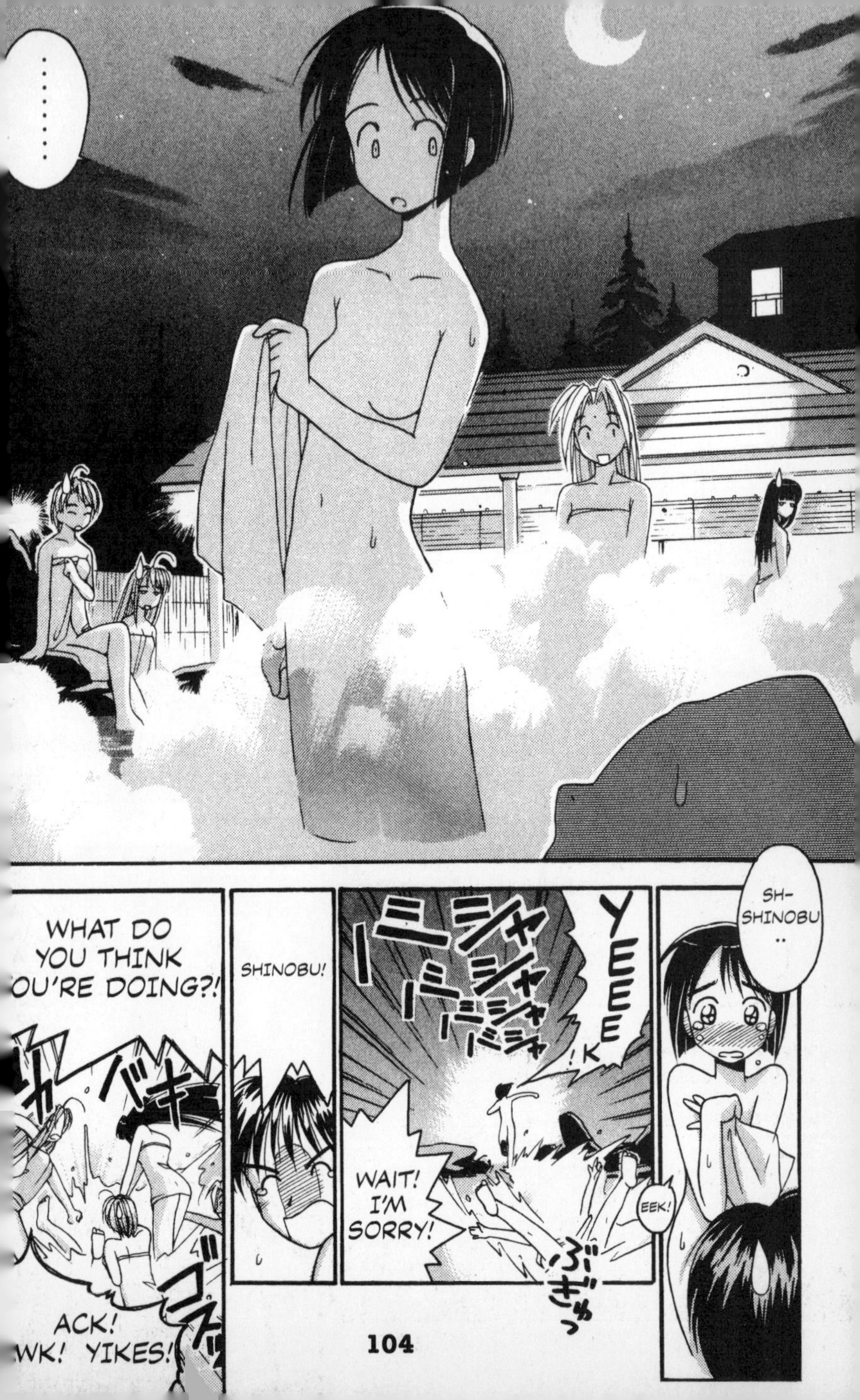
......
SH-SHINOBU..
EEK!
YEEEK!
WAIT! I'M SORRY!
ぶぎゅっ
SHINOBU!
WHAT DO YOU THINK OU'RE DOING?!
バキ
ACK! WK! YIKES!

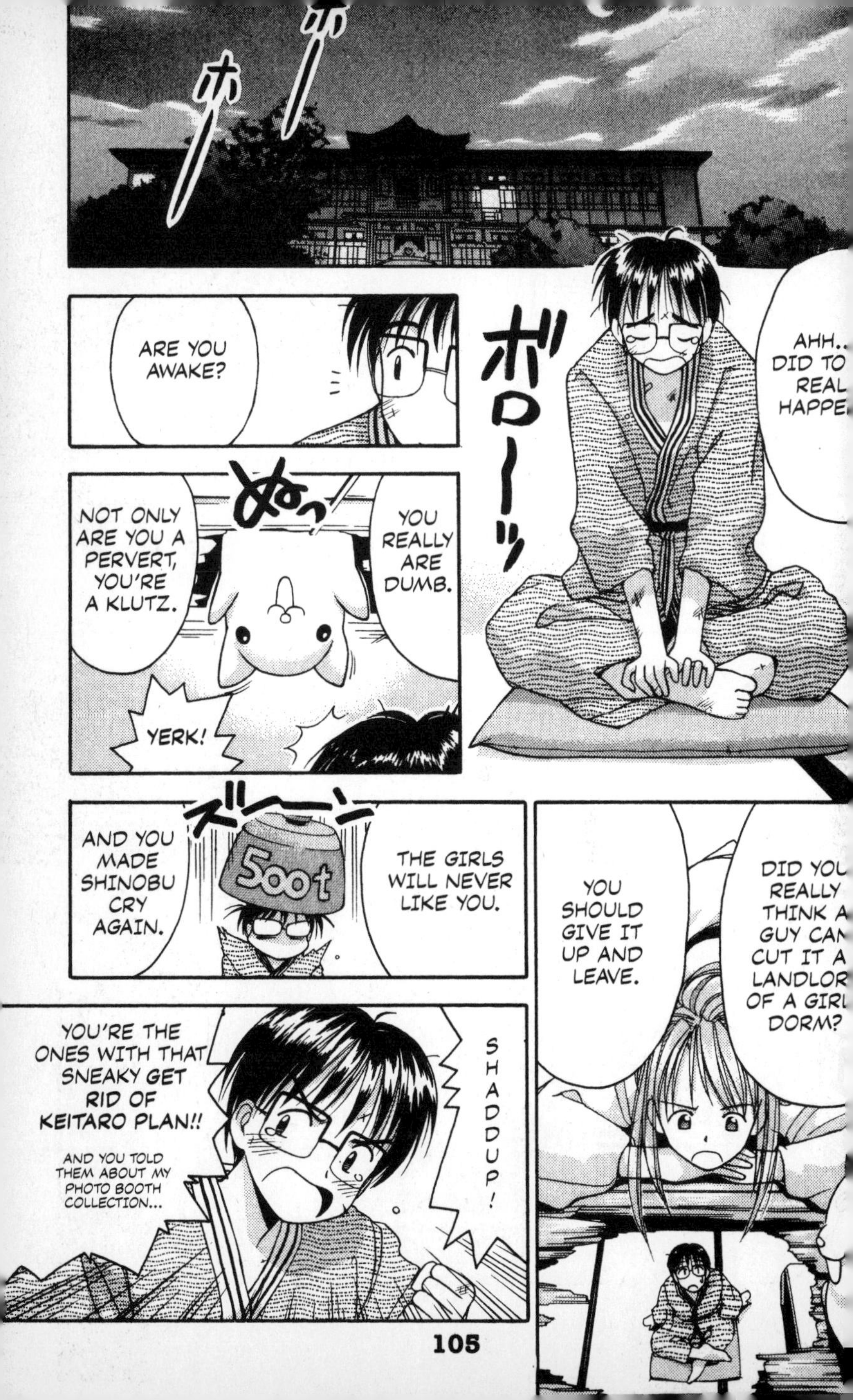

AHH.. DID TO REAL HAPPE
ボローーッ
ARE YOU AWAKE?
ぬっ
YOU REALLY ARE DUMB.
NOT ONLY ARE YOU A PERVERT, YOU'RE A KLUTZ.
YERK!
DID YOU REALLY THINK A GUY CAN CUT IT A LANDLOR OF A GIRL DORM?
YOU SHOULD GIVE IT UP AND LEAVE.
ズーン
THE GIRLS WILL NEVER LIKE YOU.
AND YOU MADE SHINOBU CRY AGAIN.
500t
SHADDUP!
YOU'RE THE ONES WITH THAT SNEAKY GET RID OF KEITARO PLAN!!
AND YOU TOLD THEM ABOUT MY PHOTO BOOTH COLLECTION...

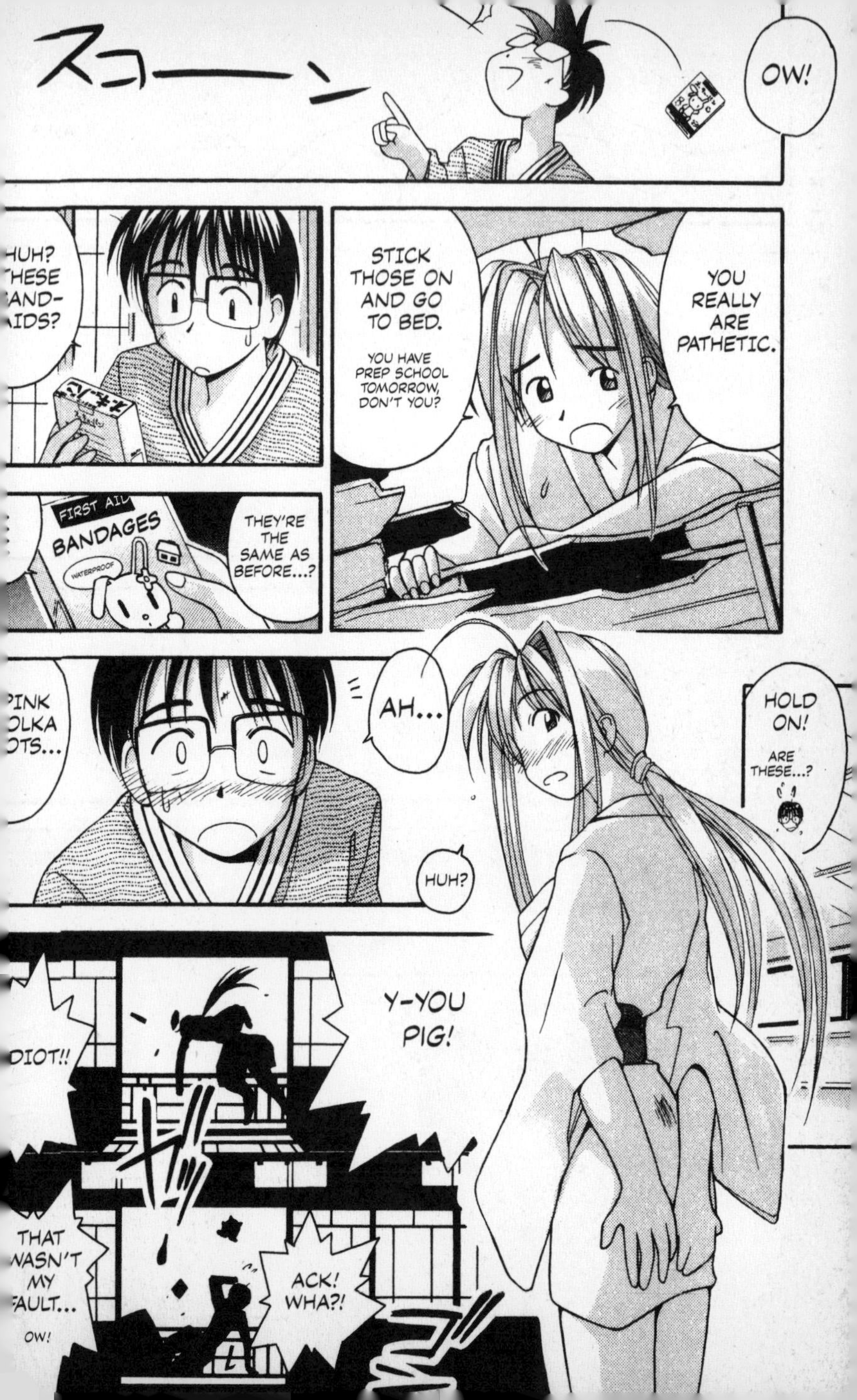
OW!
スコーーン
YOU REALLY ARE PATHETIC.
STICK THOSE ON AND GO TO BED.
YOU HAVE PREP SCHOOL TOMORROW, DON'T YOU?
HUH? HESE AND- IDS?
THEY'RE THE SAME AS BEFORE...?
FIRST AI
BANDAGES
WATERPROOF
HOLD ON!
ARE THESE...?
AH...
HUH?
PINK OLKA OTS...
Y-YOU PIG!
DIOT!!
ACK! WHA?!
THAT ASN'T MY AULT...
OW!

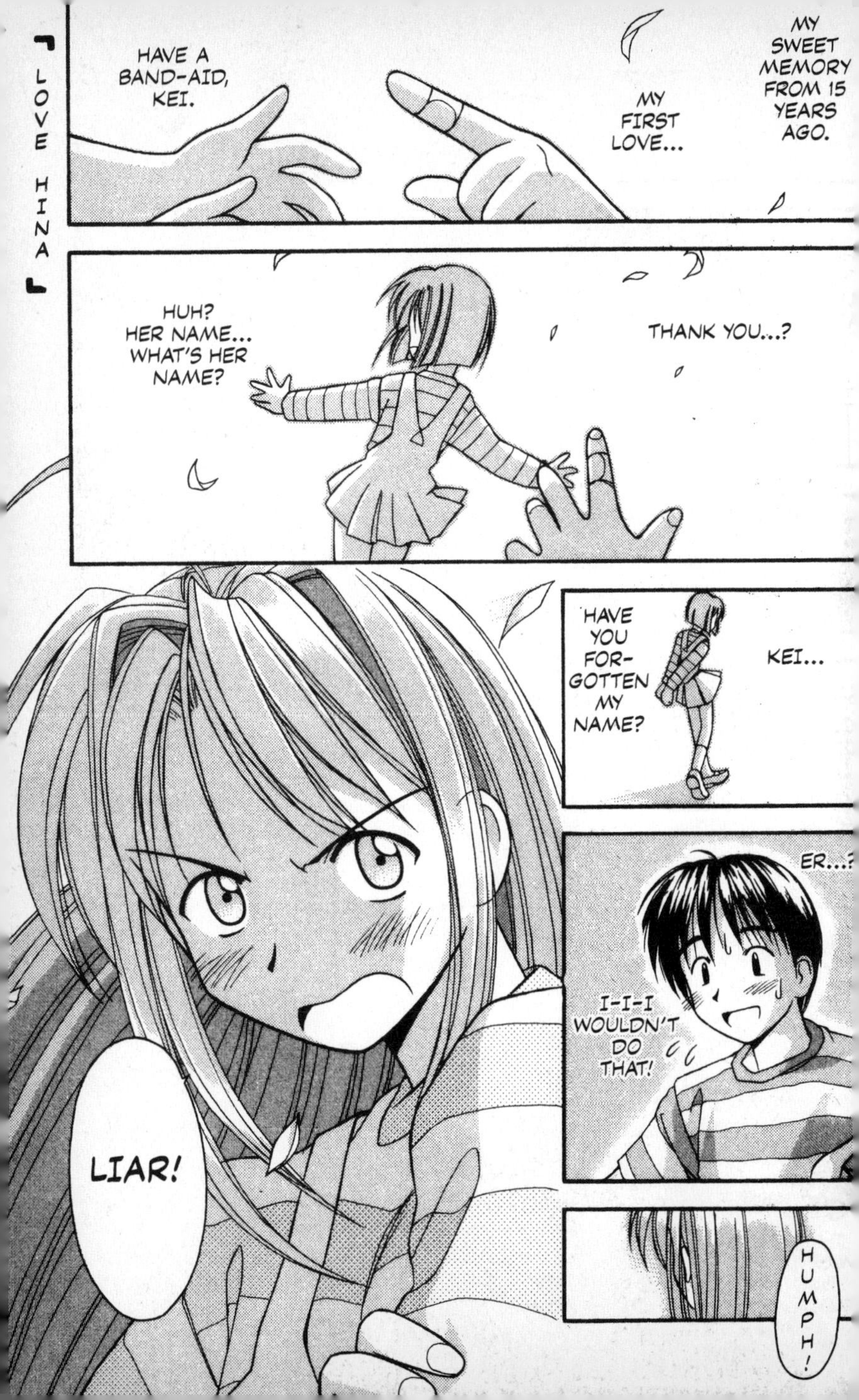
MY SWEET MEMORY FROM 15 YEARS AGO.
MY FIRST LOVE...
HAVE A BAND-AID, KEI.
THANK YOU...?
HUH? HER NAME... WHAT'S HER NAME?
KEI...
HAVE YOU FOR-GOTTEN MY NAME?
ER...?
I-I-I WOULDN'T DO THAT!
HUMPH!
LIAR!

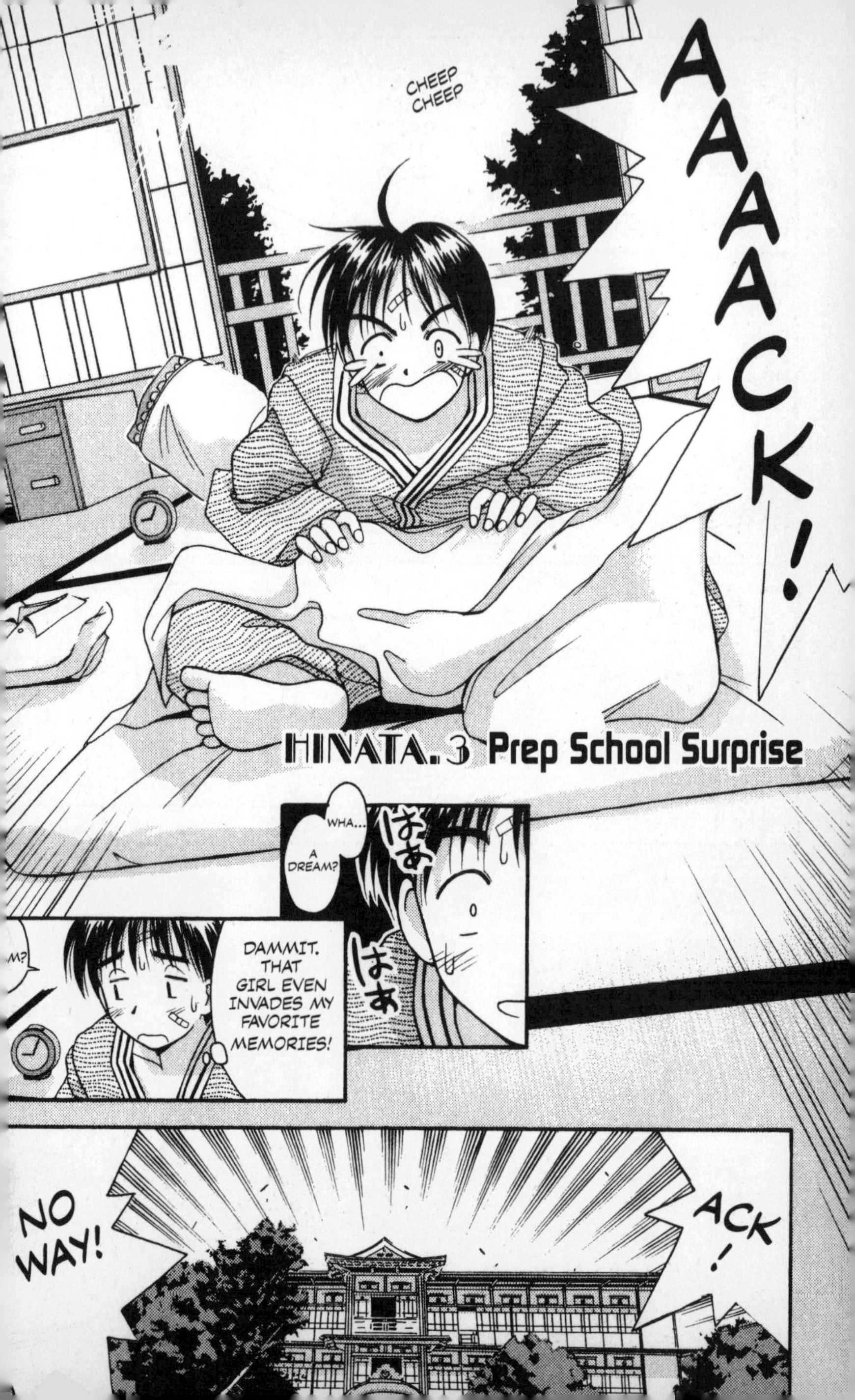
AAAACK!
CHEEP CHEEP
HINATA. 3 Prep School Surprise
WHA... A DREAM?
はあ はあ
DAMMIT. THAT GIRL EVEN INVADES MY FAVORITE MEMORIES!
ACK!
NO WAY!

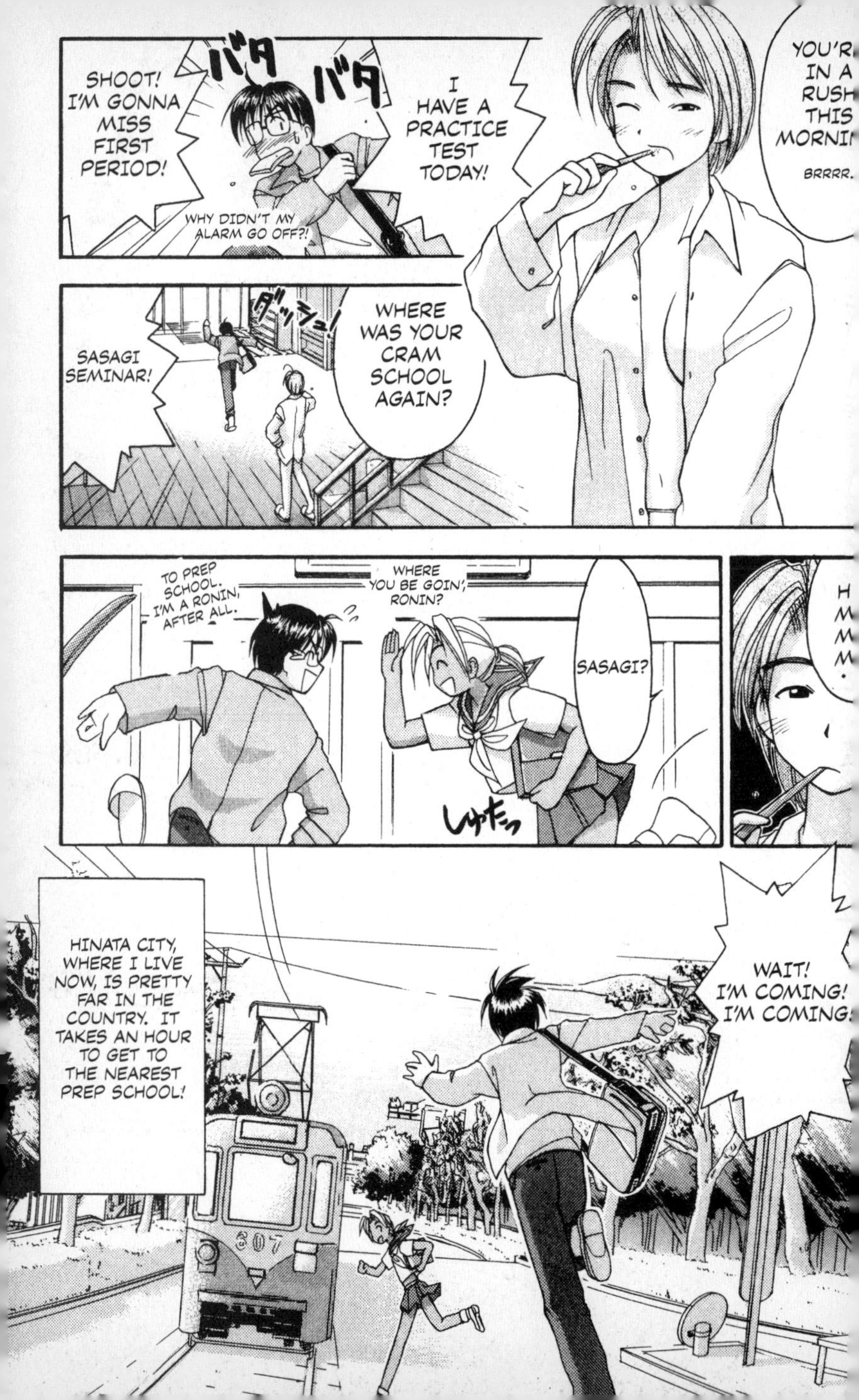
YOU'R IN A RUSH THIS MORNI
BRRRR.
バタ
バタ
SHOOT! I'M GONNA MISS FIRST PERIOD!
I HAVE A PRACTICE TEST TODAY!
WHY DIDN'T MY ALARM GO OFF?!
WHERE WAS YOUR CRAM SCHOOL AGAIN?
ダッシュ!
SASAGI SEMINAR!
HMMM.
SASAGI?
WHERE YOU BE GOIN', RONIN?
TO PREP SCHOOL. I'M A RONIN, AFTER ALL.
WAIT! I'M COMING! I'M COMING!
HINATA CITY, WHERE I LIVE NOW, IS PRETTY FAR IN THE COUNTRY. IT TAKES AN HOUR TO GET TO THE NEAREST PREP SCHOOL!

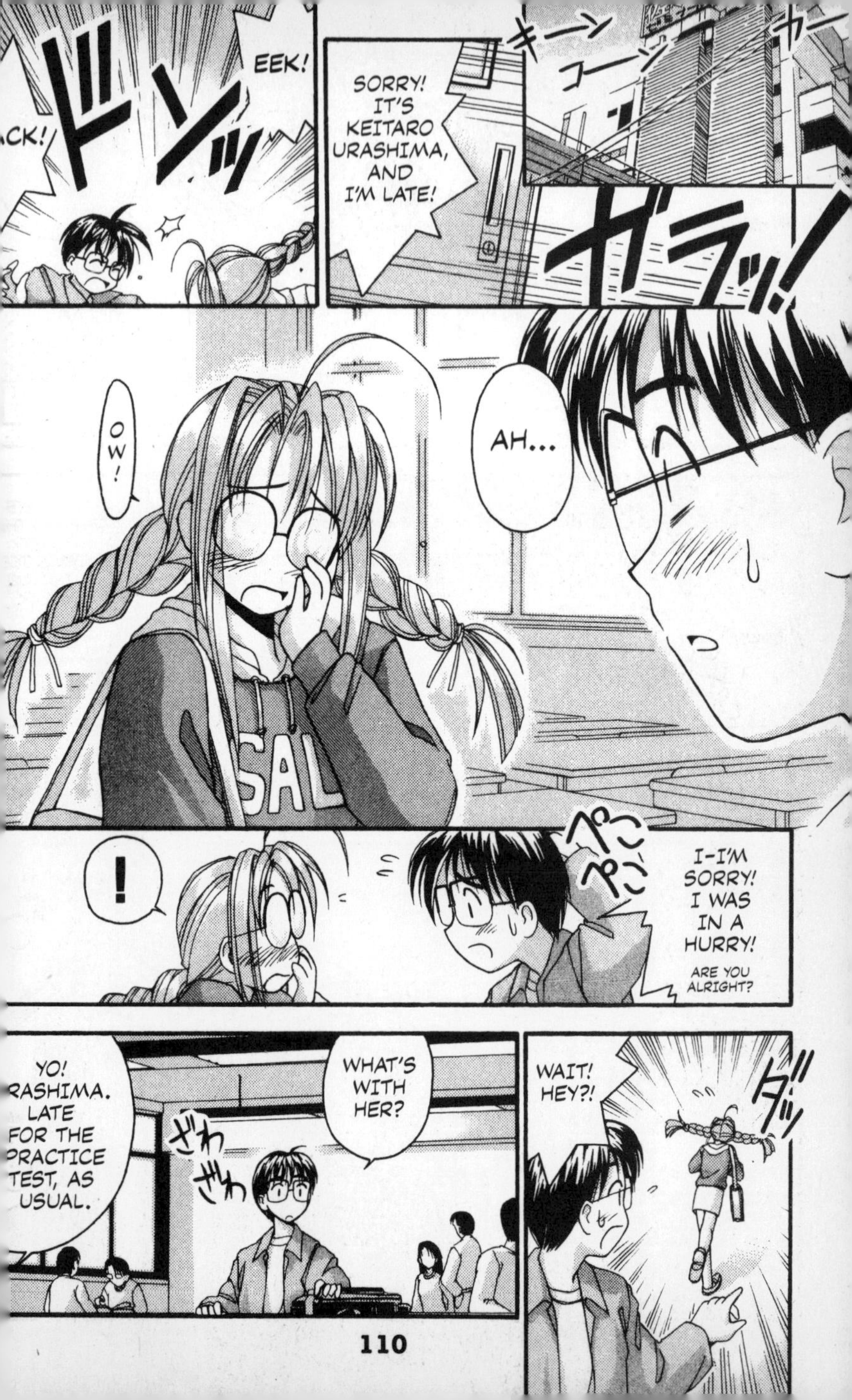

キーン
コーン
カーン
ガラッ!
SORRY! IT'S KEITARO URASHIMA, AND I'M LATE!
EEK!
ドンッ
CK!
AH...
OW!
I-I'M SORRY! I WAS IN A HURRY!
ARE YOU ALRIGHT?
ぺこぺこ
!
WAIT! HEY?!
ダッ
WHAT'S WITH HER?
ざわざわ
YO! RASHIMA. LATE FOR THE PRACTICE TEST, AS USUAL.

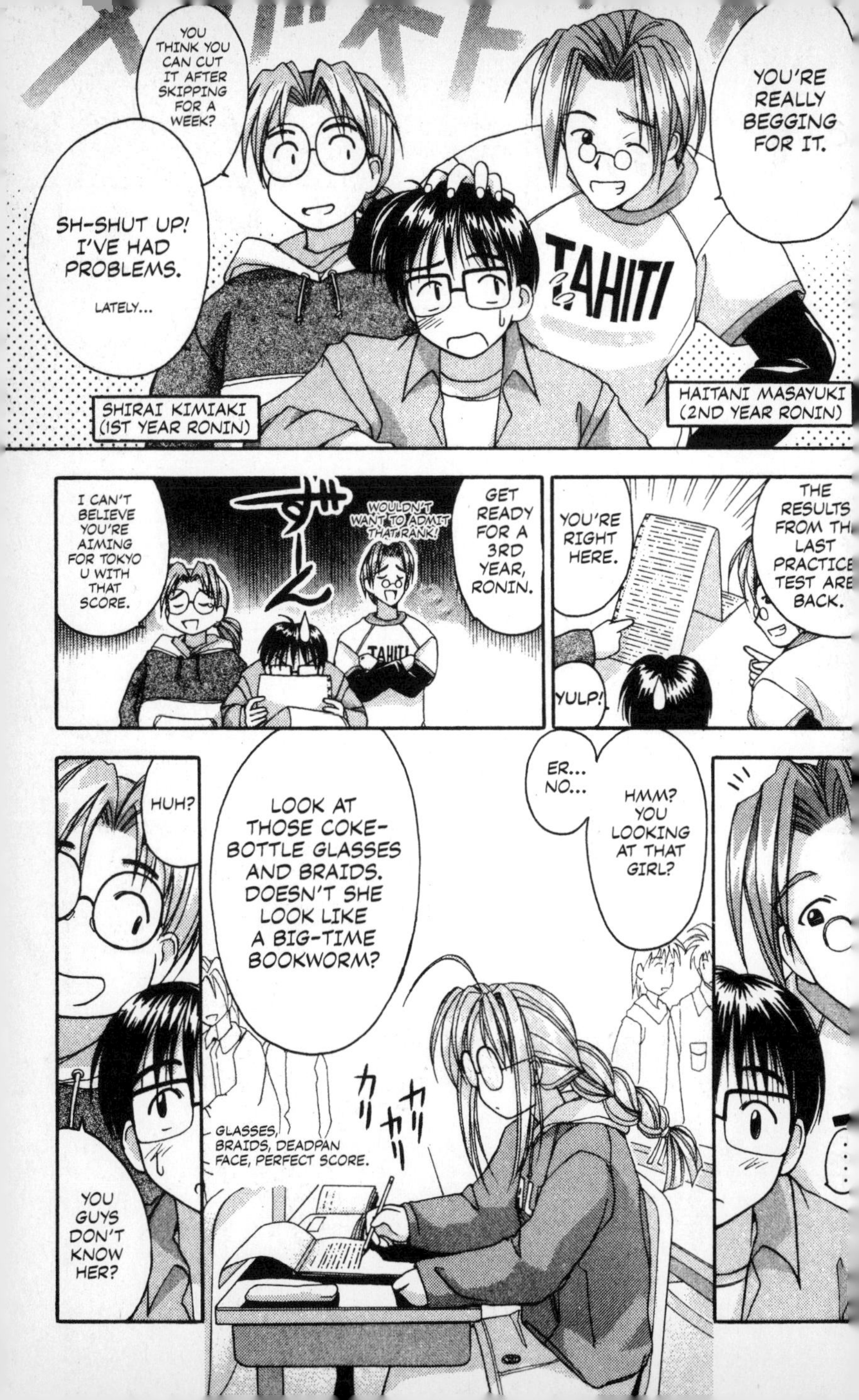
YOU'RE REALLY BEGGING FOR IT.
YOU THINK YOU CAN CUT IT AFTER SKIPPING FOR A WEEK?
SH-SHUT UP! I'VE HAD PROBLEMS.
LATELY...
HAITANI MASAYUKI (2ND YEAR RONIN)
SHIRAI KIMIAKI (1ST YEAR RONIN)
THE RESULTS FROM TH LAST PRACTICE TEST ARE BACK.
YOU'RE RIGHT HERE.
YULP!
GET READY FOR A 3RD YEAR, RONIN.
WOULDN'T WANT TO ADMIT THAT RANK!
I CAN'T BELIEVE YOU'RE AIMING FOR TOKYO U WITH THAT SCORE.
HMM? YOU LOOKING AT THAT GIRL?
ER... NO...
LOOK AT THOSE COKE-BOTTLE GLASSES AND BRAIDS. DOESN'T SHE LOOK LIKE A BIG-TIME BOOKWORM?
GLASSES, BRAIDS, DEADPAN FACE, PERFECT SCORE.
HUH?
YOU GUYS DON'T KNOW HER?

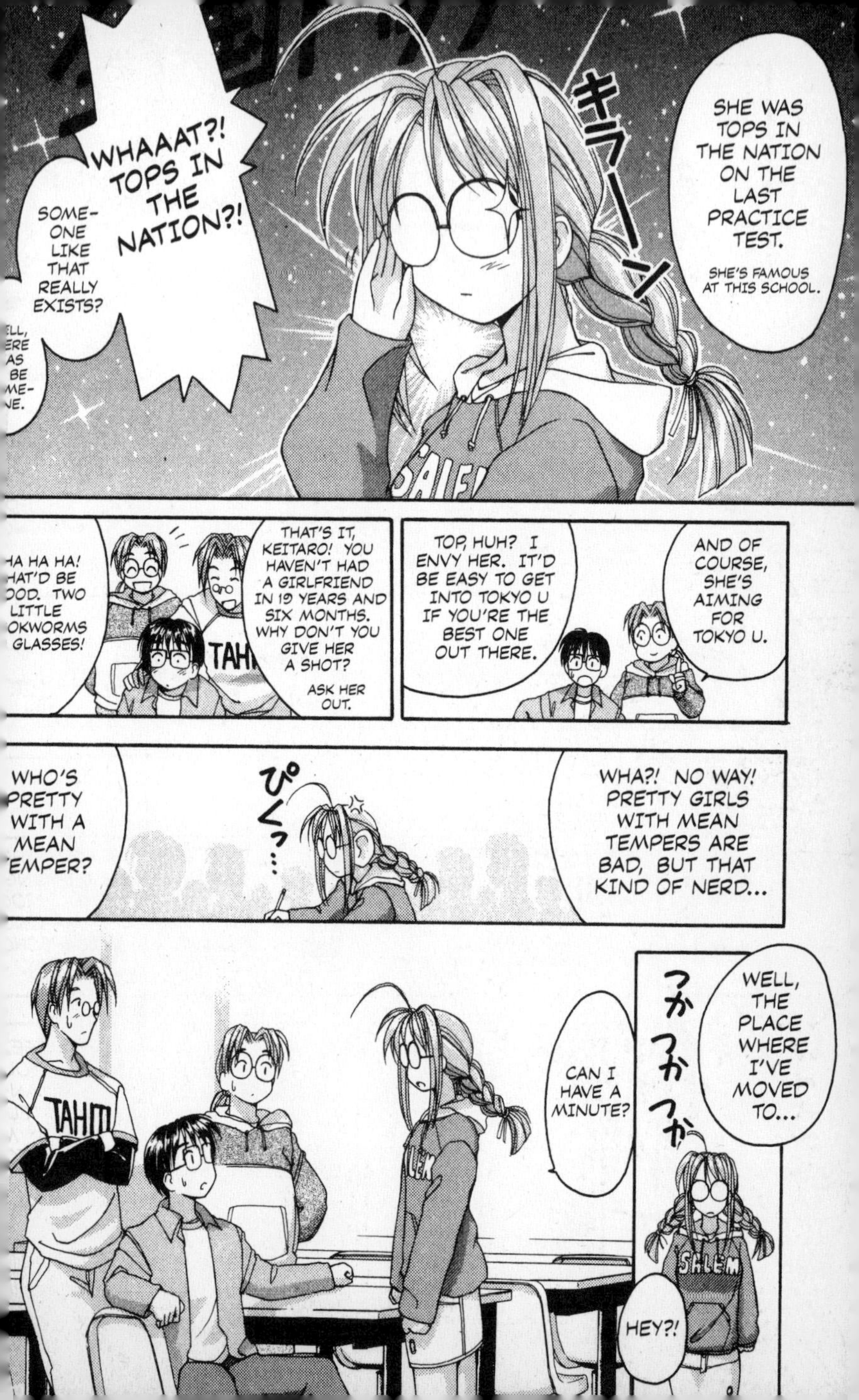
SHE WAS TOPS IN THE NATION ON THE LAST PRACTICE TEST.
SHE'S FAMOUS AT THIS SCHOOL.
キラーン
WHAAAT?! TOPS IN THE NATION?!
SOME-ONE LIKE THAT REALLY EXISTS?
ELL, ERE AS BE ME- NE.
AND OF COURSE, SHE'S AIMING FOR TOKYO U.
TOP, HUH? I ENVY HER. IT'D BE EASY TO GET INTO TOKYO U IF YOU'RE THE BEST ONE OUT THERE.
THAT'S IT, KEITARO! YOU HAVEN'T HAD A GIRLFRIEND IN 19 YEARS AND SIX MONTHS. WHY DON'T YOU GIVE HER A SHOT?
ASK HER OUT.
HA HA HA! HAT'D BE OOD. TWO LITTLE OKWORMS GLASSES!
WHA?! NO WAY! PRETTY GIRLS WITH MEAN TEMPERS ARE BAD, BUT THAT KIND OF NERD...
ぴくっ...
WHO'S PRETTY WITH A MEAN EMPER?
WELL, THE PLACE WHERE I'VE MOVED TO...
つかつかつか
HEY?!
CAN I HAVE A MINUTE?

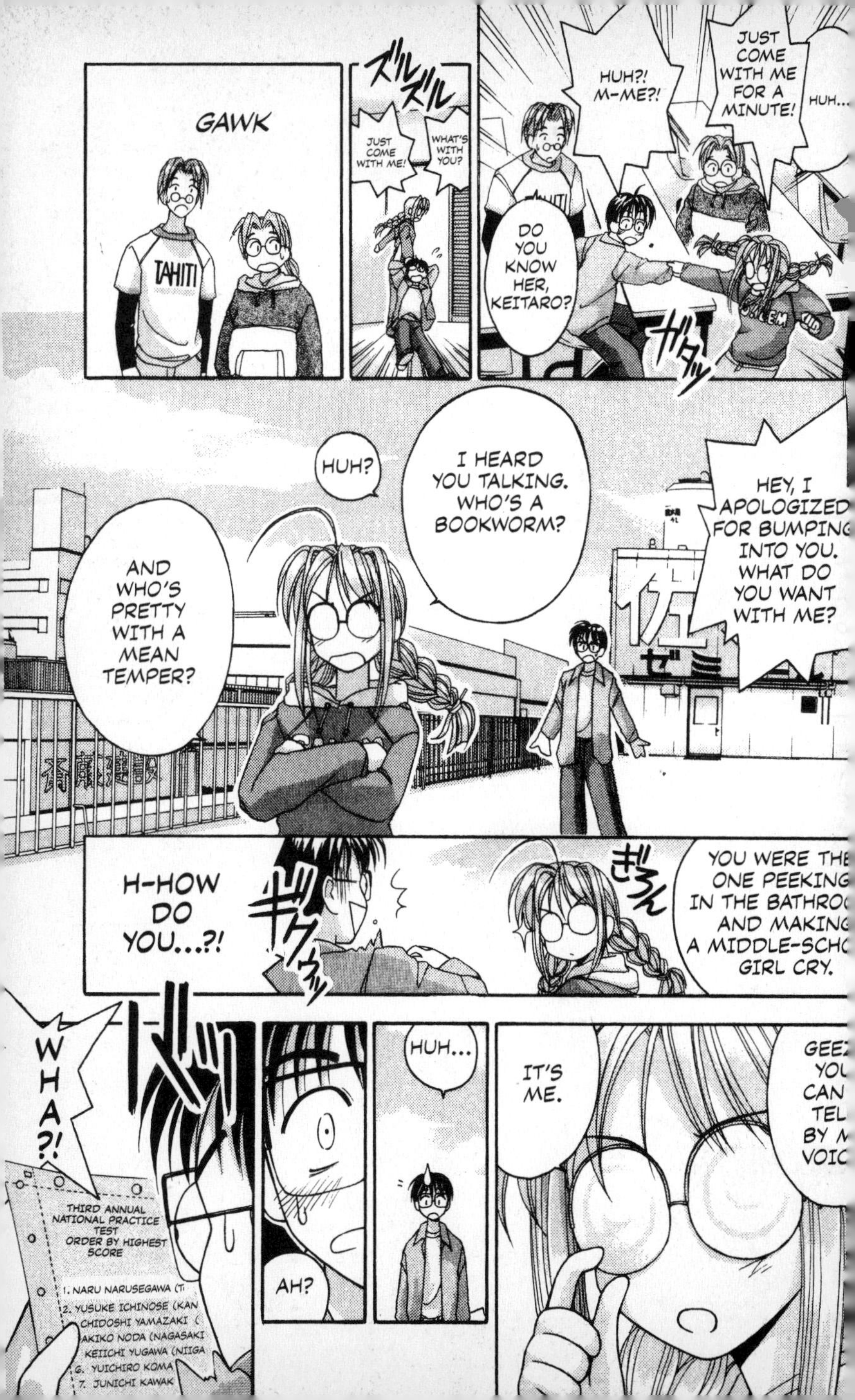
HUH...
JUST COME WITH ME FOR A MINUTE!
HUH?! M-ME?!
DO YOU KNOW HER, KEITARO?
ガタッ
ズルズル
WHAT'S WITH YOU?
JUST COME WITH ME!
GAWK
HEY, I APOLOGIZED FOR BUMPING INTO YOU. WHAT DO YOU WANT WITH ME?
I HEARD YOU TALKING. WHO'S A BOOKWORM?
HUH?
AND WHO'S PRETTY WITH A MEAN TEMPER?
YOU WERE THE ONE PEEKING IN THE BATHROO AND MAKING A MIDDLE-SCHO GIRL CRY.
ぎろん
ギクウッ
H-HOW DO YOU...?!
GEEZ YOU CAN TEL BY M VOIC
IT'S ME.
HUH...
AH?
WHA?!
THIRD ANNUAL NATIONAL PRACTICE TEST ORDER BY HIGHEST SCORE
1. NARU NARUSEGAWA (T
2. YUSUKE ICHINOSE (KAN
CHIDOSHI YAMAZAKI (
AKIKO NODA (NAGASAKI
KEIICHI YUGAWA (NIIGA
6. YUICHIRO KOMA
7. JUNICHI KAWAK

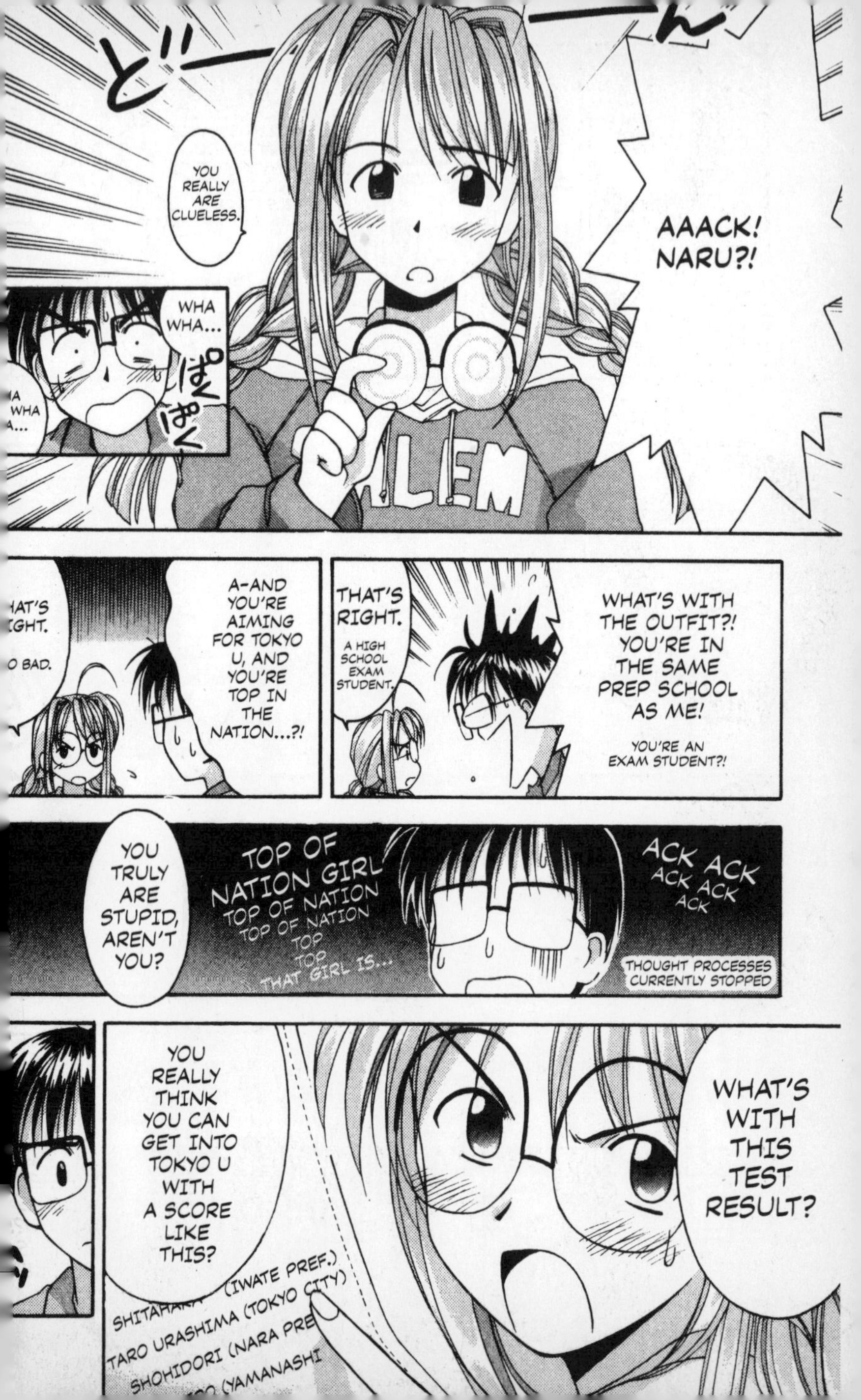
どーーーん
AAACK! NARU?!
YOU REALLY ARE CLUELESS.
WHA WHA...
ぱくぱく
WHAT'S WITH THE OUTFIT?! YOU'RE IN THE SAME PREP SCHOOL AS ME!
YOU'RE AN EXAM STUDENT?!
THAT'S RIGHT.
A HIGH SCHOOL EXAM STUDENT.
A-AND YOU'RE AIMING FOR TOKYO U, AND YOU'RE TOP IN THE NATION...?!
ACK ACK ACK ACK ACK
THOUGHT PROCESSES CURRENTLY STOPPED
TOP OF NATION GIRL
TOP OF NATION
TOP OF NATION
TOP
TOP
THAT GIRL IS...
YOU TRULY ARE STUPID, AREN'T YOU?
WHAT'S WITH THIS TEST RESULT?
YOU REALLY THINK YOU CAN GET INTO TOKYO U WITH A SCORE LIKE THIS?
SHITAHARA (IWATE PREF.)
TARO URASHIMA (TOKYO CITY)
SHOHIDORI (NARA PRE
(YAMANASHI

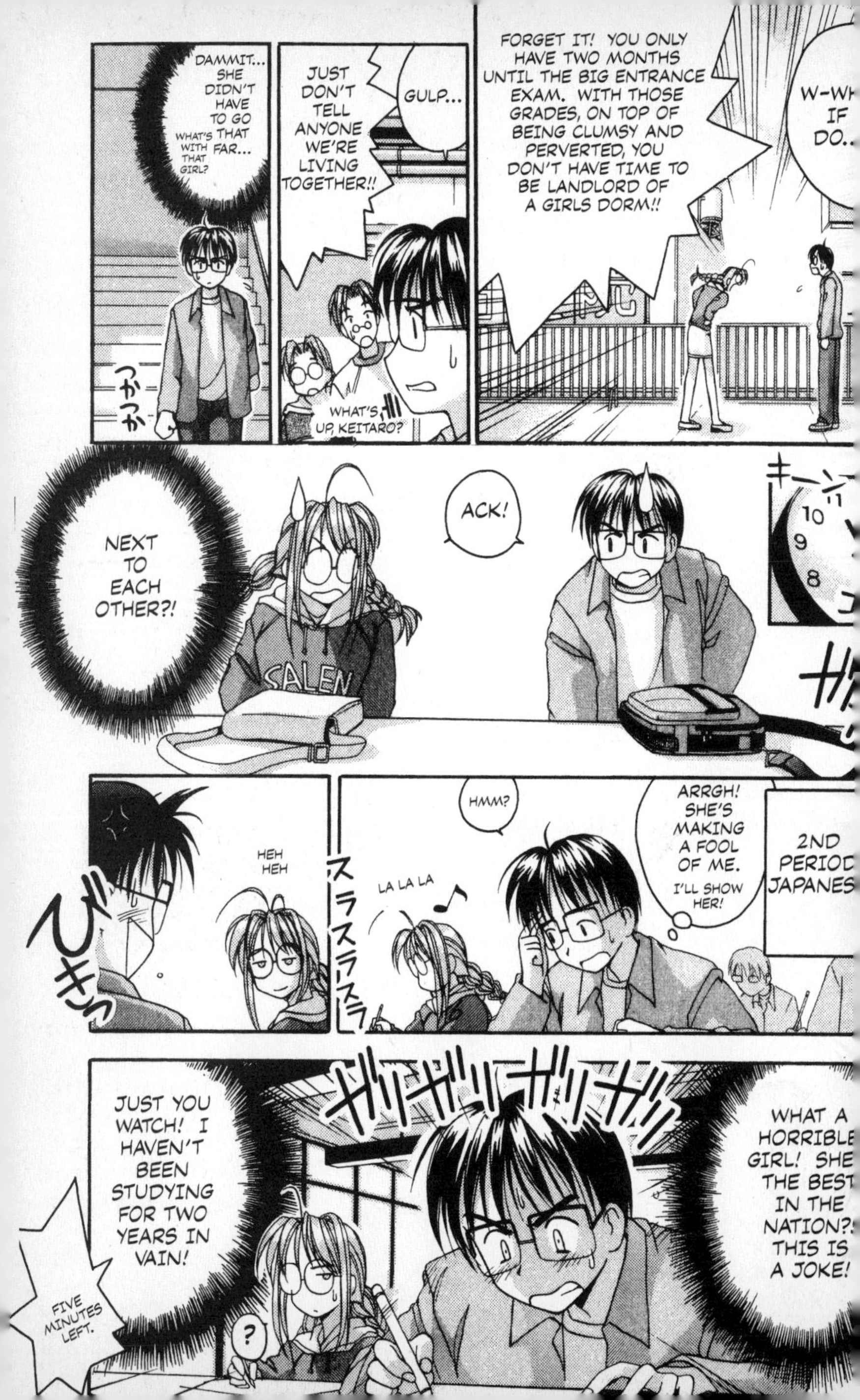

W-WH
IF
DO..
FORGET IT! YOU ONLY HAVE TWO MONTHS UNTIL THE BIG ENTRANCE EXAM. WITH THOSE GRADES, ON TOP OF BEING CLUMSY AND PERVERTED, YOU DON'T HAVE TIME TO BE LANDLORD OF A GIRLS DORM!!
GULP...
JUST DON'T TELL ANYONE WE'RE LIVING TOGETHER!!
WHAT'S UP, KEITARO?
DAMMIT... SHE DIDN'T HAVE TO GO THAT FAR...
WHAT'S WITH THAT GIRL?
つかつか
ACK!
NEXT TO EACH OTHER?!
2ND PERIOD JAPANES
ARRGH! SHE'S MAKING A FOOL OF ME.
I'LL SHOW HER!
HMM?
LA LA LA
スラスラスラ
HEH HEH
びきっ
WHAT A HORRIBLE GIRL! SHE THE BEST IN THE NATION?! THIS IS A JOKE!
JUST YOU WATCH! I HAVEN'T BEEN STUDYING FOR TWO YEARS IN VAIN!
FIVE MINUTES LEFT.
?

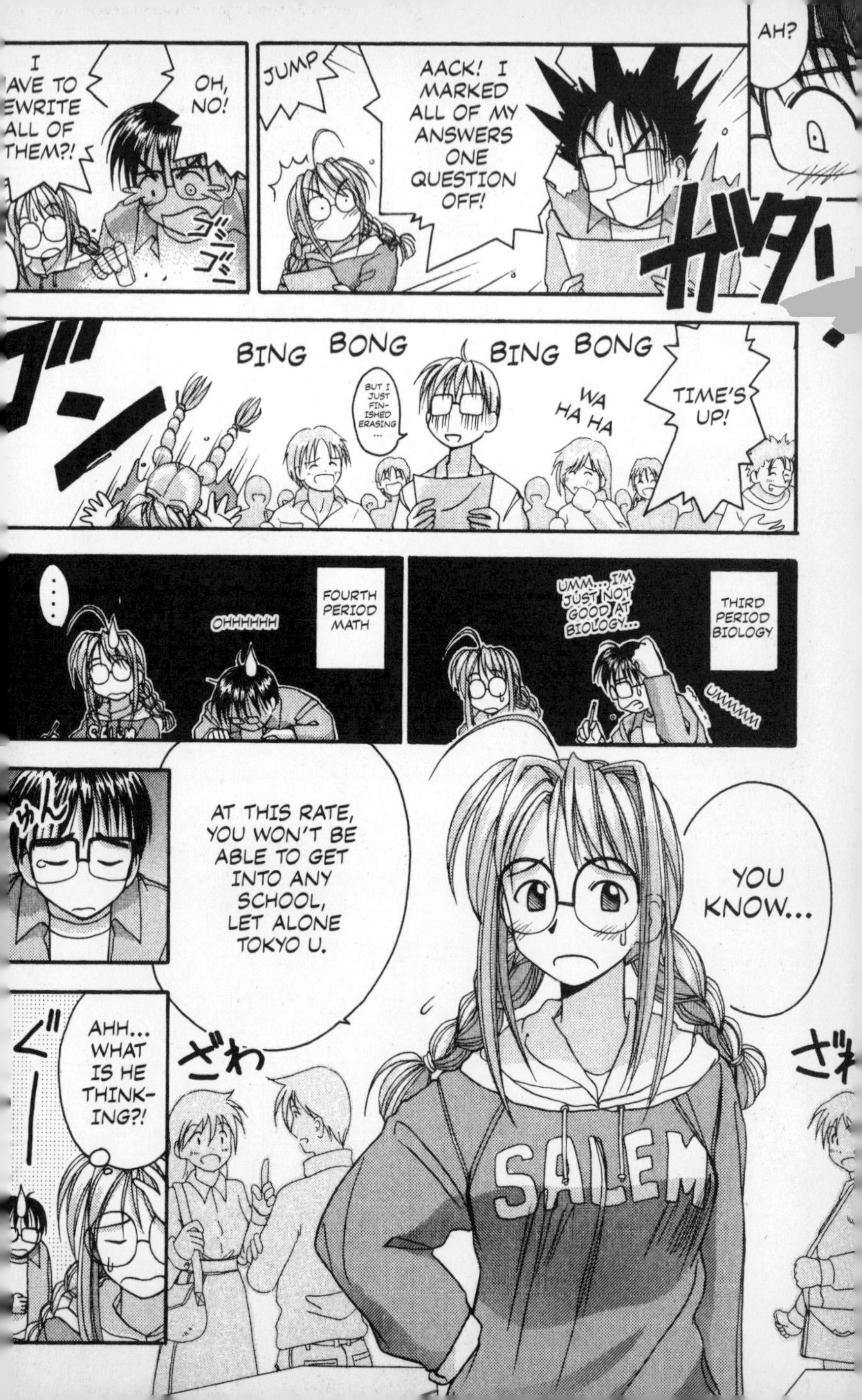
AH?
JUMP
AACK! I MARKED ALL OF MY ANSWERS ONE QUESTION OFF!
ガタッ
OH, NO!
I AVE TO EWRITE ALL OF THEM?!
TIME'S UP!
BING BONG BING BONG
WA HA HA
BUT I JUST FIN-ISHED ERASING...
THIRD PERIOD BIOLOGY
UMMMMM
UMM... I'M JUST NOT GOOD AT BIOLOGY...
FOURTH PERIOD MATH
OHHHHHH
...
YOU KNOW...
AT THIS RATE, YOU WON'T BE ABLE TO GET INTO ANY SCHOOL, LET ALONE TOKYO U.
ざわ
SALEM
AHH... WHAT IS HE THINKING?!

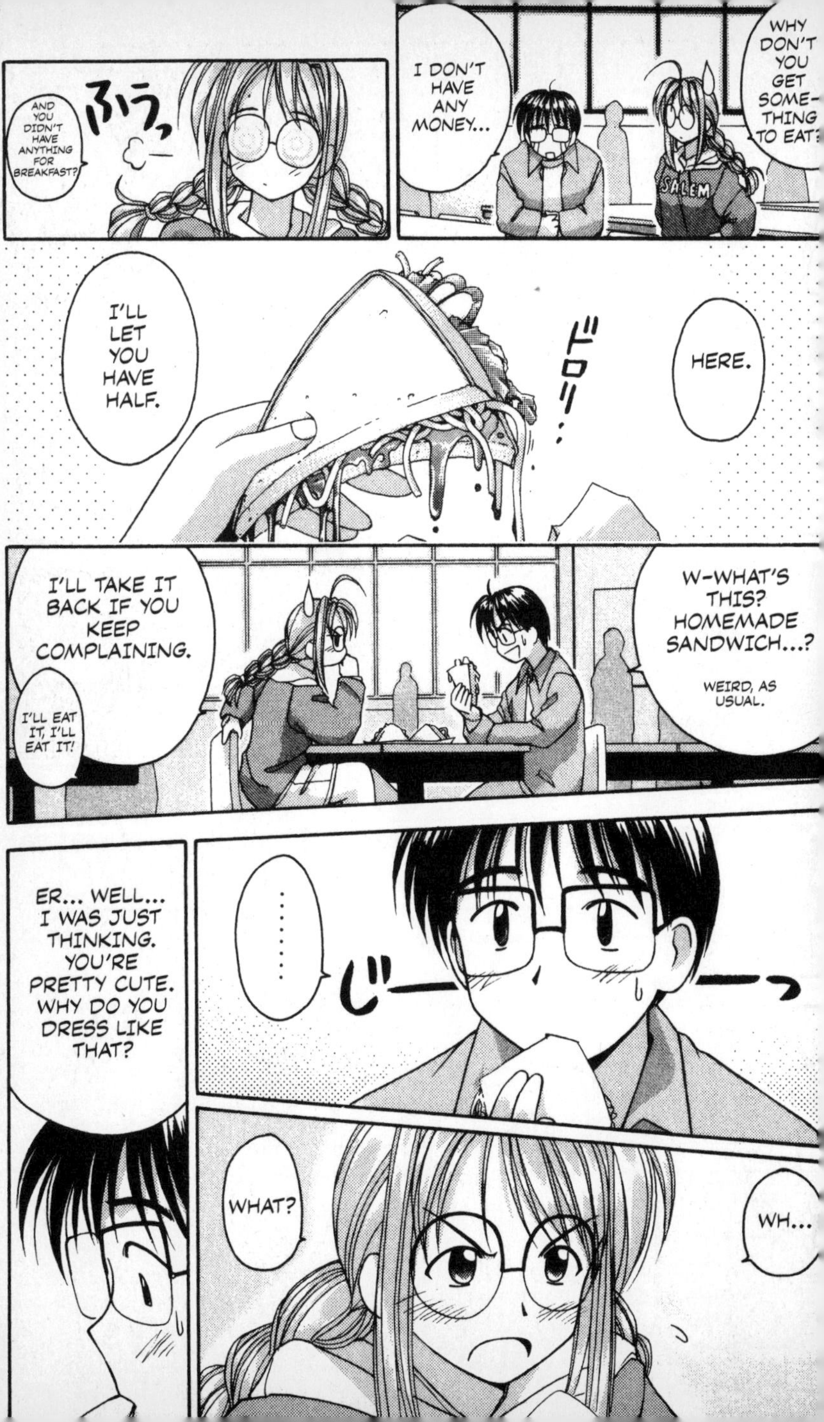
WHY DON'T YOU GET SOME-THING TO EAT?
I DON'T HAVE ANY MONEY...
ふうっ
AND YOU DIDN'T HAVE ANYTHING FOR BREAKFAST?
HERE.
ドロリ…
I'LL LET YOU HAVE HALF.
W-WHAT'S THIS? HOMEMADE SANDWICH...?
WEIRD, AS USUAL.
I'LL TAKE IT BACK IF YOU KEEP COMPLAINING.
I'LL EAT IT, I'LL EAT IT!
......
じーーっ
WH...
WHAT?
ER... WELL... I WAS JUST THINKING. YOU'RE PRETTY CUTE. WHY DO YOU DRESS LIKE THAT?

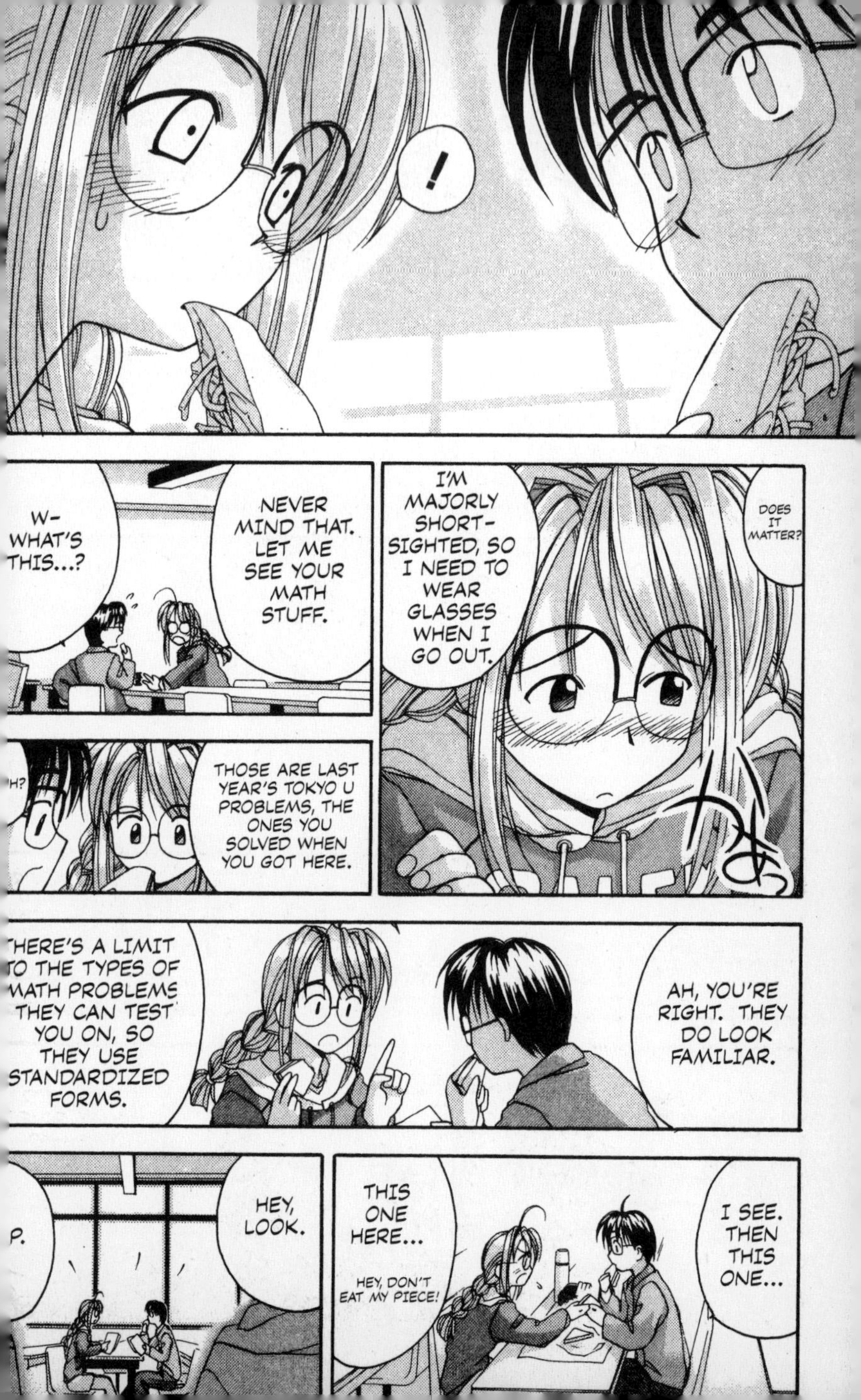

!
DOES IT MATTER?
I'M MAJORLY SHORT-SIGHTED, SO I NEED TO WEAR GLASSES WHEN I GO OUT.
NEVER MIND THAT. LET ME SEE YOUR MATH STUFF.
W- WHAT'S THIS...?
THOSE ARE LAST YEAR'S TOKYO U PROBLEMS, THE ONES YOU SOLVED WHEN YOU GOT HERE.
H?
AH, YOU'RE RIGHT. THEY DO LOOK FAMILIAR.
THERE'S A LIMIT TO THE TYPES OF MATH PROBLEMS THEY CAN TEST YOU ON, SO THEY USE STANDARDIZED FORMS.
I SEE. THEN THIS ONE...
THIS ONE HERE...
HEY, DON'T EAT MY PIECE!
HEY, LOOK.
P.

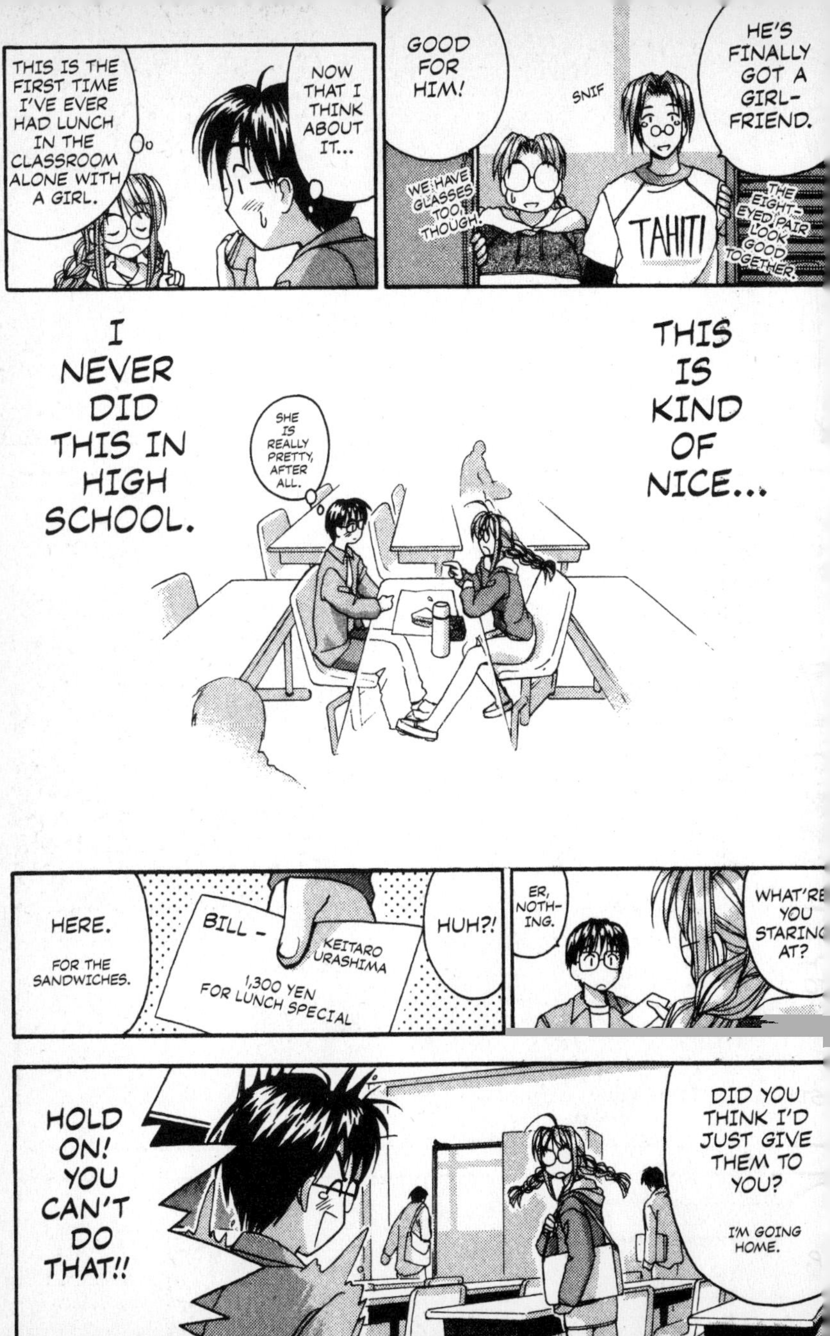
HE'S FINALLY GOT A GIRL-FRIEND.
SNIF
GOOD FOR HIM!
THE EIGHT-EYED PAIR LOOK GOOD TOGETHER.
WE HAVE GLASSES TOO, THOUGH!
NOW THAT I THINK ABOUT IT...
THIS IS THE FIRST TIME I'VE EVER HAD LUNCH IN THE CLASSROOM ALONE WITH A GIRL.
THIS IS KIND OF NICE...
SHE IS REALLY PRETTY, AFTER ALL.
I NEVER DID THIS IN HIGH SCHOOL.
WHAT'RE YOU STARING AT?
ER, NOTHING.
HUH?!
BILL -
KEITARO URASHIMA
1,300 YEN FOR LUNCH SPECIAL
HERE.
FOR THE SANDWICHES.
DID YOU THINK I'D JUST GIVE THEM TO YOU?
I'M GOING HOME.
HOLD ON! YOU CAN'T DO THAT!!

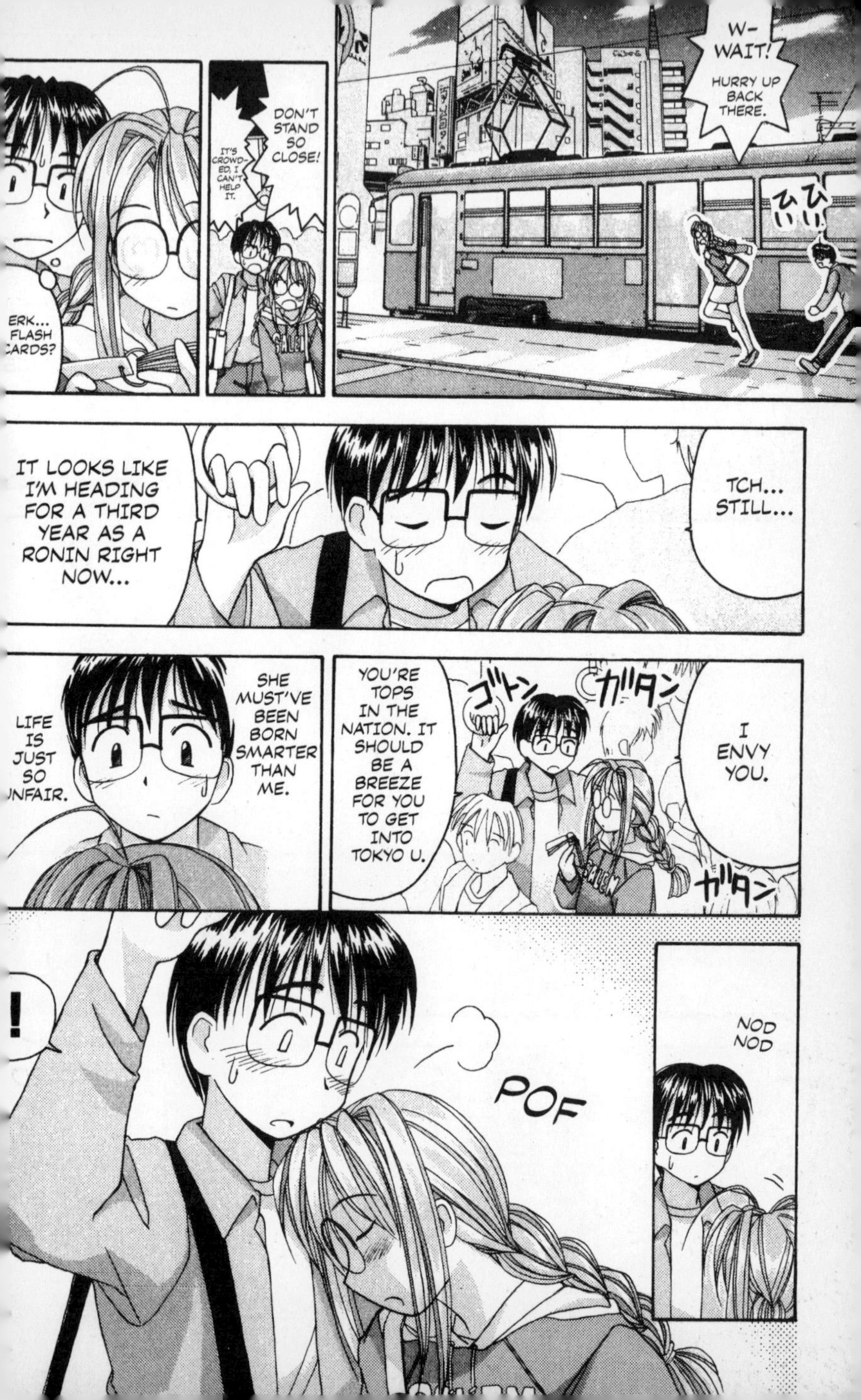
W-WAIT!
HURRY UP BACK THERE.
ひいひい
DON'T STAND SO CLOSE!
IT'S CROWDED, I CAN'T HELP IT.
ERK... FLASH CARDS?
TCH... STILL...
IT LOOKS LIKE I'M HEADING FOR A THIRD YEAR AS A RONIN RIGHT NOW...
I ENVY YOU.
ガタン
ゴトン
YOU'RE TOPS IN THE NATION. IT SHOULD BE A BREEZE FOR YOU TO GET INTO TOKYO U.
ガタン
SHE MUST'VE BEEN BORN SMARTER THAN ME.
LIFE IS JUST SO UNFAIR.
NOD NOD
POF
!

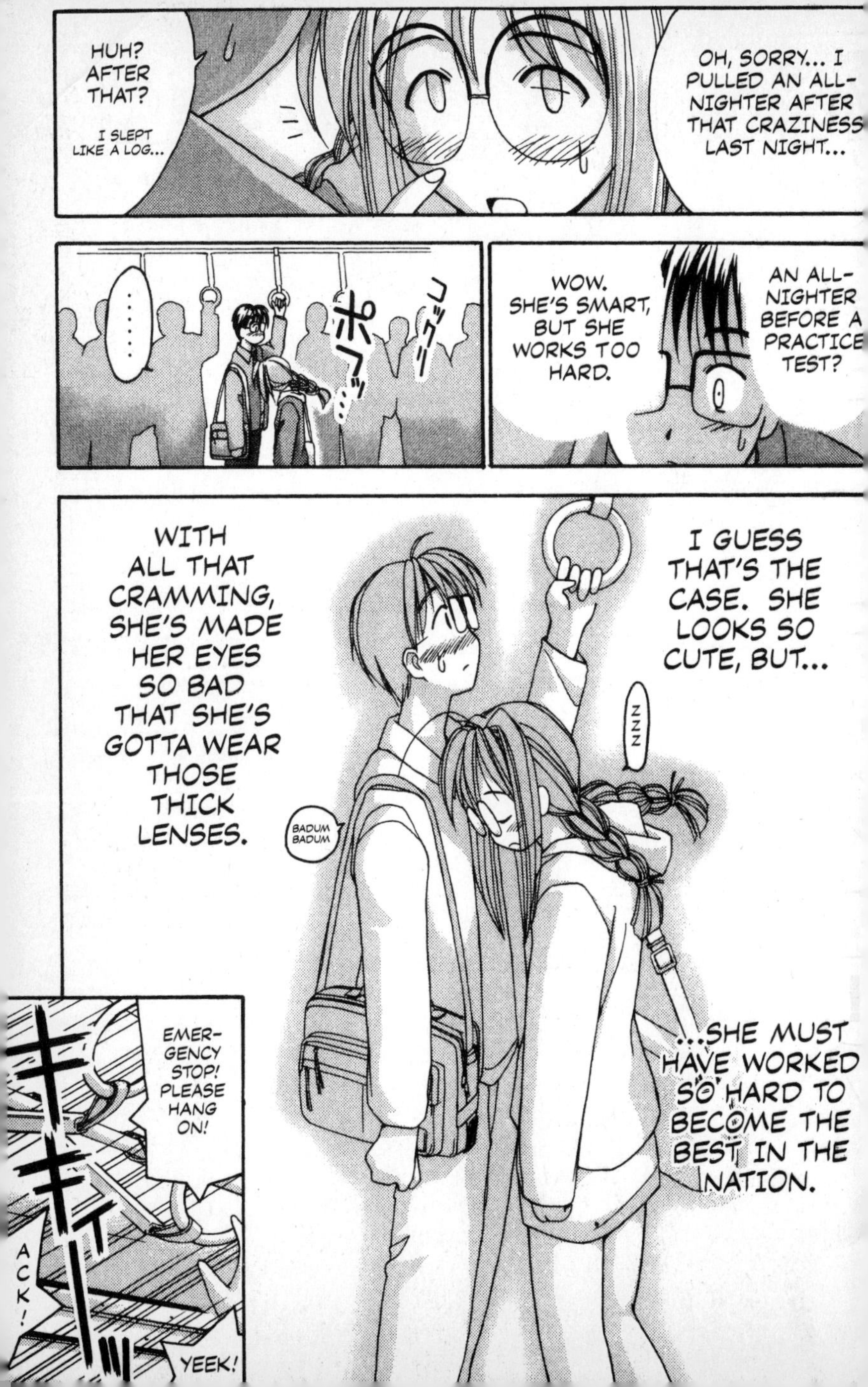
OH, SORRY... I PULLED AN ALL-NIGHTER AFTER THAT CRAZINESS LAST NIGHT...
HUH? AFTER THAT?
I SLEPT LIKE A LOG...
AN ALL-NIGHTER BEFORE A PRACTICE TEST?
WOW. SHE'S SMART, BUT SHE WORKS TOO HARD.
コックリ
ポフッ…
......
I GUESS THAT'S THE CASE. SHE LOOKS SO CUTE, BUT...
ZZZ
WITH ALL THAT CRAMMING, SHE'S MADE HER EYES SO BAD THAT SHE'S GOTTA WEAR THOSE THICK LENSES.
BADUM BADUM
...SHE MUST HAVE WORKED SO HARD TO BECOME THE BEST IN THE NATION.
EMERGENCY STOP! PLEASE HANG ON!
ACK!
YEEK!

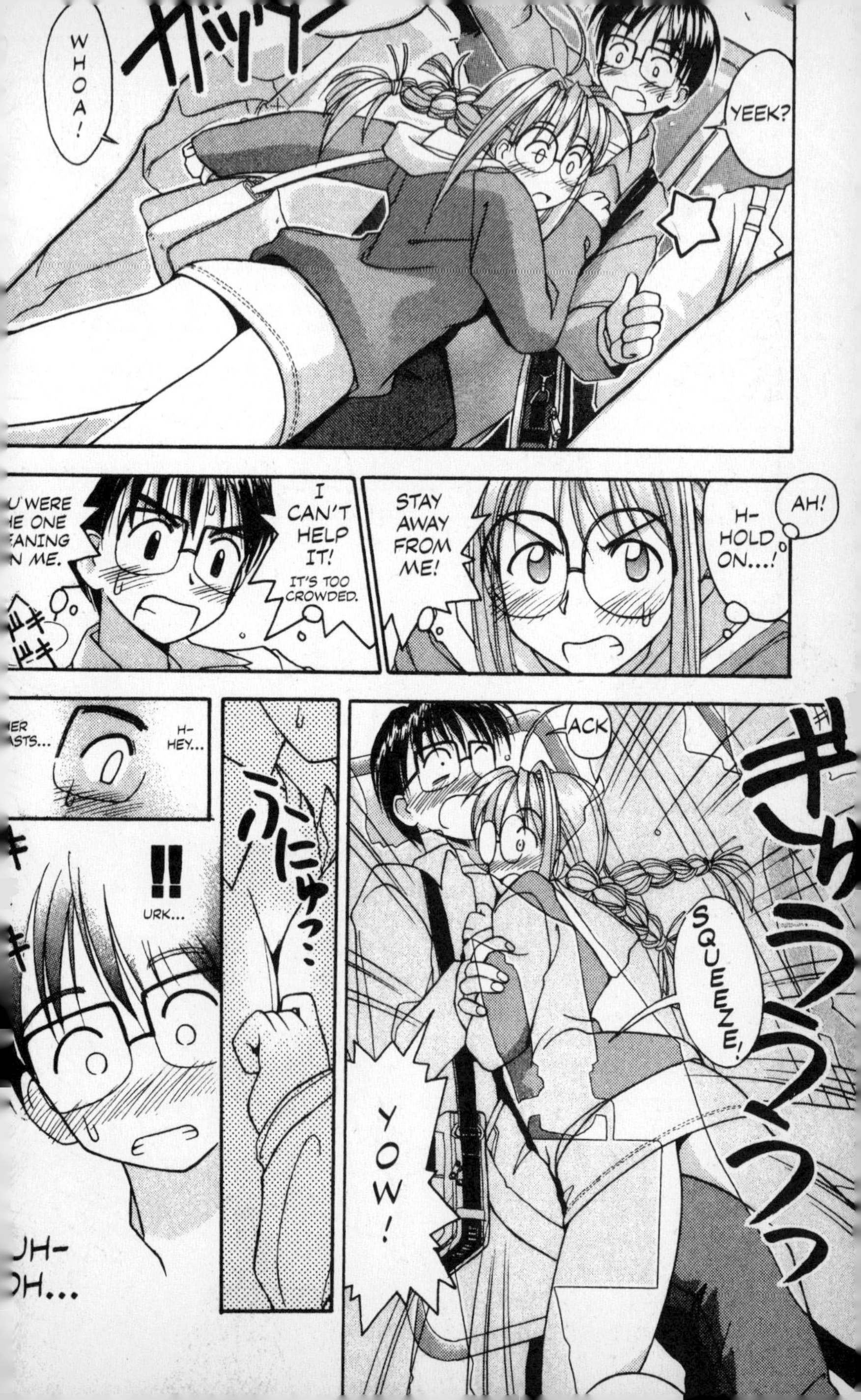
YEEK?
WHOA!
AH!
H-HOLD ON....!
STAY AWAY FROM ME!
I CAN'T HELP IT! IT'S TOO CROWDED.
U WERE HE ONE EANING N ME.
ACK
SQUEEZE!
YOW!
ふにゅっ
H-HEY...
ER ASTS...
!!
URK...
UH-OH...

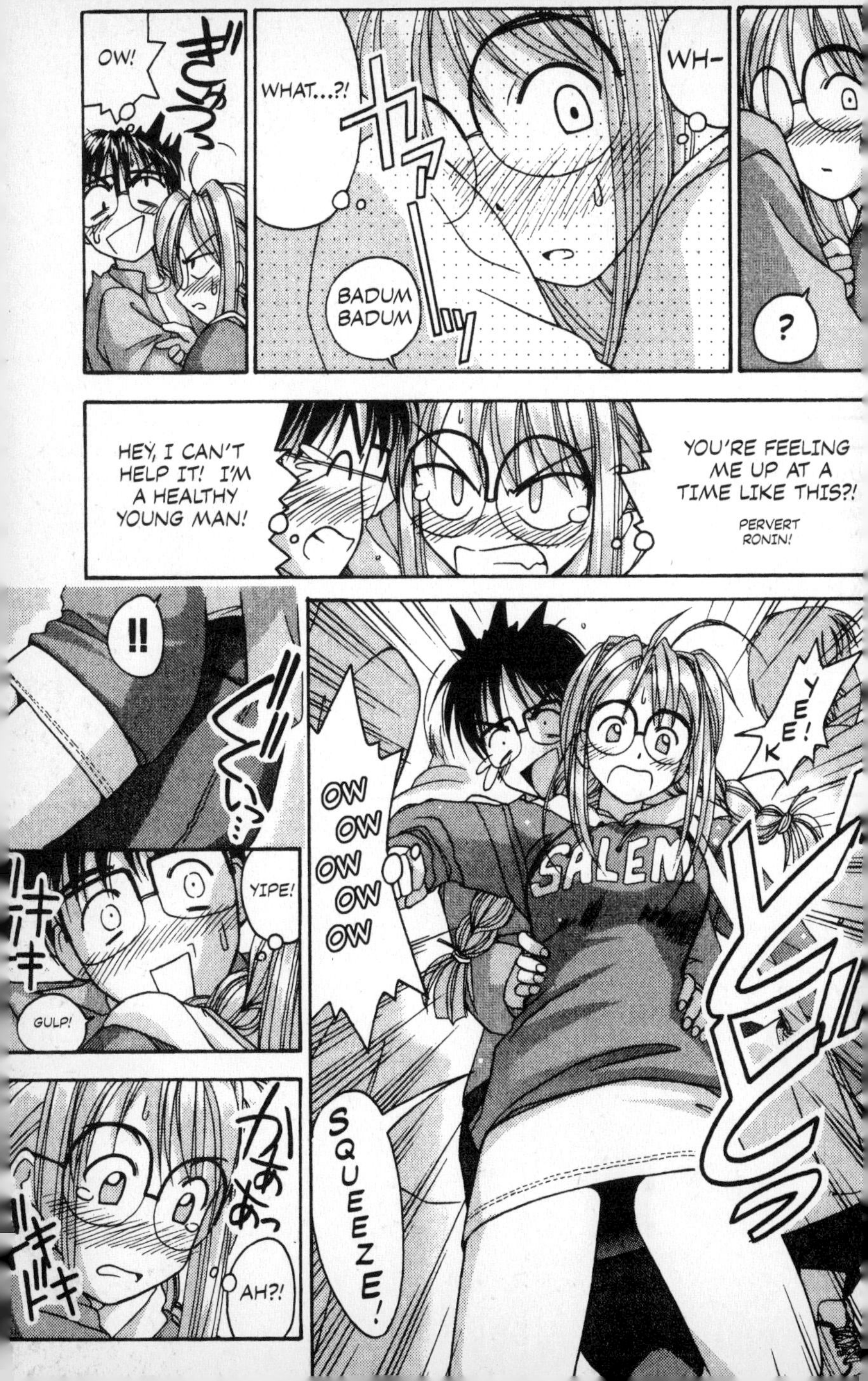
?
WH-
WHAT...?!
BADUM BADUM
OW!
YOU'RE FEELING ME UP AT A TIME LIKE THIS?!
PERVERT RONIN!
HEY, I CAN'T HELP IT! I'M A HEALTHY YOUNG MAN!
YEEK!
OW OW OW OW OW
SQUEEZE!
!!
YIPE!
GULP!
AH?!

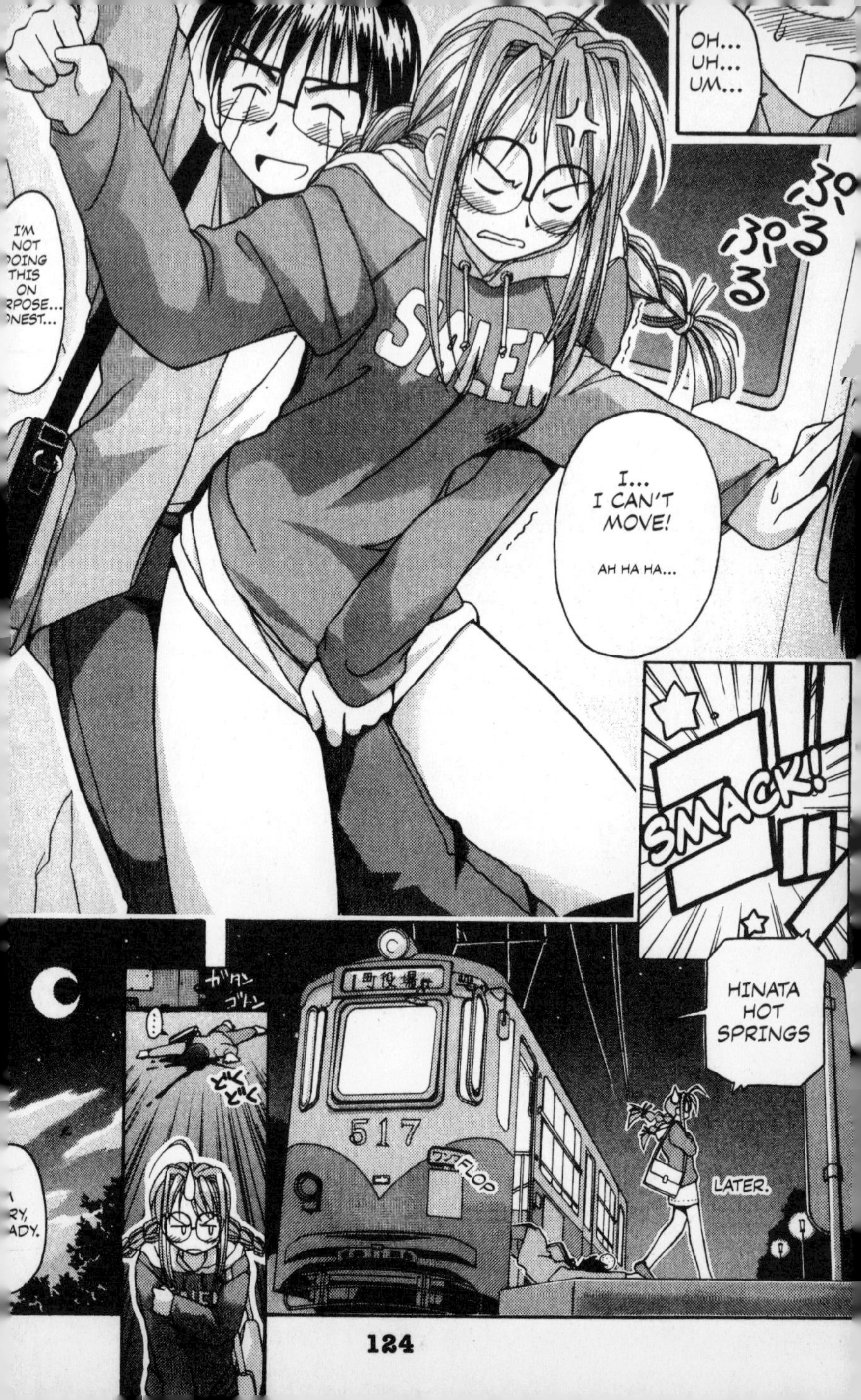
OH... UH... UM...
I... I CAN'T MOVE!
AH HA HA...
I'M NOT DOING THIS ON PURPOSE... HONEST...
SMACK!!
HINATA HOT SPRINGS
LATER.
FLOP
...

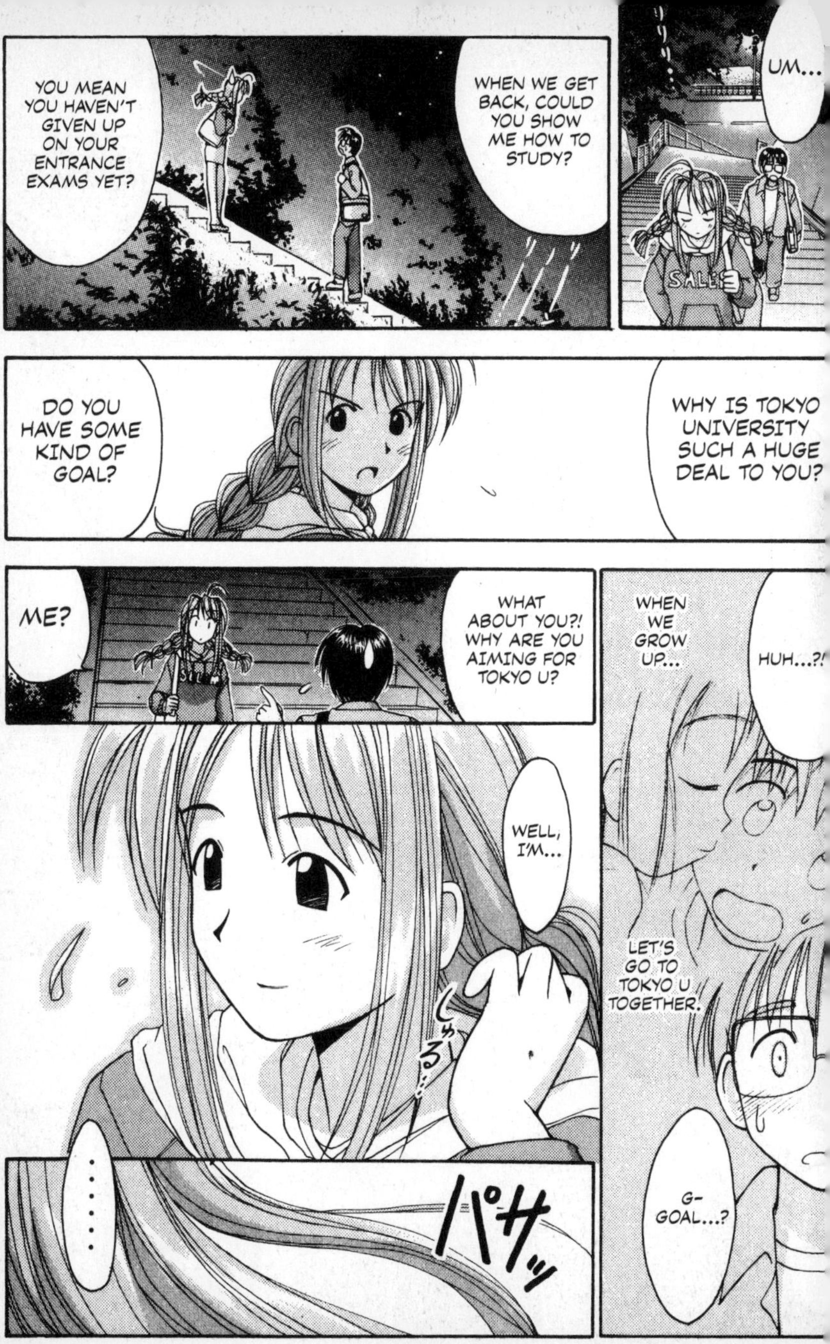
UM...
WHEN WE GET BACK, COULD YOU SHOW ME HOW TO STUDY?
YOU MEAN YOU HAVEN'T GIVEN UP ON YOUR ENTRANCE EXAMS YET?
WHY IS TOKYO UNIVERSITY SUCH A HUGE DEAL TO YOU?
DO YOU HAVE SOME KIND OF GOAL?
HUH...?!
WHEN WE GROW UP...
LET'S GO TO TOKYO U TOGETHER.
G-GOAL...?
WHAT ABOUT YOU?! WHY ARE YOU AIMING FOR TOKYO U?
ME?
WELL, I'M...
しゅる…
......
パサッ

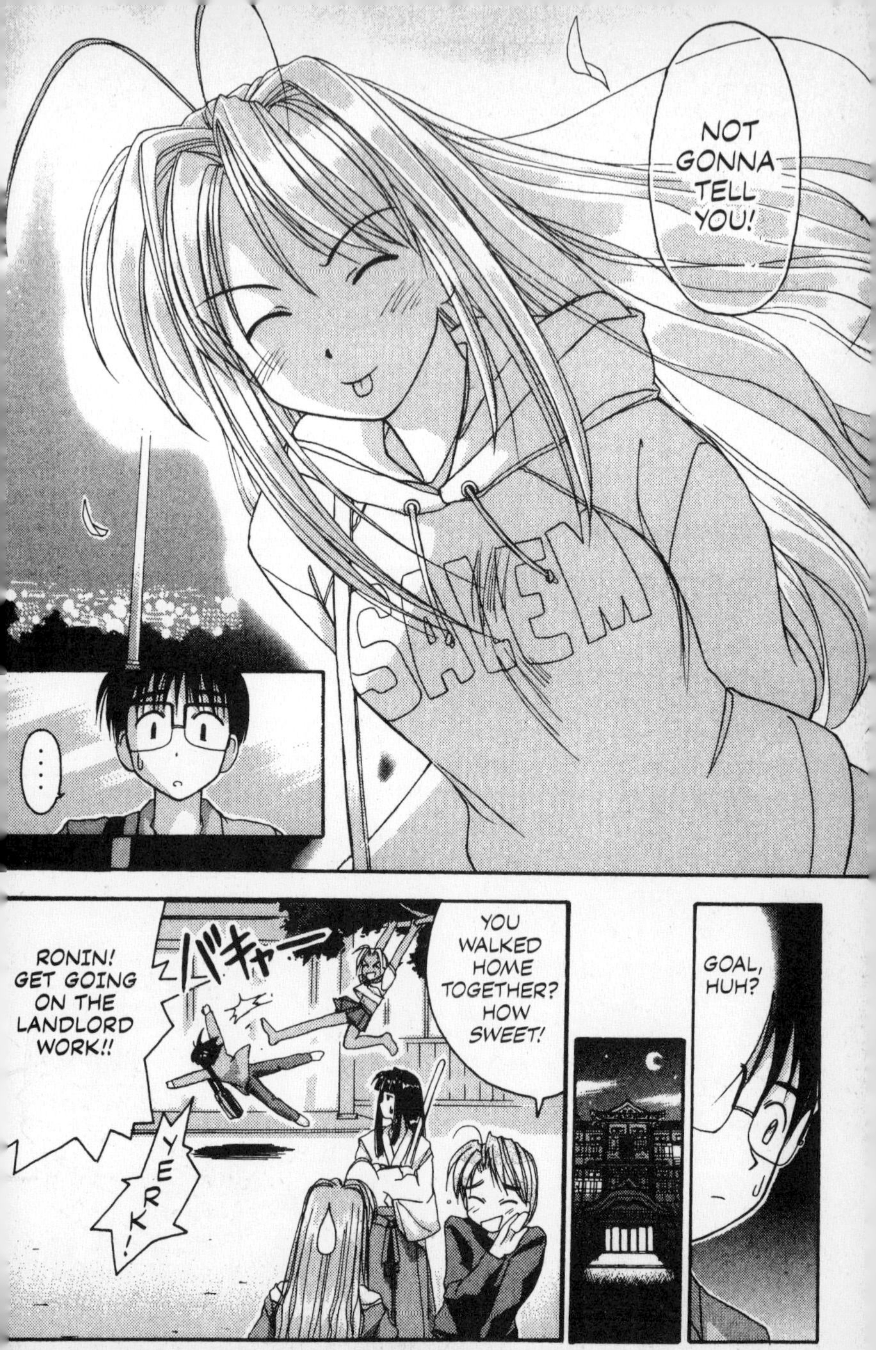
NOT GONNA TELL YOU!
....
GOAL, HUH?
YOU WALKED HOME TOGETHER? HOW SWEET!
バキャー
RONIN! GET GOING ON THE LANDLORD WORK!!
YERK!

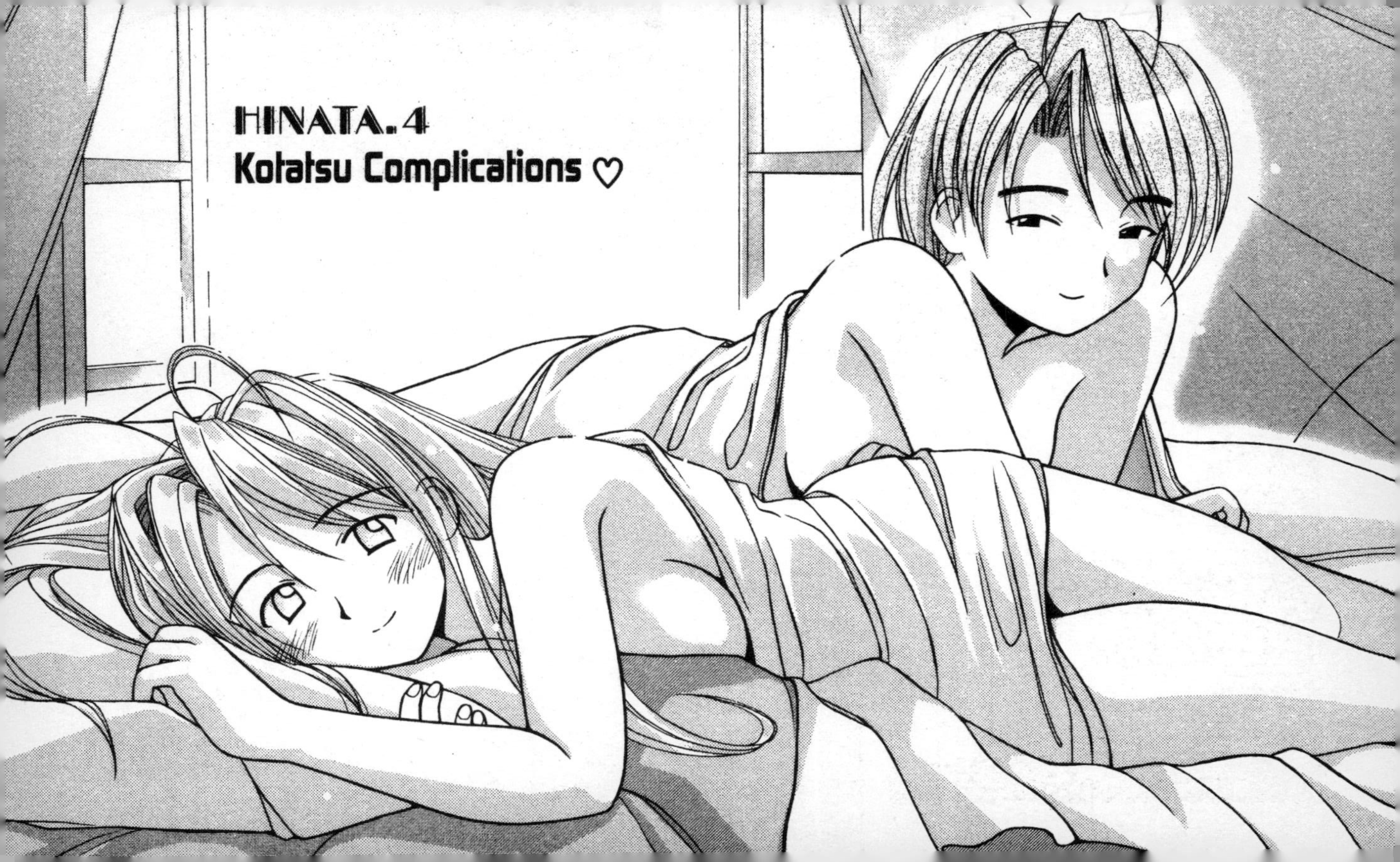
HINATA.4
Kotatsu Complications ♡

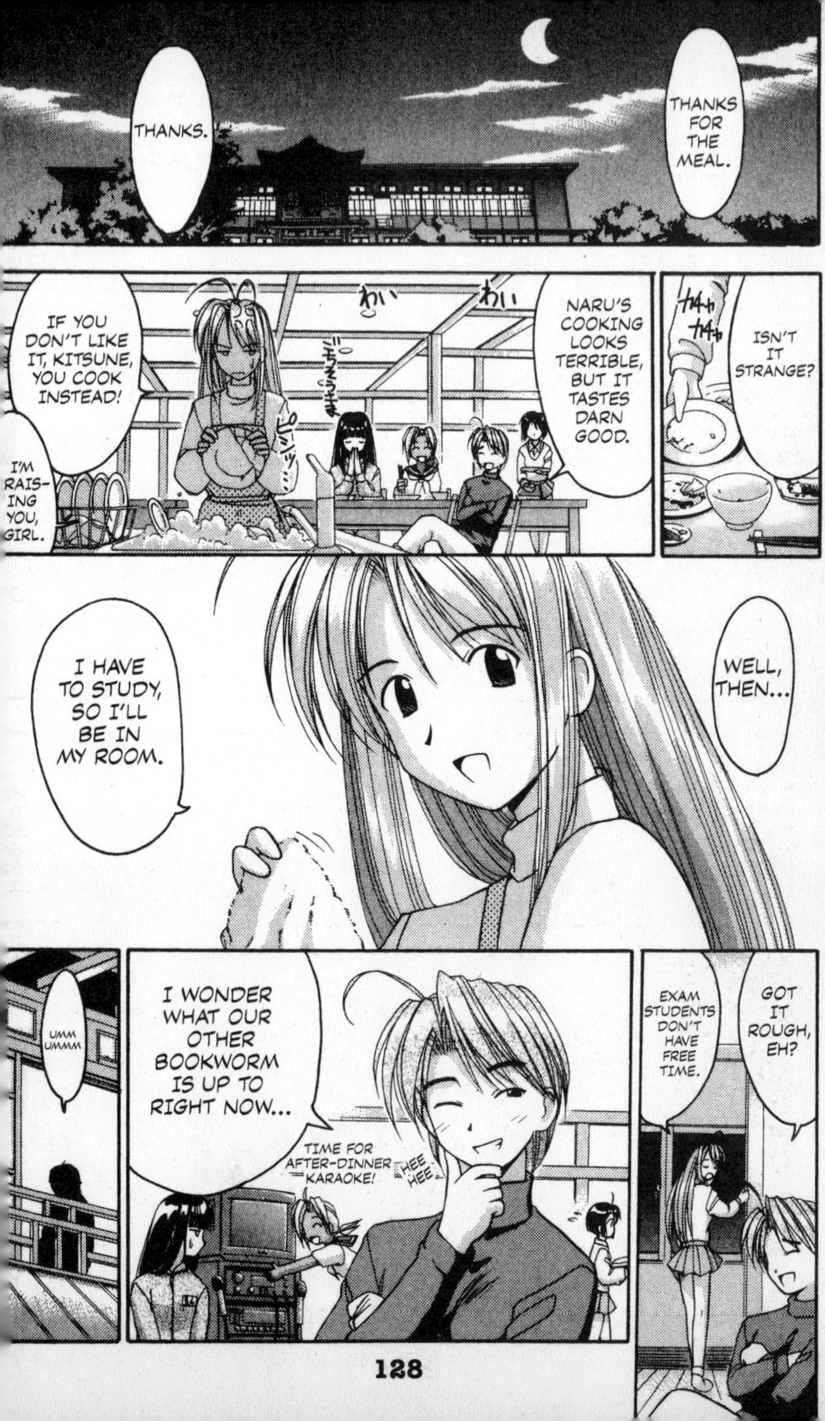
THANKS FOR THE MEAL.
THANKS.
ISN'T IT STRANGE?
NARU'S COOKING LOOKS TERRIBLE, BUT IT TASTES DARN GOOD.
IF YOU DON'T LIKE IT, KITSUNE, YOU COOK INSTEAD!
I'M RAISING YOU, GIRL.
WELL, THEN...
I HAVE TO STUDY, SO I'LL BE IN MY ROOM.
GOT IT ROUGH, EH?
EXAM STUDENTS DON'T HAVE FREE TIME.
I WONDER WHAT OUR OTHER BOOKWORM IS UP TO RIGHT NOW...
HEE HEE
TIME FOR AFTER-DINNER KARAOKE!
UMM UMMM

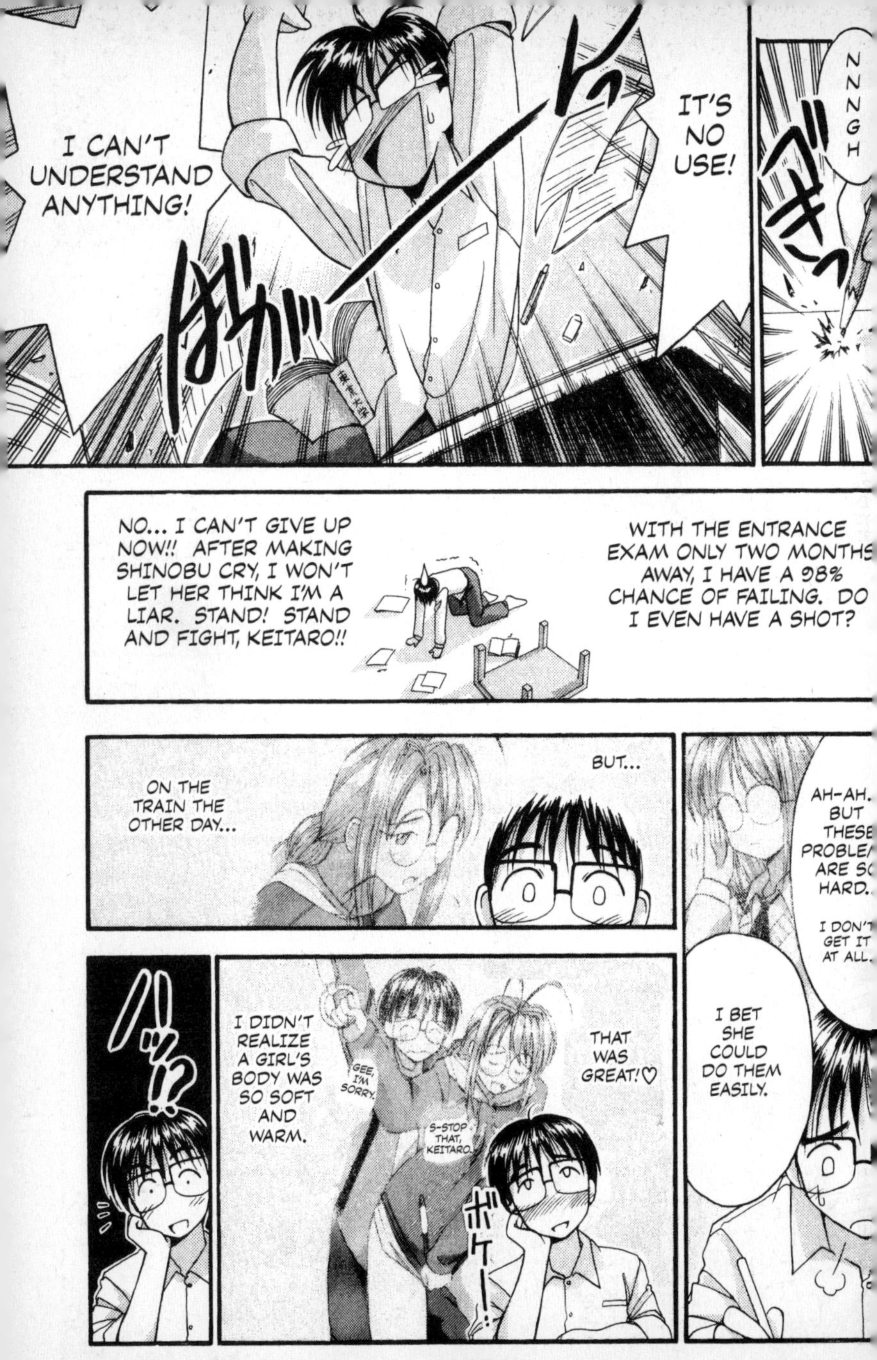
NNNGH
IT'S NO USE!
I CAN'T UNDERSTAND ANYTHING!
WITH THE ENTRANCE EXAM ONLY TWO MONTHS AWAY, I HAVE A 98% CHANCE OF FAILING. DO I EVEN HAVE A SHOT?
NO... I CAN'T GIVE UP NOW!! AFTER MAKING SHINOBU CRY, I WON'T LET HER THINK I'M A LIAR. STAND! STAND AND FIGHT, KEITARO!!
AH-AH. BUT THESE PROBLE ARE S HARD...
I DON'T GET IT AT ALL.
I BET SHE COULD DO THEM EASILY.
BUT...
ON THE TRAIN THE OTHER DAY...
THAT WAS GREAT!♡
I DIDN'T REALIZE A GIRL'S BODY WAS SO SOFT AND WARM.
GEE, I'M SORRY.
S-STOP THAT, KEITARO.

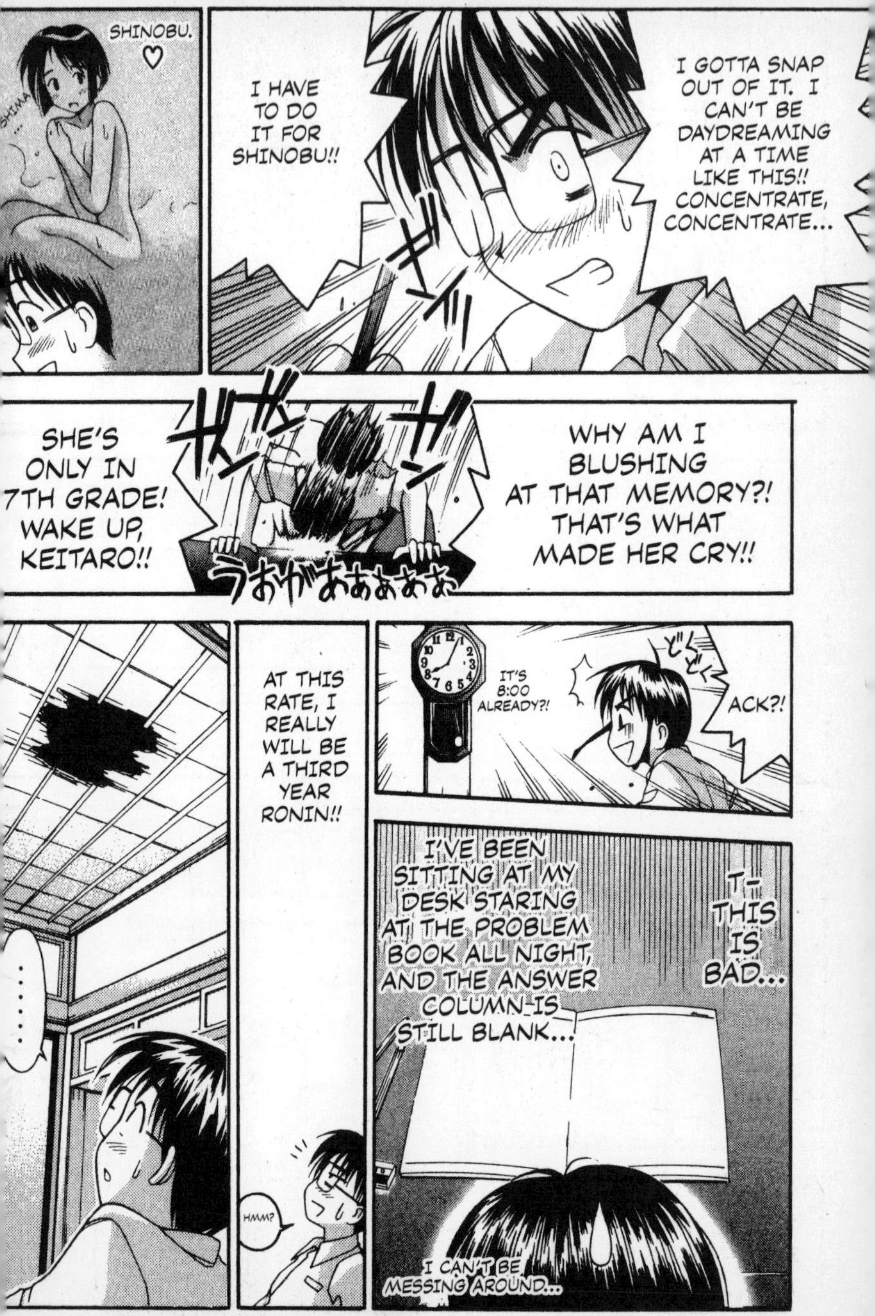
I GOTTA SNAP OUT OF IT. I CAN'T BE DAYDREAMING AT A TIME LIKE THIS!! CONCENTRATE, CONCENTRATE...
I HAVE TO DO IT FOR SHINOBU!!
SHINOBU. ♡
WHY AM I BLUSHING AT THAT MEMORY?! THAT'S WHAT MADE HER CRY!!
SHE'S ONLY IN 7TH GRADE! WAKE UP, KEITARO!!
うおがあああああ
ACK?!
どくどく
IT'S 8:00 ALREADY?!
T-THIS IS BAD...
I'VE BEEN SITTING AT MY DESK STARING AT THE PROBLEM BOOK ALL NIGHT, AND THE ANSWER COLUMN IS STILL BLANK...
I CAN'T BE MESSING AROUND...
AT THIS RATE, I REALLY WILL BE A THIRD YEAR RONIN!!
HMM?
......

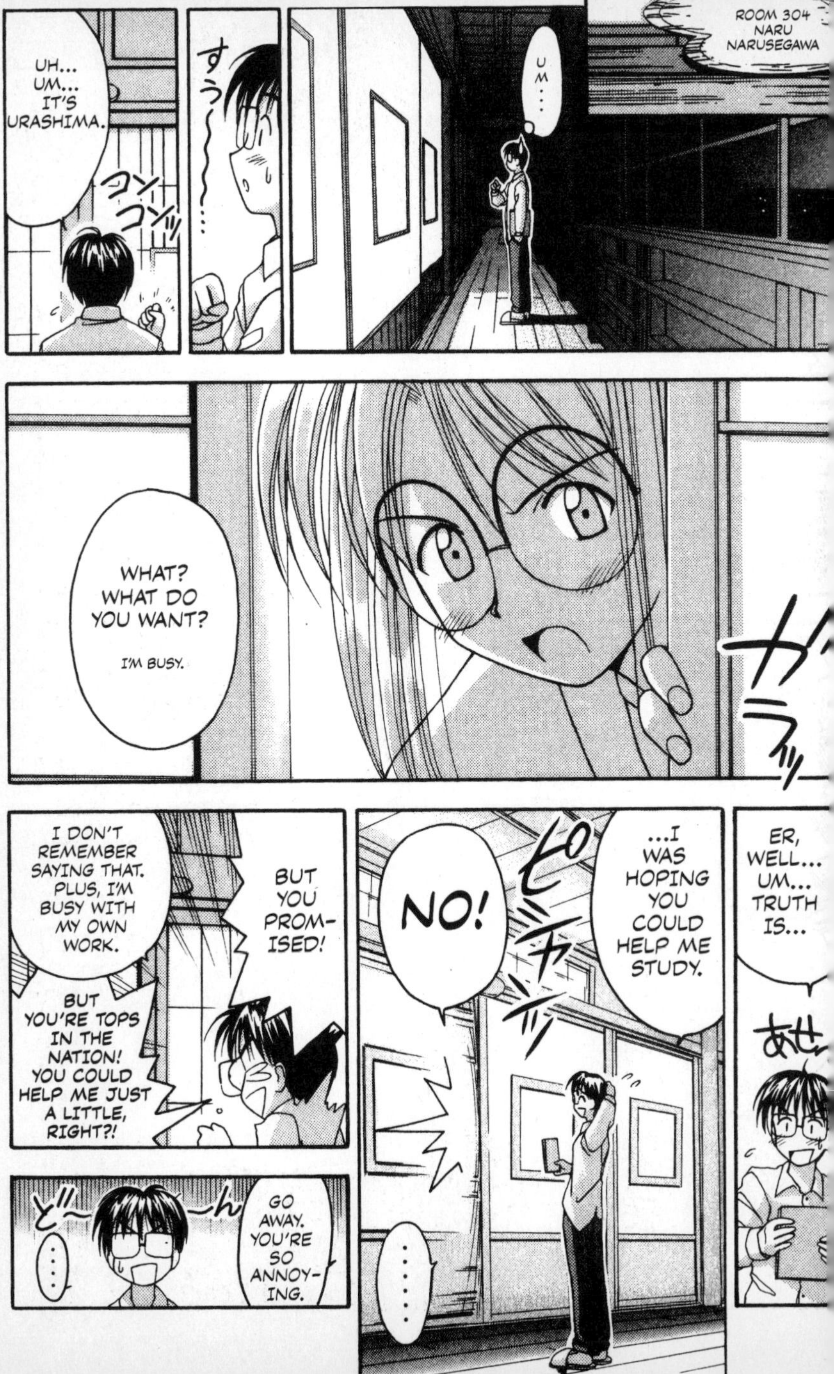
ROOM 304 NARU NARUSEGAWA
UM...
すう~...
UH... UM... IT'S URASHIMA.
コンコンッ
ガラッ
WHAT? WHAT DO YOU WANT?
I'M BUSY.
ER, WELL... UM... TRUTH IS...
あせ
...I WAS HOPING YOU COULD HELP ME STUDY.
ピシャッ
NO!
......
BUT YOU PROMISED!
I DON'T REMEMBER SAYING THAT. PLUS, I'M BUSY WITH MY OWN WORK.
BUT YOU'RE TOPS IN THE NATION! YOU COULD HELP ME JUST A LITTLE, RIGHT?!
GO AWAY. YOU'RE SO ANNOYING.
....

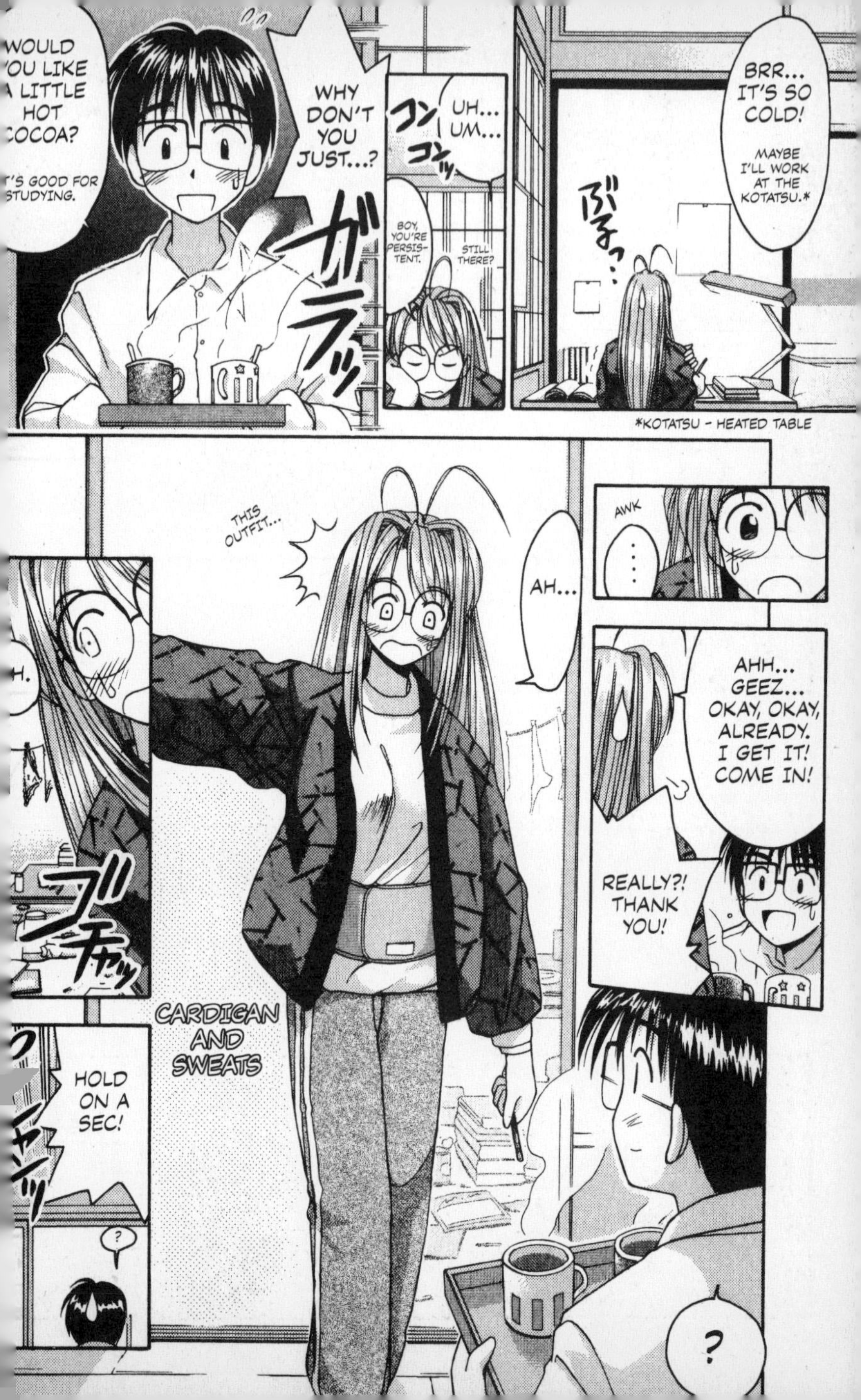
BRR... IT'S SO COLD!
MAYBE I'LL WORK AT THE KOTATSU.*
ぶるっ
UH... UM...
コンコンッ
STILL THERE?
BOY, YOU'RE PERSIST-TENT.
WHY DON'T YOU JUST...?
ガラッ
WOULD OU LIKE A LITTLE HOT COCOA?
T'S GOOD FOR STUDYING.
AWK
...
AHH... GEEZ... OKAY, OKAY, ALREADY. I GET IT! COME IN!
REALLY?! THANK YOU!
?
AH...
THIS OUTFIT...
CARDIGAN AND SWEATS
H.
ブチャッ
HOLD ON A SEC!
?
*KOTATSU - HEATED TABLE

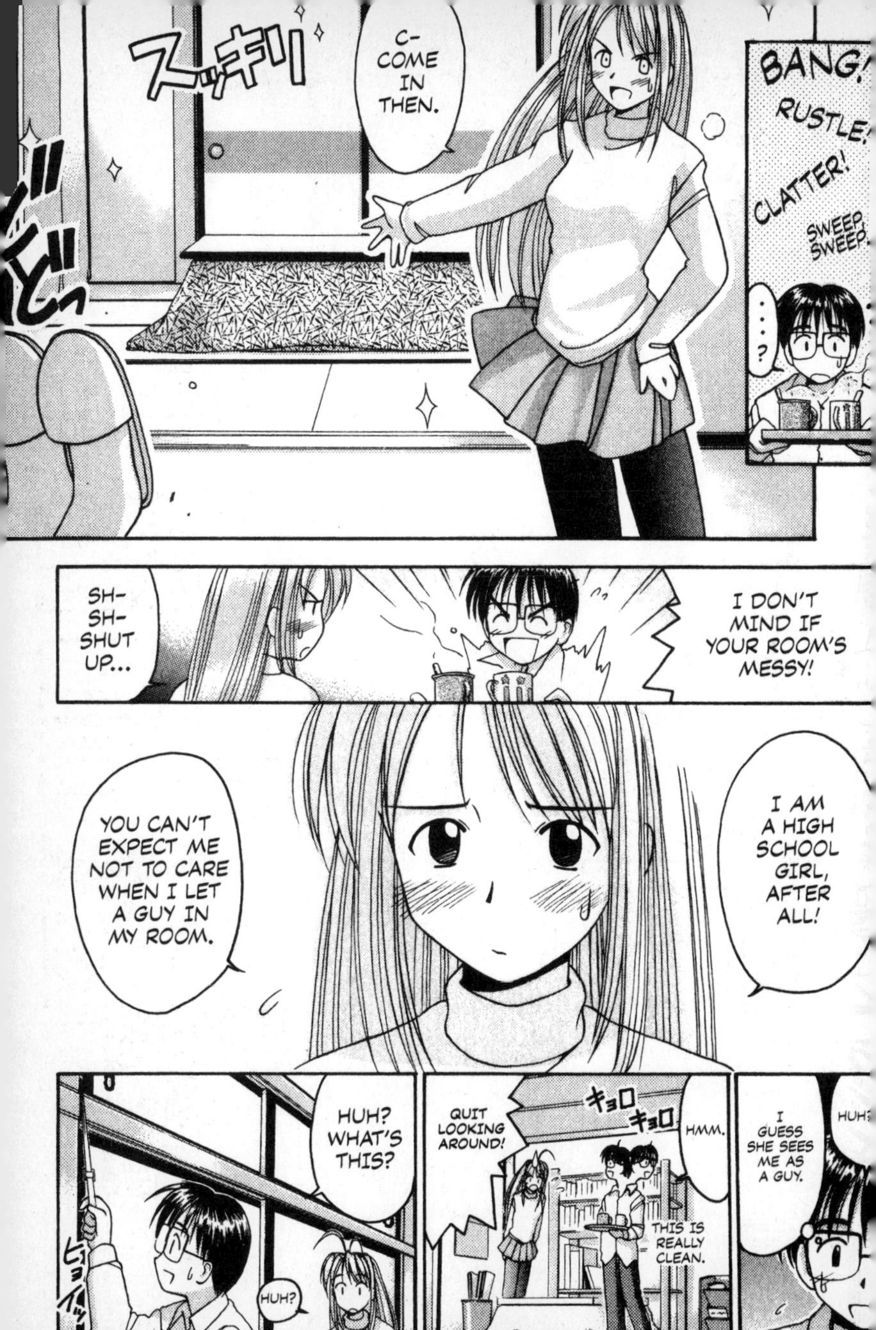
BANG!
RUSTLE!
CLATTER!
SWEEP SWEEP!
...?
C-COME IN THEN.
スッキリ
I DON'T MIND IF YOUR ROOM'S MESSY!
SH-SH-SHUT UP...
I AM A HIGH SCHOOL GIRL, AFTER ALL!
YOU CAN'T EXPECT ME NOT TO CARE WHEN I LET A GUY IN MY ROOM.
HUH?
I GUESS SHE SEES ME AS A GUY.
HMM.
キョロ キョロ
QUIT LOOKING AROUND!
THIS IS REALLY CLEAN.
HUH? WHAT'S THIS?
HUH?

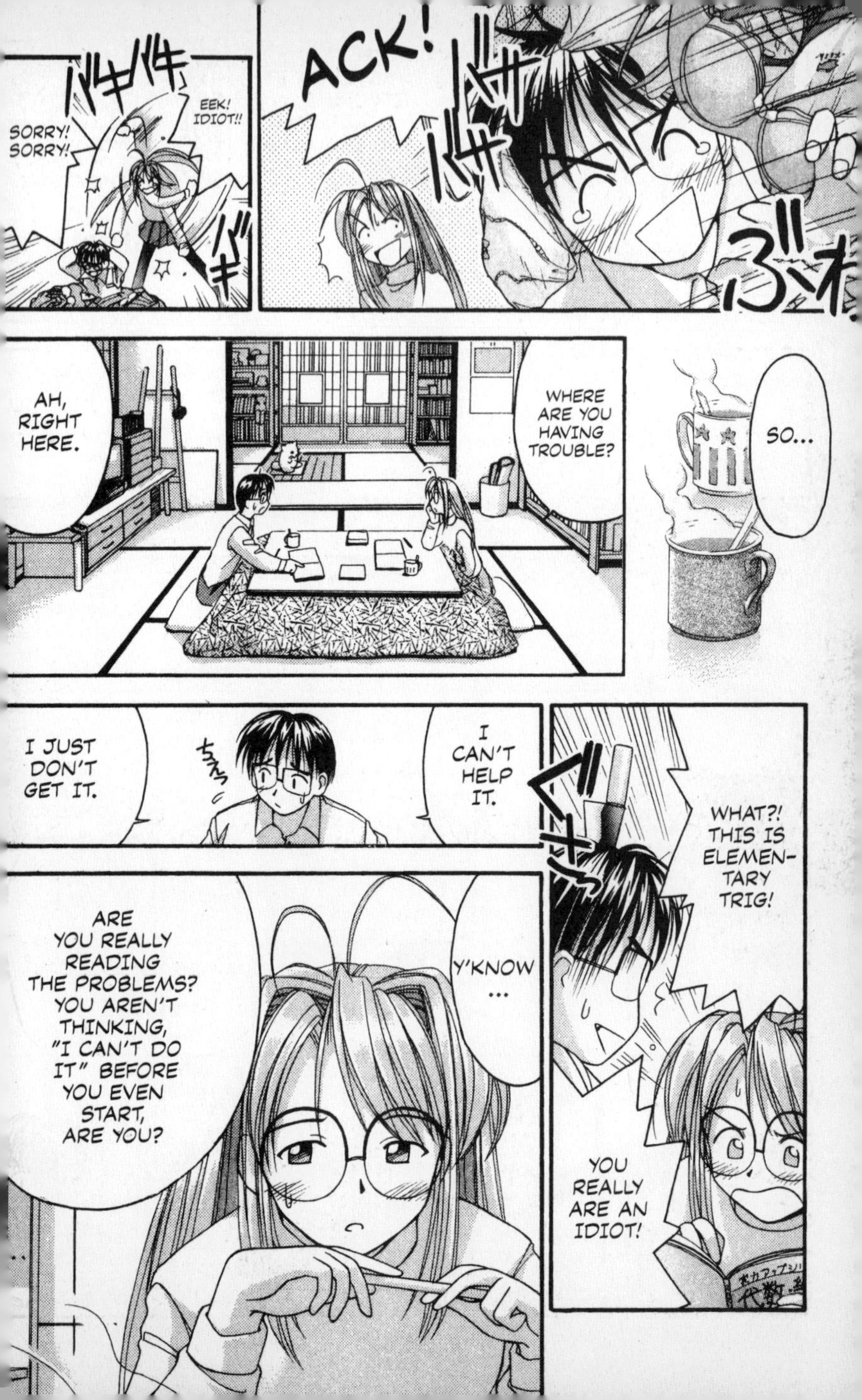
ACK!
EEK! IDIOT!!
SORRY! SORRY!
SO...
WHERE ARE YOU HAVING TROUBLE?
AH, RIGHT HERE.
WHAT?! THIS IS ELEMENTARY TRIG!
YOU REALLY ARE AN IDIOT!
I CAN'T HELP IT.
I JUST DON'T GET IT.
Y'KNOW ...
ARE YOU REALLY READING THE PROBLEMS? YOU AREN'T THINKING, "I CAN'T DO IT" BEFORE YOU EVEN START, ARE YOU?

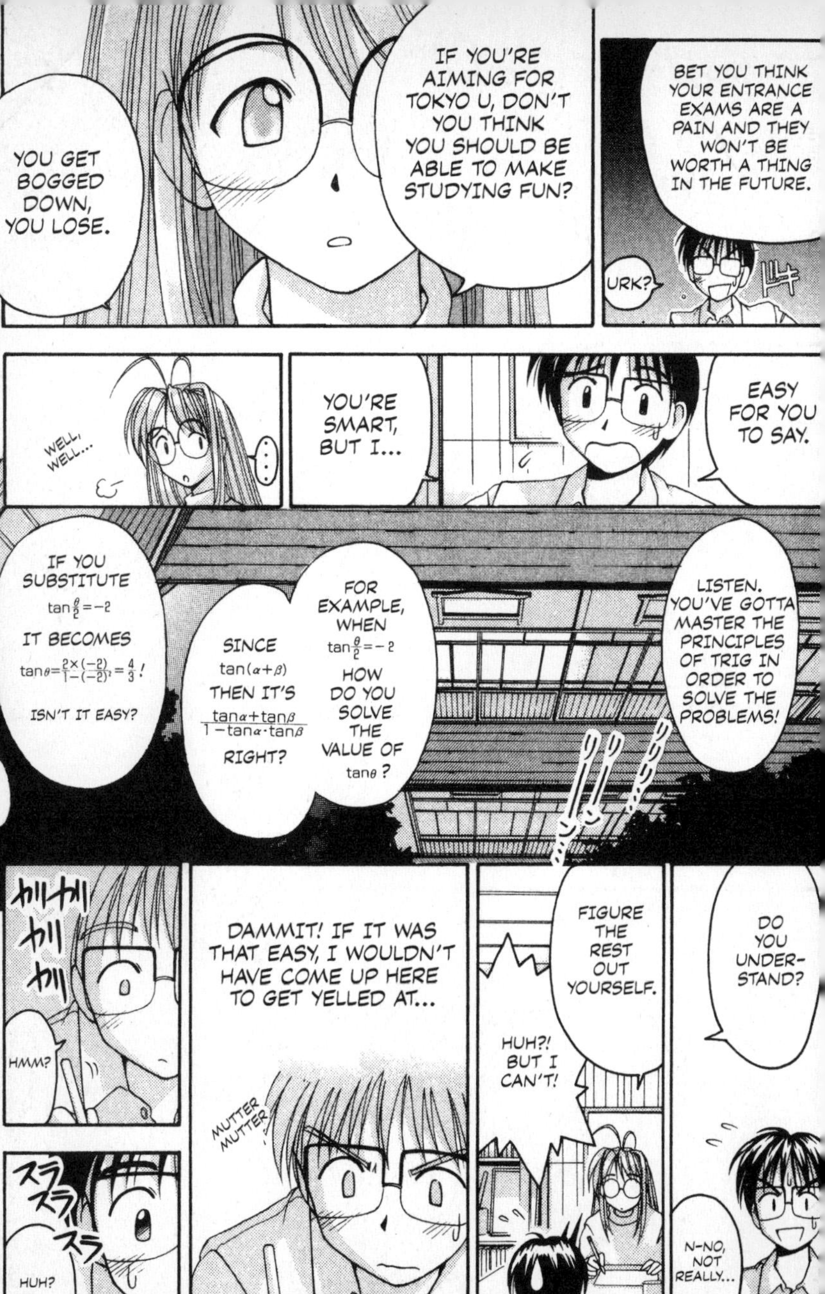

BET YOU THINK YOUR ENTRANCE EXAMS ARE A PAIN AND THEY WON'T BE WORTH A THING IN THE FUTURE.
URK?
ドキ
IF YOU'RE AIMING FOR TOKYO U, DON'T YOU THINK YOU SHOULD BE ABLE TO MAKE STUDYING FUN?
YOU GET BOGGED DOWN, YOU LOSE.
EASY FOR YOU TO SAY.
YOU'RE SMART, BUT I...
...
WELL, WELL...
LISTEN. YOU'VE GOTTA MASTER THE PRINCIPLES OF TRIG IN ORDER TO SOLVE THE PROBLEMS!
FOR EXAMPLE, WHEN $\tan\frac{\theta}{2}=-2$ HOW DO YOU SOLVE THE VALUE OF $\tan\theta$?
SINCE $\tan(\alpha+\beta)$ THEN IT'S $\frac{\tan\alpha+\tan\beta}{1-\tan\alpha\cdot\tan\beta}$ RIGHT?
IF YOU SUBSTITUTE $\tan\frac{\theta}{2}=-2$ IT BECOMES $\tan\theta=\frac{2\times(-2)}{1-(-2)^2}=\frac{4}{3}$! ISN'T IT EASY?
....
DO YOU UNDERSTAND?
N-NO, NOT REALLY...
FIGURE THE REST OUT YOURSELF.
HUH?! BUT I CAN'T!
DAMMIT! IF IT WAS THAT EASY, I WOULDN'T HAVE COME UP HERE TO GET YELLED AT...
MUTTER MUTTER
カリカリカリカリ
HMM?
スラスラスラ
HUH?

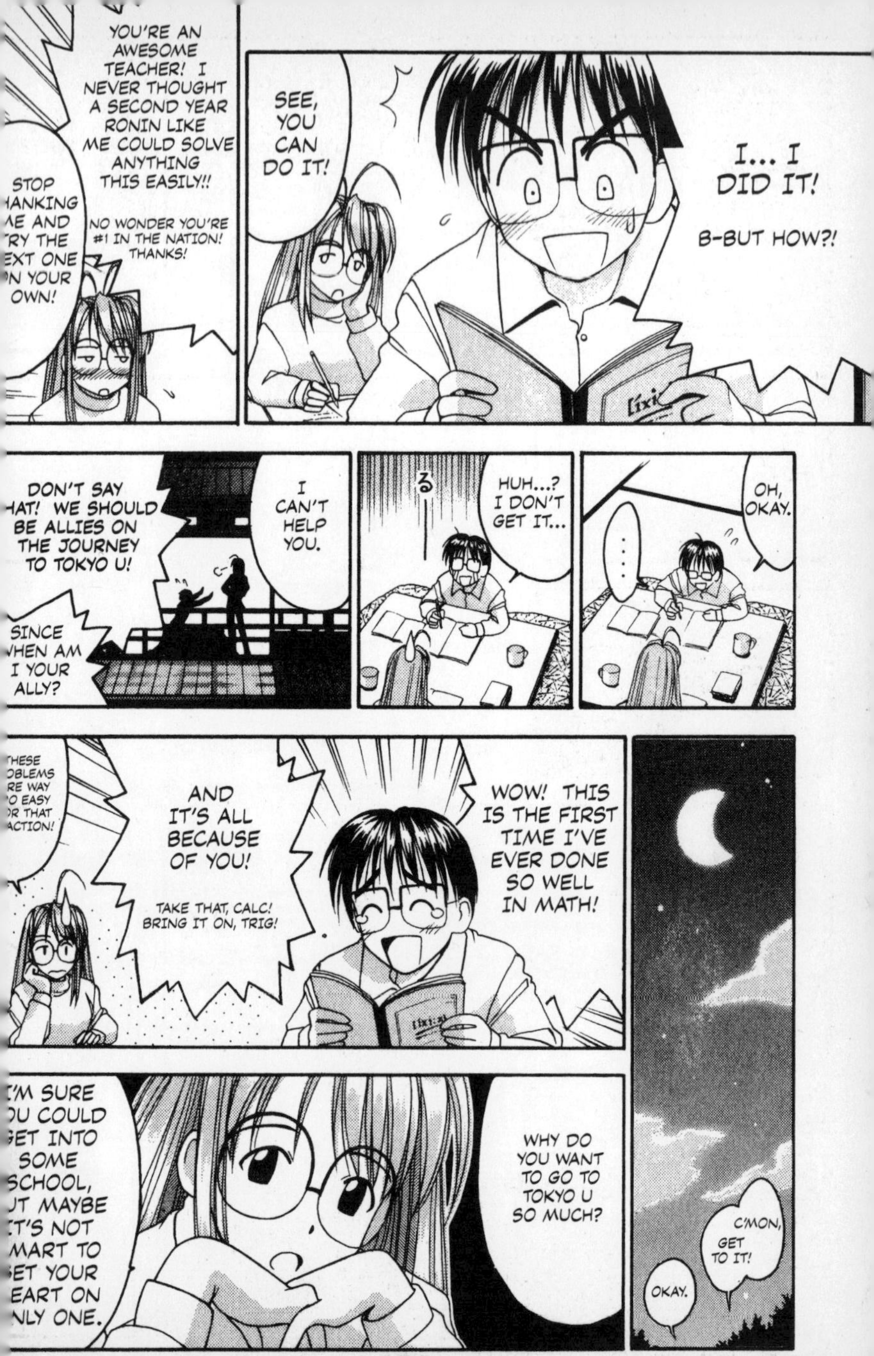
I... I DID IT!
B-BUT HOW?!
SEE, YOU CAN DO IT!
YOU'RE AN AWESOME TEACHER! I NEVER THOUGHT A SECOND YEAR RONIN LIKE ME COULD SOLVE ANYTHING THIS EASILY!!
NO WONDER YOU'RE #1 IN THE NATION! THANKS!
STOP HANKING ME AND RY THE EXT ONE N YOUR OWN!
OH, OKAY.
...
HUH...? I DON'T GET IT...
る
I CAN'T HELP YOU.
DON'T SAY HAT! WE SHOULD BE ALLIES ON THE JOURNEY TO TOKYO U!
SINCE VHEN AM I YOUR ALLY?
C'MON, GET TO IT!
OKAY.
WOW! THIS IS THE FIRST TIME I'VE EVER DONE SO WELL IN MATH!
AND IT'S ALL BECAUSE OF YOU!
TAKE THAT, CALC! BRING IT ON, TRIG!
HESE OBLEMS RE WAY O EASY OR THAT ACTION!
WHY DO YOU WANT TO GO TO TOKYO U SO MUCH?
'M SURE OU COULD GET INTO SOME SCHOOL, UT MAYBE T'S NOT MART TO ET YOUR EART ON NLY ONE.

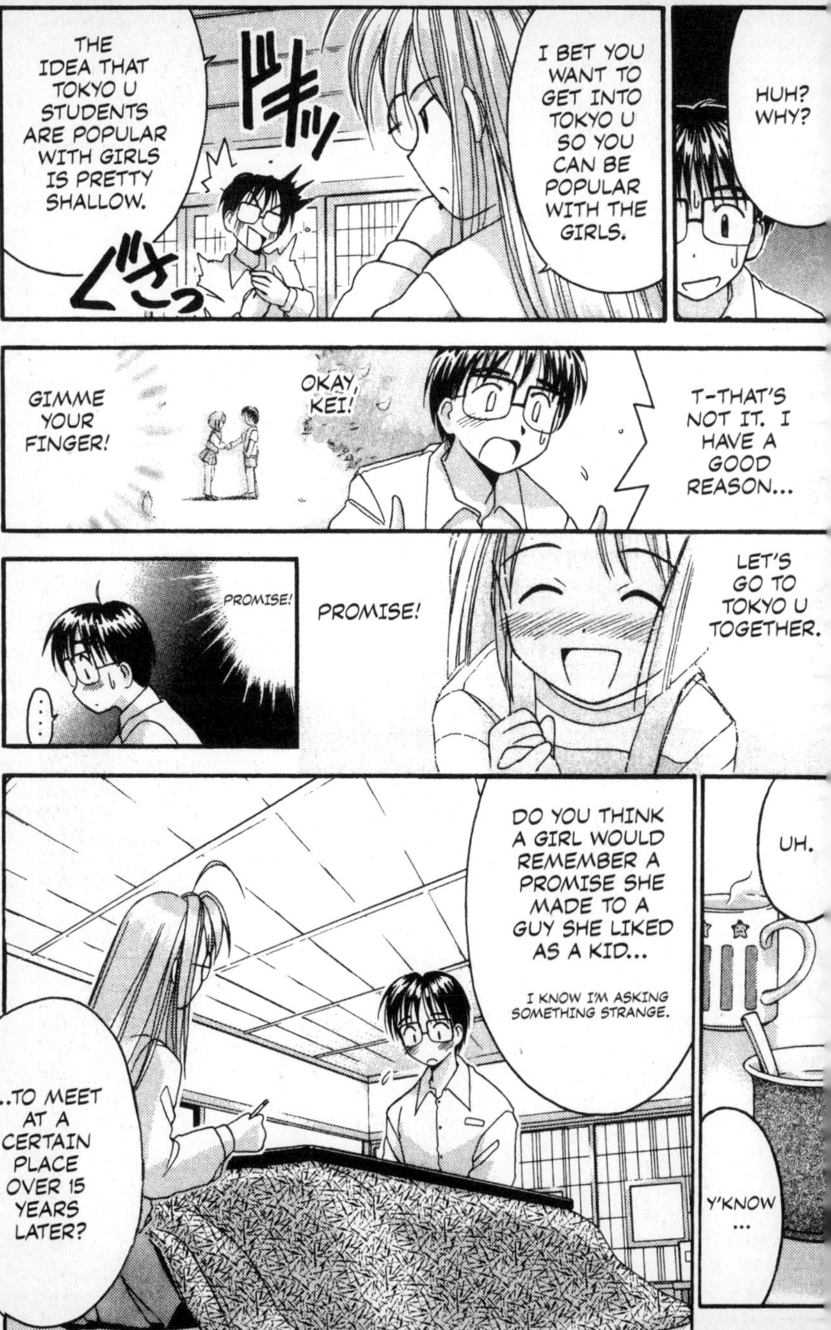
HUH? WHY?
I BET YOU WANT TO GET INTO TOKYO U SO YOU CAN BE POPULAR WITH THE GIRLS.
ドキッ
THE IDEA THAT TOKYO U STUDENTS ARE POPULAR WITH GIRLS IS PRETTY SHALLOW.
ぐさっ
T-THAT'S NOT IT. I HAVE A GOOD REASON...
OKAY, KEI!
GIMME YOUR FINGER!
LET'S GO TO TOKYO U TOGETHER.
PROMISE!
PROMISE!
....
UH.
Y'KNOW ...
DO YOU THINK A GIRL WOULD REMEMBER A PROMISE SHE MADE TO A GUY SHE LIKED AS A KID...
I KNOW I'M ASKING SOMETHING STRANGE.
...TO MEET AT A CERTAIN PLACE OVER 15 YEARS LATER?

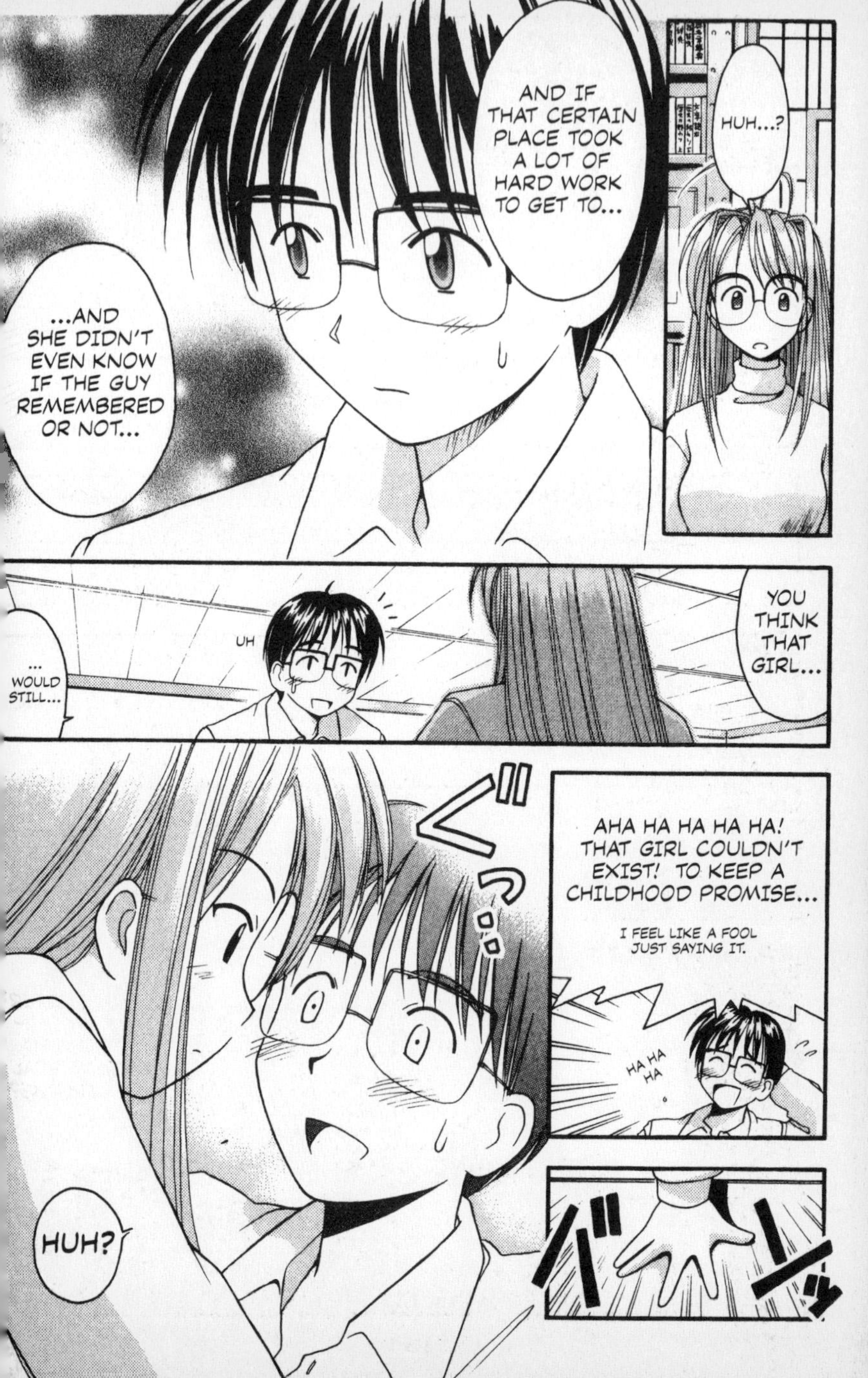
HUH...?
AND IF THAT CERTAIN PLACE TOOK A LOT OF HARD WORK TO GET TO...
...AND SHE DIDN'T EVEN KNOW IF THE GUY REMEMBERED OR NOT...
YOU THINK THAT GIRL...
UH
...WOULD STILL...
AHA HA HA HA HA! THAT GIRL COULDN'T EXIST! TO KEEP A CHILDHOOD PROMISE...
I FEEL LIKE A FOOL JUST SAYING IT.
HA HA HA
HUH?

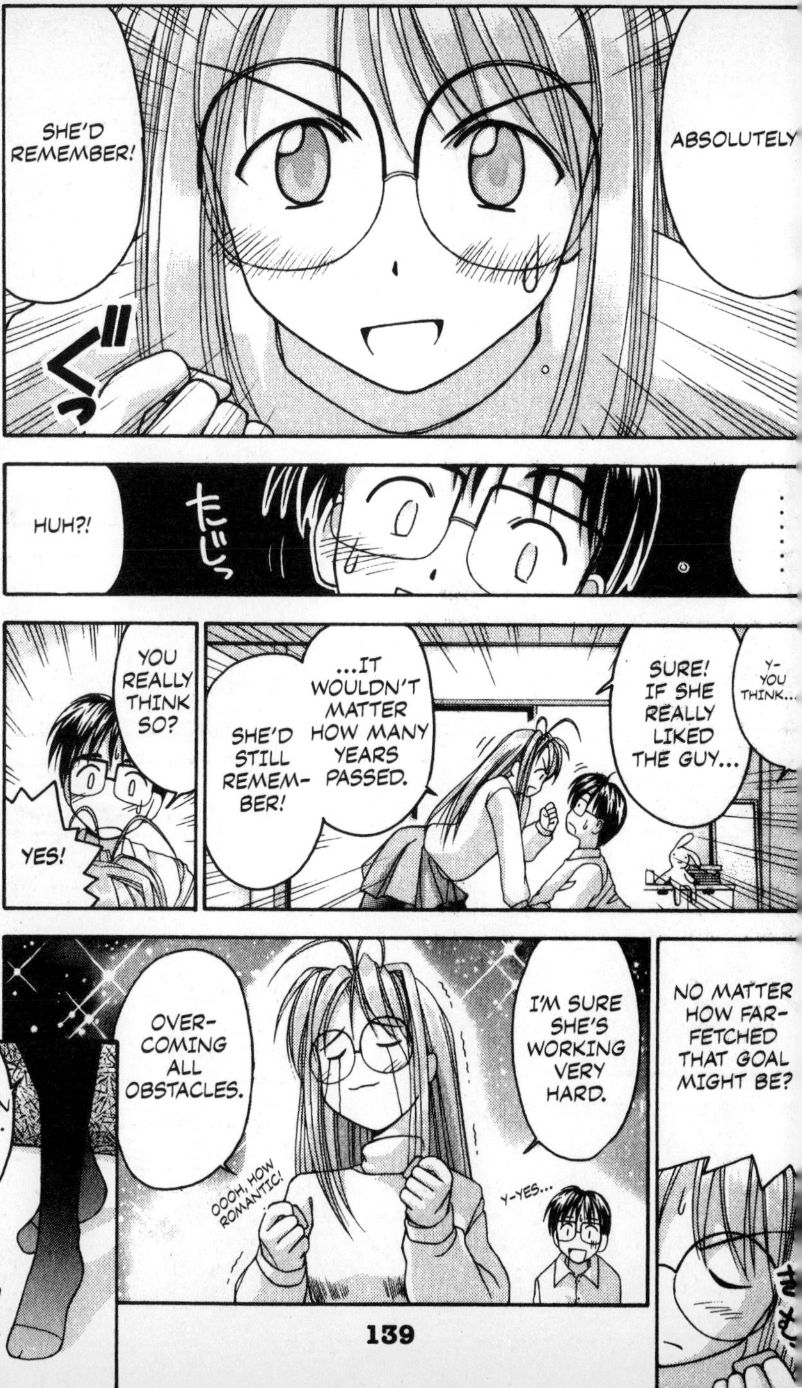
ABSOLUTELY
SHE'D REMEMBER!
ぐっ
...
たじっ
HUH?!
Y-YOU THINK...
SURE! IF SHE REALLY LIKED THE GUY...
...IT WOULDN'T MATTER HOW MANY YEARS PASSED.
SHE'D STILL REMEM-BER!
YOU REALLY THINK SO?
YES!
NO MATTER HOW FAR-FETCHED THAT GOAL MIGHT BE?
I'M SURE SHE'S WORKING VERY HARD.
OVER-COMING ALL OBSTACLES.
OOOH, HOW ROMANTIC!
Y-YES...
EVEN IF...
ギッ

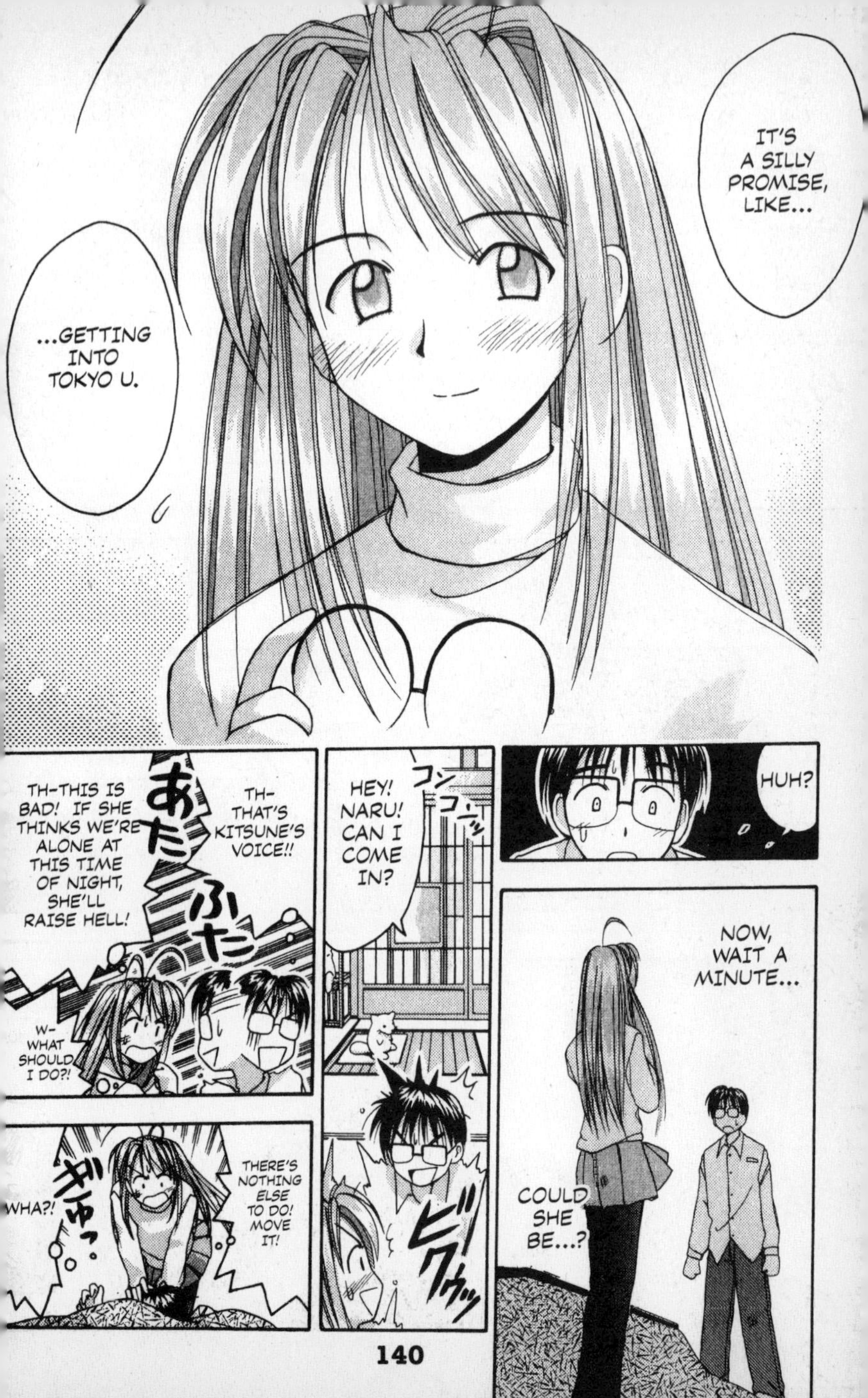
IT'S A SILLY PROMISE, LIKE...
...GETTING INTO TOKYO U.
HUH?
NOW, WAIT A MINUTE...
COULD SHE BE...?
コンコンッ
HEY! NARU! CAN I COME IN?
ビクゥッ
TH-THAT'S KITSUNE'S VOICE!!
TH-THIS IS BAD! IF SHE THINKS WE'RE ALONE AT THIS TIME OF NIGHT, SHE'LL RAISE HELL!
あたふた
W-WHAT SHOULD I DO?!
THERE'S NOTHING ELSE TO DO! MOVE IT!
ぎゅっ
WHA?!

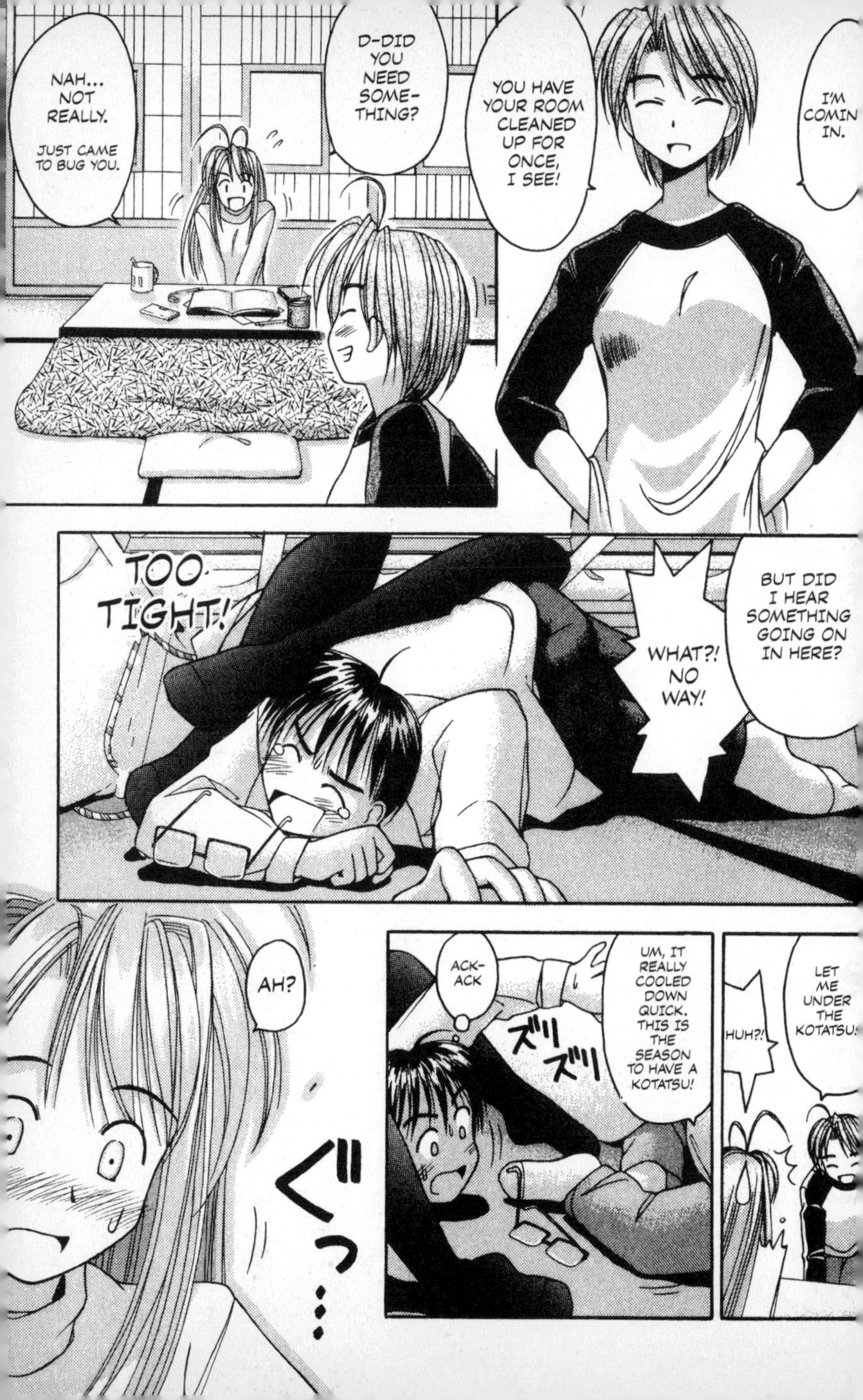
I'M COMIN IN.
YOU HAVE YOUR ROOM CLEANED UP FOR ONCE, I SEE!
D-DID YOU NEED SOMETHING?
NAH... NOT REALLY.
JUST CAME TO BUG YOU.
BUT DID I HEAR SOMETHING GOING ON IN HERE?
WHAT?! NO WAY!
TOO TIGHT!
LET ME UNDER THE KOTATSU.
HUH?!
UM, IT REALLY COOLED DOWN QUICK. THIS IS THE SEASON TO HAVE A KOTATSU!
ACK-ACK
ズリズリ
AH?
ぐっ…

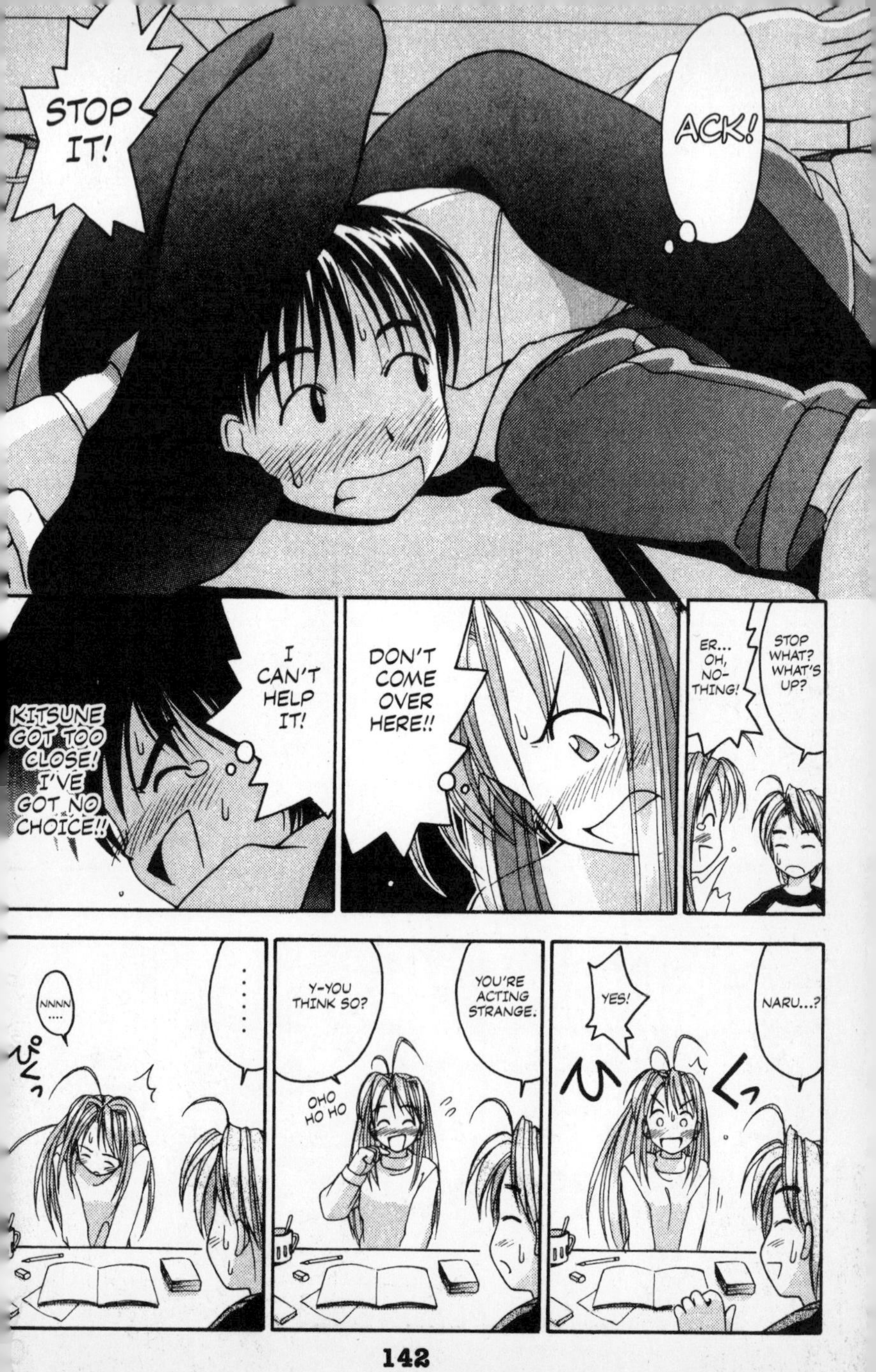
ACK!
STOP IT!
STOP WHAT? WHAT'S UP?
ER... OH, NO-THING!
DON'T COME OVER HERE!!
I CAN'T HELP IT!
KITSUNE GOT TOO CLOSE! I'VE GOT NO CHOICE!!
NARU...?
YES!
YOU'RE ACTING STRANGE.
Y-YOU THINK SO?
OHO HO HO
......
NNNN ....

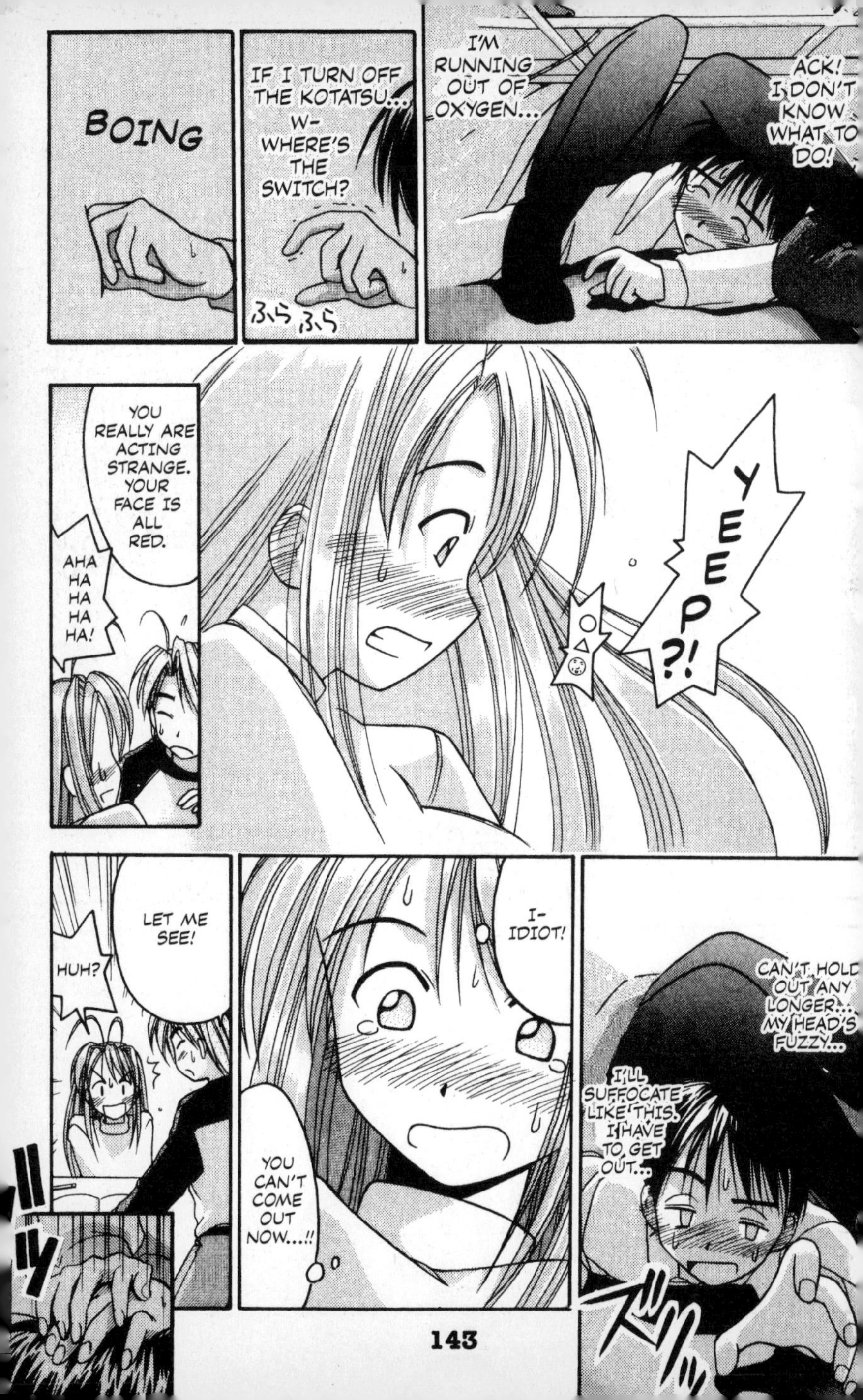
I'M RUNNING OUT OF OXYGEN...
ACK! I DON'T KNOW WHAT TO DO!
IF I TURN OFF THE KOTATSU...
W-WHERE'S THE SWITCH?
ふらふら
BOING
YEEP?!
YOU REALLY ARE ACTING STRANGE. YOUR FACE IS ALL RED.
AHA HA HA HA HA!
CAN'T HOLD OUT ANY LONGER... MY HEAD'S FUZZY...
I'LL SUFFOCATE LIKE THIS. I HAVE TO GET OUT...
I-IDIOT!
YOU CAN'T COME OUT NOW...!!
LET ME SEE!
HUH?

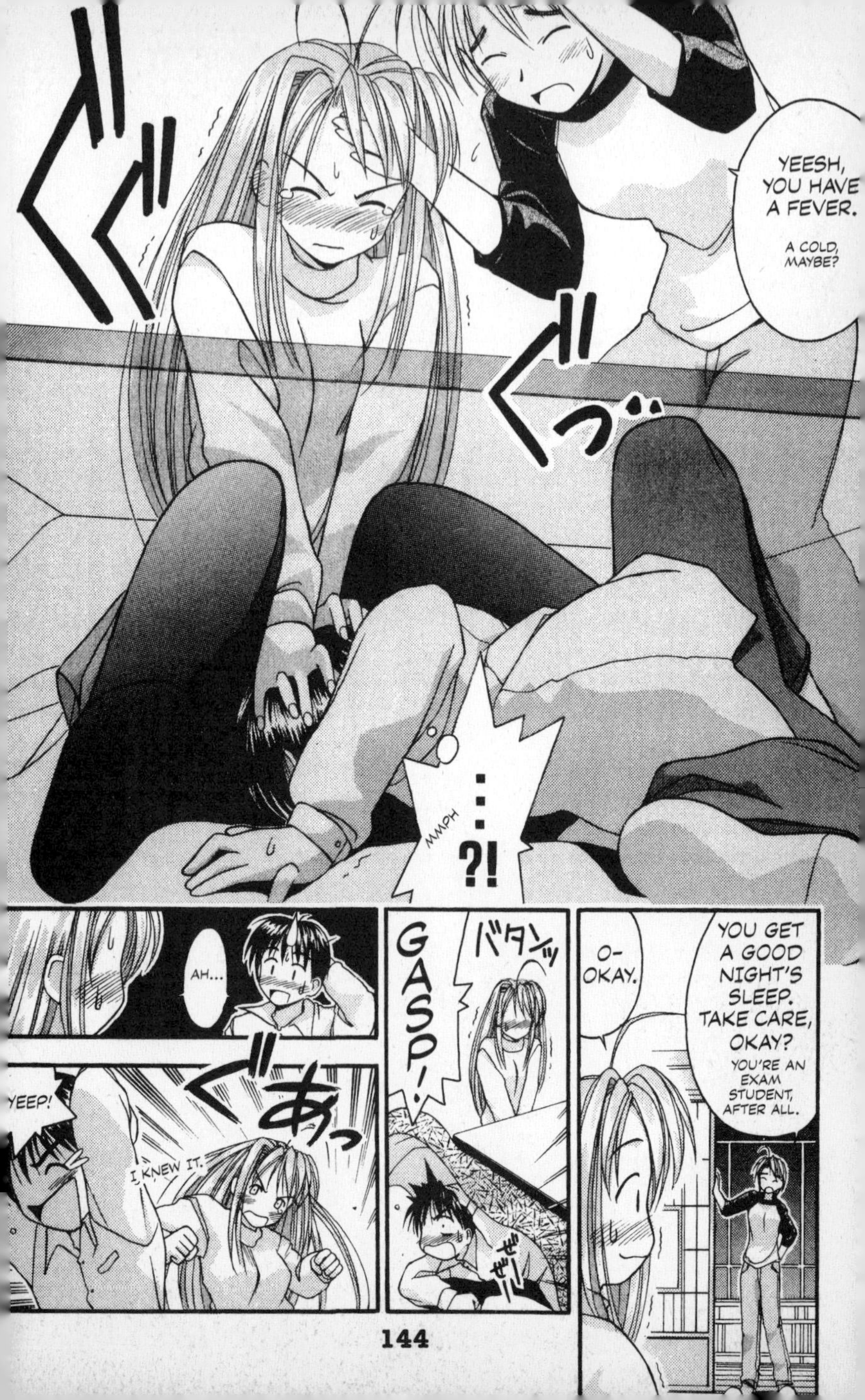
YEESH, YOU HAVE A FEVER.
A COLD, MAYBE?
MMPH
...?!
YOU GET A GOOD NIGHT'S SLEEP. TAKE CARE, OKAY?
YOU'RE AN EXAM STUDENT, AFTER ALL.
O- OKAY.
バタンッ
GASP!
ぜーぜー
AH...
YEEP!
ぐあっ
I KNEW IT.

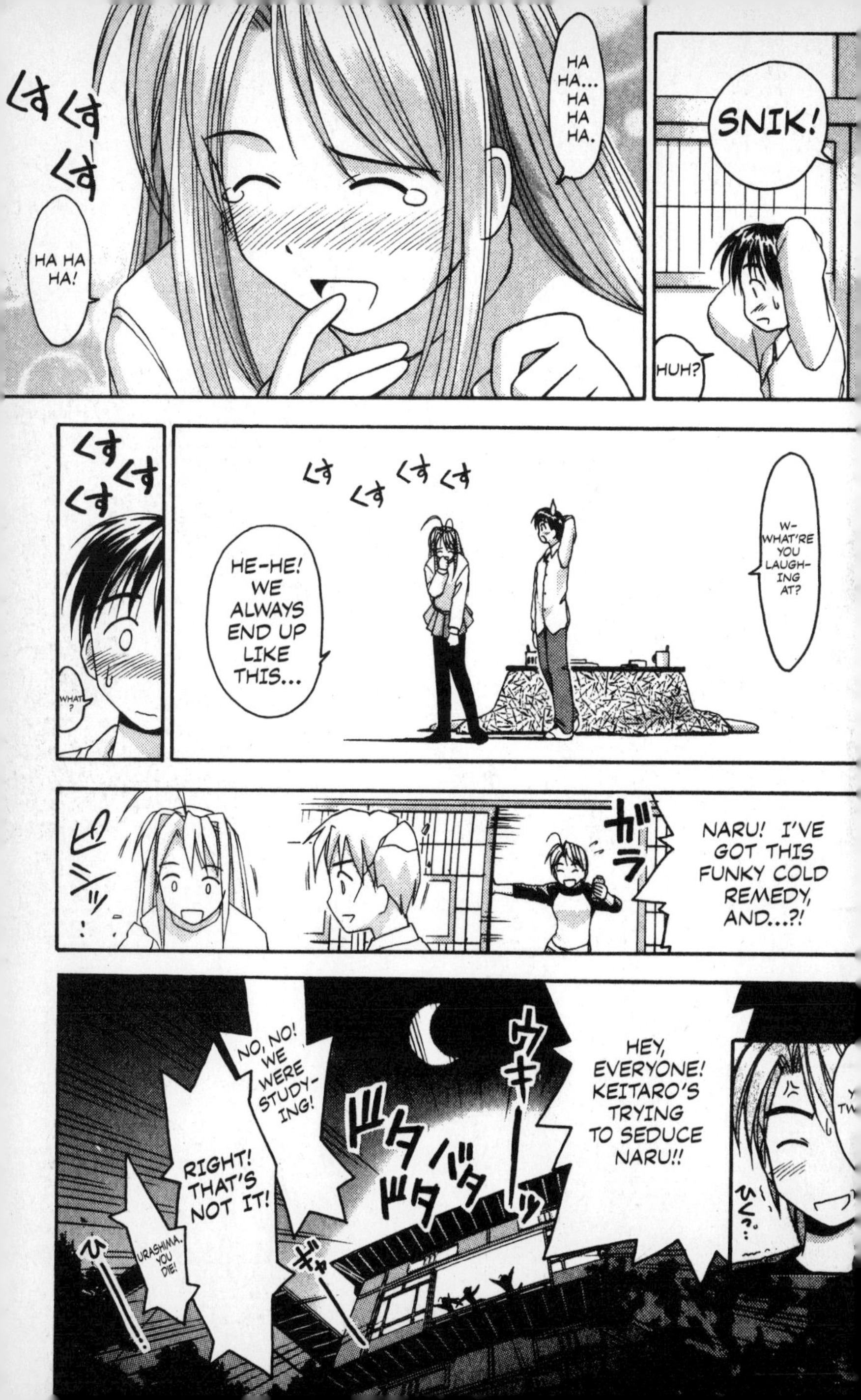
SNIK!
HUH?
HA HA... HA HA HA.
くすくす
くす
HA HA HA!
W-WHAT'RE YOU LAUGH-ING AT?
くす くす くす くす
HE-HE! WE ALWAYS END UP LIKE THIS...
くすくす
くす
WHAT?
NARU! I'VE GOT THIS FUNKY COLD REMEDY, AND...?!
ガラ
ピシッ
ひくっ
HEY, EVERYONE! KEITARO'S TRYING TO SEDUCE NARU!!
ウキーッ
ドタバタ
ドタ
NO, NO! WE WERE STUDY-ING!
RIGHT! THAT'S NOT IT!
ギャー
URASHIMA, YOU DIE!
ひ

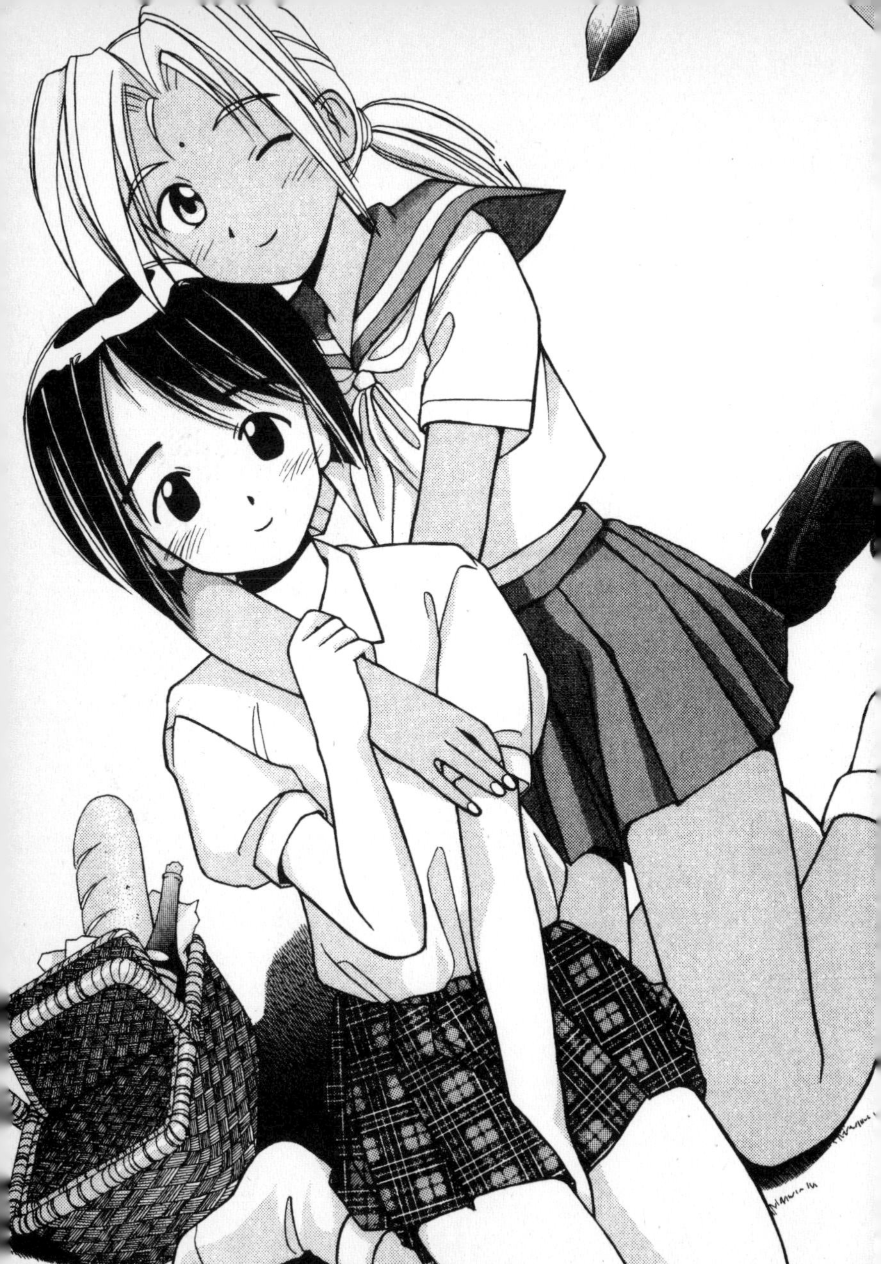

HINATA. 5 Don't Cry, Shinobu

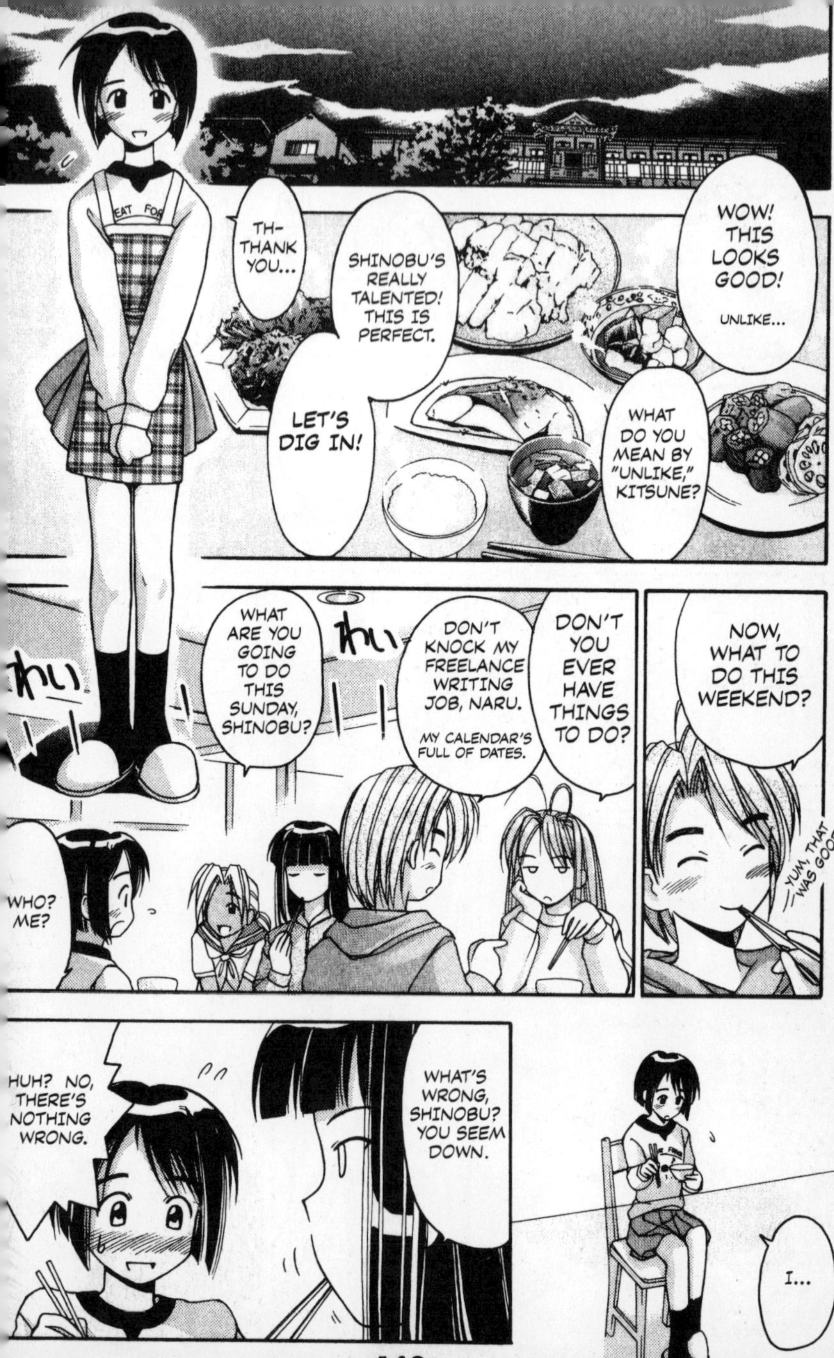
WOW! THIS LOOKS GOOD!
UNLIKE...
WHAT DO YOU MEAN BY "UNLIKE," KITSUNE?
SHINOBU'S REALLY TALENTED! THIS IS PERFECT.
LET'S DIG IN!
TH-THANK YOU...
NOW, WHAT TO DO THIS WEEKEND?
YUM, THAT WAS GOOD.
DON'T YOU EVER HAVE THINGS TO DO?
DON'T KNOCK MY FREELANCE WRITING JOB, NARU.
MY CALENDAR'S FULL OF DATES.
WHAT ARE YOU GOING TO DO THIS SUNDAY, SHINOBU?
WHO? ME?
I...
WHAT'S WRONG, SHINOBU? YOU SEEM DOWN.
HUH? NO, THERE'S NOTHING WRONG.

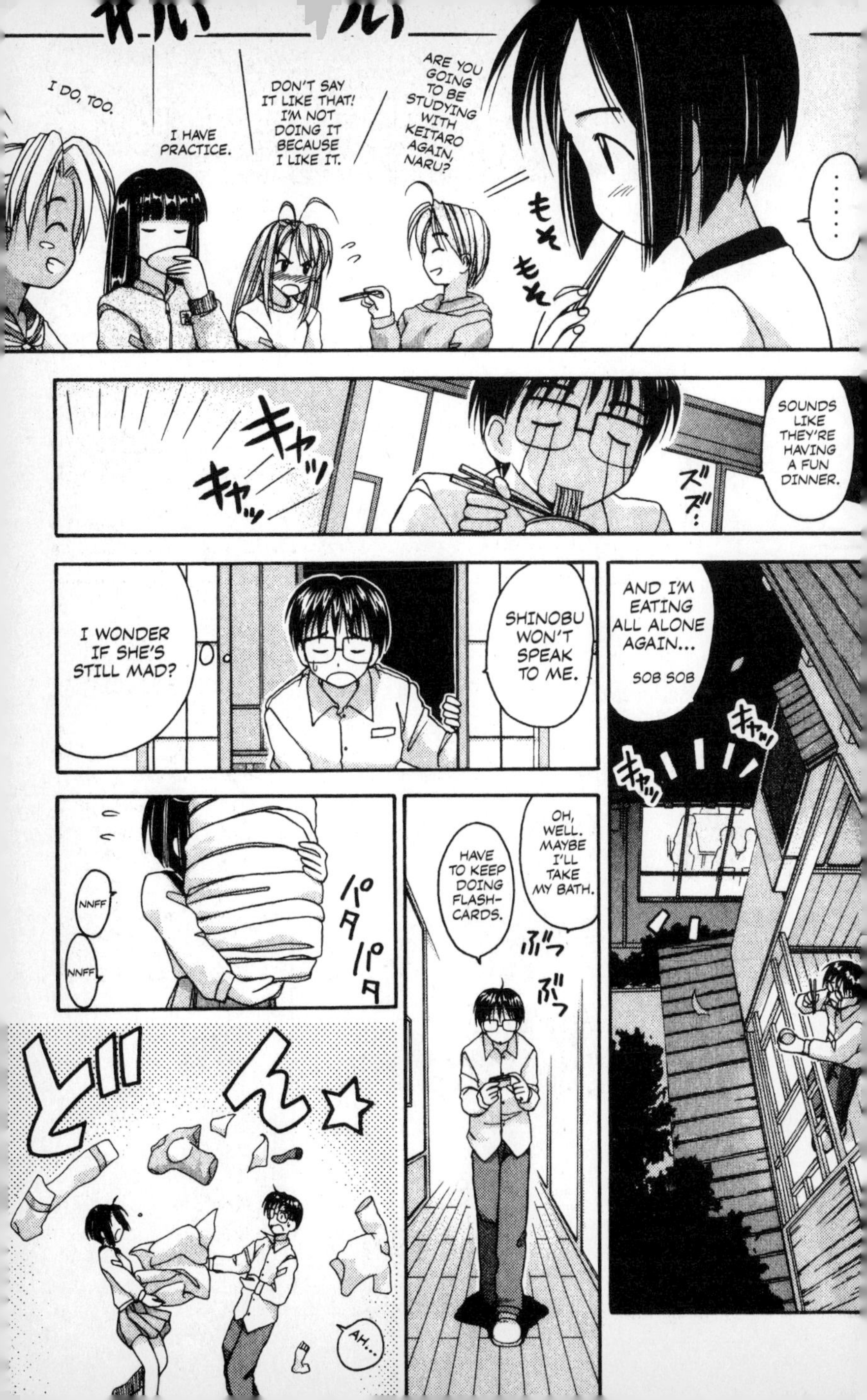
.....
ARE YOU GOING TO BE STUDYING WITH KEITARO AGAIN, NARU?
もそもそ
DON'T SAY IT LIKE THAT! I'M NOT DOING IT BECAUSE I LIKE IT.
I HAVE PRACTICE.
I DO, TOO.
SOUNDS LIKE THEY'RE HAVING A FUN DINNER.
ズズ…
キャッ キャッ
AND I'M EATING ALL ALONE AGAIN...
SOB SOB
キャッ キャッ
SHINOBU WON'T SPEAK TO ME.
I WONDER IF SHE'S STILL MAD?
OH, WELL. MAYBE I'LL TAKE MY BATH.
HAVE TO KEEP DOING FLASH-CARDS.
ぶつぶつ
NNFF
NNFF
パタパタ
どてん☆
AH...

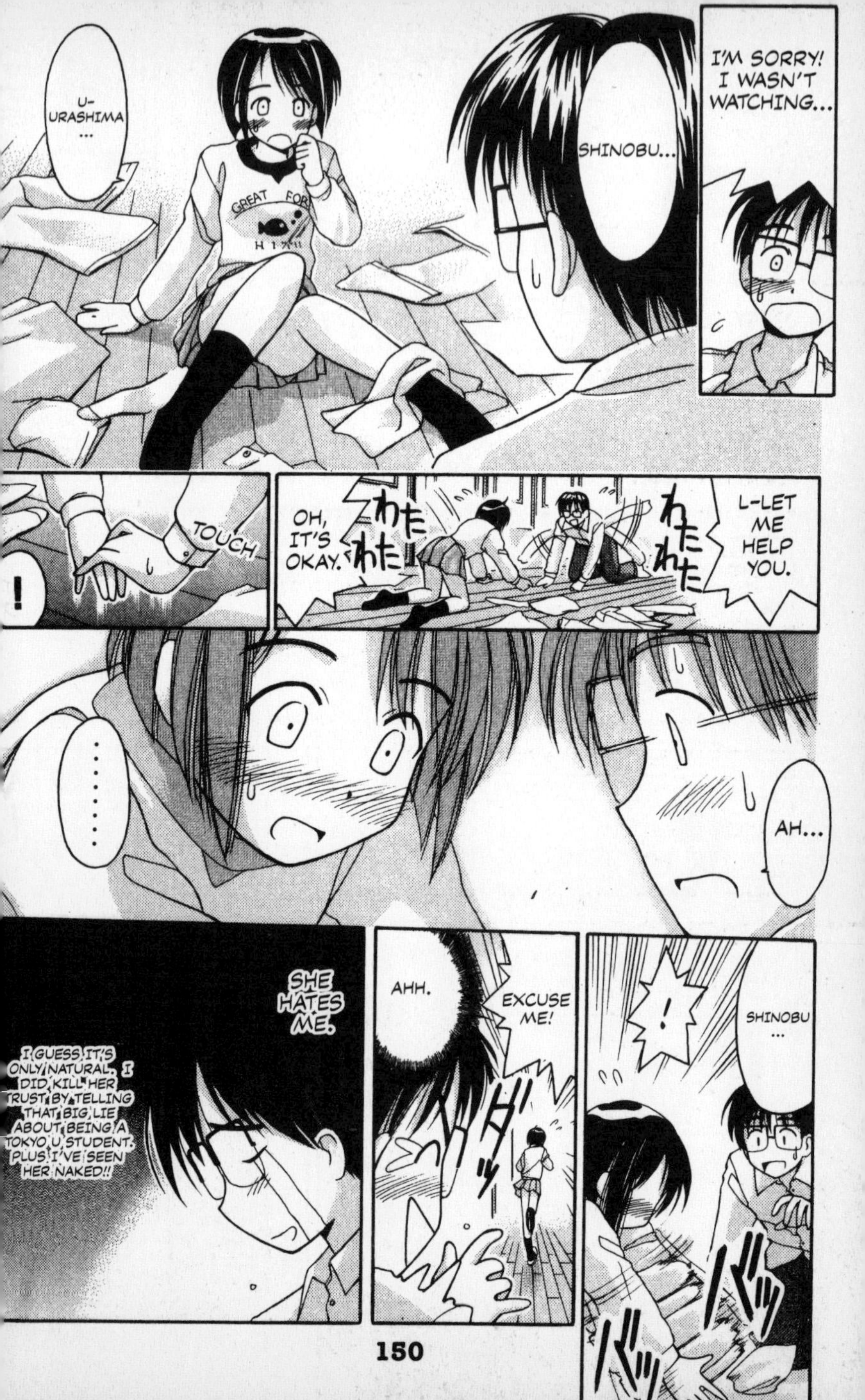
I'M SORRY! I WASN'T WATCHING...
SHINOBU...
U-URASHIMA...
L-LET ME HELP YOU.
わたわた
OH, IT'S OKAY.
わたわた
TOUCH
!
AH...
....
!
SHINOBU...
バッ
EXCUSE ME!
AHH.
ダッ
SHE HATES ME.
I GUESS IT'S ONLY NATURAL. I DID KILL HER TRUST BY TELLING THAT BIG LIE ABOUT BEING A TOKYO U STUDENT. PLUS I'VE SEEN HER NAKED!!

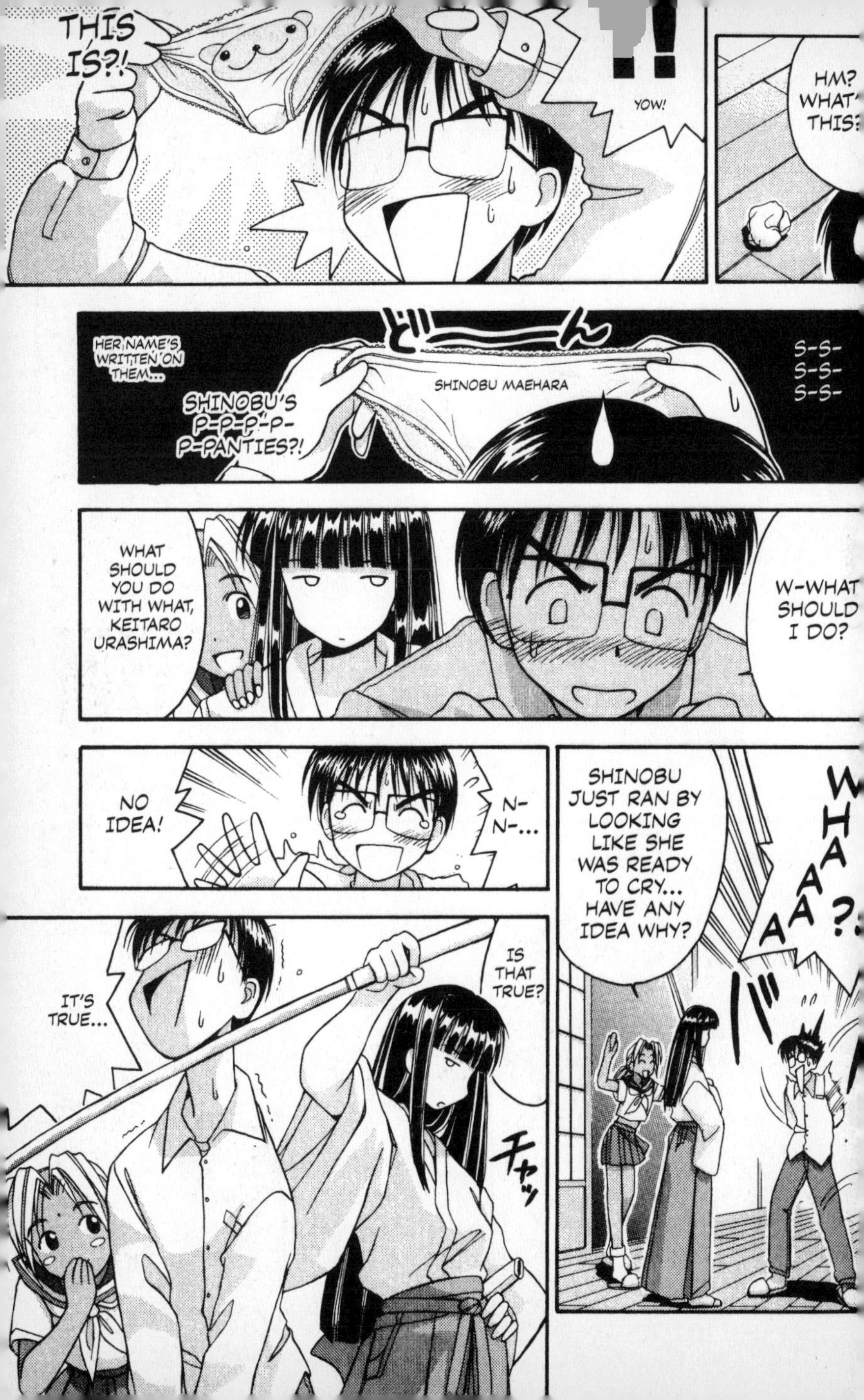
HM? WHAT' THIS?
!!
YOW!
THIS IS?!
S-S-S-S-S-S-
どーーーん
SHINOBU MAEHARA
HER NAME'S WRITTEN ON THEM...
SHINOBU'S P-P-P-P-P-PANTIES?!
W-WHAT SHOULD I DO?
WHAT SHOULD YOU DO WITH WHAT, KEITARO URASHIMA?
WHAAAAA?!
ド
SHINOBU JUST RAN BY LOOKING LIKE SHE WAS READY TO CRY... HAVE ANY IDEA WHY?
N-N-...
NO IDEA!
IS THAT TRUE?
IT'S TRUE...
チャッ

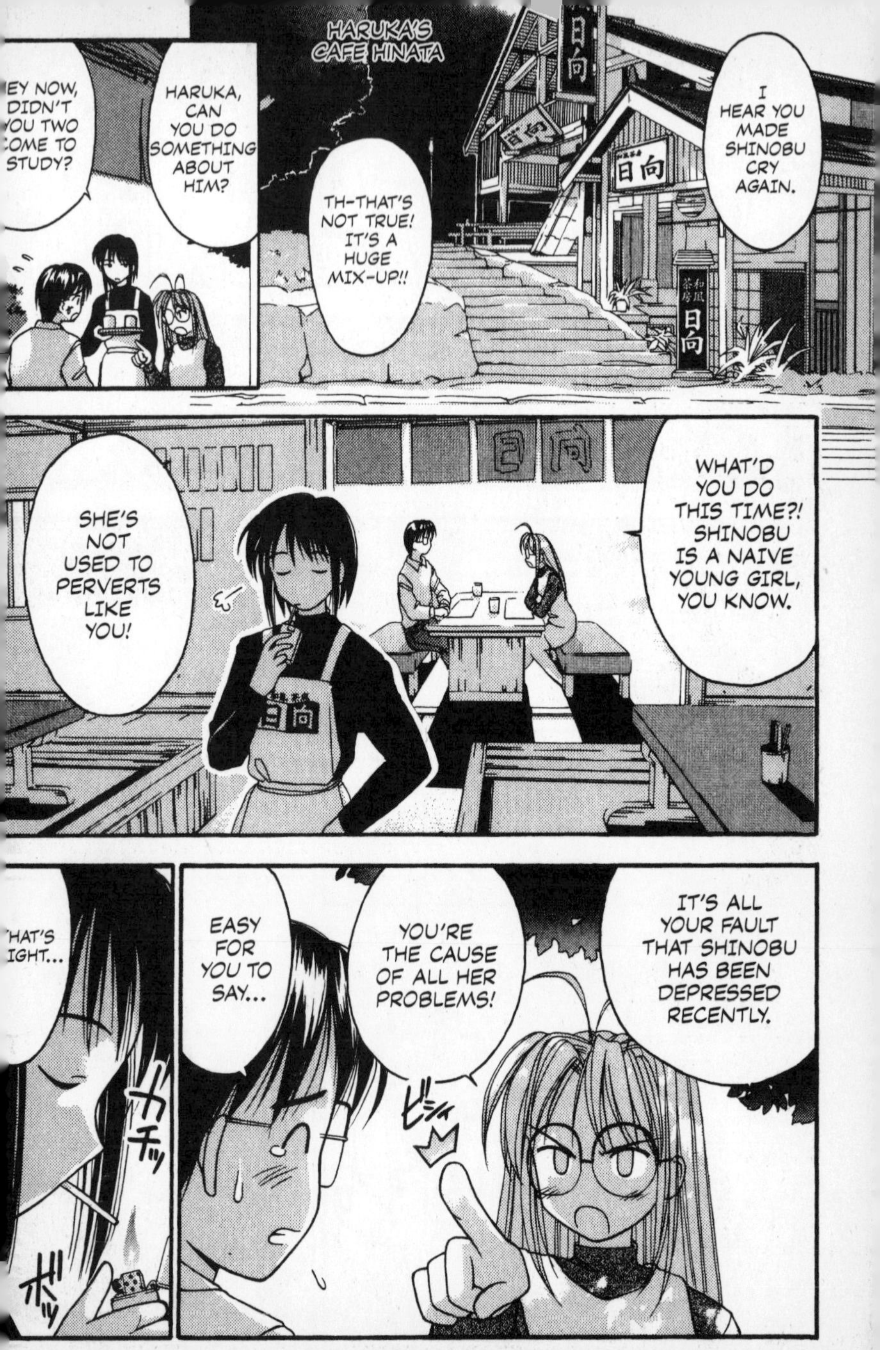
HARUKA'S CAFE HINATA
I HEAR YOU MADE SHINOBU CRY AGAIN.
TH-THAT'S NOT TRUE! IT'S A HUGE MIX-UP!!
HARUKA, CAN YOU DO SOMETHING ABOUT HIM?
EY NOW, DIDN'T OU TWO OME TO STUDY?
WHAT'D YOU DO THIS TIME?! SHINOBU IS A NAIVE YOUNG GIRL, YOU KNOW.
SHE'S NOT USED TO PERVERTS LIKE YOU!
IT'S ALL YOUR FAULT THAT SHINOBU HAS BEEN DEPRESSED RECENTLY.
YOU'RE THE CAUSE OF ALL HER PROBLEMS!
EASY FOR YOU TO SAY...
HAT'S IGHT...

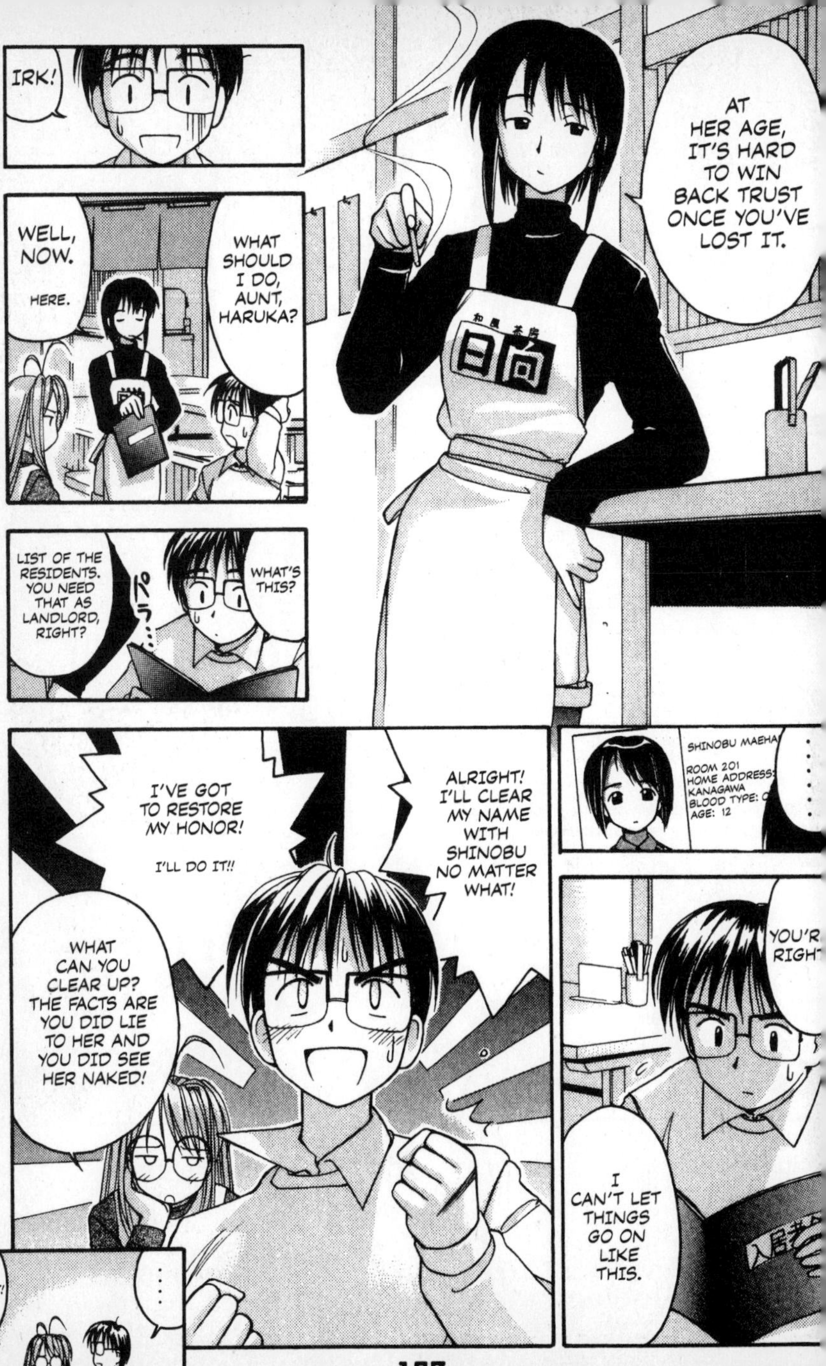
AT HER AGE, IT'S HARD TO WIN BACK TRUST ONCE YOU'VE LOST IT.
日向
IRK!
WHAT SHOULD I DO, AUNT, HARUKA?
WELL, NOW.
HERE.
WHAT'S THIS?
LIST OF THE RESIDENTS. YOU NEED THAT AS LANDLORD, RIGHT?
パラ…
. . . .
SHINOBU MAEHA
ROOM 201
HOME ADDRESS:
KANAGAWA
BLOOD TYPE:
AGE: 12
YOU'R
RIGHT
I CAN'T LET THINGS GO ON LIKE THIS.
ALRIGHT! I'LL CLEAR MY NAME WITH SHINOBU NO MATTER WHAT!
I'VE GOT TO RESTORE MY HONOR!
I'LL DO IT!!
WHAT CAN YOU CLEAR UP? THE FACTS ARE YOU DID LIE TO HER AND YOU DID SEE HER NAKED!
. . . .
IDIOT!

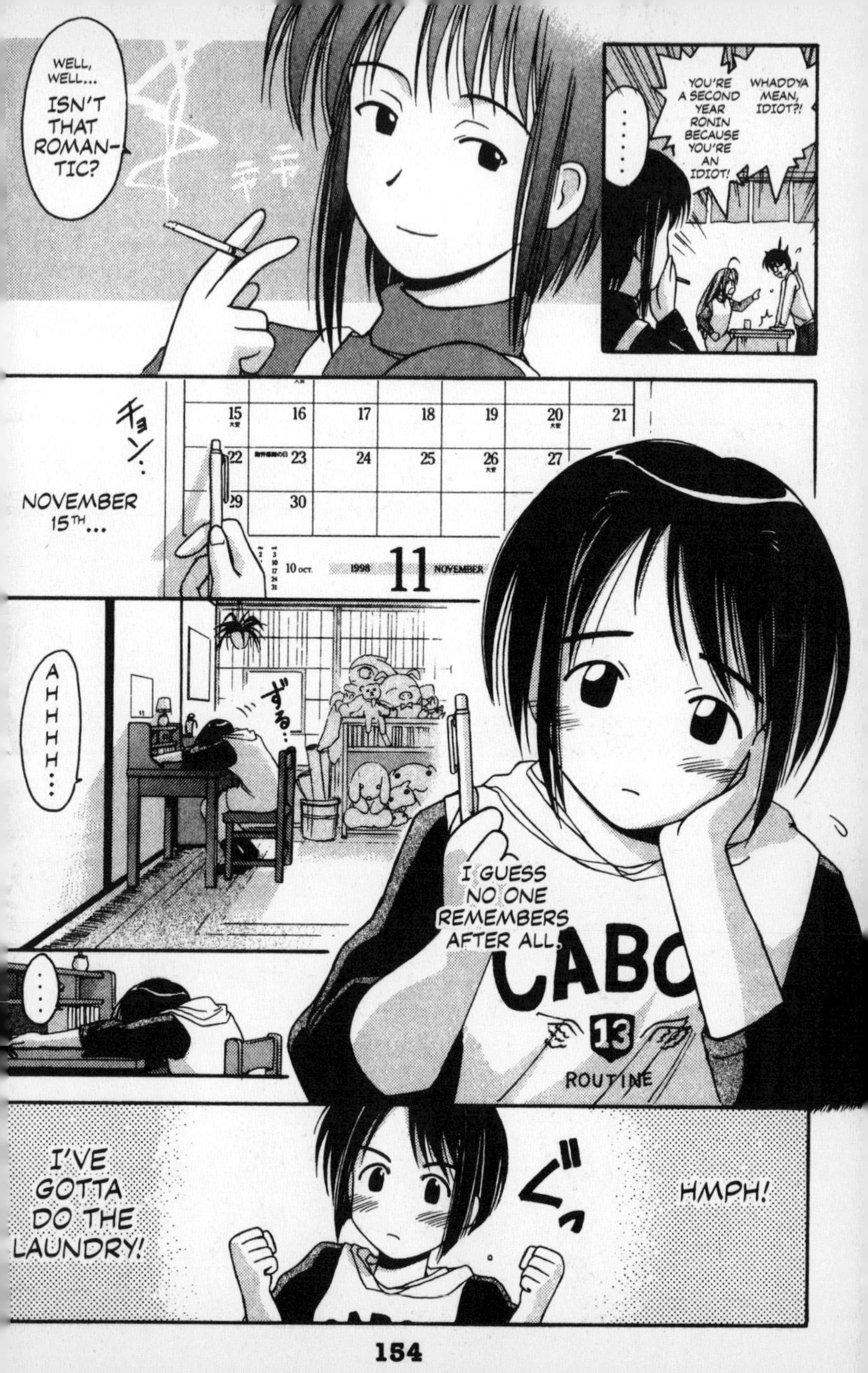
WHADDYA MEAN, IDIOT?!
YOU'RE A SECOND YEAR RONIN BECAUSE YOU'RE AN IDIOT!
......
WELL, WELL... ISN'T THAT ROMANTIC?
チョン...
NOVEMBER 15TH...
15 16 17 18 19 20 21
22 23 24 25 26 27
29 30
10 OCT.
1998
11
NOVEMBER
I GUESS NO ONE REMEMBERS AFTER ALL.
CABO
13
ROUTINE
AHHHH...
ずる...
......
HMPH!
ぐっ
I'VE GOTTA DO THE LAUNDRY!

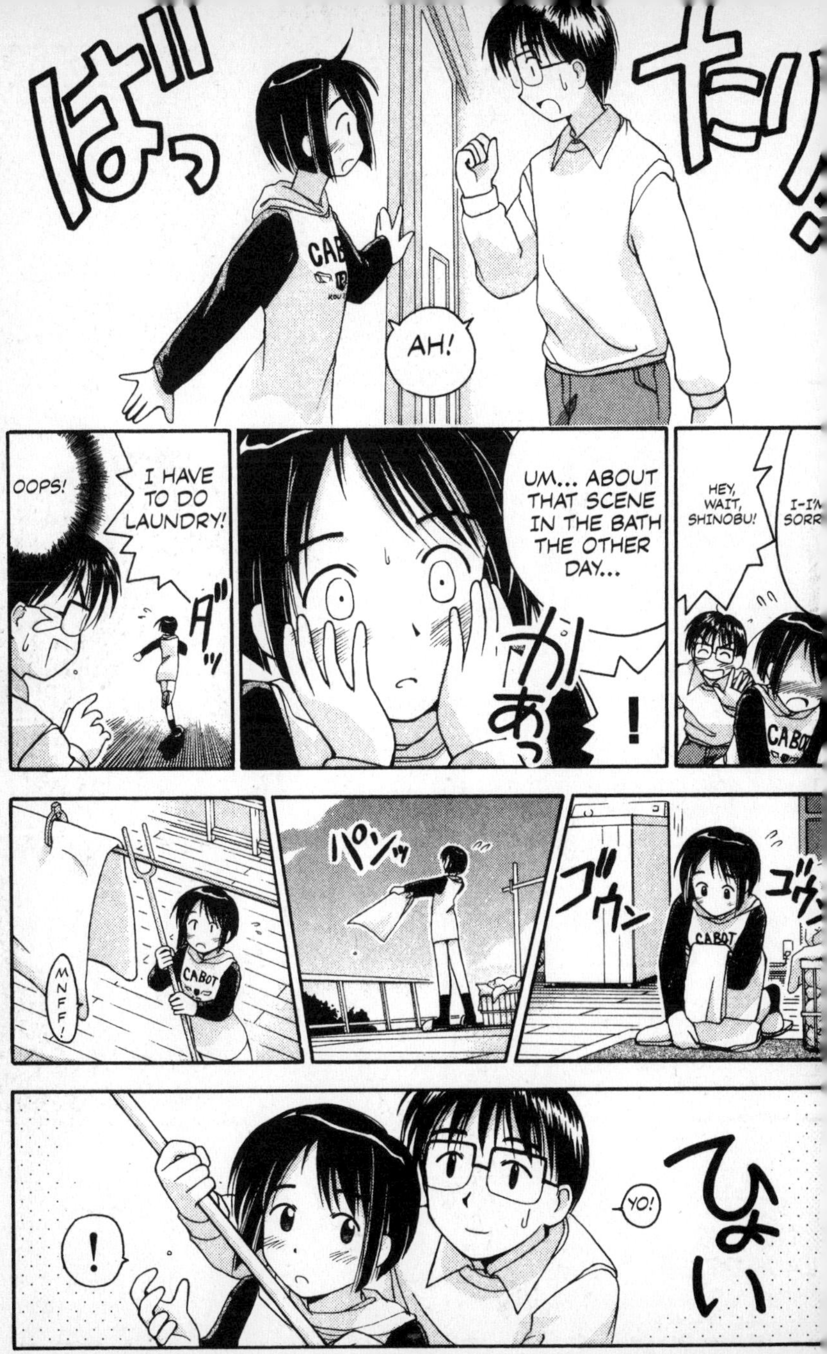
ばっ
AH!
I-I'M SORR
HEY, WAIT, SHINOBU!
UM... ABOUT THAT SCENE IN THE BATH THE OTHER DAY...
かあっ
!
I HAVE TO DO LAUNDRY!
OOPS!
ダッ
ゴウン
ゴウン
パンッ
MNFF!
ひょい
YO!
!

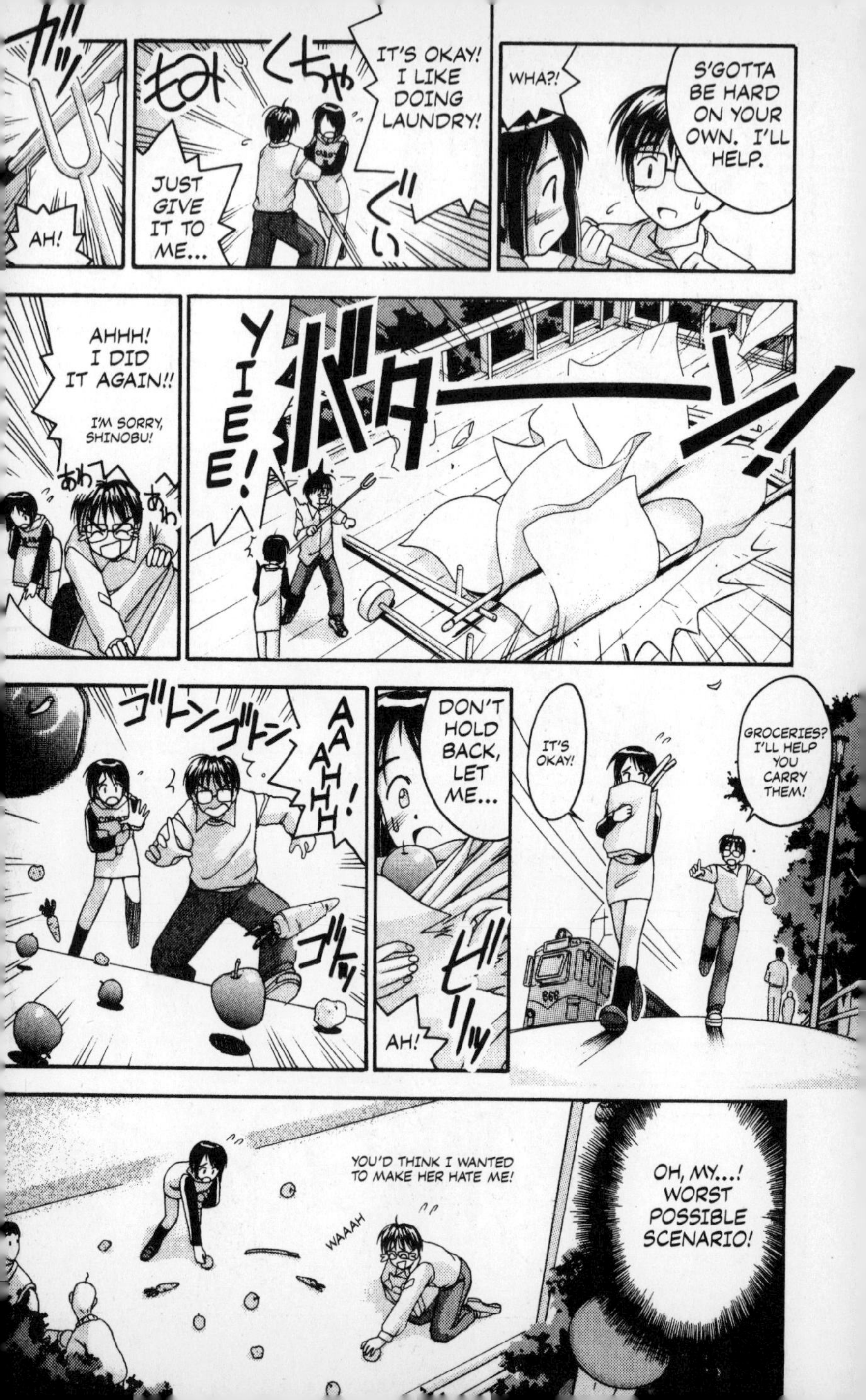
S'GOTTA BE HARD ON YOUR OWN. I'LL HELP.
WHA?!
IT'S OKAY! I LIKE DOING LAUNDRY!
もみ くちゃ
JUST GIVE IT TO ME...
ぐい
ガッ
AH!
バターーン!!
YIEE!
AHHH! I DID IT AGAIN!!
I'M SORRY, SHINOBU!
あわ
あわ
GROCERIES? I'LL HELP YOU CARRY THEM!
IT'S OKAY!
DON'T HOLD BACK, LET ME...
ビリッ
AH!
ゴトッ
AAAHHH!
ゴトンゴトン
OH, MY...! WORST POSSIBLE SCENARIO!
YOU'D THINK I WANTED TO MAKE HER HATE ME!
WAAAH

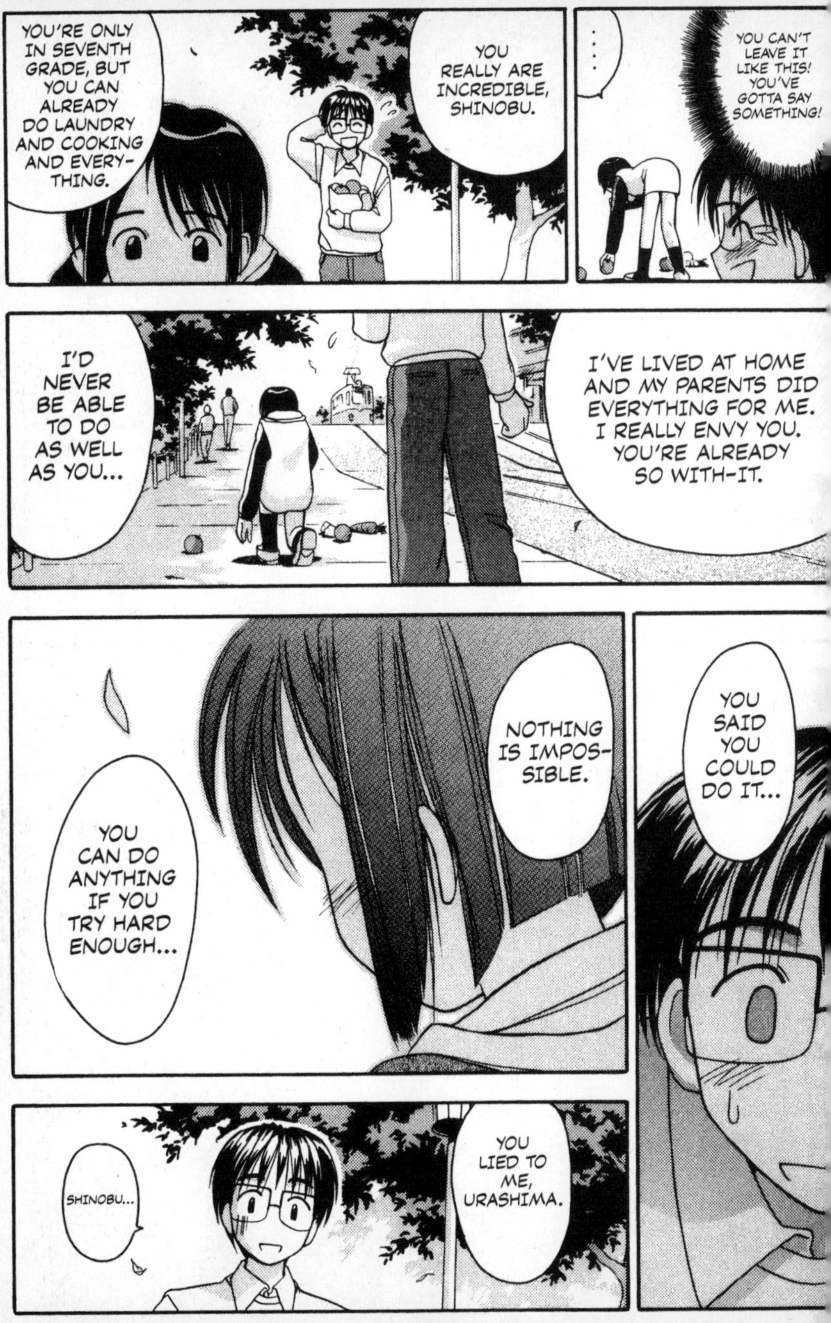
. . . .
YOU CAN'T LEAVE IT LIKE THIS! YOU'VE GOTTA SAY SOMETHING!
YOU REALLY ARE INCREDIBLE, SHINOBU.
YOU'RE ONLY IN SEVENTH GRADE, BUT YOU CAN ALREADY DO LAUNDRY AND COOKING AND EVERY-THING.
I'VE LIVED AT HOME AND MY PARENTS DID EVERYTHING FOR ME. I REALLY ENVY YOU. YOU'RE ALREADY SO WITH-IT.
I'D NEVER BE ABLE TO DO AS WELL AS YOU...
YOU SAID YOU COULD DO IT...
NOTHING IS IMPOS-SIBLE.
YOU CAN DO ANYTHING IF YOU TRY HARD ENOUGH...
YOU LIED TO ME, URASHIMA.
SHINOBU...

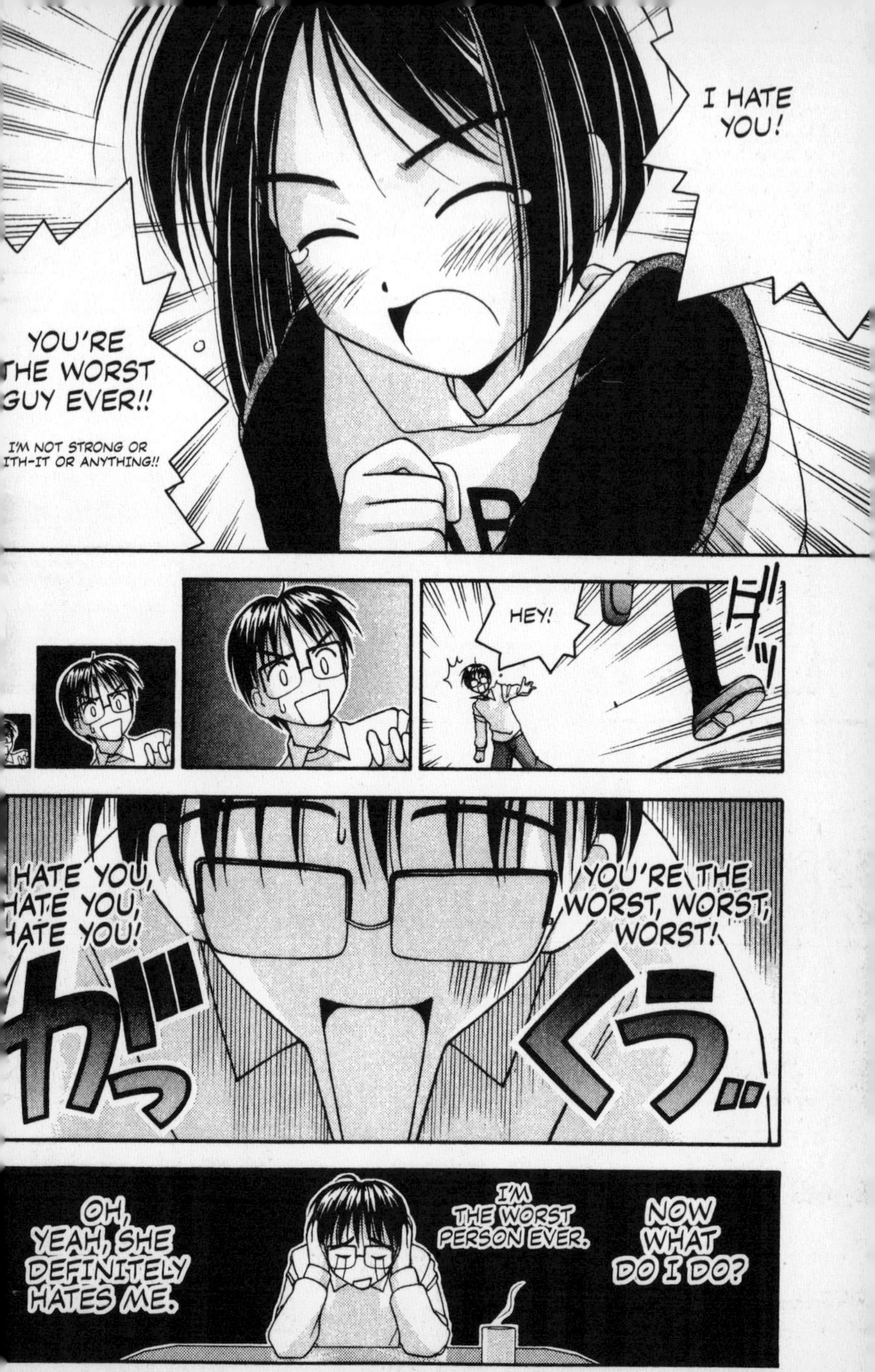
I HATE YOU!
YOU'RE THE WORST GUY EVER!!
I'M NOT STRONG OR ITH-IT OR ANYTHING!!
HEY!
ダッ
YOU'RE THE WORST, WORST, WORST!
くぅ
HATE YOU, HATE YOU, HATE YOU!
がっ
NOW WHAT DO I DO?
I'M THE WORST PERSON EVER.
OH, YEAH, SHE DEFINITELY HATES ME.

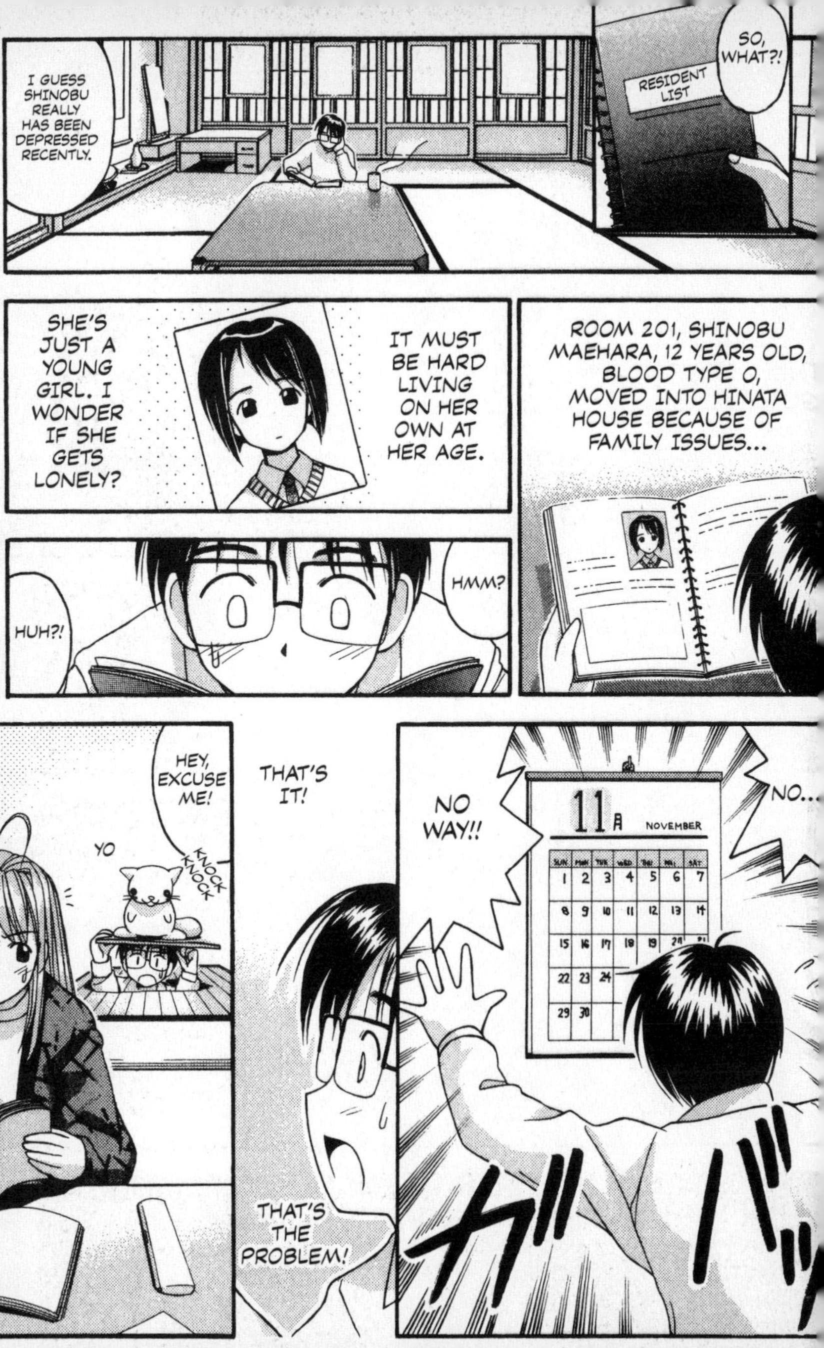
SO, WHAT?!
RESIDENT LIST
I GUESS SHINOBU REALLY HAS BEEN DEPRESSED RECENTLY.
ROOM 201, SHINOBU MAEHARA, 12 YEARS OLD, BLOOD TYPE O, MOVED INTO HINATA HOUSE BECAUSE OF FAMILY ISSUES...
IT MUST BE HARD LIVING ON HER OWN AT HER AGE.
SHE'S JUST A YOUNG GIRL. I WONDER IF SHE GETS LONELY?
HMM?
HUH?!
NO...
11月 NOVEMBER
NO WAY!!
THAT'S IT!
HEY, EXCUSE ME!
KNOCK KNOCK
YO
THAT'S THE PROBLEM!

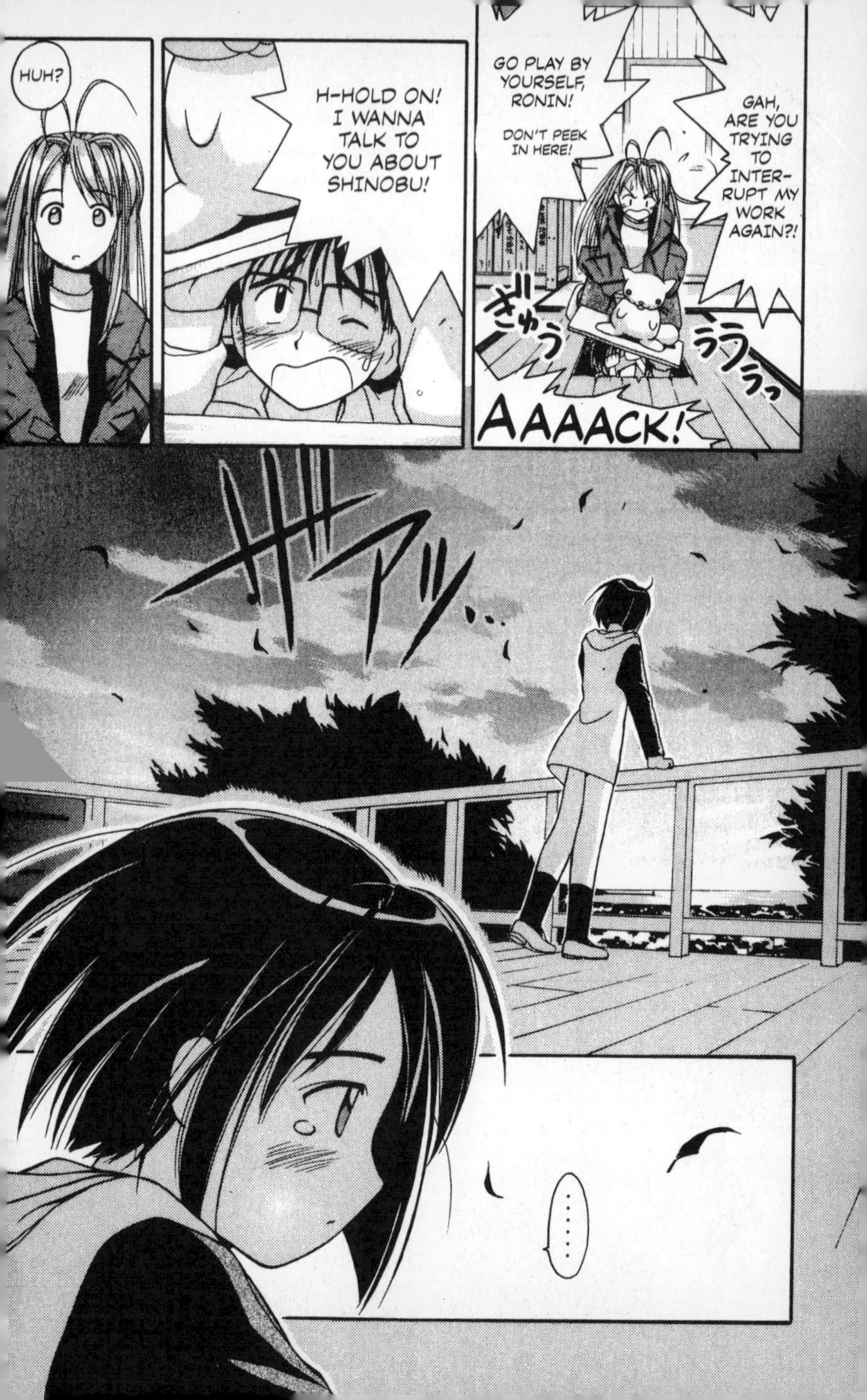
GAH, ARE YOU TRYING TO INTER-RUPT MY WORK AGAIN?!
GO PLAY BY YOURSELF, RONIN!
DON'T PEEK IN HERE!
ぎゅう
AAAACK!
H-HOLD ON! I WANNA TALK TO YOU ABOUT SHINOBU!
HUH?
......

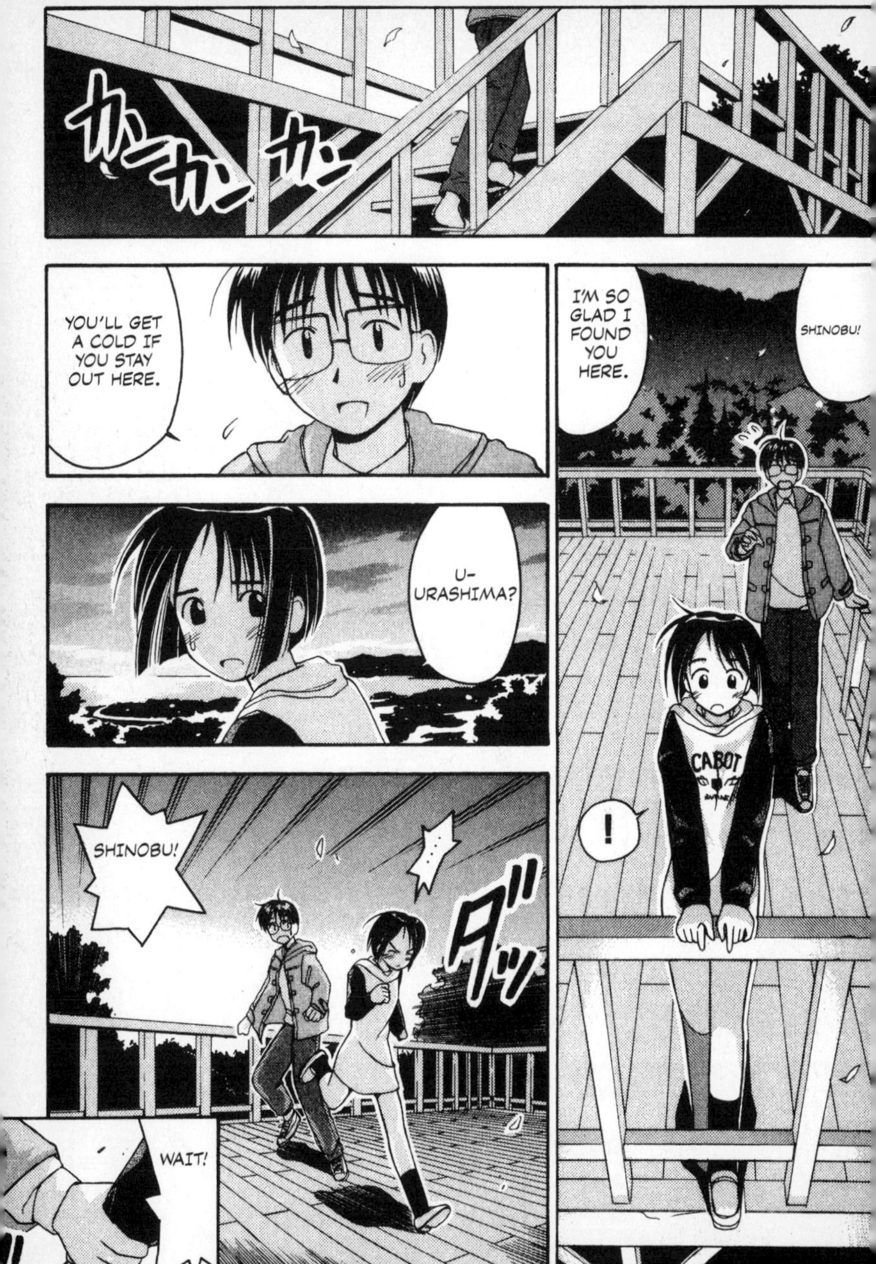

カーカン カン
SHINOBU!
I'M SO GLAD I FOUND YOU HERE.
!
YOU'LL GET A COLD IF YOU STAY OUT HERE.
U-URASHIMA?
SHINOBU!
...
ダッ
WAIT!

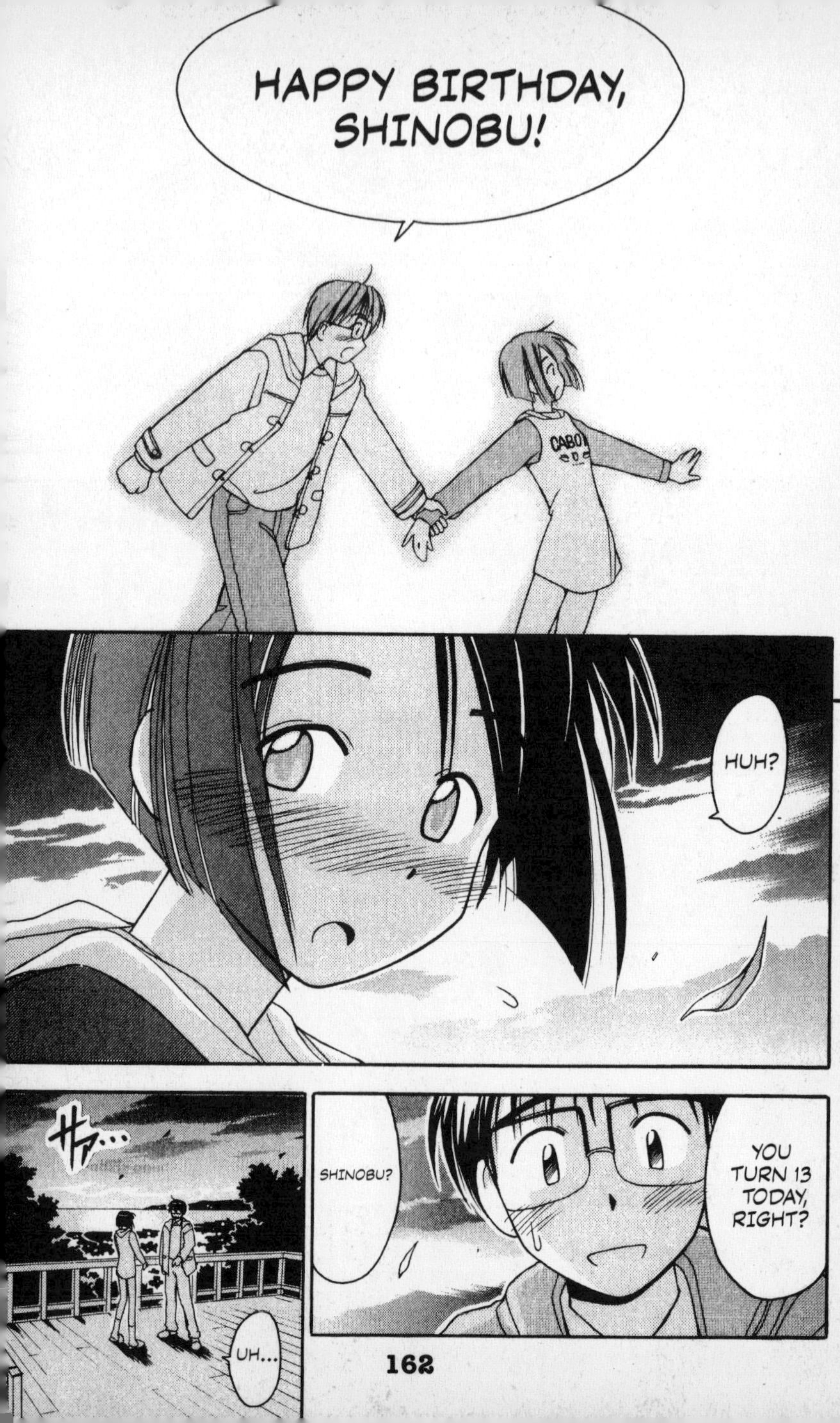
HAPPY BIRTHDAY, SHINOBU!
HUH?
YOU TURN 13 TODAY, RIGHT?
SHINOBU?
サァ…
UH...

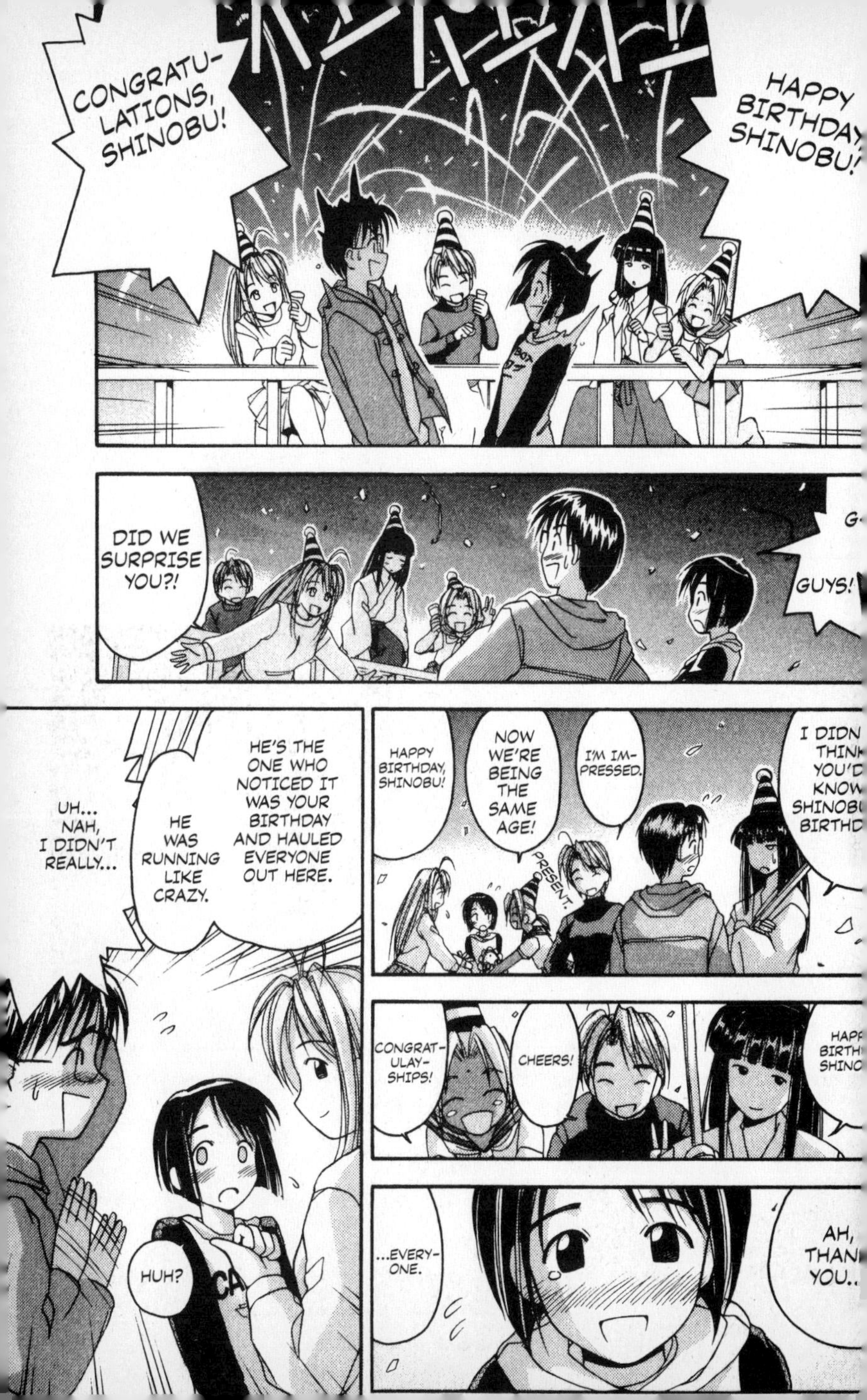
HAPPY BIRTHDAY SHINOBU!
CONGRATULATIONS, SHINOBU!
G-
GUYS!
DID WE SURPRISE YOU?!
I DIDN THINK YOU'D KNOW SHINOBU BIRTHD
I'M IM-PRESSED.
NOW WE'RE BEING THE SAME AGE!
HAPPY BIRTHDAY, SHINOBU!
PRESENT.
HAPP BIRTH SHINO
CHEERS!
CONGRAT-ULAY-SHIPS!
AH, THAN YOU..
...EVERY-ONE.
HE'S THE ONE WHO NOTICED IT WAS YOUR BIRTHDAY AND HAULED EVERYONE OUT HERE.
HE WAS RUNNING LIKE CRAZY.
UH... NAH, I DIDN'T REALLY...
HUH?

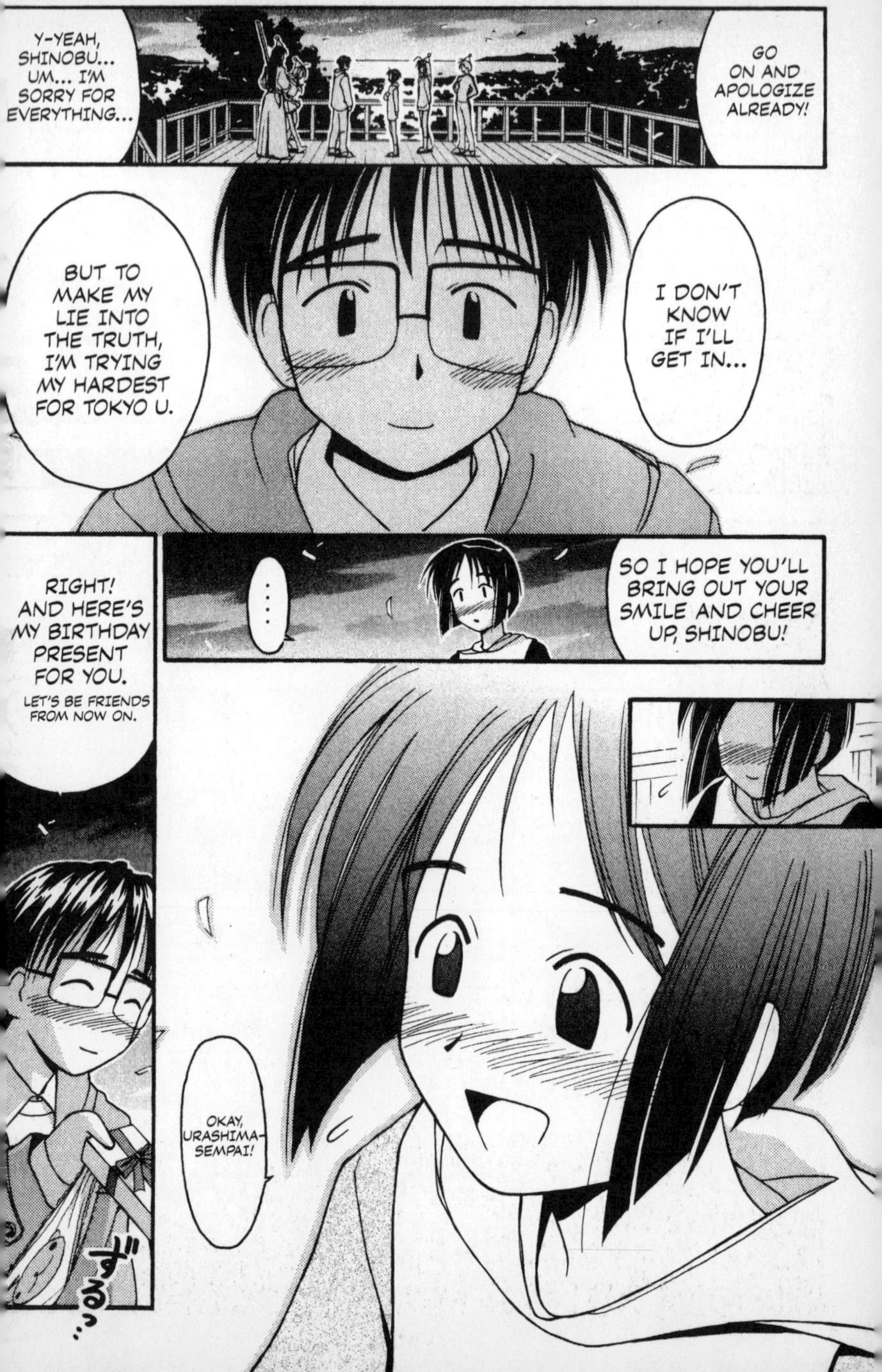
GO ON AND APOLOGIZE ALREADY!
Y-YEAH, SHINOBU... UM... I'M SORRY FOR EVERYTHING...
I DON'T KNOW IF I'LL GET IN...
BUT TO MAKE MY LIE INTO THE TRUTH, I'M TRYING MY HARDEST FOR TOKYO U.
SO I HOPE YOU'LL BRING OUT YOUR SMILE AND CHEER UP, SHINOBU!
.....
OKAY, URASHIMA-SEMPAI!
RIGHT! AND HERE'S MY BIRTHDAY PRESENT FOR YOU.
LET'S BE FRIENDS FROM NOW ON.
ずるっ...

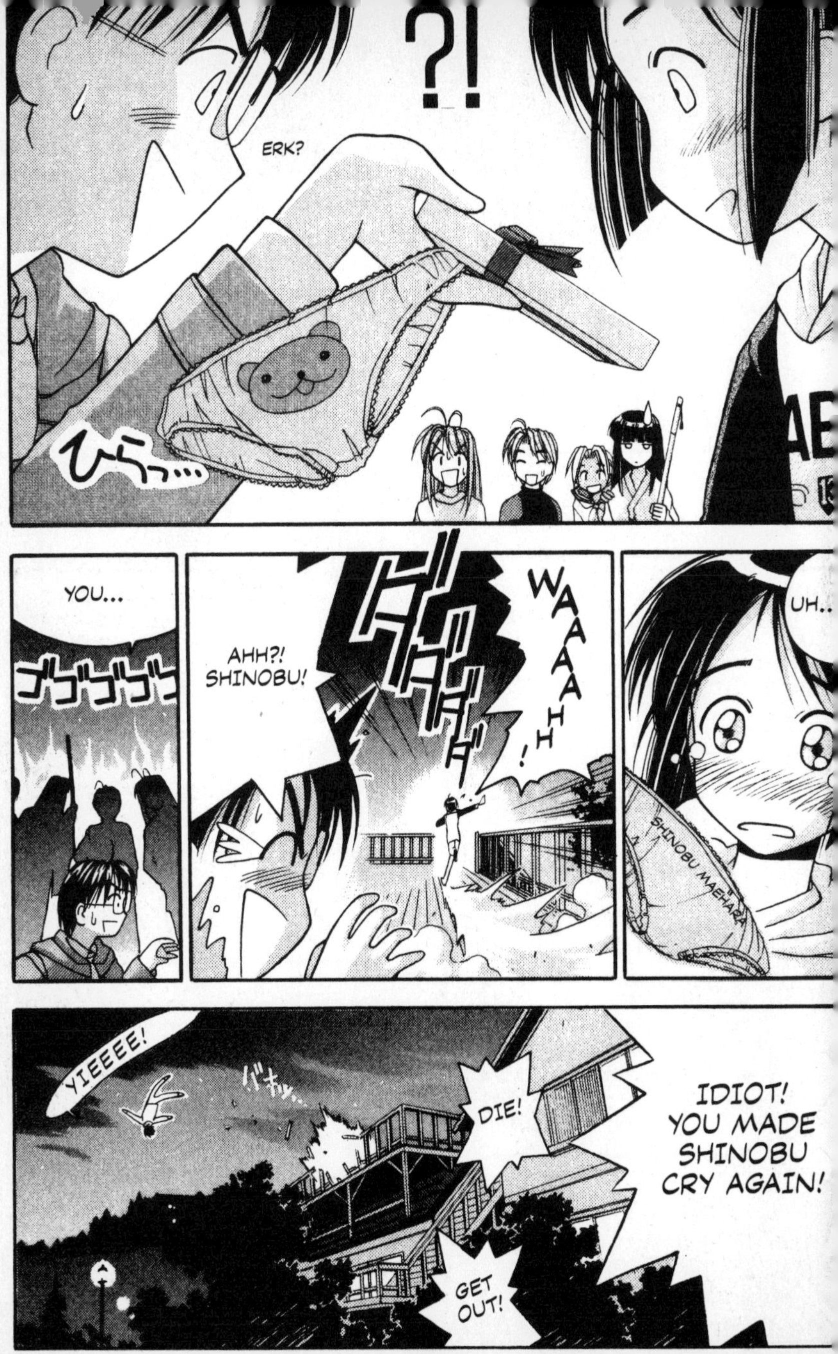
?!
ERK?
ひらっ…
UH...
SHINOBU MAEHARA
WAAAAHH!
AHH?! SHINOBU!
YOU...
ゴゴゴゴ
IDIOT! YOU MADE SHINOBU CRY AGAIN!
GET OUT!
DIE!
バキッ…
YIEEEE!

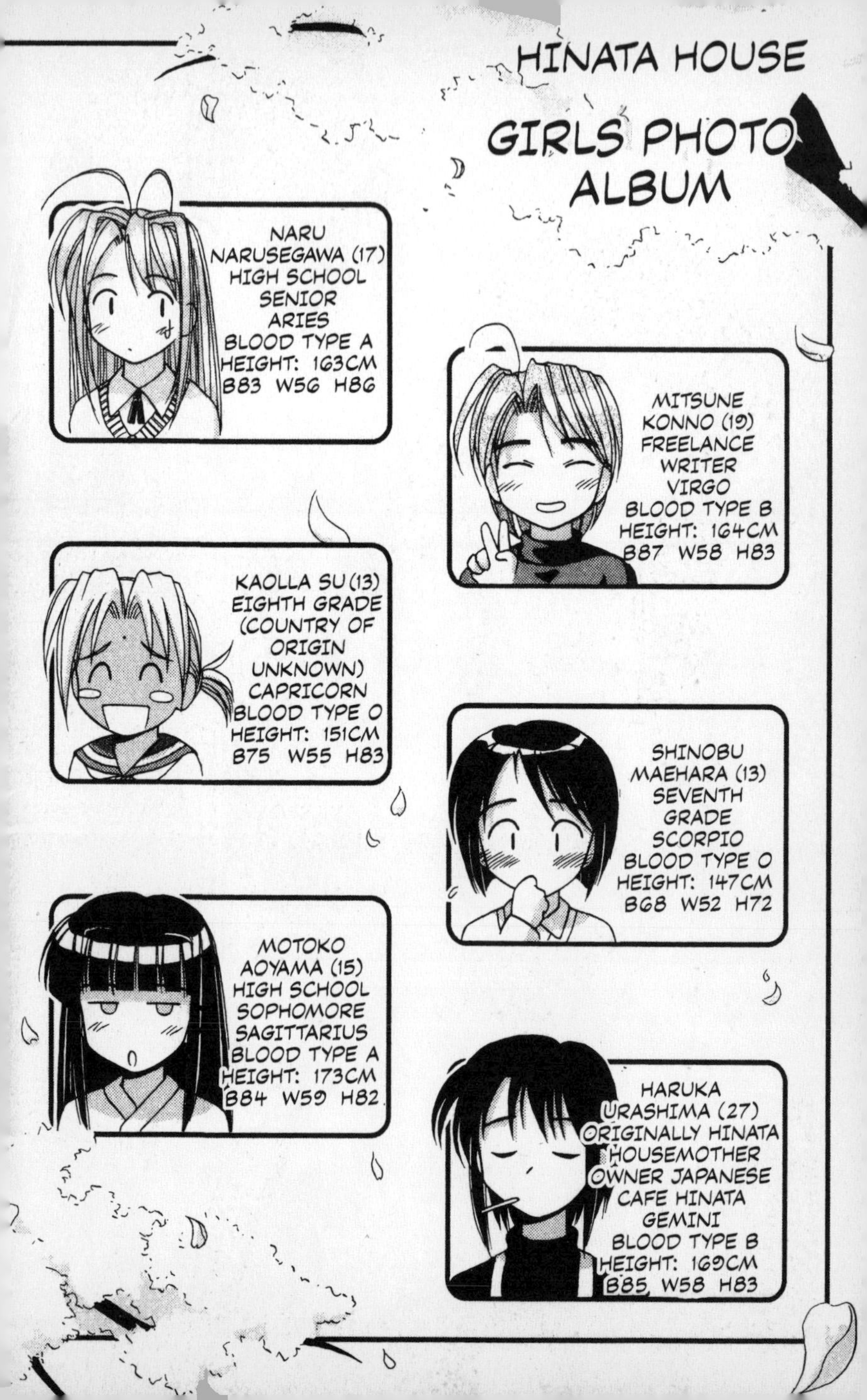
HINATA HOUSE GIRLS PHOTO ALBUM
NARU NARUSEGAWA (17) HIGH SCHOOL SENIOR ARIES BLOOD TYPE A HEIGHT: 163CM B83 W56 H86
MITSUNE KONNO (19) FREELANCE WRITER VIRGO BLOOD TYPE B HEIGHT: 164CM B87 W58 H83
KAOLLA SU (13) EIGHTH GRADE (COUNTRY OF ORIGIN UNKNOWN) CAPRICORN BLOOD TYPE O HEIGHT: 151CM B75 W55 H83
SHINOBU MAEHARA (13) SEVENTH GRADE SCORPIO BLOOD TYPE O HEIGHT: 147CM B68 W52 H72
MOTOKO AOYAMA (15) HIGH SCHOOL SOPHOMORE SAGITTARIUS BLOOD TYPE A HEIGHT: 173CM B84 W59 H82
HARUKA URASHIMA (27) ORIGINALLY HINATA HOUSEMOTHER OWNER JAPANESE CAFE HINATA GEMINI BLOOD TYPE B HEIGHT: 169CM B85, W58 H83

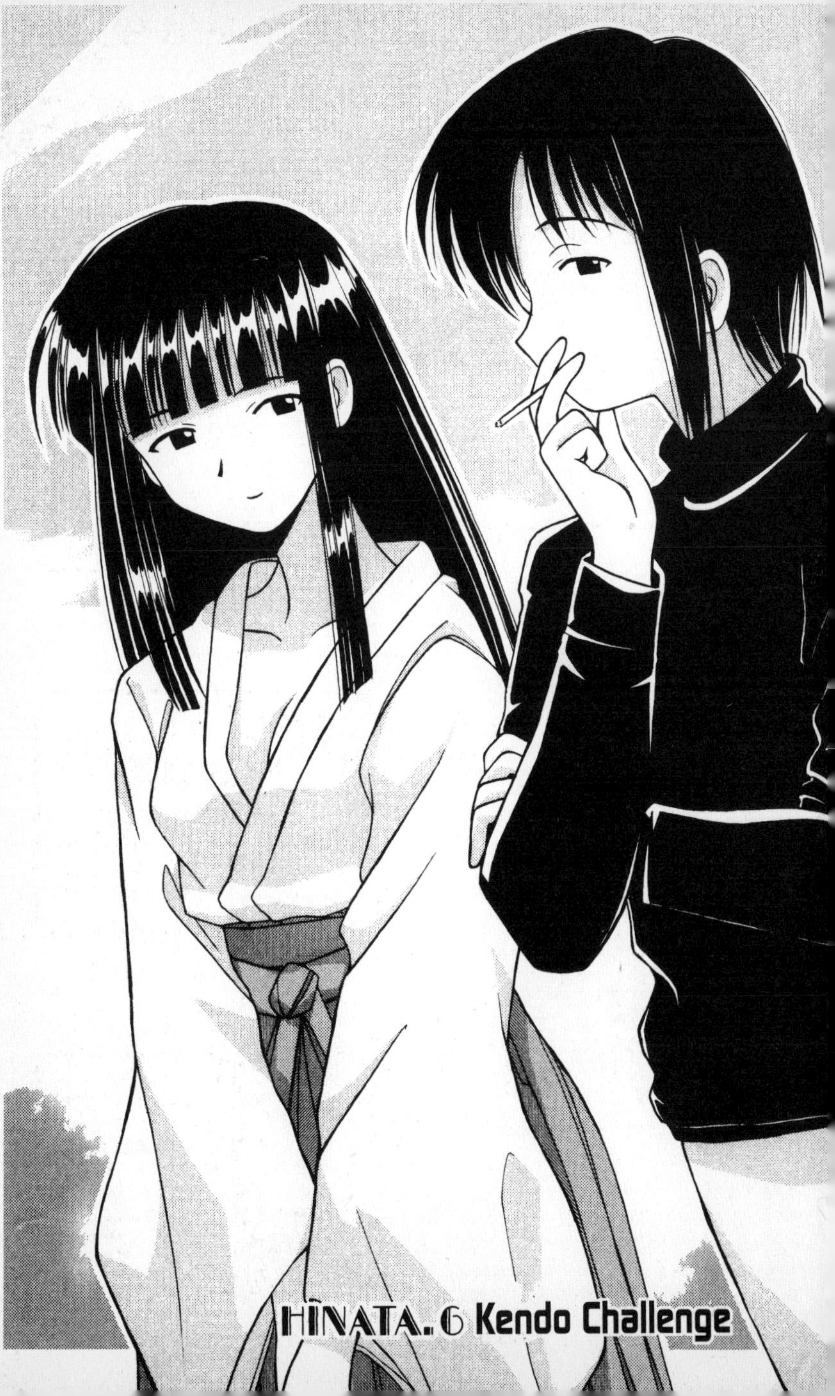
HINATA. 6 Kendo Challenge

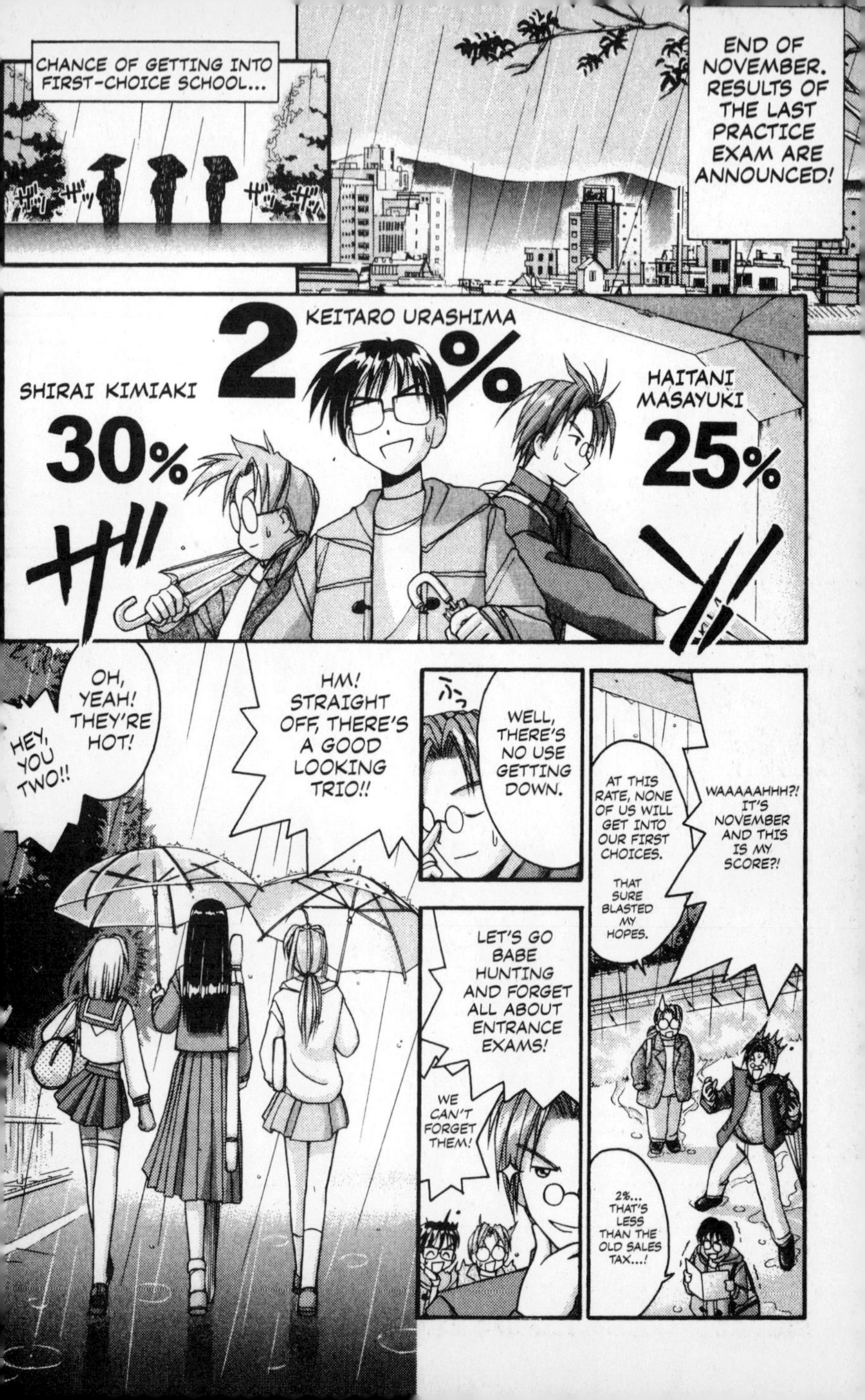
END OF NOVEMBER. RESULTS OF THE LAST PRACTICE EXAM ARE ANNOUNCED!
CHANCE OF GETTING INTO FIRST-CHOICE SCHOOL...
HAITANI MASAYUKI
25%
KEITARO URASHIMA
2%
SHIRAI KIMIAKI
30%
WAAAAAHHH?! IT'S NOVEMBER AND THIS IS MY SCORE?!
AT THIS RATE, NONE OF US WILL GET INTO OUR FIRST CHOICES.
THAT SURE BLASTED MY HOPES.
2%... THAT'S LESS THAN THE OLD SALES TAX...!
WELL, THERE'S NO USE GETTING DOWN.
LET'S GO BABE HUNTING AND FORGET ALL ABOUT ENTRANCE EXAMS!
WE CAN'T FORGET THEM!
HM! STRAIGHT OFF, THERE'S A GOOD LOOKING TRIO!!
OH, YEAH! THEY'RE HOT!
HEY, YOU TWO!!

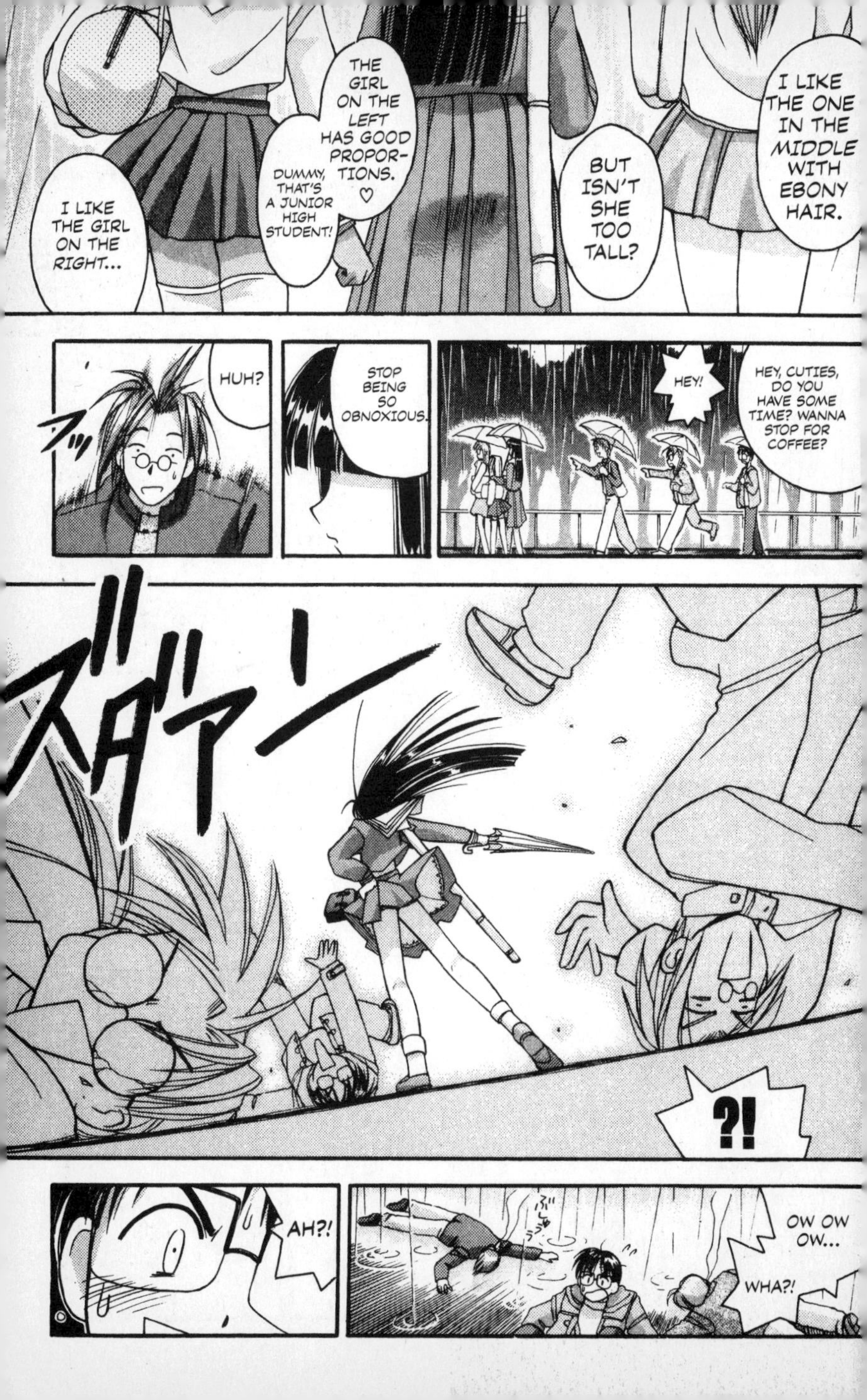
I LIKE THE ONE IN THE MIDDLE WITH EBONY HAIR.
BUT ISN'T SHE TOO TALL?
THE GIRL ON THE LEFT HAS GOOD PROPORTIONS. ♡
DUMMY, THAT'S A JUNIOR HIGH STUDENT!
I LIKE THE GIRL ON THE RIGHT...
HEY, CUTIES, DO YOU HAVE SOME TIME? WANNA STOP FOR COFFEE?
HEY!
STOP BEING SO OBNOXIOUS.
HUH?
?!
OW OW OW...
WHA?!
AH?!

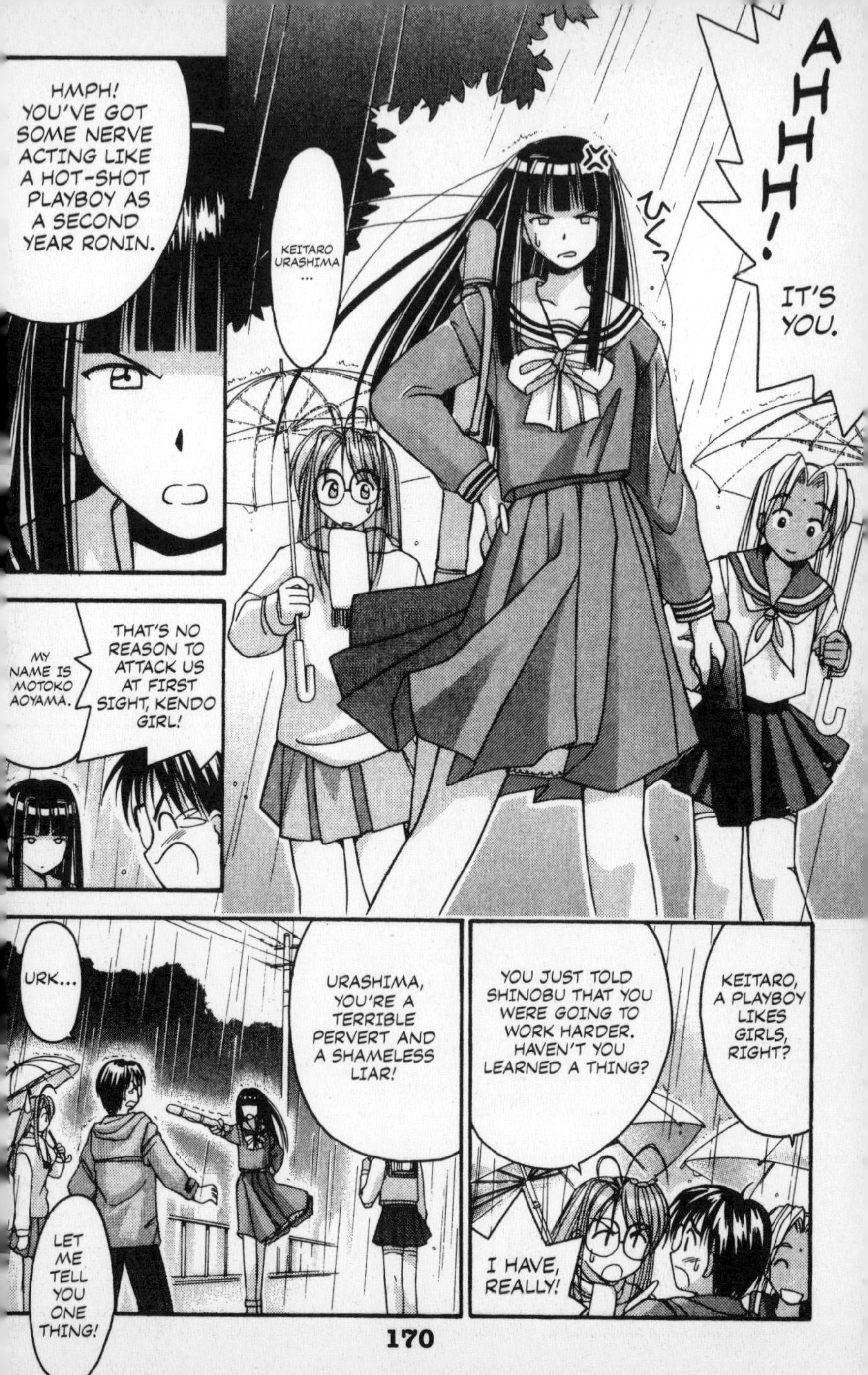
AHHHH!
IT'S YOU.
KEITARO URASHIMA ...
HMPH! YOU'VE GOT SOME NERVE ACTING LIKE A HOT-SHOT PLAYBOY AS A SECOND YEAR RONIN.
THAT'S NO REASON TO ATTACK US AT FIRST SIGHT, KENDO GIRL!
MY NAME IS MOTOKO AOYAMA.
KEITARO, A PLAYBOY LIKES GIRLS, RIGHT?
YOU JUST TOLD SHINOBU THAT YOU WERE GOING TO WORK HARDER. HAVEN'T YOU LEARNED A THING?
I HAVE, REALLY!
URASHIMA, YOU'RE A TERRIBLE PERVERT AND A SHAMELESS LIAR!
URK...
LET ME TELL YOU ONE THING!

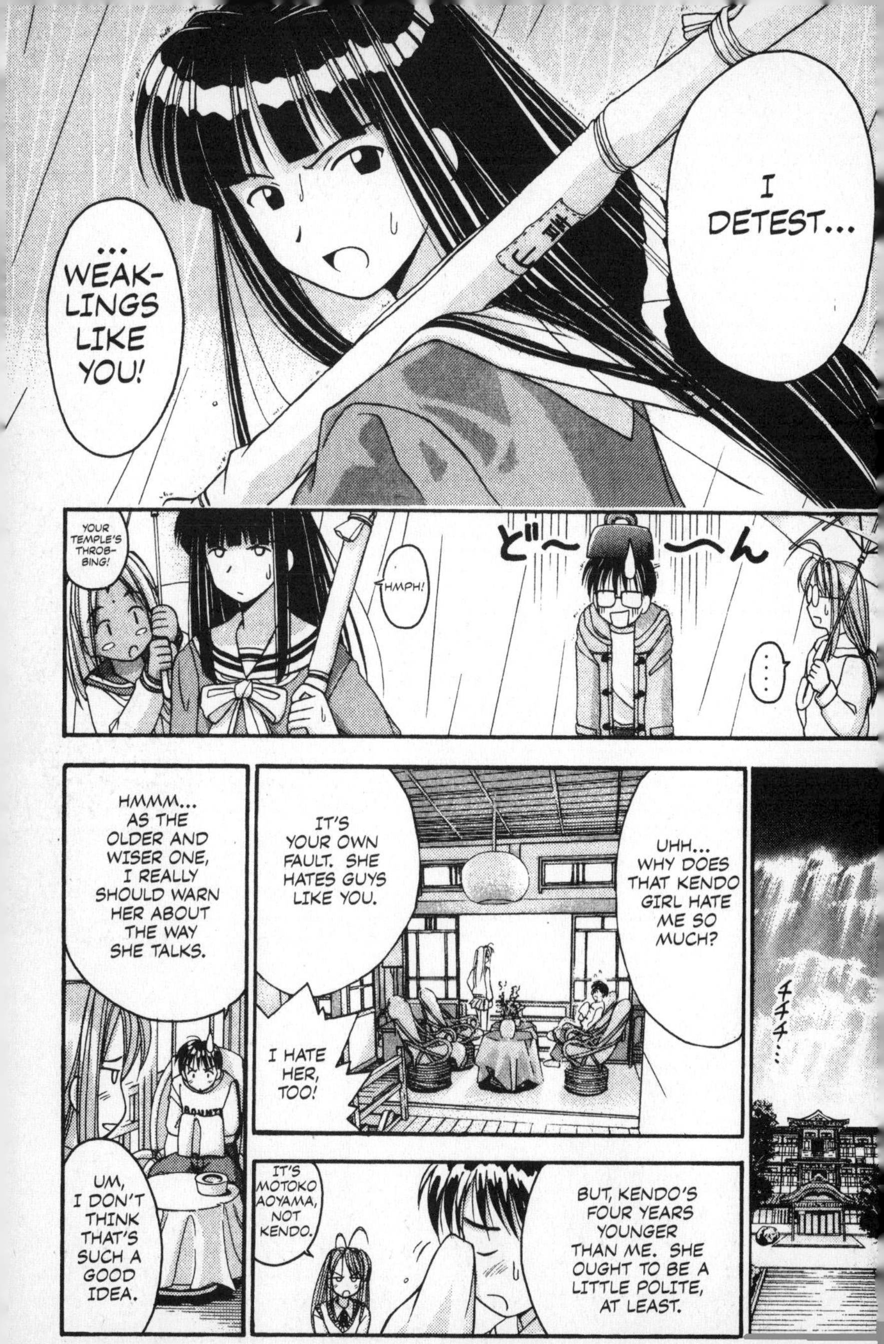
I DETEST...
...WEAK-LINGS LIKE YOU!
どーーーん
....
HMPH!
YOUR TEMPLE'S THROB-BING!
チチチ...
UHH... WHY DOES THAT KENDO GIRL HATE ME SO MUCH?
IT'S YOUR OWN FAULT. SHE HATES GUYS LIKE YOU.
I HATE HER, TOO!
BUT, KENDO'S FOUR YEARS YOUNGER THAN ME. SHE OUGHT TO BE A LITTLE POLITE, AT LEAST.
IT'S MOTOKO AOYAMA, NOT KENDO.
HMMM... AS THE OLDER AND WISER ONE, I REALLY SHOULD WARN HER ABOUT THE WAY SHE TALKS.
UM, I DON'T THINK THAT'S SUCH A GOOD IDEA.

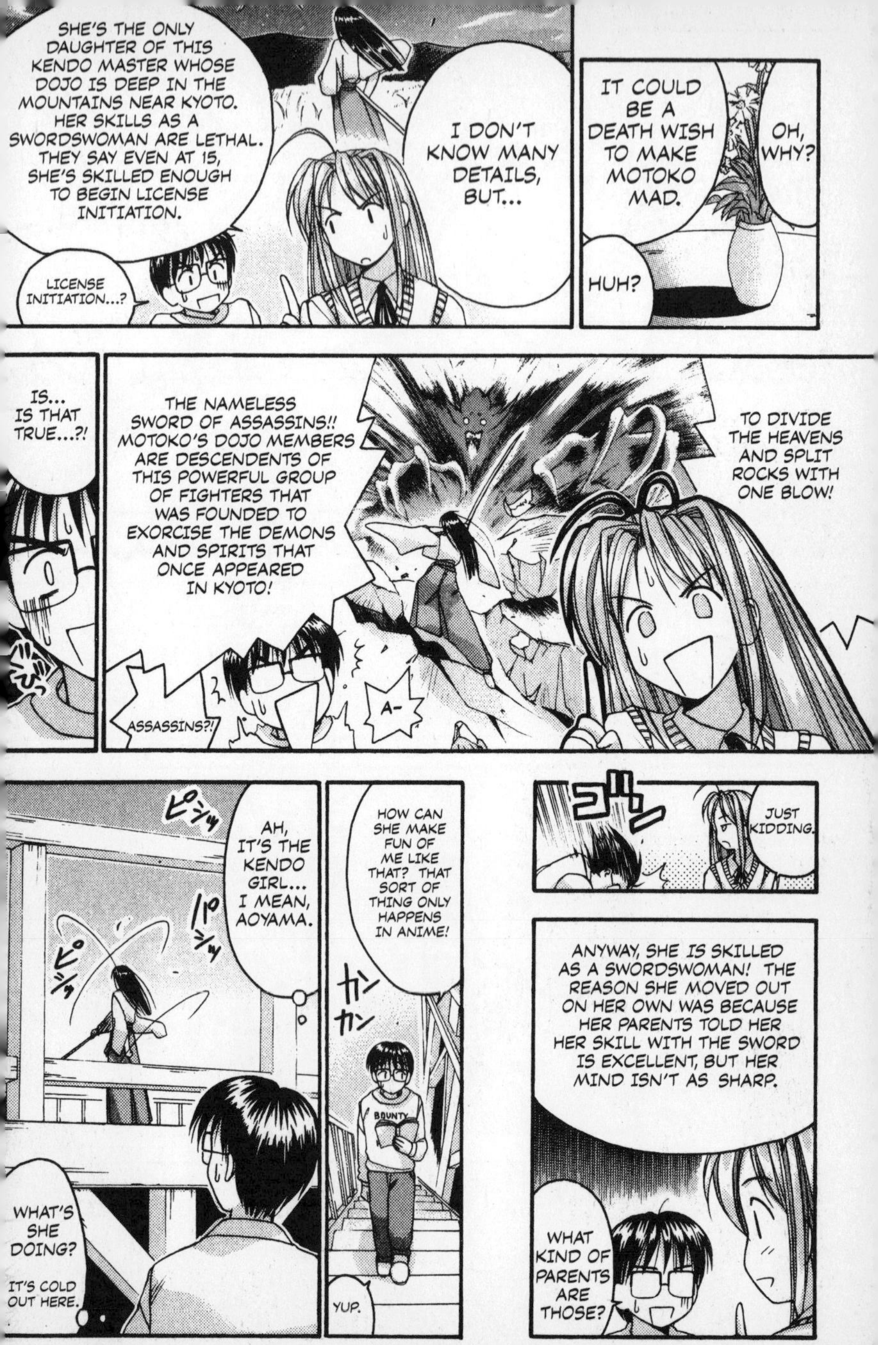
IT COULD BE A DEATH WISH TO MAKE MOTOKO MAD.
HUH?
OH, WHY?
I DON'T KNOW MANY DETAILS, BUT...
SHE'S THE ONLY DAUGHTER OF THIS KENDO MASTER WHOSE DOJO IS DEEP IN THE MOUNTAINS NEAR KYOTO. HER SKILLS AS A SWORDSWOMAN ARE LETHAL. THEY SAY EVEN AT 15, SHE'S SKILLED ENOUGH TO BEGIN LICENSE INITIATION.
LICENSE INITIATION...?
TO DIVIDE THE HEAVENS AND SPLIT ROCKS WITH ONE BLOW!
THE NAMELESS SWORD OF ASSASSINS!! MOTOKO'S DOJO MEMBERS ARE DESCENDENTS OF THIS POWERFUL GROUP OF FIGHTERS THAT WAS FOUNDED TO EXORCISE THE DEMONS AND SPIRITS THAT ONCE APPEARED IN KYOTO!
A-
ASSASSINS?!
IS... IS THAT TRUE...?!
JUST KIDDING.
ANYWAY, SHE IS SKILLED AS A SWORDSWOMAN! THE REASON SHE MOVED OUT ON HER OWN WAS BECAUSE HER PARENTS TOLD HER HER SKILL WITH THE SWORD IS EXCELLENT, BUT HER MIND ISN'T AS SHARP.
WHAT KIND OF PARENTS ARE THOSE?
HOW CAN SHE MAKE FUN OF ME LIKE THAT? THAT SORT OF THING ONLY HAPPENS IN ANIME!
BOUNTY
YUP.
AH, IT'S THE KENDO GIRL... I MEAN, AOYAMA.
WHAT'S SHE DOING?
IT'S COLD OUT HERE.

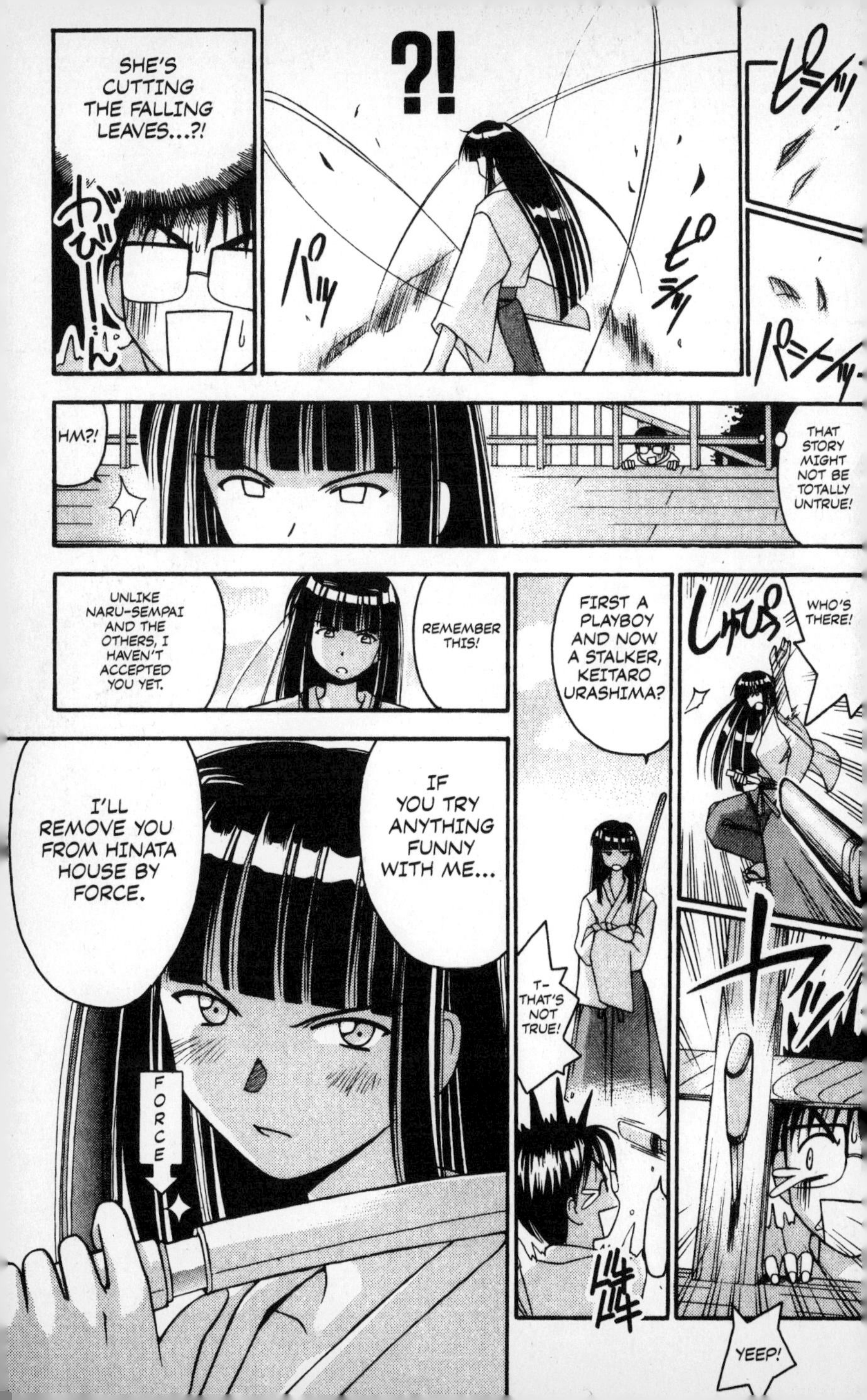
?!
SHE'S CUTTING THE FALLING LEAVES...?!
THAT STORY MIGHT NOT BE TOTALLY UNTRUE!
HM?!
WHO'S THERE!
YEEP!
FIRST A PLAYBOY AND NOW A STALKER, KEITARO URASHIMA?
T-THAT'S NOT TRUE!
REMEMBER THIS!
UNLIKE NARU-SEMPAI AND THE OTHERS, I HAVEN'T ACCEPTED YOU YET.
IF YOU TRY ANYTHING FUNNY WITH ME...
I'LL REMOVE YOU FROM HINATA HOUSE BY FORCE.
FORCE

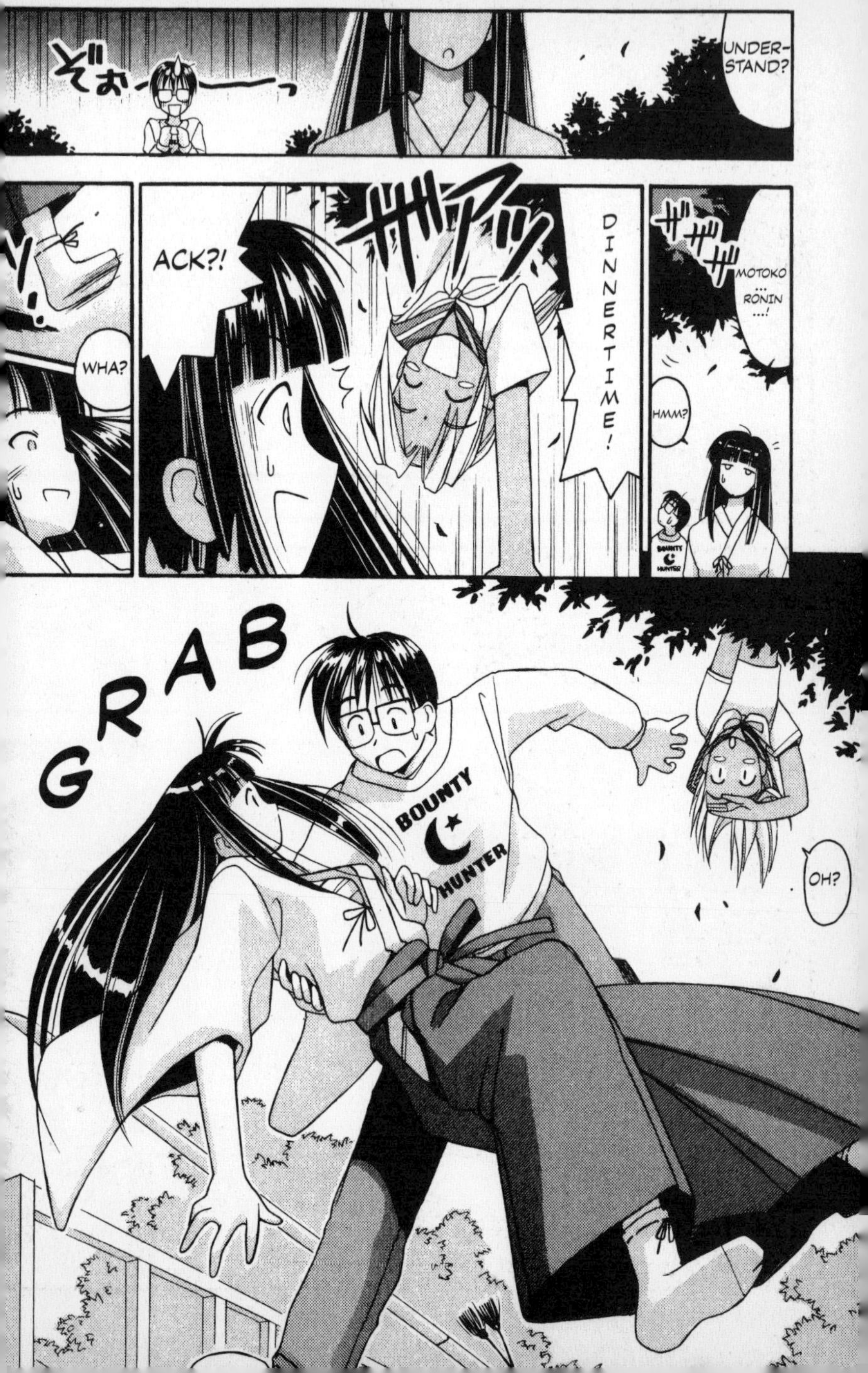
UNDER-STAND?
ぞぉーーーっ
ザザザ
MOTOKO ... RONIN ...!
HMM?
BOUNTY HUNTER
ザザアッ
DINNERTIME!
ACK?!
WHA?
OH?
GRAB
BOUNTY HUNTER

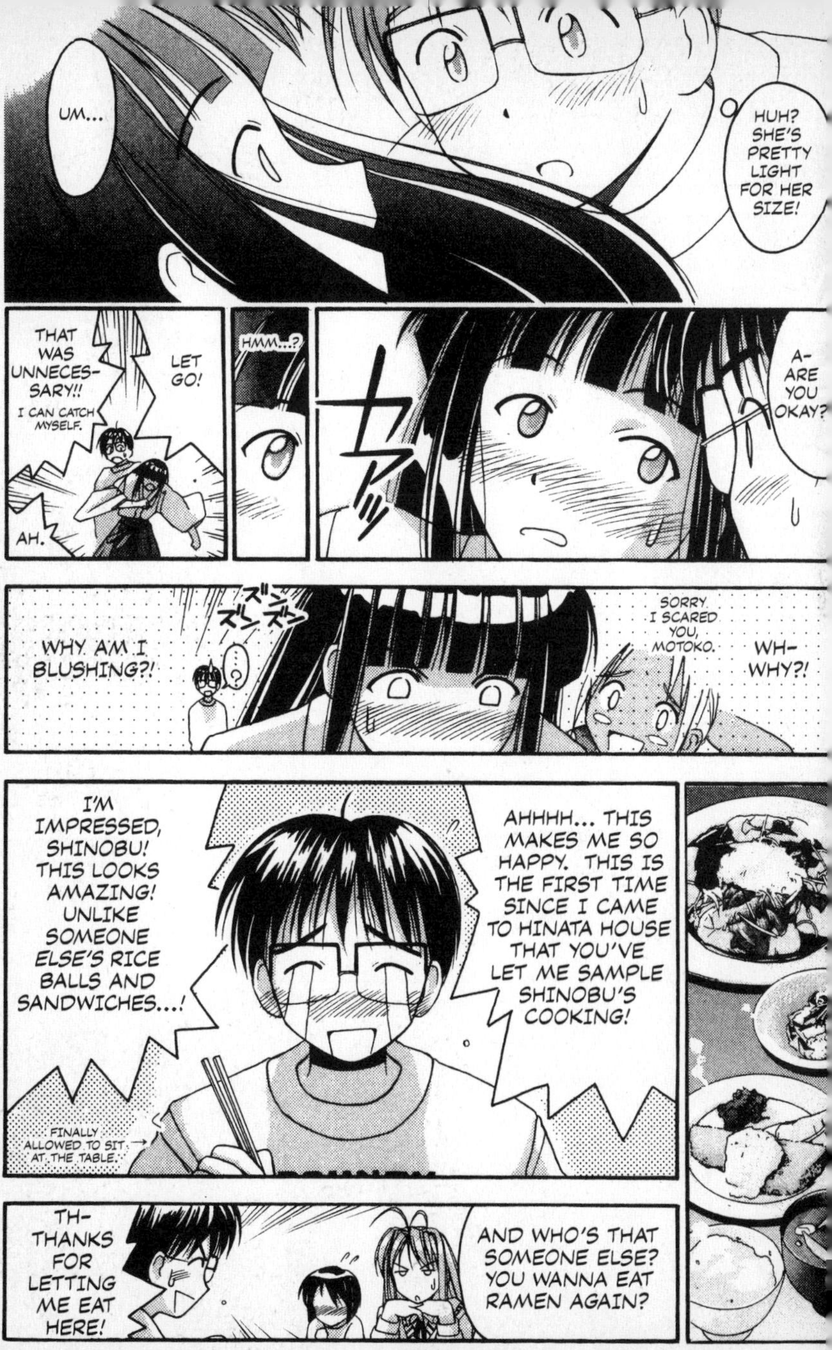
HUH? SHE'S PRETTY LIGHT FOR HER SIZE!
UM...
A- ARE YOU OKAY?
HMM...?
LET GO!
THAT WAS UNNECES-SARY!!
I CAN CATCH MYSELF.
AH.
WH-WHY?!
SORRY. I SCARED YOU, MOTOKO.
...?
WHY AM I BLUSHING?!
AHHHH... THIS MAKES ME SO HAPPY. THIS IS THE FIRST TIME SINCE I CAME TO HINATA HOUSE THAT YOU'VE LET ME SAMPLE SHINOBU'S COOKING!
I'M IMPRESSED, SHINOBU! THIS LOOKS AMAZING! UNLIKE SOMEONE ELSE'S RICE BALLS AND SANDWICHES...!
FINALLY ALLOWED TO SIT AT THE TABLE.
AND WHO'S THAT SOMEONE ELSE? YOU WANNA EAT RAMEN AGAIN?
TH- THANKS FOR LETTING ME EAT HERE!

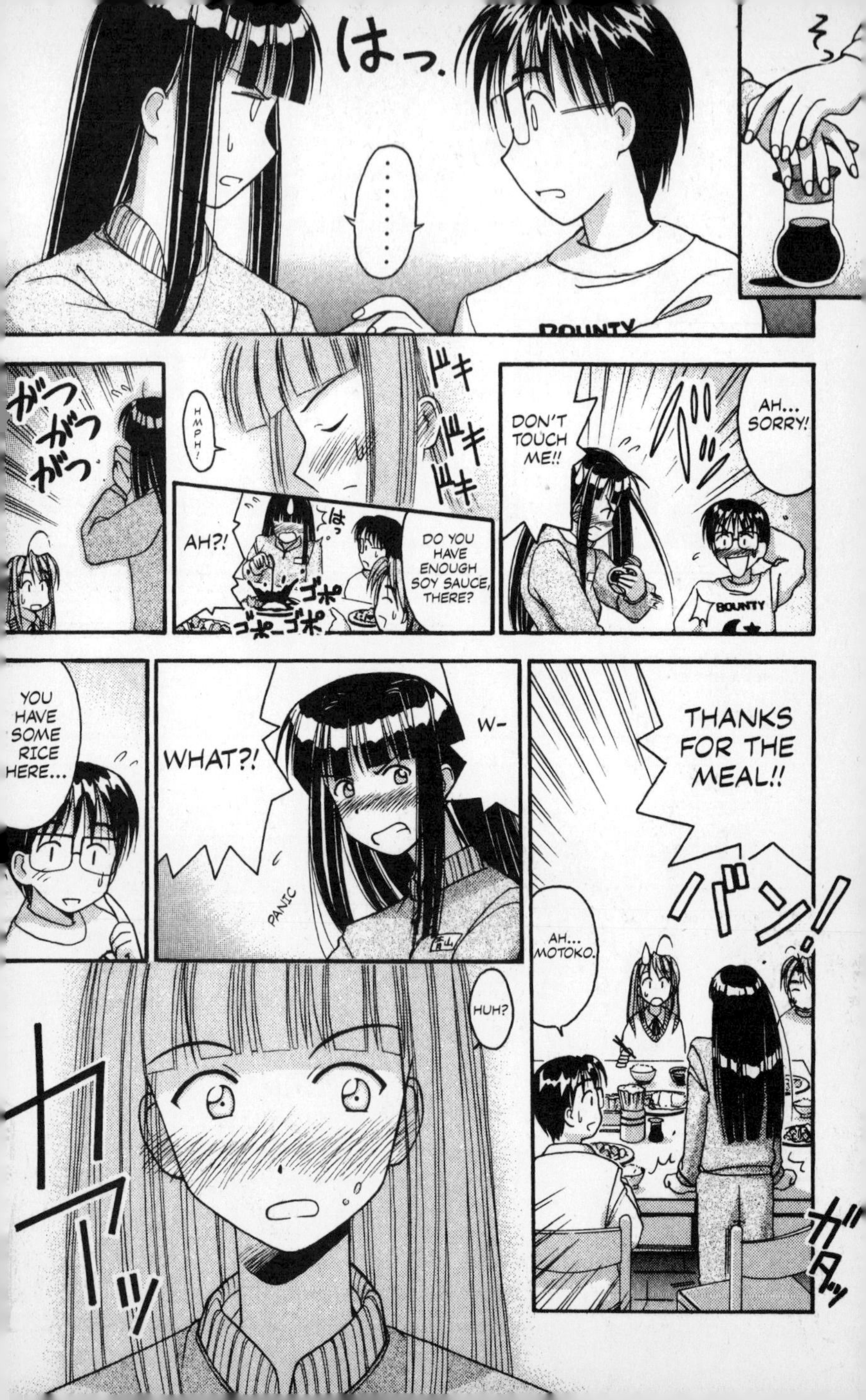
そっ
はっ.
……
AH... SORRY!
DON'T TOUCH ME!!
ドキ ドキ ドキ
HMPH!
DO YOU HAVE ENOUGH SOY SAUCE, THERE?
はっ
AH?!
ゴポ ゴポ ゴポ
がつ がつ がつ
THANKS FOR THE MEAL!!
バン!
AH... MOTOKO.
ガタッ
W-
WHAT?!
PANIC
YOU HAVE SOME RICE HERE...
HUH?
カァーッ

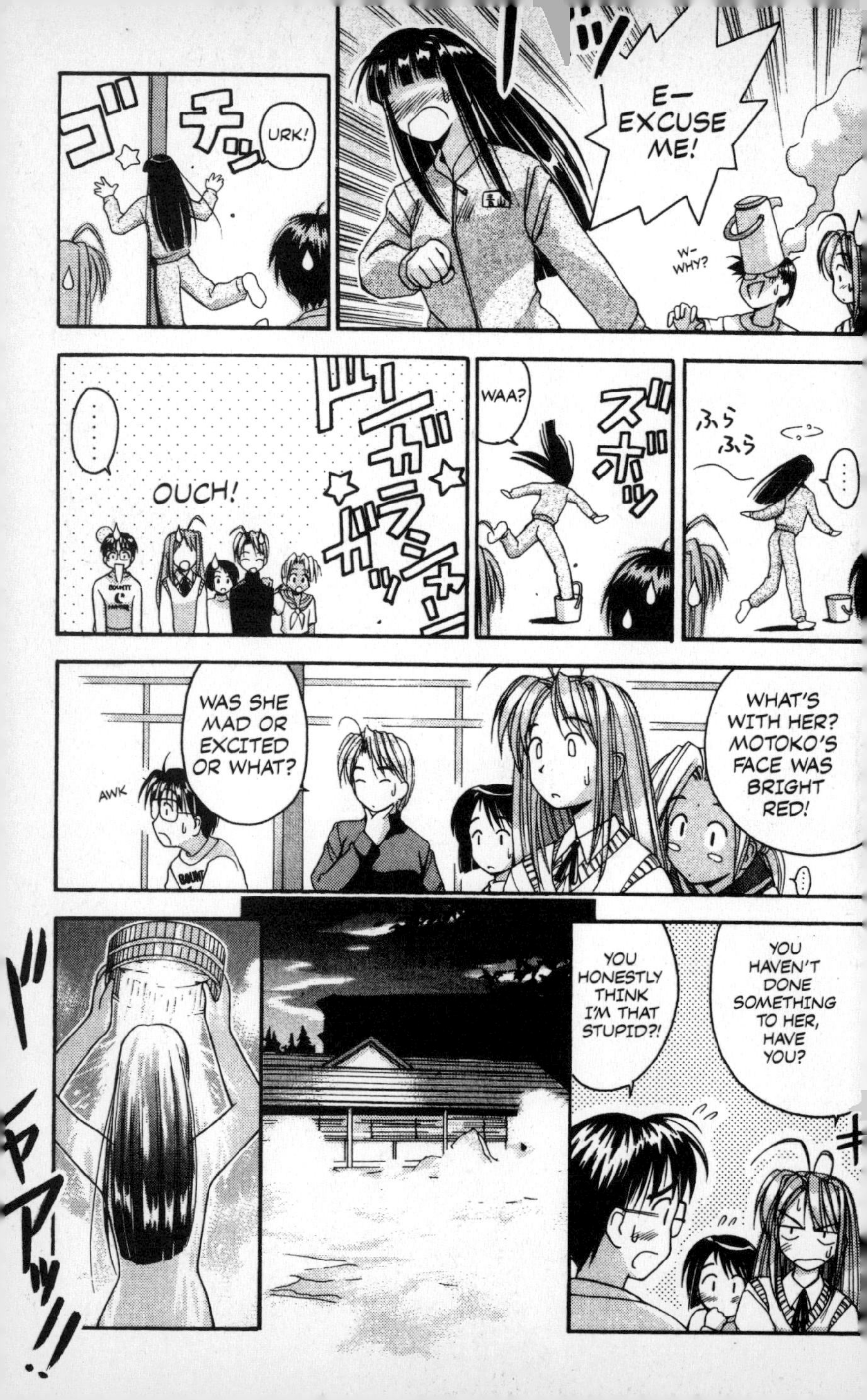
E— EXCUSE ME!
W— WHY?
ゴチッ
URK!
ふら ふら
...
WAA?
ズボッ
ドンガラガッシャーン
...
OUCH!
WHAT'S WITH HER? MOTOKO'S FACE WAS BRIGHT RED!
...
WAS SHE MAD OR EXCITED OR WHAT?
AWK
YOU HAVEN'T DONE SOMETHING TO HER, HAVE YOU?
YOU HONESTLY THINK I'M THAT STUPID?!

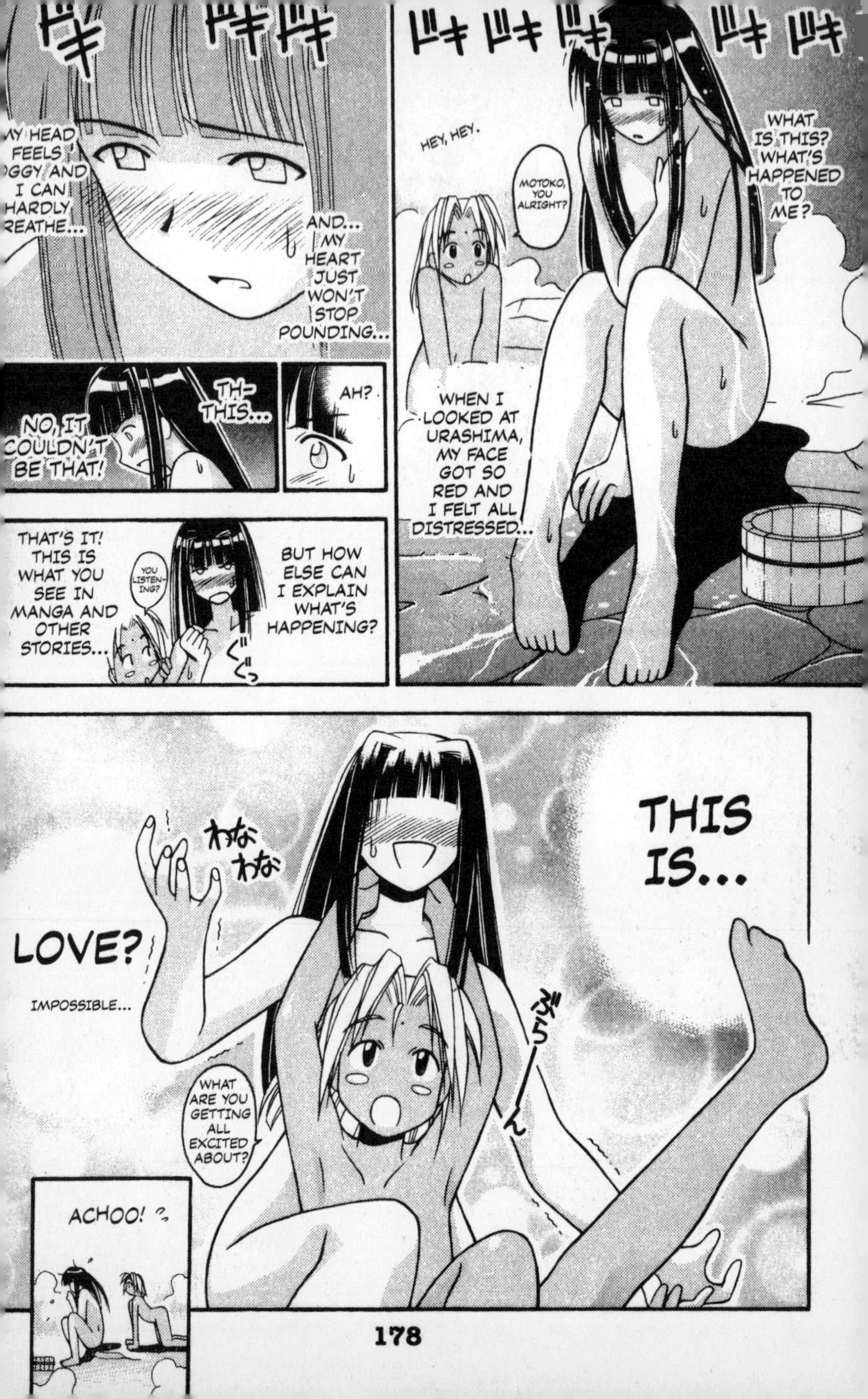

ドキドキドキ ドキドキ
WHAT IS THIS? WHAT'S HAPPENED TO ME?
HEY, HEY.
MOTOKO, YOU ALRIGHT?
WHEN I LOOKED AT URASHIMA, MY FACE GOT SO RED AND I FELT ALL DISTRESSED...
ドキ ドキドキ
MY HEAD FEELS OGGY AND I CAN HARDLY REATHE...
AND... MY HEART JUST WON'T STOP POUNDING...
AH?
TH-THIS...
NO, IT COULDN'T BE THAT!
BUT HOW ELSE CAN I EXPLAIN WHAT'S HAPPENING?
YOU LISTENING?
ぐぐっ
THAT'S IT! THIS IS WHAT YOU SEE IN MANGA AND OTHER STORIES...
THIS IS...
LOVE?
IMPOSSIBLE...
わなわな
ぷら～ん
WHAT ARE YOU GETTING ALL EXCITED ABOUT?
ACHOO!

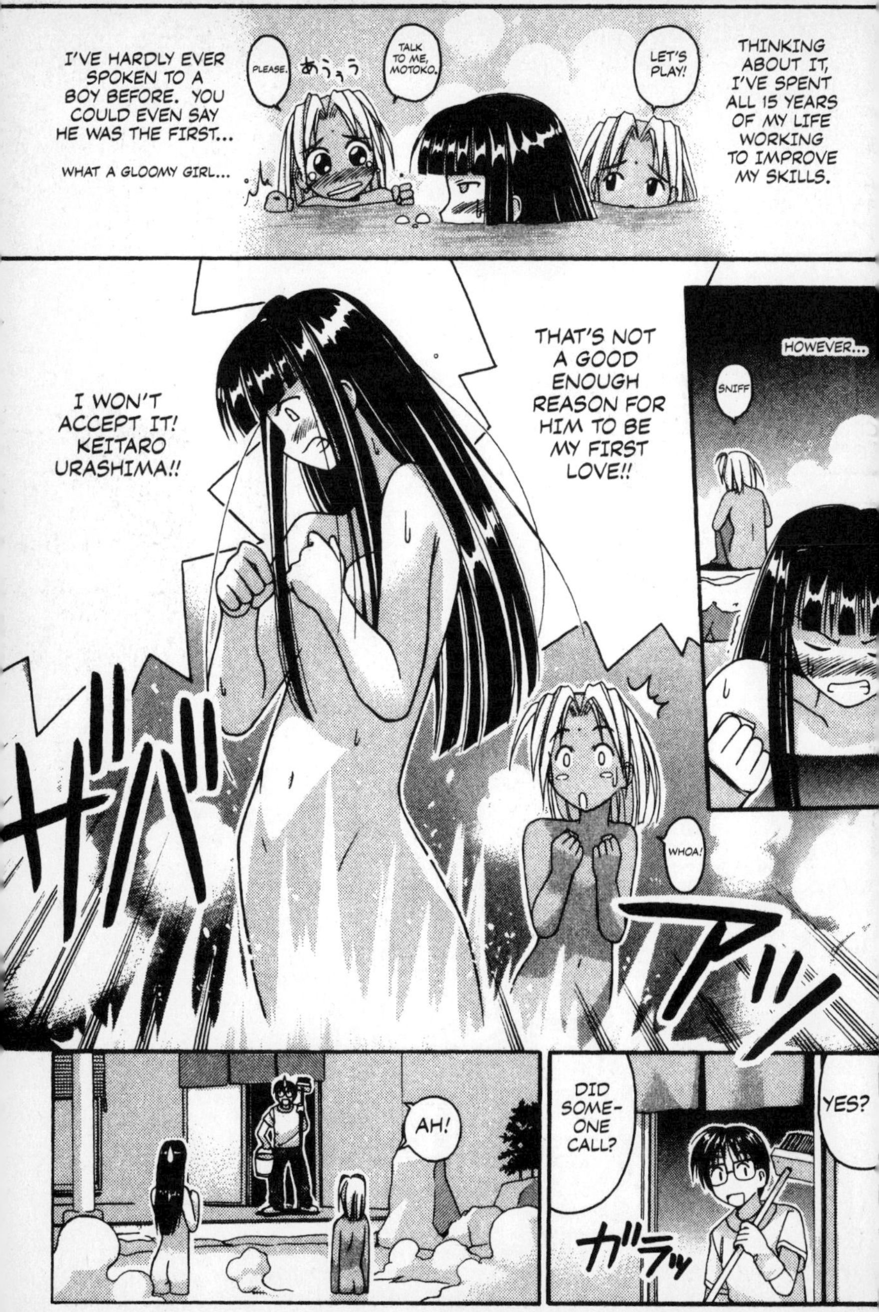
THINKING ABOUT IT, I'VE SPENT ALL 15 YEARS OF MY LIFE WORKING TO IMPROVE MY SKILLS.
LET'S PLAY!
TALK TO ME, MOTOKO.
あうぅう
PLEASE.
I'VE HARDLY EVER SPOKEN TO A BOY BEFORE. YOU COULD EVEN SAY HE WAS THE FIRST...
WHAT A GLOOMY GIRL...
HOWEVER...
SNIFF
THAT'S NOT A GOOD ENOUGH REASON FOR HIM TO BE MY FIRST LOVE!!
I WON'T ACCEPT IT! KEITARO URASHIMA!!
WHOA!
アッ
ザバ
YES?
DID SOMEONE CALL?
ガラッ
AH!

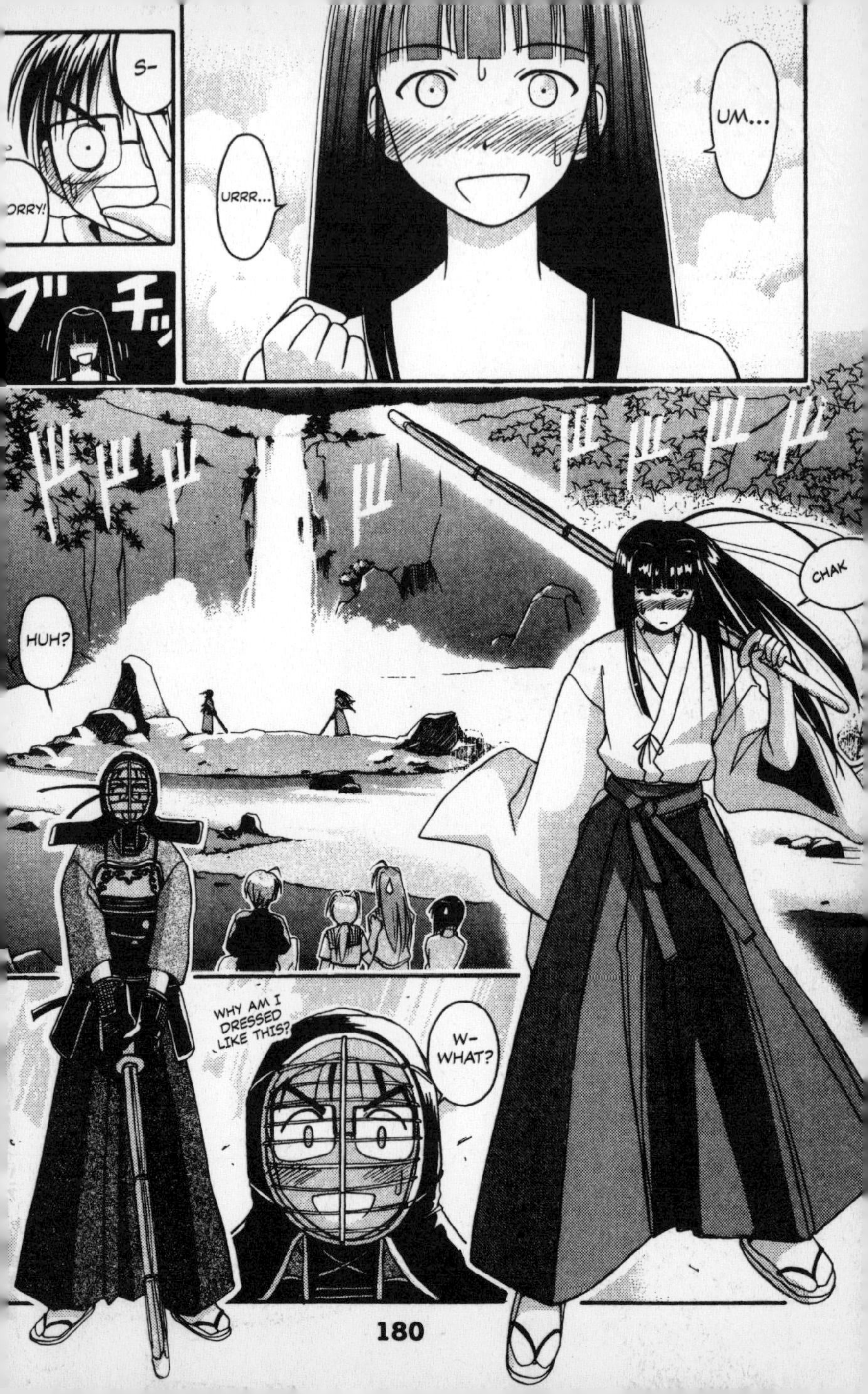
UM...
URRR...
S-
ORRY!
ブチッ
CHAK
HUH?
W- WHAT?
WHY AM I DRESSED LIKE THIS?

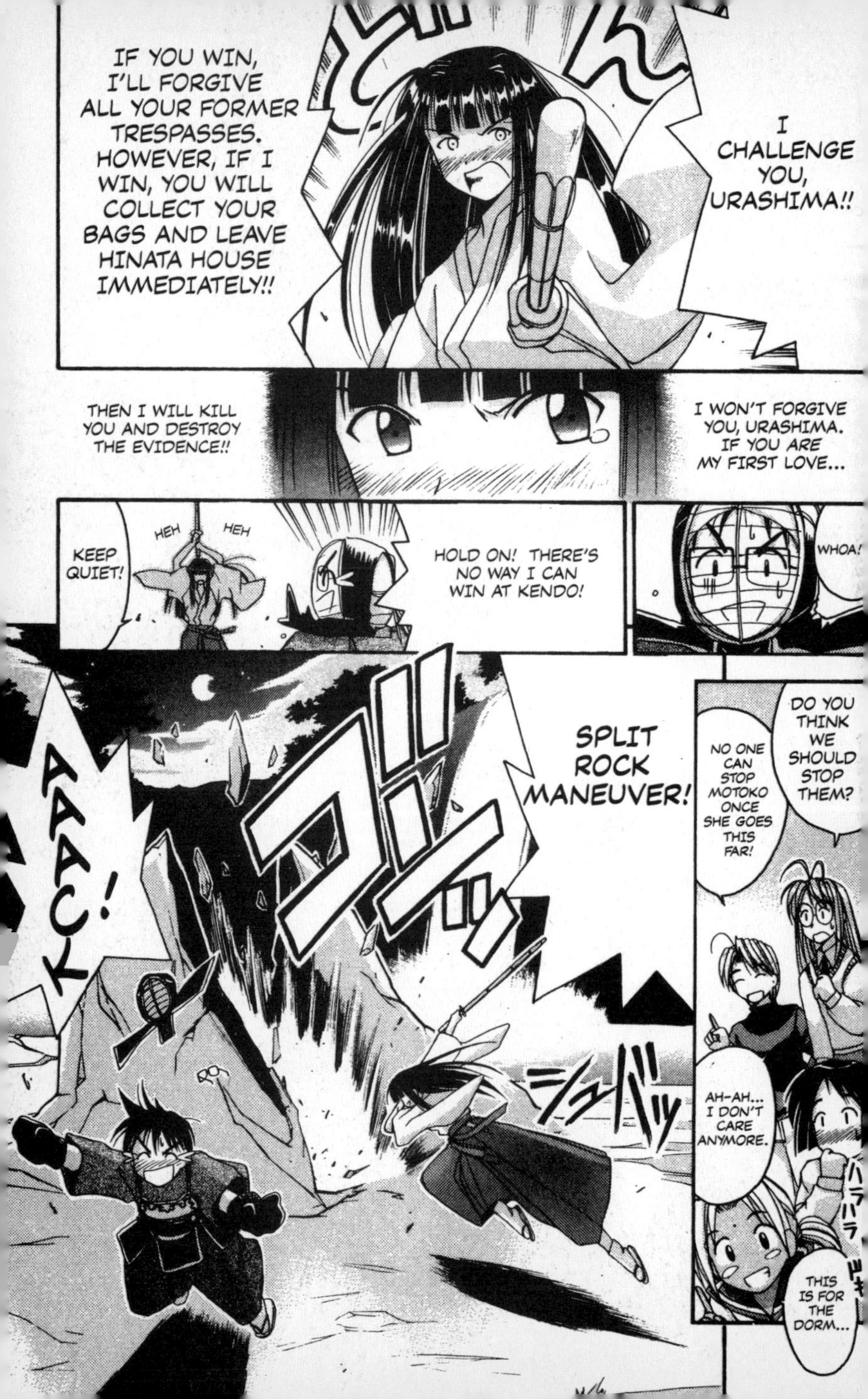
I CHALLENGE YOU, URASHIMA!!
IF YOU WIN, I'LL FORGIVE ALL YOUR FORMER TRESPASSES. HOWEVER, IF I WIN, YOU WILL COLLECT YOUR BAGS AND LEAVE HINATA HOUSE IMMEDIATELY!!
I WON'T FORGIVE YOU, URASHIMA. IF YOU ARE MY FIRST LOVE...
THEN I WILL KILL YOU AND DESTROY THE EVIDENCE!!
WHOA!
HOLD ON! THERE'S NO WAY I CAN WIN AT KENDO!
HEH HEH
KEEP QUIET!
DO YOU THINK WE SHOULD STOP THEM?
NO ONE CAN STOP MOTOKO ONCE SHE GOES THIS FAR!
AH-AH... I DON'T CARE ANYMORE.
THIS IS FOR THE DORM...
SPLIT ROCK MANEUVER!
AAACK!

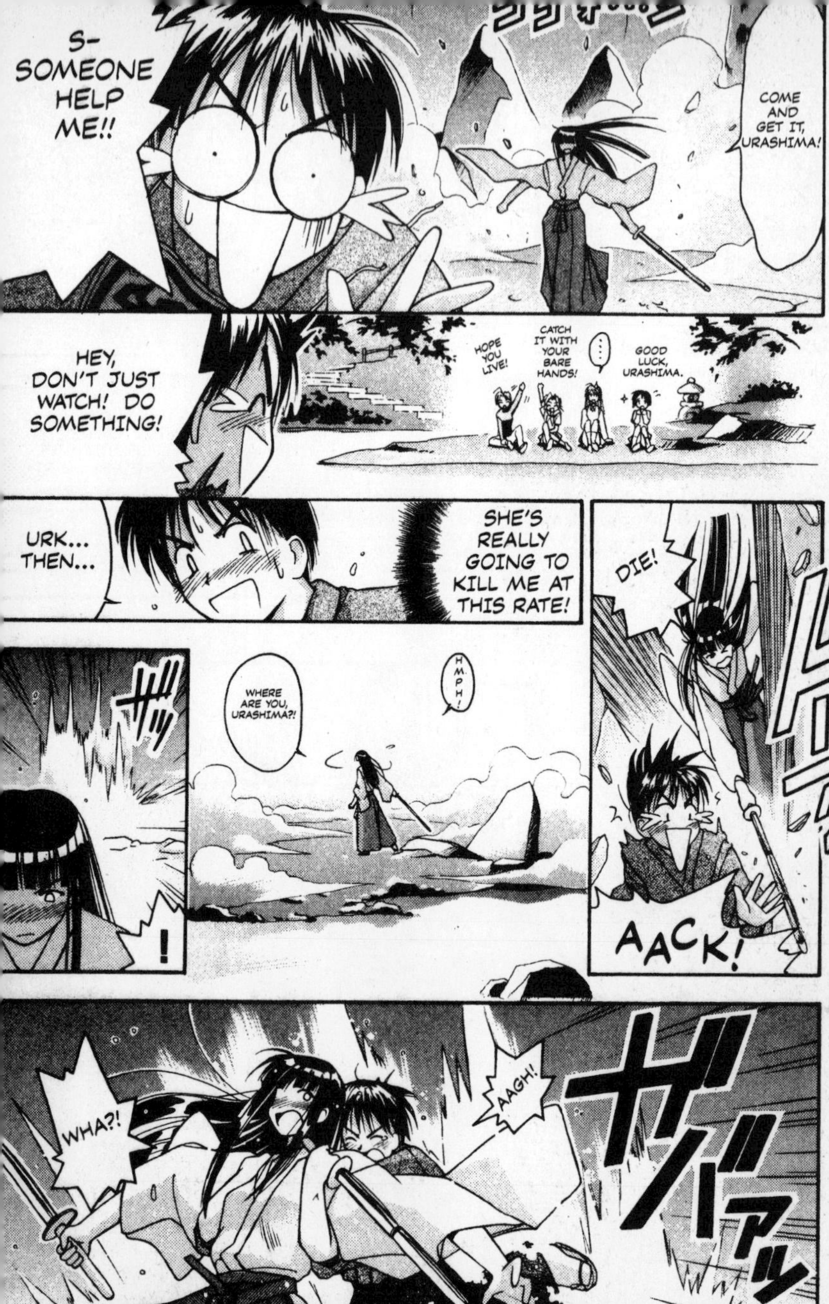
COME AND GET IT, URASHIMA!
S-SOMEONE HELP ME!!
GOOD LUCK, URASHIMA.
...
CATCH IT WITH YOUR BARE HANDS!
HOPE YOU LIVE!
HEY, DON'T JUST WATCH! DO SOMETHING!
DIE!
AACK!
SHE'S REALLY GOING TO KILL ME AT THIS RATE!
URK... THEN...
HMPH!
WHERE ARE YOU, URASHIMA?!
!
AAGH!
WHA?!

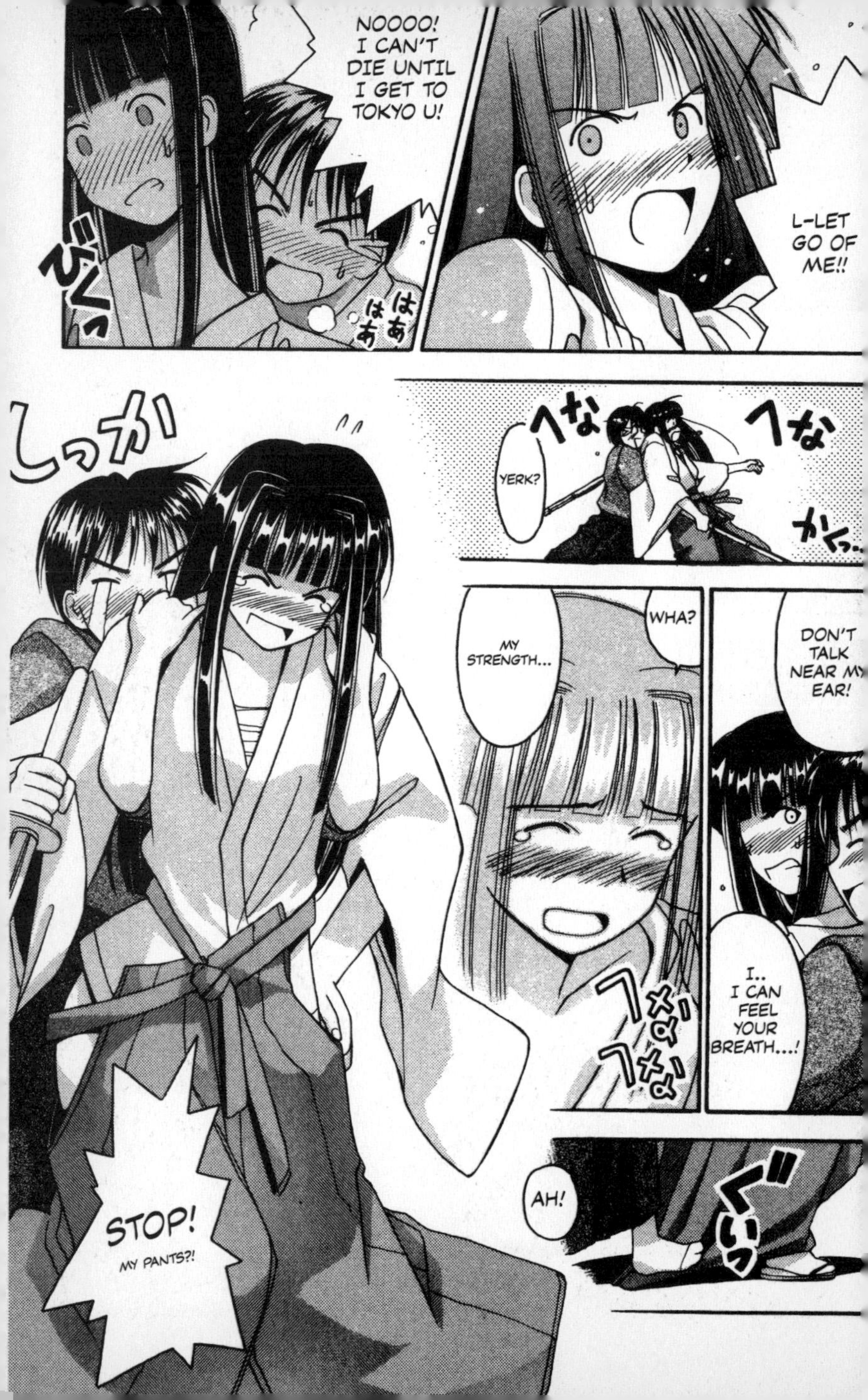
L-LET GO OF ME!!
NOOOO! I CAN'T DIE UNTIL I GET TO TOKYO U!
びくっ
はあはあ
へな
へな
YERK?
かくっ…
DON'T TALK NEAR MY EAR!
I.. I CAN FEEL YOUR BREATH...!
WHA?
MY STRENGTH...
へなへな
AH!
ぐいっ
しっかり
STOP!
MY PANTS?!

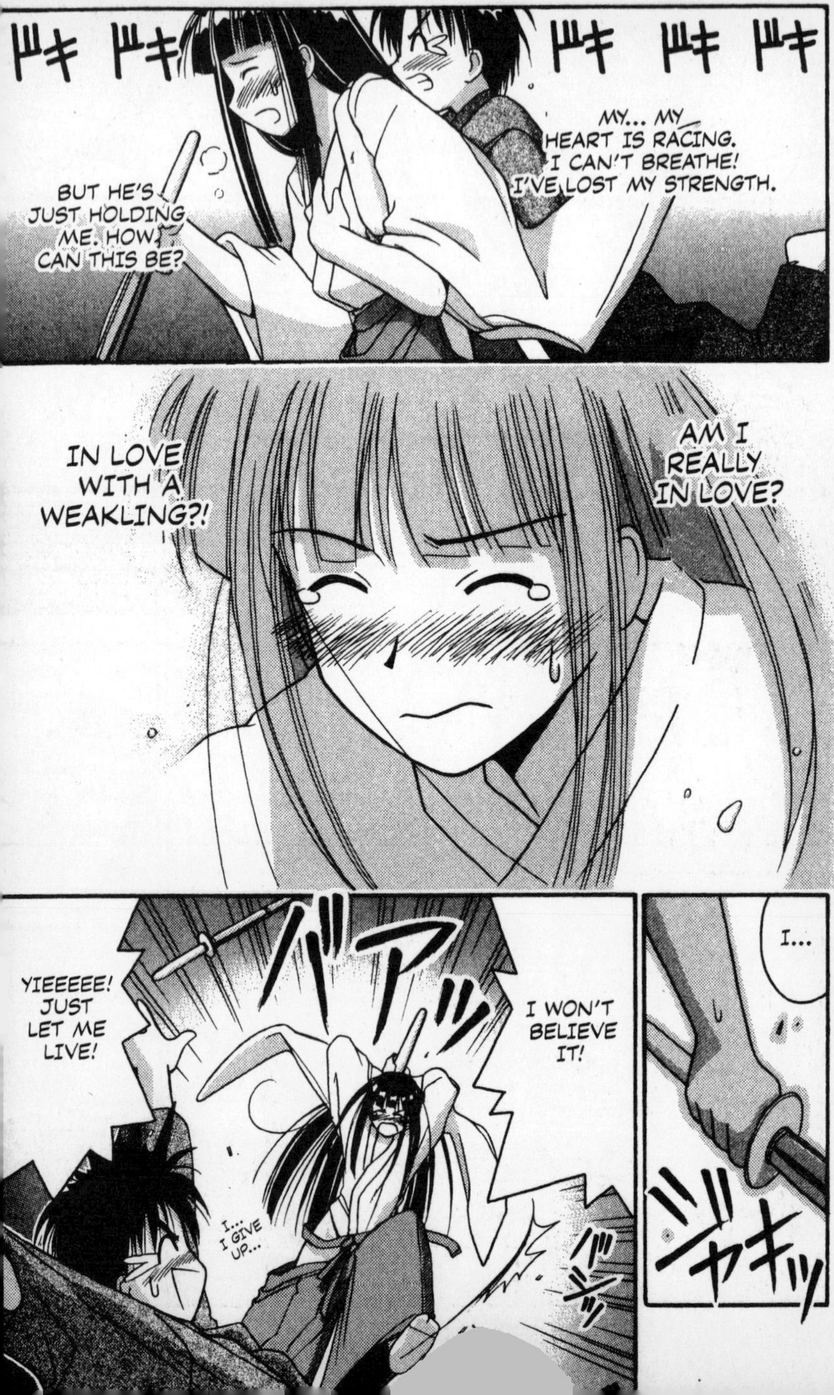
ドキ ドキ ドキ
ドキ ドキ
MY... MY HEART IS RACING. I CAN'T BREATHE! I'VE LOST MY STRENGTH.
BUT HE'S JUST HOLDING ME. HOW CAN THIS BE?
AM I REALLY IN LOVE?
IN LOVE WITH A WEAKLING?!
I...
ジャキッ
バアッ
I WON'T BELIEVE IT!
YIEEEEE! JUST LET ME LIVE!
I... I GIVE UP...

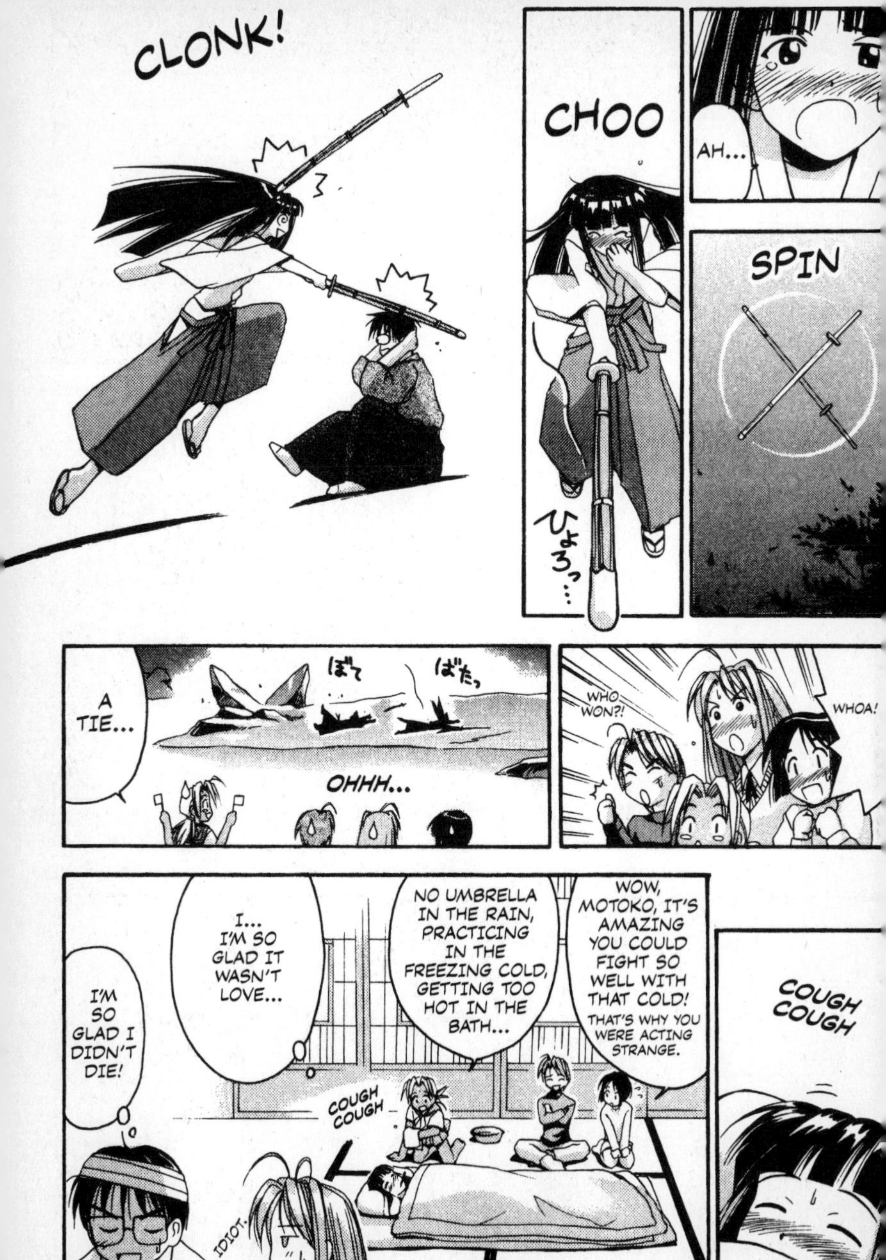
AH...
SPIN
CHOO
ひょろっ…
CLONK!
WHOA!
WHO WON?!
ばたっ
ぼて
A TIE...
OHHH...
COUGH COUGH
WOW, MOTOKO, IT'S AMAZING YOU COULD FIGHT SO WELL WITH THAT COLD!
THAT'S WHY YOU WERE ACTING STRANGE.
NO UMBRELLA IN THE RAIN, PRACTICING IN THE FREEZING COLD, GETTING TOO HOT IN THE BATH...
I... I'M SO GLAD IT WASN'T LOVE...
COUGH COUGH
I'M SO GLAD I DIDN'T DIE!
IDIOT.

BOOK 1- END

STAFF

Ken Akamatsu
Takashi Takemoto
Kenichi Nakamura
Takaaki Miyahara
Tomohiko Saito

EDITOR

Noboru Ohno
Tomoyuki Shiratsuchi

KC Editor

Mitsuei Ishii

[LOVEHINA]

THE EARLY CHARACTER DESIGNS
AND ROUGH DRAWINGS
(HALF A YEAR BEFORE THE LAUNCH OF THE SERIES)

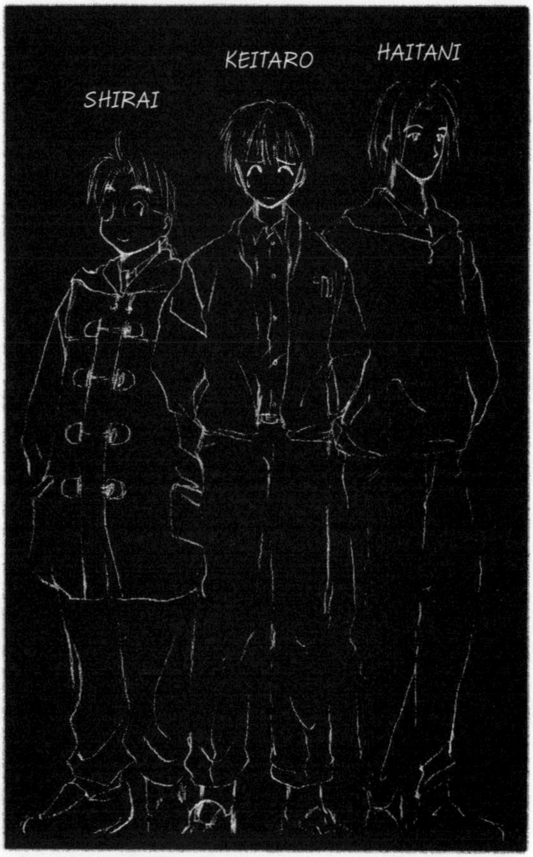
KEITARO
HAITANI
SHIRAI

COMMENTS BY ASSISTANT M

MIDORI

NARU - WHO'S MIDORI ?

THIS IS A RATHER VAGUE CHARACTER DESCRIPTION

- SHE FALLS NAKED THROUGH THE CEILING
- WHEN IT HAPPENS, SHE HITS HER HEAD ON THE MAIN CHARACTER'S AND LOSES HER MEMORY
- HER NAME AND PAST ARE UNKNOWN. THE MAIN CHARACTER GIVES HER A NAME
- SHE HAS HER OWN PACE, AND DURING CONVERSATION TENDS TO REACT SLOWLY
- BONEHEADED; PHILANTHROPIST - THE OPPOSITE OF NOW (LAUGH)
- THE MAIN CHARACTER FALLS IN LOVE WTIH HER AND SHE GETS A LITTLE BEWILDERED, BUT SHE ALSO KIND OF LIKES HIM, TOO
- A RESIDENT OF THE RYOKAN (JAPANESE STYLE HOTEL), WANTS TO BE A FRIEND OF EVERYONE

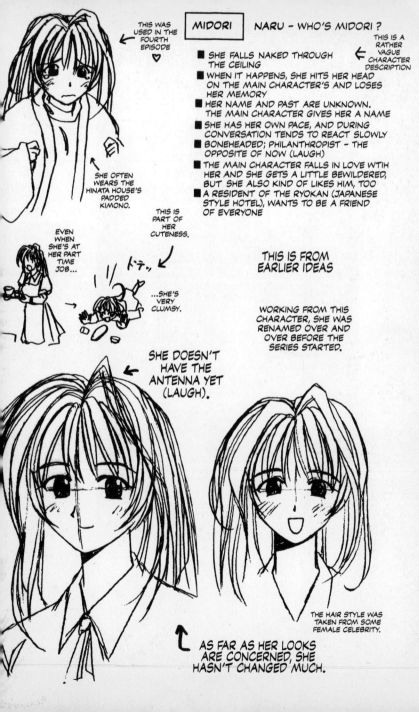

THIS WAS USED IN THE FOURTH EPISODE ♡
SHE OFTEN WEARS THE HINATA HOUSE'S PADDED KIMONO.

EVEN WHEN SHE'S AT HER PART TIME JOB...
THIS IS PART OF HER CUTENESS.
ドテッ
...SHE'S VERY CLUMSY.

THIS IS FROM EARLIER IDEAS

WORKING FROM THIS CHARACTER, SHE WAS RENAMED OVER AND OVER BEFORE THE SERIES STARTED.

SHE DOESN'T HAVE THE ANTENNA YET (LAUGH).

THE HAIR STYLE WAS TAKEN FROM SOME FEMALE CELEBRITY.

AS FAR AS HER LOOKS ARE CONCERNED, SHE HASN'T CHANGED MUCH.

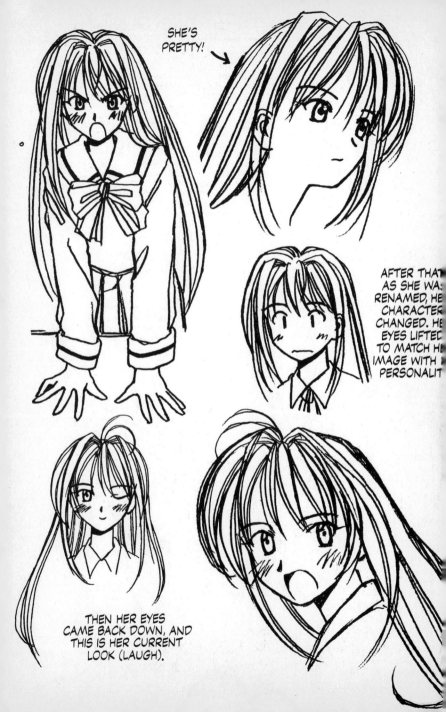

SHE'S PRETTY!

AFTER THAT
AS SHE WA:
RENAMED, HE
CHARACTEI
CHANGED. HE
EYES LIFTED
TO MATCH HI
IMAGE WITH
PERSONALIT

THEN HER EYES
CAME BACK DOWN, AND
THIS IS HER CURRENT
LOOK (LAUGH).

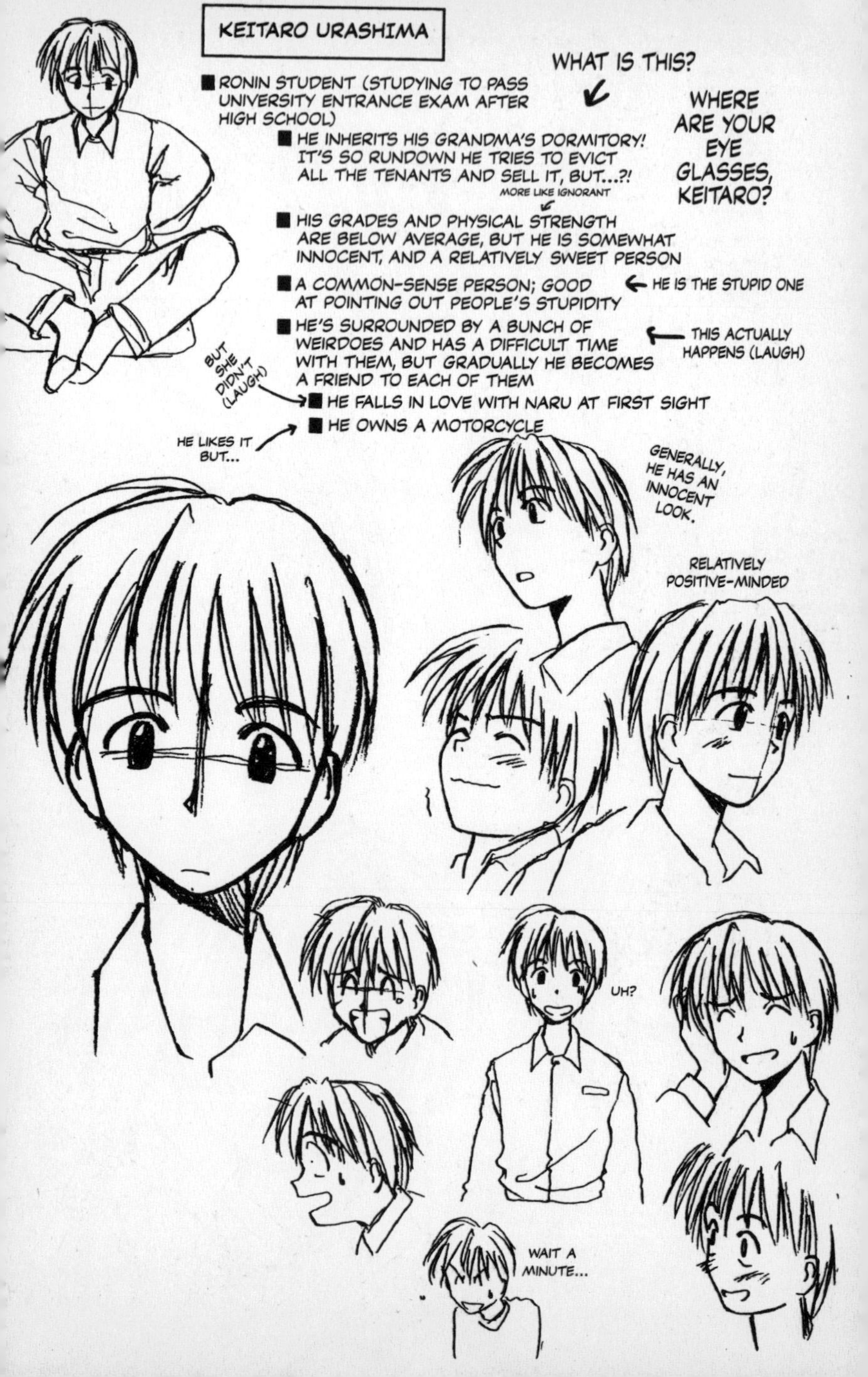
KEITARO URASHIMA
■ RONIN STUDENT (STUDYING TO PASS UNIVERSITY ENTRANCE EXAM AFTER HIGH SCHOOL)
WHAT IS THIS?
WHERE ARE YOUR EYE GLASSES, KEITARO?
■ HE INHERITS HIS GRANDMA'S DORMITORY! IT'S SO RUNDOWN HE TRIES TO EVICT ALL THE TENANTS AND SELL IT, BUT...?!
MORE LIKE IGNORANT
■ HIS GRADES AND PHYSICAL STRENGTH ARE BELOW AVERAGE, BUT HE IS SOMEWHAT INNOCENT, AND A RELATIVELY SWEET PERSON
■ A COMMON-SENSE PERSON; GOOD AT POINTING OUT PEOPLE'S STUPIDITY
HE IS THE STUPID ONE
■ HE'S SURROUNDED BY A BUNCH OF WEIRDOES AND HAS A DIFFICULT TIME WITH THEM, BUT GRADUALLY HE BECOMES A FRIEND TO EACH OF THEM
THIS ACTUALLY HAPPENS (LAUGH)
BUT SHE DIDN'T (LAUGH)
■ HE FALLS IN LOVE WITH NARU AT FIRST SIGHT
■ HE OWNS A MOTORCYCLE
HE LIKES IT BUT...
GENERALLY, HE HAS AN INNOCENT LOOK.
RELATIVELY POSITIVE-MINDED
UH?
WAIT A MINUTE...

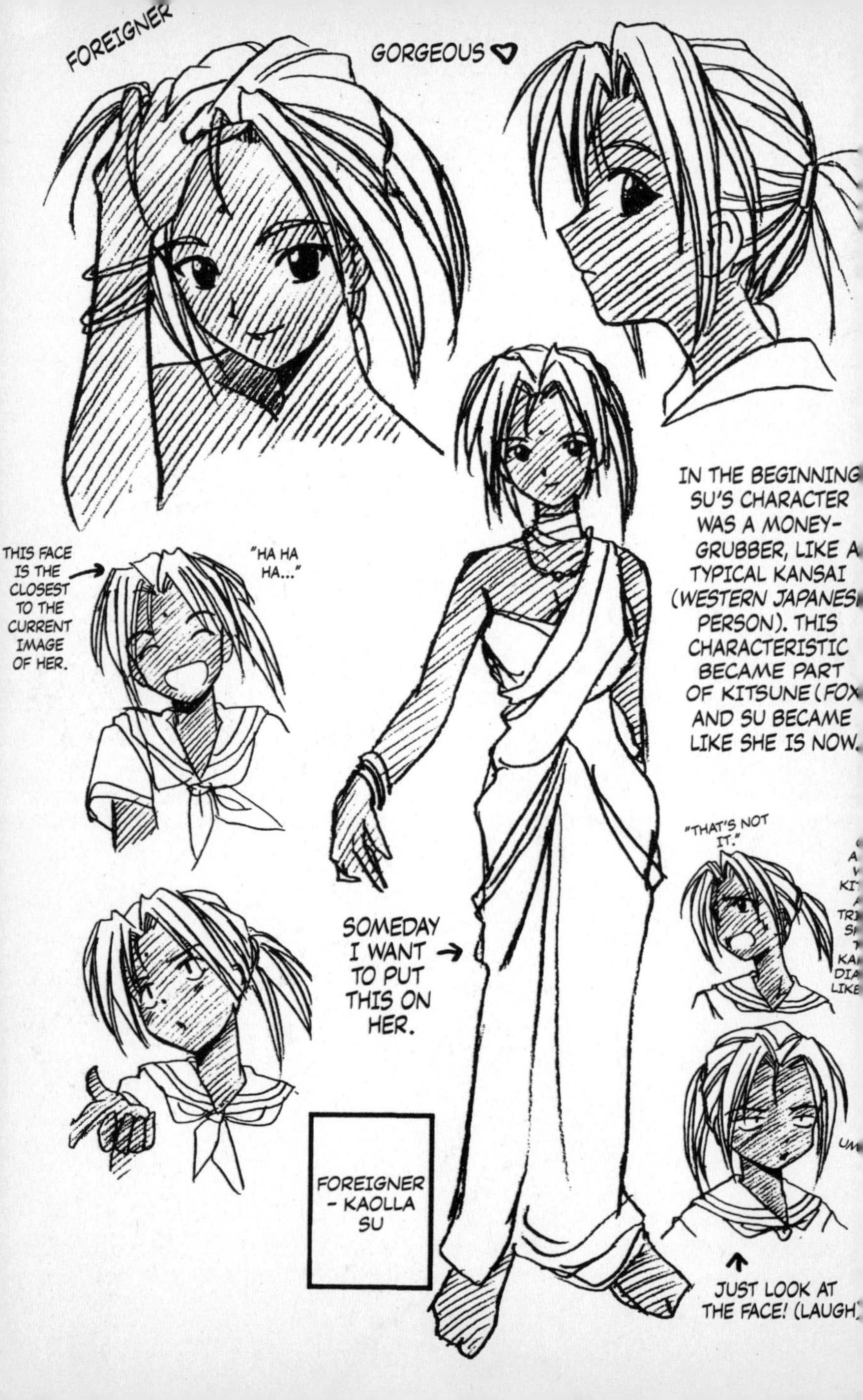
GORGEOUS ♡
FOREIGNER
IN THE BEGINNING SU'S CHARACTER WAS A MONEY-GRUBBER, LIKE A TYPICAL KANSAI (WESTERN JAPANES PERSON). THIS CHARACTERISTIC BECAME PART OF KITSUNE(FOX AND SU BECAME LIKE SHE IS NOW.
"HA HA HA..."
THIS FACE IS THE CLOSEST TO THE CURRENT IMAGE OF HER.
"THAT'S NOT IT."
SOMEDAY I WANT TO PUT THIS ON HER.
JUST LOOK AT THE FACE! (LAUGH)
FOREIGNER - KAOLLA SU

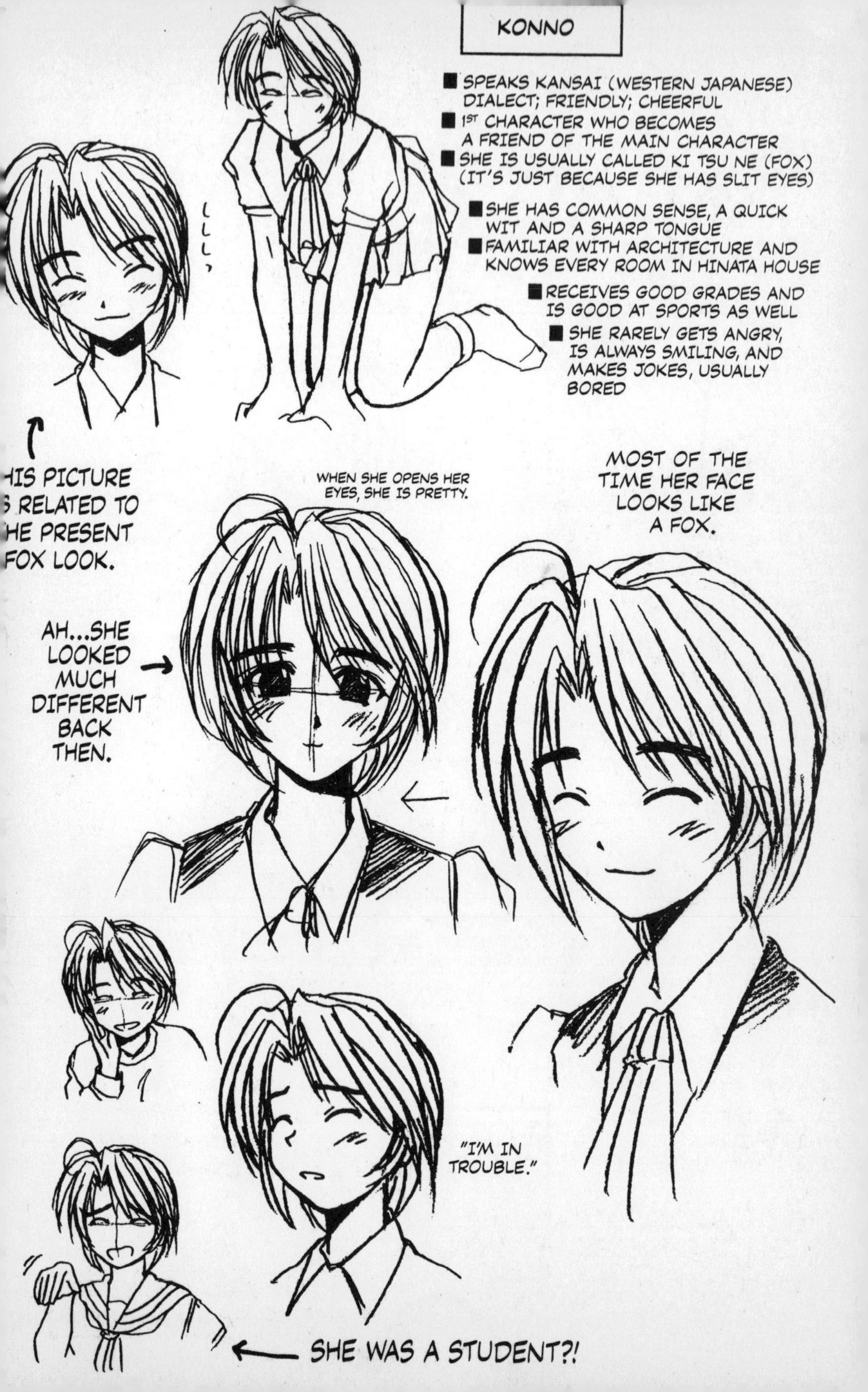
KONNO
■ SPEAKS KANSAI (WESTERN JAPANESE) DIALECT; FRIENDLY; CHEERFUL
■ 1ST CHARACTER WHO BECOMES A FRIEND OF THE MAIN CHARACTER
■ SHE IS USUALLY CALLED KI TSU NE (FOX) (IT'S JUST BECAUSE SHE HAS SLIT EYES)
■ SHE HAS COMMON SENSE, A QUICK WIT AND A SHARP TONGUE
■ FAMILIAR WITH ARCHITECTURE AND KNOWS EVERY ROOM IN HINATA HOUSE
■ RECEIVES GOOD GRADES AND IS GOOD AT SPORTS AS WELL
■ SHE RARELY GETS ANGRY, IS ALWAYS SMILING, AND MAKES JOKES, USUALLY BORED
HIS PICTURE S RELATED TO HE PRESENT FOX LOOK.
MOST OF THE TIME HER FACE LOOKS LIKE A FOX.
WHEN SHE OPENS HER EYES, SHE IS PRETTY.
AH...SHE LOOKED MUCH DIFFERENT BACK THEN.
"I'M IN TROUBLE."
SHE WAS A STUDENT?!

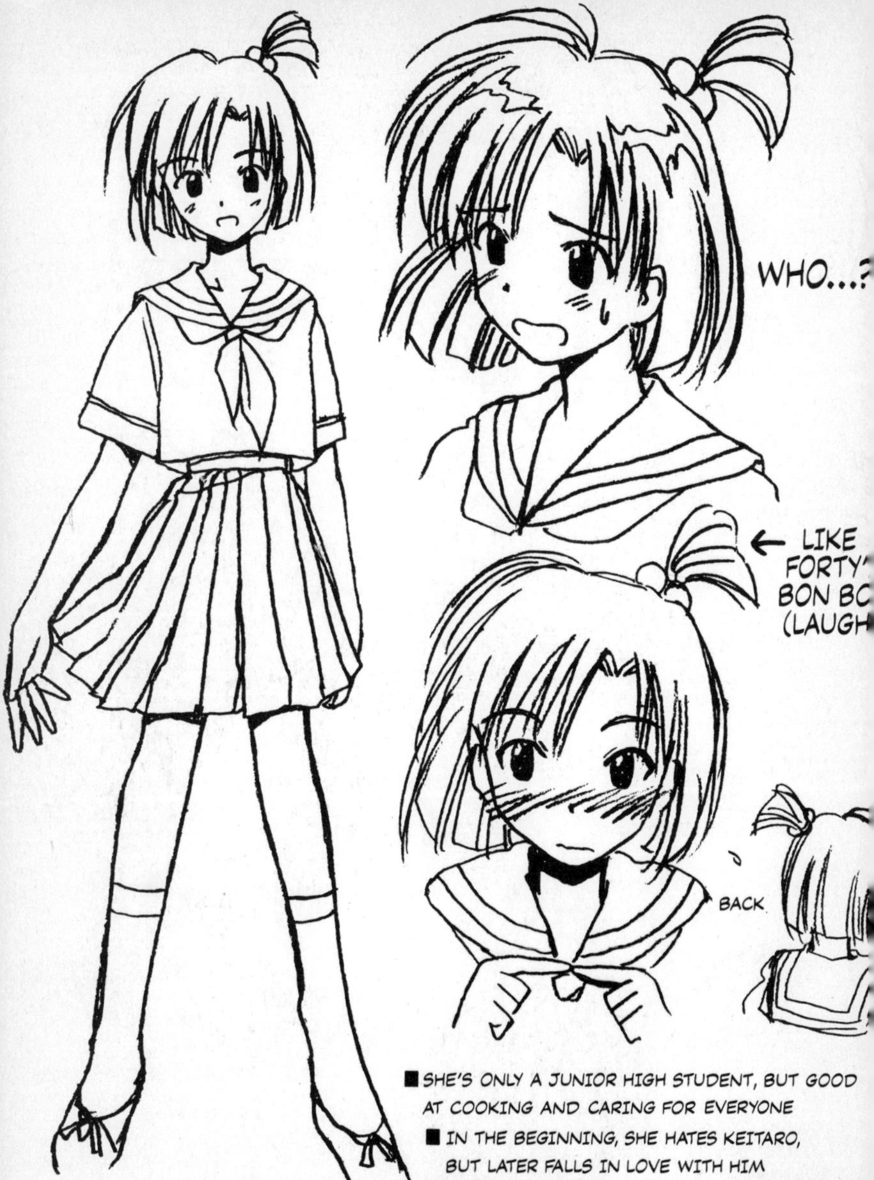
WHO...?
← LIKE
FORTY'
BON BC
(LAUGH
BACK

- SHE'S ONLY A JUNIOR HIGH STUDENT, BUT GOOD AT COOKING AND CARING FOR EVERYONE
- IN THE BEGINNING, SHE HATES KEITARO, BUT LATER FALLS IN LOVE WITH HIM
- SHY AND MOODY

SHINOBU CHANGED THE MOST. UNTIL RIGHT BEFORE THE DRAWING STAGE, I WORKED ON HER DESIGN AGAIN AND AGAIN.

JUNIOR HIGH SCHOOL STUDENT - SHINOBU

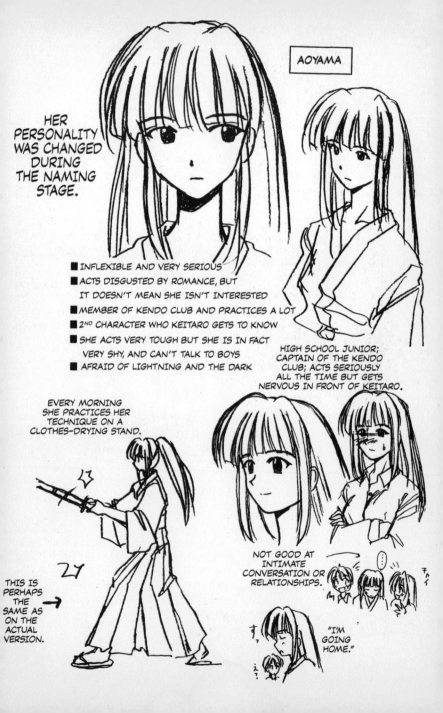

AOYAMA

HER PERSONALITY WAS CHANGED DURING THE NAMING STAGE.

- INFLEXIBLE AND VERY SERIOUS
- ACTS DISGUSTED BY ROMANCE, BUT IT DOESN'T MEAN SHE ISN'T INTERESTED
- MEMBER OF KENDO CLUB AND PRACTICES A LOT
- 2ND CHARACTER WHO KEITARO GETS TO KNOW
- SHE ACTS VERY TOUGH BUT SHE IS IN FACT VERY SHY, AND CAN'T TALK TO BOYS
- AFRAID OF LIGHTNING AND THE DARK

HIGH SCHOOL JUNIOR; CAPTAIN OF THE KENDO CLUB; ACTS SERIOUSLY ALL THE TIME BUT GETS NERVOUS IN FRONT OF KEITARO.

EVERY MORNING SHE PRACTICES HER TECHNIQUE ON A CLOTHES-DRYING STAND.

THIS IS PERHAPS THE SAME AS ON THE ACTUAL VERSION.

NOT GOOD AT INTIMATE CONVERSATION OR RELATIONSHIPS.

"I'M GOING HOME."

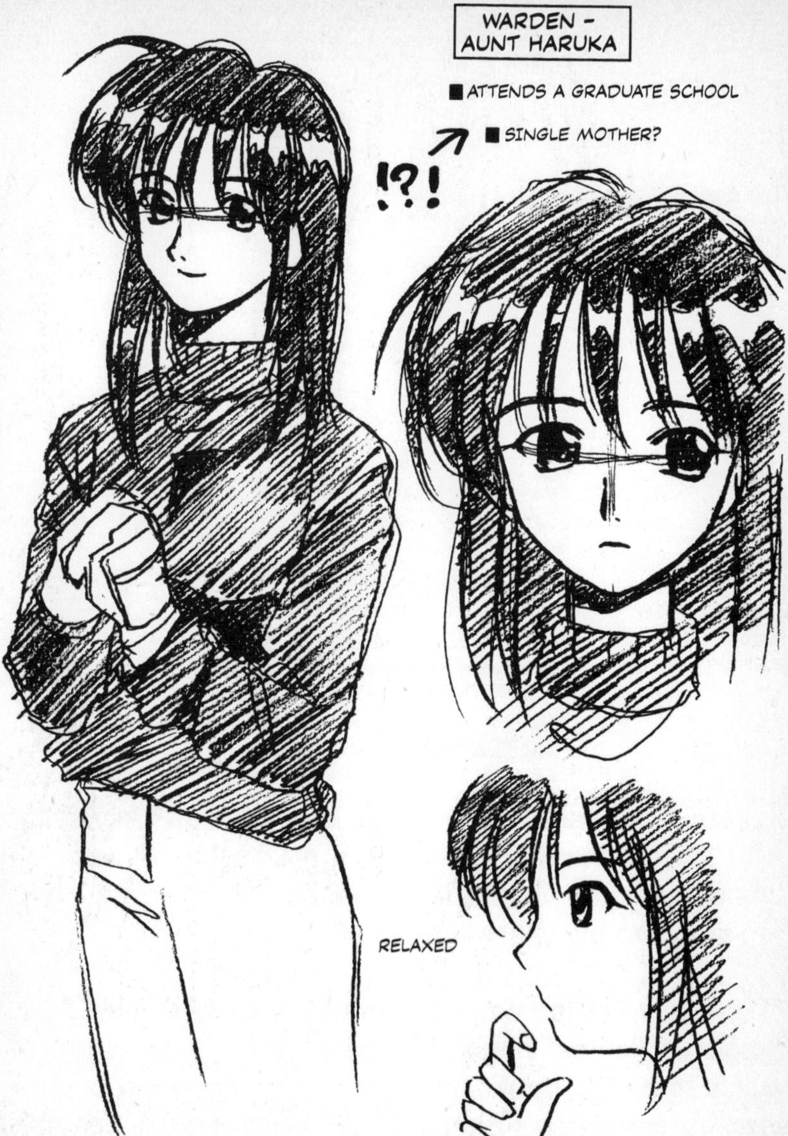
WARDEN - AUNT HARUKA
■ATTENDS A GRADUATE SCHOOL
■SINGLE MOTHER?
!?!
RELAXED

WOW?! DIFFERENT PERSON?!
HARUKA HAS ONLY A FEW SCENES

Keitaro Urashima's dream is to attend Tokyo University with his childhood sweetheart, a girl he hasn't seen in years. But when he fails the entrance exams, he's in danger of losing his chance for good.

Meanwhile, his job as caretaker of a girls dorm filled with gorgeous ladies keeps him more than busy. Keitaro wants to hit the books, but first he's got to see if one of the girls really is his old crush! Working together, can the two finally make the grade, or will Keitaro be seduced by the temptations that surround him?

ON SALE NOW!

COWBOY BEBOP
shooting star

Story & Art by:
Cain Kuga

Original Concept by:
Hajime Yatate
©Sunrise

100% AUTHENTIC MANGA

TOKYOPOP

MORE SPIKE
MORE JET
MORE COWBOY BEBOP

Also Available:
Cowboy Bebop Volumes 1, 2, 3 & Boxed Set
Cowboy Bebop Anime Guides
Volumes 1-6 in stores now! Collect them all!!

T TEEN AGE 13+

www.TOKYOPOP.com

BY CLAMP

America's must-have manga

"Chobits... is a wonderfully entertaining story that would be a great installment in anybody's Manga collection."

— Tony Chen,
Anime News Network.com

CHOBITS AVAILABLE AT YOUR FAVORITE BOOK AND COMIC STORES

STOP!

This is the back of the book.
You wouldn't want to spoil a great ending!

This book is printed "manga-style," in the authentic Japanese right-to-left format. Since none of the artwork has been flipped or altered, readers get to experience the story just as the creator intended. You've been asking for it, so TOKYOPOP® delivered: authentic, hot-off-the-press, and far more fun!

DIRECTIONS

If this is your first time reading manga-style, here's a quick guide to help you understand how it works.

It's easy... just start in the top right panel and follow the numbers. Have fun, and look for more 100% authentic manga from TOKYOPOP®!

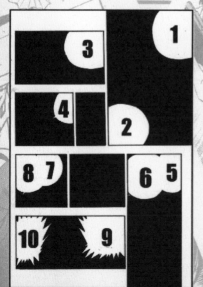

100% AUTHENTIC MANGA